Jan. Morn.	Jan. Even.	Feb. Morn.	Feb. Even.	Mar. Morn.	Mar. Even.	Apr. Morn.	Apr. Even.	May Morn.	May Even.	Jun. Morn.	Jun. Even.	Days
11 51	—	0 41	1 4	11 52	—	0 30	0 50	0 35	0 55	1 44	2 8	5
0 15	0 36	1 24	1 45	0 18	0 41	1 10	1 29	1 17	1 38	2 33	2 58	6
0 57	1 17	2 4	2 24	1 3	1 24	1 47	2 5	2 0	2 22	3 24	3 50	7
1 38	1 58	2 43	3 0	1 43	2 0	2 25	2 45	2 43	3 6	4 14	4 39	8
2 17	2 37	3 19	3 37	2 18	2 37	3 5	3 26	3 30	3 55	5 5	5 31	9
2 57	3 15	3 56	4 15	2 55	3 13	3 47	4 9	4 20	4 46	5 59	6 26	10
3 35	3 55	4 34	4 53	3 33	3 52	4 32	4 55	5 13	5 41	6 54	7 22	11
4 15	4 35	5 14	5 34	4 12	4 32	5 19	5 45	6 13	6 47	7 52	8 24	12
4 55	5 16	5 55	6 19	4 51	5 11	6 17	6 54	7 23	8 2	8 57	9 29	13
5 39	6 3	6 46	7 17	5 34	5 58	7 36	8 24	8 42	9 23	9 57	10 25	14
6 28	6 54	7 55	8 37	6 26	6 58	9 16	10 4	9 58	10 28	10 53	11 19	15
7 21	7 51	9 26	10 18	7 36	8 25	10 42	11 12	10 54	11 18	11 42	—	16
8 27	9 5	11 5	11 42	9 21	10 15	11 37	—	11 39	11 59	0 4	0 26	17
9 48	10 30	—	[illegible]	[illegible]	[illegible]	[illegible]	0 20	—	0 19	0 47	1 6	18
11 8	11 40	0 42	[illegible]	[illegible]	[illegible]	[illegible]	[illegible]	[illegible]	[illegible]	[illegible] 24	1 44	19
—	0 9	1 29	[illegible]	[illegible]	[illegible]	[illegible]	[illegible]	[illegible]	[illegible]	[illegible]	2 20	20
0 39	1 8	2 7	[illegible]	[illegible]	[illegible]	[illegible]	[illegible]	[illegible]	[illegible]	[illegible]	2 55	21
1 35	1 57	2 44	[illegible]	[illegible]	[illegible]	[illegible]	[illegible]	[illegible]	[illegible]	[illegible]	3 32	22
2 19	2 40	3 15	[illegible]	[illegible]	[illegible]	[illegible]	[illegible]	[illegible]	[illegible]	[illegible]	4 12	23
3 1	3 20	3 47	[illegible]	[illegible]	[illegible]	[illegible]	[illegible]	[illegible]	[illegible]	[illegible]	4 52	24
3 39	3 58	4 16	[illegible]	[illegible]	[illegible]	[illegible]	[illegible]	[illegible]	[illegible]	[illegible]	5 38	25
4 16	4 34	4 45	[illegible]	[illegible]	[illegible]	[illegible]	[illegible]	[illegible]	[illegible]	[illegible]	6 29	26
4 50	5 6	5 16	[illegible]	[illegible]	[illegible]	[illegible]	[illegible]	[illegible]	[illegible]	[illegible]	7 26	27
5 24	5 42	5 50	[illegible]	[illegible]	[illegible]	[illegible]	[illegible]	[illegible]	[illegible]	[illegible]	8 27	28
6 0	6 18			[illegible]	[illegible]	[illegible]	[illegible]	[illegible]	[illegible]	[illegible]	9 33	29
6 27	7 0			[illegible]	[illegible]	[illegible]	[illegible]	[illegible]	[illegible]	[illegible]	10 39	30
7 27	7 59			6 58	7 40			[illegible]	[illegible]			31

MEAN TIME OF HIGH WATER AT GLASGOW, 1875.

JULY.		AUGUST.		SEPT.		OCTOBER.		NOV.		DEC.		Days.
MORN.	EVEN.	MORN.	EVEN.	MORN.	EVEN.	MORN.	EVEN.	MORN.	EVEN.	MORN.	EVEN.	
11 10	11 42	0 42	1 10	2 3	2 21	2 8	2 23	2 40	2 55	2 55	3 14	1
—	0 11	1 35	1 58	2 37	2 55	2 39	2 55	3 12	3 29	3 31	3 48	2
0 39	1 6	2 20	2 41	3 11	3 28	3 9	3 25	3 45	4 1	4 6	4 24	3
1 33	1 59	3 2	3 22	3 43	3 59	3 39	3 54	4 19	4 38	4 46	5 9	4
2 25	2 53	3 42	4 1	4 13	4 28	4 9	4 23	4 59	5 22	5 31	5 57	5
3 18	3 40	4 19	4 36	4 43	4 58	4 39	5 0	5 50	6 21	6 25	6 54	6
4 3	4 25	4 52	5 10	5 16	5 35	5 23	5 48	6 56	7 36	7 25	7 59	7
4 47	5 8	5 27	5 45	5 56	6 19	6 16	6 48	8 18	9 12	8 34	9 12	8
5 30	5 51	6 3	6 23	6 49	7 24	7 31	8 19	9 40	10 14	9 46	10 16	9
6 13	6 36	6 45	7 11	8 6	8 58	9 10	9 56	10 42	11 7	10 44	11 10	10
6 59	7 22	7 42	8 17	9 49	10 33	10 34	11 5	11 30	11 50	11 36	—	11
7 48	8 17	9 0	9 45	11 9	11 38	11 29	11 49	—	0 10	0 2	0 27	12
8 49	9 23	10 26	11 2	—	0 2	—	0 8	0 30	0 52	0 53	1 19	13
9 59	10 32	11 34	—	0 25	0 45	0 26	0 45	1 15	1 36	1 44	2 10	14
11 2	11 30	0 3	0 29	1 4	1 22	1 4	1 22	1 57	2 20	2 36	3 2	15
11 57	—	0 51	1 11	1 39	1 56	1 39	1 57	2 43	3 6	3 29	3 54	16
0 22	0 45	1 30	1 49	2 12	2 29	2 17	2 37	3 32	3 57	4 17	4 42	17
1 8	1 29	2 7	2 24	2 47	3 5	2 59	3 20	4 22	4 49	5 9	5 35	18
1 47	2 4	2 40	2 57	3 24	3 43	3 42	4 5	5 18	5 48	5 59	6 25	19
2 23	2 41	3 15	3 33	4 1	4 21	4 29	4 53	6 20	6 54	6 52	7 20	20
3 0	3 17	3 52	4 10	4 42	5 4	5 19	5 50	7 31	8 9	7 49	8 21	21
3 37	3 57	4 27	4 46	5 28	5 56	6 25	7 5	8 50	9 29	8 54	9 29	22
4 15	4 35	5 6	5 28	6 29	7 7	7 51	8 44	10 2	10 32	10 2	10 33	23
4 55	5 15	5 51	6 16	7 53	8 47	9 34	10 14	10 58	11 20	11 1	11 27	24
5 36	5 59	6 45	7 19	9 42	10 30	10 45	11 11	11 42	—	11 51	—	25
6 22	6 49	7 57	8 43	11 6	11 36	11 35	11 56	0 3	0 23	0 13	0 35	26
7 16	7 45	9 36	10 28	—	0 3	—	0 16	0 41	0 59	0 55	1 15	27
8 19	9 0	11 8	11 42	0 25	0 46	0 33	0 51	1 15	1 32	1 34	1 53	28
9 44	10 26	—	0 12	1 4	1 21	1 8	1 23	1 48	2 5	2 10	2 29	29
11 4	11 38	0 39	1 3	1 37	1 52	1 38	1 54	2 21	2 38	2 46	3 4	30
—	0 11	1 25	1 46			2 10	2 26			3 23	3 40	31

find the time of HIGH WATER at the following places, add to or subtract from the time given in the Table, as required:—

Place	H. M.	Place	H. M.	Place	H. M.
erdeen, .	sub. 0 17	Dublin, . .	sub. 2 5	Limerick, . .	sub. 1 12
drossan, .	sub. 1 35	Dunbar, . .	add 0 50	London, .	add 0 40
r, ,	sub. 1 45	Dundalk, . .	sub. 2 21	Londonderry,	add 4 31
llyshannon, .	add 4 0	Dundee, . .	add 1 15	Montrose, . .	add 0 10
nff, . .	sub. 0 49	Falmouth, . .	add 3 40	Newcastle, . .	add 3 6
ntry Harbour,	add 2 30	Fort-William, .	add 4 2	Oban, . .	add 3 45
lfast, .	sub. 2 34	Galloway, Mull .	sub. 2 2	Peterhead, . .	sub. 0 43
rwick, .	add 1 0	Galway, . .	add 3 18	Portpatrick, .	sub. 2 5
istol, . .	add 5 56	Grangemouth, .	add 1 15	Port Rush, . .	sub. 4 41
mpbelton, .	sub. 1 45	Greenock, . .	sub. 1 12	Rothesay, . .	sub. 1 25
ntyre, Mull of,	sub. 2 42	Havre, . .	sub. 3 26	Sligo, . .	add 4 0
rnarvon, .	sub. 3 44	Hull, . .	add 5 12	Stirling. . .	add 2 12
rk Harbour, .	add 3 44	Inveraray, . .	sub. 1 30	Stranraer, .	sub. 2 10
omarty, .	sub. 1 23	Inverness, . .	sub. 1 22	Tobermory, .	add 3 48
naghadee, .	sub. 2 4	Kirkcudbright, .	sub. 2 7	Waterford, . .	add 4 50
negal, . .	add 4 0	Leith Pier, . .	add 1 0	Wick, . .	sub. 1 55
uglas, . .	sub. 2 5	Liverpool, . .	sub. 1 54	Wicklow, . .	sub. 2 50

he mean duration of the ebb and flow of a tide is about 12 hours 25 min., that is, half e lunar day of 24 h. 50 min., the period elapsing between successive returns of the oon to the same meridian.

When — occurs it indicates that there is no tide. The height to which the tide rises ries every day. Spring tide—or when the tide rises to the highest—is about two ys after new and full moon. A tide occupies more than 12 hours. The tide previous the — occurs so near to 12 o'clock that the next tide is thrown over the next 12 hours to the following morning or evening. Morning commences immediately after 12 clock midnight, and evening immediately after 12 o'clock noon.

TIDES.

In 1875 the highest tides will be those of 9th March, 8th April, 7th May, 17th ptember, 16th October and 15th November.

RECEIPT AND BILL STAMPS.

ECEIPT for £2 & upwards, ONE PENNY.

The person receiving the money pays the

bills, or drafts already stamped. Receipts for money passing between master and servant, but this will not apply to travellers who travel for several houses.

BILLS AND PROMISSORY NOTES.

IN AVOIRDUPOIS WEIGHT 16 drams are 1 oz., 16 oz. 1 lb., 28 lbs. 1 quarter, 4 quarters or 112 lbs. 1 cwt., and 20 cwt. 1 ton. 14 lbs. are 1 stone, and 8 stones 1 cwt. The lb. contains 7,000 grains. 80 oz. avoirdupois are 73 oz. troy. 175 lbs. troy are equal to 144 lbs. avoirdupois, and 14 lbs. avoirdupois are 80 grains above 17 lbs. troy. Avoirdupois weight is generally used in commerce.

MEASURES.—4 gills are 1 pint, 2 pints a quart and 4 quarts a gallon. The preceding is used for liquids and dry goods, but the following is used for dry goods only —2 gallons are a peck, 4 pecks a bushel, 8 bushels a quarter. An imperial gill is 5 oz., and an imperial gallon 10 lbs. avoirdupois, or 12·15 lb. troy. This is the only measure allowed now by law for liquids, and all dry goods not sold by heaped measure. A Scotch pint is 104·2 cubic inches, and weighs 55 oz. troy. In the old beer measure—which is still in use in several places —18 gallons of 282 cubic inches are a kilderkin, 2 kilderkins a barrel, and 3 kilderkins or 54 gallons a hogshead, 2 hogsheads a butt. In the wine and spirit measure 84 gallons are a puncheon, 63 gallons a hogshead, 2 hogsheads a pipe, and 2 pipes a tun.

LENGTHS.—A palm is 3 and a span 9

miles a degree.

SQUARES.— in a sq. foot, 9 s sq feet in an ac 40 square poles i acre, each conta 34 yards 28 inche square yards, o way. Two acr each way; 3 acr and 640 acres a mile, or 880 yar a quarter of a m is 40 acres; a f way, is 10 acres. 36 square ells m 4 roods an acre. each way, 48 old lish. The Engli America.

CUBIC OR S cubic inches in are a cubic yar timber, or 50 cu 28 cubic feet of of clay, are deem is 42 cubic feet, o

Paper—24 shee are 1 ream.

GERMAN AND FRENCH STANDARD M

453·25 grammes, 1 lb. avoirdupois, English.
372·96 do. 1 lb. troy, English.
1 gramme, 15·433 grains troy, E.
1 kilogramme, 2 lbs. 3 oz. 4½ dr. or 2·2049 lbs. avoirdupois, or 2·6794 lbs. troy, E.
1 myriagramme, 22·0485 lb. avoirdupois E.
1 quintal, 100 kilogrammes, or 1·97 cwt. E.
1 millier, 1000 kilogrammes, or 1 French ton, or 19·7 cwt. E.
4000 metres, 1 league, E.
1609·31 metres, 1 mile, E.
1 metre, 39·37079 inch, or 3 feet 3½ inches, E.
1 decametre, 10 metres 10·93633 yards, E.
1 kilometre, 39370·79 inch, or 5-8 of a m. E.
1 myriametre, 6·2138 ms. or 6 ms. 376 yds. E.
1 litre, 61·02705 cubic inches. E.
1 litre, 1·760773 pint or 0·220097 gal. E.
1 decalitre, 2·20097 gals. E.
1 hectolitre, 2·7512 bushels, E.
1 hectolitre, 22·00297 gals. E.
1 kilolitre, 220·0297 gals. E.
1 stere, 35·3158 cubic feet, E.
1 decistere, 3·53158 cubic feet, E
1 hectare 2·4736 inches, E.
1 arpen, 1·0430 acres, E.
1 are, 1076·4414 square feet, E.

A kilolitre is a little over 6 brls. E.; a bush. is 36·347664 litres; a qrt. is 1·13586 litres; a gal. 4·543458 litres; a rood 10·116775 ares; an acre 0·404671 hectares. To reduce English

cubic inches to g reduce English c by 61·02705, and

To reduce metr ply by 1·09364 yar by 0·914318. To pounds avoirdup or pounds into To convert litres ply by 61·02705; To convert hecto multiply by 2·75 convert hectares 2·473614; acres i For kilometres i miles into kilom eral calculation reckoned as 5-8th

These are read ples of the stand 10 times, by *hect* 1000 times, as ki and by merely ch one place furthe two for hundred *deci* for the 10th part, and *milli* fo gramme, the 100t terms for the mu for dividing are I

LENGTHS.—A palm is 3 and a span 9 are 1 ream.

GERMAN AND FRENCH STANDARD MEASURES.

453·25 grammes, 1 lb. avoirdupois, English.
372·96 do. 1 lb. troy, English.
1 gramme, 15·433 grains troy, E.
1 kilogramme, 2 lbs. 3 oz. 4½ dr. or 2·2049 lbs. avoirdupois, or 2·6794 lbs. troy, E.
1 myriagramme, 22·0485 lb. avoirdupois E.
1 quintal, 100 kilogrammes, or 1·97 cwt. E.
1 millier, 1000 kilogrammes, or 1 French ton, or 19·7 cwt. E.
4000 metres, 1 league, E.
1609·31 metres, 1 mile, E.
1 metre, 39·37079 inch, or 3 feet 3½ inches, E.
1 decametre, 10 metres 10·93633 yards, E.
1 kilometre, 39370·79 inch, or 5-8 of a m. E.
1 myriametre, 6·2138 ms. or 6 ms. 376 yds. E.
1 litre, 61·02705 cubic inches. E.
1 litre, 1·760773 pint or 0·220097 gal. E.
1 decalitre, 2·20097 gals. E.
1 hectolitre, 2·7512 bushels, E.
1 hectolitre, 22·00297 gals. E.
1 kilolitre, 220·0297 gals. E.
1 stere, 35·3158 cubic feet, E.
1 decistere, 3·53158 cubic feet, E
1 hectare 2·4736 inches, E.
1 arpen, 1·0430 acres, E.
1 are, 1076·4414 square feet, E.

A kilolitre is a little over 6 brls. E.; a bush. is 36·347664 litres; a qrt. is 1·13586 litres; a gal. 4·543458 litres; a rood 10·116775 ares; an acre 0·404671 hectares. To reduce English cubic inches to *gallons*, divide by 2 reduce English cubic inches to *litr* by 61·02705, and *vice versa*.

To reduce metres into our yarc ply by 1·09364 yards, and yards int by 0·914318. To convert kilogram pounds avoirdupois, multiply by or pounds into kilogrammes by To convert litres into cubic inch ply by 61·02705; the contrary b To convert hectolitres into imperi multiply by 2·7513; contrary, 0·3 convert hectares into acres, mu 2·473614; acres into hectares by For kilometres into miles, by 0·6 miles into kilometres, by 1·6102. eral calculations, the kilometre reckoned as 5-8ths of a mile.

These are readily converted int ples of the standards, by prefixing 10 times, by *hecto* for 100 times, b 1000 times, as kilogramme, 1000 g and by merely changing the decin one place further to the right two for hundreds, &c. To divid *deci* for the 10th part, *centi* for t part, and *milli* for the 1000th part, gramme, the 100th part of a gram terms for the multiplying are Gre for dividing are Latin.

MEAN TIME OF HIGH WATER AT GLASGOW, 1875.

Days.	JULY.		AUGUST.		SEPT.		OCTOBER.		NOV.		D
	MORN.	EVEN.	MORN.	EVEN.	MORN.	EVEN.	MORN.	EVEN.	MORN.	EVEN.	MORN.
1	11 10	11 42	0 42	1 10	2 3	2 21	2 8	2 23	2 40	2 55	2 55
2	—	0 11	1 35	1 58	2 37	2 55	2 39	2 55	3 12	3 29	3 31
3	0 39	1 6	2 20	2 41	3 11	3 28	3 9	3 25	3 45	4 1	4 6
4	1 33	1 59	3 2	3 22	3 43	3 59	3 39	3 54	4 19	4 38	4 46
5	2 25	2 53	3 42	4 1	4 13	4 28	4 9	4 23	4 59	5 22	5 31
6	3 18	3 40	4 19	4 36	4 43	4 58	4 39	5 0	5 50	6 21	6 25
7	4 3	4 25	4 52	5 10	5 16	5 35	5 23	5 48	6 56	7 36	7 25
8	4 47	5 8	5 27	5 45	5 56	6 19	6 16	6 48	8 18	9 12	8 34
9	5 30	5 51	6 3	6 23	6 49	7 24	7 31	8 19	9 40	10 14	9 46
10	6 13	6 36	6 45	7 11	8 6	8 58	9 10	9 56	10 42	11 7	10 44
11	6 59	7 22	7 42	8 17	9 49	10 33	10 34	11 5	11 30	11 50	11 36
12	7 48	8 17	9 0	9 45	11 9	11 38	11 29	11 49	—	0 10	0 2
13	8 49	9 23	10 26	11 2	—	0 2	—	0 8	0 30	0 52	0 53
14	9 59	10 32	11 34	—	0 25	0 45	0 26	0 45	1 15	1 36	1 44
15	11 2	11 30	0 3	0 29	1 4	1 22	1 4	1 22	1 57	2 20	2 36
16	11 57	—	0 51	1 11	1 39	1 56	1 39	1 57	2 43	3 6	3 29
17	0 22	0 45	1 30	1 49	2 12	2 29	2 17	2 37	3 32	3 57	4 17
18	1 8	1 29	2 7	2 24	2 47	3 5	2 59	3 20	4 22	4 49	5 9
19	1 47	2 4	2 40	2 57	3 24	3 43	3 42	4 5	5 18	5 48	5 59
20	2 23	2 41	3 15	3 33	4 1	4 21	4 29	4 53	6 20	6 54	6 52
21	3 0	3 17	3 52	4 10	4 42	5 4	5 19	5 50	7 31	8 9	7 49
22	3 37	3 57	4 27	4 46	5 28	5 56	6 25	7 5	8 50	9 29	8 54
23	4 15	4 35	5 6	5 28	6 29	7 7	7 51	8 44	10 2	10 32	10 2
24	4 55	5 15	5 51	6 16	7 53	8 47	9 34	10 14	10 58	11 20	11 1
25	5 36	5 59	6 45	7 19	9 42	10 30	10 45	11 11	11 42	—	11 51
26	6 22	6 49	7 57	8 43	11 6	11 36	11 35	11 56	0 3	0 23	0 13
27	7 16	7 45	9 36	10 28	—	0 3	—	0 16	0 41	0 59	0 55
28	8 19	9 0	11 8	11 42	0 25	0 46	0 33	0 51	1 15	1 32	1 34
29	9 44	10 26	—	0 12	1 4	1 21	1 8	1 23	1 48	2 5	2 10
30	11 4	11 38	0 39	1 3	1 37	1 52	1 38	1 54	2 21	2 38	2 46
31	—	0 11	1 25	1 46			2 10	2 26			3 23

To find the time of **HIGH WATER** at the following places, add to or subtr the time given in the Table, as required:—

	H. M.		H. M.	
Aberdeen, .	sub. 0 17	Dublin, . .	sub. 2 5	Limerick, . .
Ardrossan, .	sub. 1 35	Dunbar, . .	add 0 50	London, .
Ayr, ,	sub. 1 45	Dundalk, . .	sub. 2 21	Londonderry,
Ballyshannon, .	add 4 0	Dundee, . .	add 1 15	Montrose, . .
Banff, . .	sub. 0 49	Falmouth, . .	add 3 40	Newcastle, . .
Bantry Harbour,	add 2 30	Fort-William, .	add 4 2	Oban, . .
Belfast, .	sub. 2 34	Galloway, Mull .	sub. 2 2	Peterhead, . .
Berwick, .	add 1 0	Galway, . .	add 3 18	Portpatrick, .
Bristol, . .	add 5 56	Grangemouth, .	add 1 15	Port Rush, . .
Campbelton, .	sub. 1 45	Greenock, . .	sub. 1 12	Rothesay, .
Cantyre, Mull of,	sub. 2 42	Havre, . .	sub. 3 26	Sligo, . .
Carnarvon, .	sub. 3 44	Hull, . .	add 5 12	Stirling. .
Cork Harbour, .	add 3 44	Inveraray, . .	sub. 1 30	Stranraer, .
Cromarty, .	sub. 1 23	Inverness, . .	sub. 1 22	Tobermory, .
Donaghadee, .	sub. 2 4	Kirkcudbright, .	sub. 2 7	Waterford, . .
Donegal, . .	add 4 0	Leith Pier, . .	add 1 0	Wick, . .
Douglas, . .	sub. 2 5	Liverpool, . .	sub. 1 54	Wicklow, . .

The mean duration of the ebb and flow of a tide is about 12 hours

												Days
1	—	0 41	1 4	11 52	—	0 30	0 50	0 35	0 55	1 44	2 8	5
5	0 36	1 24	1 45	0 18	0 41	1 10	1 29	1 17	1 38	2 33	2 58	6
7	1 17	2 4	2 24	1 3	1 24	1 47	2 5	2 0	2 22	3 24	3 50	7
3	1 58	2 43	3 0	1 43	2 0	2 25	2 45	2 43	3 6	4 14	4 39	8
7	2 37	3 19	3 37	2 18	2 37	3 5	3 26	3 30	3 55	5 5	5 31	9
7	3 15	3 56	4 15	2 55	3 13	3 47	4 9	4 20	4 46	5 59	6 26	10
5	3 55	4 34	4 53	3 33	3 52	4 32	4 55	5 13	5 41	6 54	7 22	11
5	4 35	5 14	5 34	4 12	4 32	5 19	5 45	6 13	6 47	7 52	8 24	12
5	5 16	5 55	6 19	4 51	5 11	6 17	6 54	7 23	8 2	8 57	9 29	13
9	6 3	6 46	7 17	5 34	5 58	7 36	8 24	8 42	9 23	9 57	10 25	14
3	6 54	7 55	8 37	6 26	6 58	9 16	10 4	9 58	10 28	10 53	11 19	15
3	7 51	9 26	10 18	7 36	8 25	10 42	11 12	10 54	11 18	11 42	—	16
7	9 5	11 5	11 42	9 21	10 15	11 37	—	11 39	11 59	0 4	0 26	17
3	10 30	—	0 13	11 1	11 37	0 1	0 20	—	0 19	0 47	1 6	18
3	11 40	0 42	1 7	—	0 6	0 38	0 56	0 39	0 57	1 24	1 44	19
	0 9	1 29	1 49	0 30	0 52	1 12	1 27	1 13	1 29	2 3	2 20	20
	1 8	2 7	2 26	1 11	1 29	1 42	1 57	1 45	2 3	2 38	2 55	21
	1 57	2 44	3 0	1 45	2 1	2 12	2 26	2 20	2 35	3 13	3 32	22
	2 40	3 15	3 31	2 16	2 30	2 41	2 55	2 50	3 8	3 51	4 12	23
	3 20	3 47	4 1	2 43	2 58	3 11	3 27	3 27	3 44	4 33	4 52	24
	3 58	4 16	4 31	3 13	3 29	3 44	4 0	4 1	4 19	5 14	5 38	25
	4 34	4 45	5 0	3 43	3 56	4 17	4 34	4 40	5 4	6 3	6 29	26
	5 6	5 16	5 33	4 10	4 24	4 52	5 13	5 29	5 55	6 57	7 26	27
	5 42	5 50	6 10	4 39	4 56	5 37	6 6	6 23	6 55	7 56	8 27	28
	6 18			5 14	5 36	6 38	7 16	7 28	8 3	8 59	9 33	29
	7 0			6 0	6 27	7 59	8 43	8 39	9 14	10 7	10 39	30
	7 59			6 58	7 40			9 47	10 16			31

MEAN TIME OF HIGH WATER AT GLASGOW, 1875.

JLY.		AUGUST.		SEPT.		OCTOBER.		NOV.		DEC.		Days.
.	EVEN.	MORN.	EVEN.	MORN.	EVEN.	MORN.	EVEN.	MORN.	EVEN.	MORN.	EVEN.	
.	11 42	0 42	1 10	2 3	2 21	2 8	2 23	2 40	2 55	2 55	3 14	1
	0 11	1 35	1 58	2 37	2 55	2 39	2 55	3 12	3 29	3 31	3 48	2
	1 6	2 20	2 41	3 11	3 28	3 9	3 25	3 45	4 1	4 6	4 24	3
	1 59	3 2	3 22	3 43	3 59	3 39	3 54	4 19	4 38	4 46	5 9	4
	2 53	3 42	4 1	4 13	4 28	4 9	4 23	4 59	5 22	5 31	5 57	5
	3 40	4 19	4 36	4 43	4 58	4 39	5 0	5 50	6 21	6 25	6 54	6
	4 25	4 52	5 10	5 16	5 35	5 23	5 48	6 56	7 36	7 25	7 59	7
	5 8	5 27	5 45	5 56	6 19	6 16	6 48	8 13	9 12	8 34	9 12	8
	5 51	6 3	6 23	6 49	7 24	7 31	8 19	9 40	10 14	9 46	10 16	9
	6 36	6 45	7 11	8 6	8 58	9 10	9 56	10 42	11 7	10 44	11 10	10
	7 22	7 42	8 17	9 49	10 33	10 34	11 5	11 30	11 50	11 36	—	11
	8 17	9 0	9 45	11 9	11 38	11 29	11 49	—	0 10	0 2	0 27	12
	9 23	10 26	11 2	—	0 2	—	0 8	0 30	0 52	0 53	1 19	13
	10 32	11 34	—	0 25	0 45	0 26	0 45	1 15	1 36	1 44	2 10	14
	11 30	0 3	0 29	1 4	1 22	1 4	1 22	1 57	2 20	2 36	3 2	15
	—	0 51	1 11	1 39	1 56	1 39	1 57	2 43	3 6	3 29	3 54	16
	0 45	1 30	1 49	2 12	2 29	2 17	2 37	3 32	3 57	4 17	4 42	17
	1 29	2 7	2 24	2 47	3 5	2 59	3 20	4 22	4 49	5 9	5 35	18
	2 4	2 40	2 57	3 24	3 43	3 42	4 5	5 18	5 48	5 59	6 25	19
	2 41	3 15	3 33	4 1	4 21	4 29	4 53	6 20	6 54	6 52	7 20	20
	3 17	3 52	4 10	4 42	5 4	5 19	5 50	7 31	8 9	7 49	8 21	21
	3 57	4 27	4 46	5 28	5 56	6 25	7 5	8 50	9 29	8 54	9 29	22
	4 35	5 6	5 28	6 29	7 7	7 51	8 44	10 2	10 32	10 2	10 33	23
	5 15	5 51	6 16	7 53	8 47	9 34	10 14	10 58	11 20	11 1	11 27	24
	5 59	6 45	7 19	9 42	10 30	10 45	11 11	11 42	—	11 51	—	25
	6 49	7 57	8 43	11 6	11 36	11 35	11 56	0 3	0 23	0 13	0 35	26
	7 45	9 36	10 28	—	0 3	—	0 16	0 41	0 59	0 55	1 15	27
	9 0	11 8	11 42	0 25	0 46	0 33	0 51	1 15	1 32	1 34	1 53	28
	10 26	—	0 12	1 4	1 21	1 8	1 23	1 48	2 5	2 10	2 29	29
	11 38	0 39	1 3	1 37	1 52	1 38	1 54	2 21	2 38	2 46	3 4	30
	0 11	1 25	1 46			2 10	2 26			3 23	3 40	31

ıe time of HIGH WATER at the following places, add to or subtract from the time given in the Table, as required:—

	H. M.		H. M.		H. M.
.	sub. 0 17	Dublin, .	sub. 2 5	Limerick, .	sub. 1 12
n, .	sub. 1 35	Dunbar, .	add 0 50	London, .	add 0 40
.	sub. 1 45	Dundalk, .	sub. 2 21	Londonderry,	add 4 31
nnon, .	add 4 0	Dundee, .	add 1 15	Montrose, .	add 0 10
.	sub. 0 49	Falmouth, .	add 3 40	Newcastle, .	add 3 6
Harbour,	add 2 30	Fort-William,	add 4 2	Oban, .	add 3 45
.	sub. 2 34	Galloway, Mull	sub. 2 2	Peterhead, .	sub. 0 43
.	add 1 0	Galway, .	add 3 18	Portpatrick,	sub. 2 5
.	add 5 56	Grangemouth,	add 1 15	Port Rush, .	sub. 4 41
on, .	sub. 1 45	Greenock, .	sub. 1 12	Rothesay, .	sub. 1 25
Mull of,	sub. 2 42	Havre, .	sub. 3 26	Sligo, .	add 4 0
n, .	sub. 3 44	Hull, .	add 5 12	Stirling. .	add 2 12
bour, .	add 3 44	Inveraray, .	sub. 1 30	Stranraer, .	sub. 2 10
.	sub. 1 23	Inverness, .	sub. 1 22	Tobermory, .	add 3 48
lee, .	sub. 2 4	Kirkcudbright,	sub. 2 7	Waterford, .	add 4 50
.	add 4 0	Leith Pier, .	add 1 0	Wick, .	sub. 1 55
.	sub. 2 5	Liverpool, .	sub. 1 54	Wicklow, .	sub. 2 50

an duration of the ebb and flow of a tide is about 12 hours 25 min., that is, half day of 24 h. 50 min., the period elapsing between successive returns of the the same meridian.

— occurs it indicates that there is no tide. The height to which the tide rises ery day. Spring tide—or when the tide rises to the highest—is about two new and full moon. A tide occupies more than 12 hours. The tide previous occurs so near to 12 o'clock that the next tide is thrown over the next 12 hours following morning or evening. Morning commences immediately after 12 nidnight, and evening immediately after 12 o'clock noon.

TIDES.

the highest tides will be those of 9th March, 8th April, 7th May, 17th r, 16th October and 15th November.

EIPT AND BILL STAMPS.

T for £2 & upwards, ONE PENNY.

son receiving the money pays the hich he is required to cancel by

bills, or drafts already stamped. Receipts for money passing between master and servant, but this will not apply to travellers who travel for several houses.

BILLS AND PROMISSORY NOTES.

IN AVOIRDUPOIS WEIGHT 16 drams are 1 oz., 16 oz. 1 lb., 28 lbs. 1 quarter, 4 quarters or 112 lbs. 1 cwt., and 20 cwt. 1 ton. 14 lbs. are 1 stone, and 8 stones 1 cwt. The lb. contains 7,000 grains. 80 oz. avoirdupois are 73 oz. troy. 175 lbs. troy are equal to 144 lbs. avoirdupois, and 14 lbs. avoirdupois are 80 grains above 17 lbs. troy. Avoirdupois weight is generally used in commerce.

MEASURES.—4 gills are 1 pint, 2 pints a quart and 4 quarts a gallon. The preceding is used for liquids and dry goods, but the following is used for dry goods only —2 gallons are a peck, 4 pecks a bushel, 8 bushels a quarter. An imperial gill is 5 oz., and an imperial gallon 10 lbs. avoirdupois, or 12·15 lb. troy. This is the only measure allowed now by law for liquids, and all dry goods not sold by heaped measure. A Scotch pint is 104·2 cubic inches, and weighs 55 oz. troy. In the old beer measure—which is still in use in several places —18 gallons of 282 cubic inches are a kilderkin, 2 kilderkins a barrel, and 3 kilderkins or 54 gallons a hogshead, 2 hogsheads a butt. In the wine and spirit measure 84 gallons are a puncheon, 63 gallons a hogshead, 2 hogsheads a pipe, and 2 pipes a tun.

LENGTHS.—A palm is 3 and a span 9

miles a degree.

SQUARES.—There a in a sq. foot, 9 sq. feet i sq feet in an acre. 30 40 square poles in a rood acre, each containing 1 34 yards 28 inches each square yards, or 69 ya way. Two acres are each way; 3 acres are 12 and 640 acres are 1 sq mile, or 880 yards each a quarter of a mile, or is 40 acres; a furlong, way, is 10 acres. In the 36 square ells made a fa 4 roods an acre. The each way, 48 old Scotch lish. The English acre America.

CUBIC OR SOLIDS cubic inches in a cubic are a cubic yard. 40 c timber, or 50 cubic feet 28 cubic feet of sand, o of clay, are deemed a to is 42 cubic feet, or 3·476

Paper—24 sheets are 1 are 1 ream.

GERMAN AND FRENCH STANDARD MEASUR

453·25 grammes, 1 lb. avoirdupois, English.
372·96 do. 1 lb. troy, English.
1 gramme, 15·433 grains troy, E.
1 kilogramme, 2 lbs. 3 oz. 4½ dr. or 2·2049 lbs. avoirdupois, or 2·6794 lbs. troy, E.
1 myriagramme, 22·0485 lb. avoirdupois E.
1 quintal, 100 kilogrammes, or 1·97 cwt. E.
1 millier, 1000 kilogrammes, or 1 French ton, or 19·7 cwt. E.
4000 metres, 1 league, E.
1609·31 metres, 1 mile, E.
1 metre, 39·37079 inch, or 3 feet 3⅜ inches, E.
1 decametre, 10 metres 10·93633 yards, E.
1 kilometre, 39370·79 inch, or 5-8 of a m. E.
1 myriametre, 6·2138 ms. or 6 ms. 376 yds. E.
1 litre, 61·02705 cubic inches. E.
1 litre, 1·760773 pint or 0·220097 gal. E.
1 decalitre, 2·20097 gals. E.
1 hectolitre, 2·7512 bushels, E.
1 hectolitre, 22·00297 gals. E.
1 kilolitre, 220·0297 gals. E.
1 stere, 35·3158 cubic feet, E.
1 decistere, 3·53158 cubic feet, E
1 hectare 2·4736 inches, E.
1 arpen, 1·0430 acres, E.
1 are, 1076·4414 square feet, E.

A kilolitre is a little over 6 brls. E.; a bush. is 36·347664 litres; a qrt. is 1·13586 litres; a gal. 4·543458 litres; a rood 10·116775 ares; an acre 0·404671 hectares. To reduce English

cubic inches to *gallons*, reduce English cubic inc by 61·02705, and *vice ver*

To reduce metres into ply by 1·09364 yards, and by 0·914318. To convert pounds avoirdupois, m or pounds into kilogra To convert litres into cu ply by 61·02705; the co To convert hectolitres i multiply by 2·7513; con convert hectares into a 2·473614; acres into he For kilometres into mi miles into kilometres, b eral calculations, the reckoned as 5-8ths of a r

These are readily con ples of the standards, by 10 times, by *hecto* for 10 1000 times, as kilogram and by merely changing one place further to t two for hundreds, &c. *deci* for the 10th part, part, and *milli* for the 10 gramme, the 100th part terms for the multiplyin for dividing are Latin.

context is all

SPOT 10
柯南道爾北極犯難記
Dangerous Work: Diary of an Arctic Adventure

作者：Arthur Conan Doyle（亞瑟・柯南・道爾）
註解者：Jon Lellenberg（強・雷能柏格）
Daniel Stashower（丹尼爾・史塔蕭爾）
譯者：黃煜文
責任編輯：冼懿穎
封面設計：顏一立
美術編輯：BEATNIKS
校對：呂佳真

法律顧問：全理法律事務所董安丹律師
出版者：英屬蓋曼群島商網路與書股份有限公司台灣分公司
發行：大塊文化出版股份有限公司
台北市 10550 南京東路四段 25 號 11 樓
www.locuspublishing.com
TEL：(02)8712-3898　FAX：(02)8712-3897
讀者服務專線：0800-006689
郵撥帳號：18955675　戶名：大塊文化出版股份有限公司

總經銷：大和書報圖書股份有限公司
地址：新北市新莊區五工五路 2 號
TEL：(02)8990-2588　FAX：(02)2290-1658
製版：瑞豐實業股份有限公司

初版一刷：2014 年 8 月
定價：新台幣 520 元
ISBN：978-986-6841-56-9

國家圖書館出版品預行編目(CIP)資料

柯南道爾北極犯難記 / 亞瑟・柯南・道爾(Arthur Conan Doyle)著；強・雷能柏格(Jon Lellenberg)，丹尼爾・史塔蕭爾(Daniel Stashower)隨寫註解；黃煜文譯. -- 初版. -- 臺北市：網路與書出版：大塊文化發行，2014.08
472面；17X23公分. -- (Spot；10)
譯自：Dangerous work：diary of an arctic adventure
ISBN 978-986-6841-56-9(平裝)
1.道爾 (Doyle, Arthur Conan, Sir, 1859-1930) 2.傳記

784.18　　103013562

柯南道爾北極犯難記

Dangerous Work

Diary of an Arctic Adventure

亞瑟・柯南・道爾 著
Arthur Conan Doyle

丹尼爾・史塔蕭爾
強・雷能柏格 編註

黃煜文 譯

亞瑟・柯南・道爾（左三）攝於一八八〇年七月十二日。W.J.A. Grant 攝。（圖片鳴謝：Hull Martime Museum）

CONTENTS
目次

致謝

眾人的支持與鼓勵，是編輯得以完成這本書的動力，感謝克里斯蒂．艾倫（Christy Allen）；菲利普．伯根（Philip Bergem）；彼得．布勞（Peter Blau）；馬里波恩圖書館（Marylebone Library）的凱瑟琳．庫克（Catherine Cooke）；艾里森．寇貝特（Alison Corbett）；澳門大學約翰．寇貝特教授（John Corbett）；格林威治（Greenwich）國家航海博物館（National Maritime Museum）的理查．埃斯普里（Richard Espley）；喬治．弗萊徹（George Fletcher）；勒維克昔德蘭圖書館的道格拉斯．嘉登（Douglas Garden）；樸資茅斯中央圖書館的麥可．甘頓（Michael Gunton）；蘿拉．威斯頓（Laura Weston）與黛安．卡伍德（Dianne Cawood）；新貝德佛德捕鯨博物館（New Bedford Whaling Musuem）館長史都華．弗蘭克（Stuart N. Frank）；羅傑．強森（Roger Johnson）；明尼蘇達大學圖書館夏洛克．福爾摩斯館藏，提摩西．強森（Timothy Johnson）與茱莉亞．麥庫拉斯（Julia McKuras）；與羅伯特．卡茲博士（Robert S. Katz）。亞伯丁大學圖書館、倫敦大英圖書館、伊利諾州芝加哥紐伯里圖書館（Newberry Library）與華府國會圖書館也提供寶貴協助。最後，編輯要感謝安娜．柯南．道爾的繼承人，這幾位家族成員是亞瑟．柯南．道爾捕鯨日記的所有人，感謝他們願意提供這個日記讓我們出版：凱瑟琳．道爾．貝格斯（Catherine Doyle Beggs）、喬吉娜．道爾（Georgina Doyle）、理查．道爾（Richard Doyle）與查理．佛利（Charles Foley）。

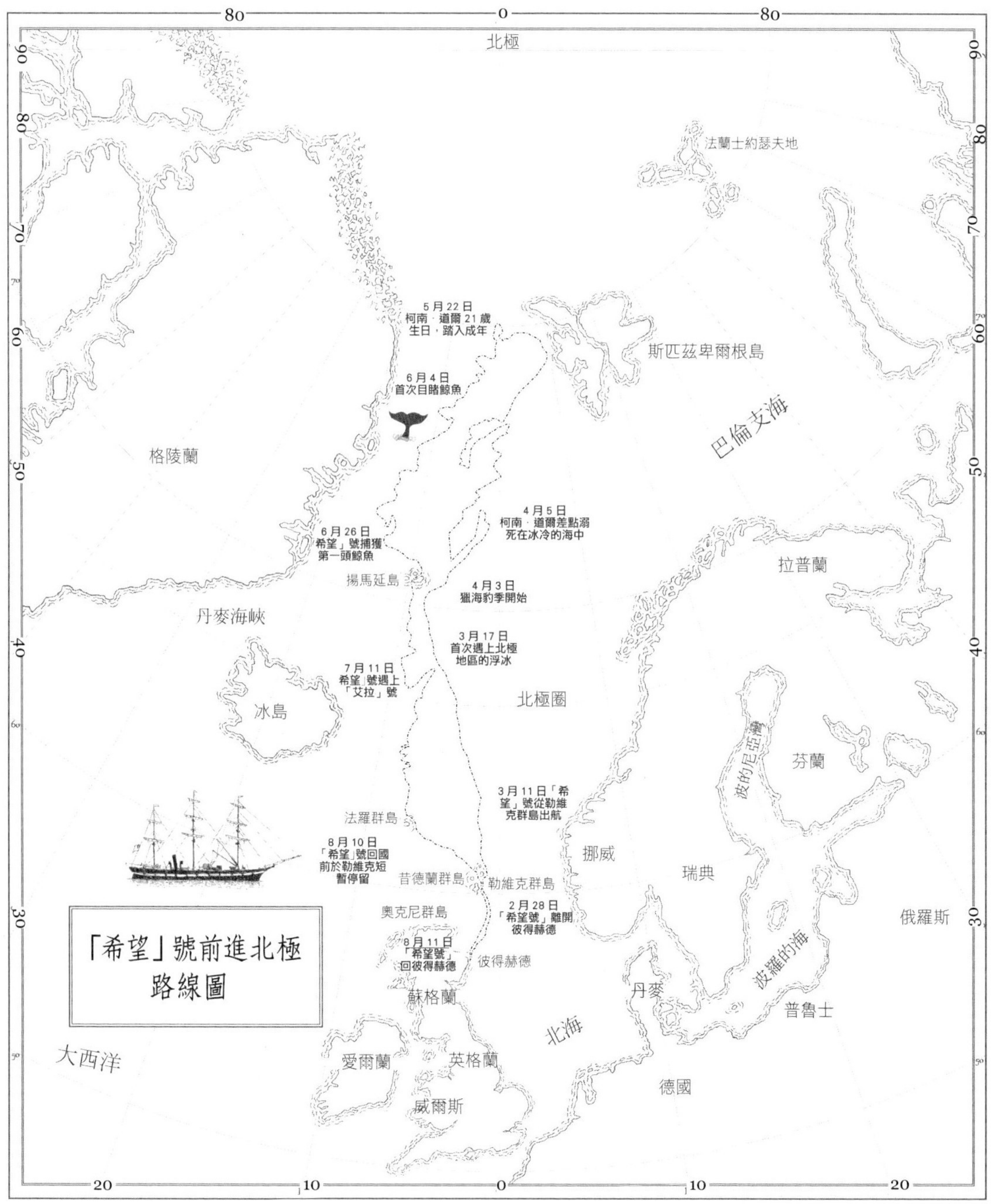
北極
法蘭士約瑟夫地
5月22日
柯南・道爾21歲
生日，踏入成年
斯匹茲卑爾根島
6月4日
首次目睹鯨魚
巴倫支海
格陵蘭
4月5日
柯南・道爾差點溺
死在冰冷的海中
6月26日
「希望」號捕獲
第一頭鯨魚
拉普蘭
揚馬延島
4月3日
獵海豹季開始
丹麥海峽
3月17日
首次遇上北極
地區的浮冰
7月11日
「希望」號遇上
「艾拉」號
北極圈
冰島
波的尼亞灣
芬蘭
3月11日「希
望」號從勒維
克群島出航
法羅群島
8月10日
「希望」號回國
前於勒維克短
暫停留
挪威
昔德蘭群島
勒維克群島
瑞典
2月28日
「希望號」離開
彼得赫德
奧克尼群島
俄羅斯
「希望」號前進北極
路線圖
8月11日
「希望號」
回彼得赫德
彼得赫德
丹麥
波羅的海
蘇格蘭
北海
普魯士
大西洋
愛爾蘭
英格蘭
德國
威爾斯

前言　「我在北緯八十度成為真正的男人」

一八八〇年三月的某個下午，一個名叫亞瑟·柯南·道爾（Arthur Conan Doyle）的年輕醫學系學生，突然一時衝動，決定暫停學業，到北極捕鯨船上擔任船醫。這趟為期六個月的航行，帶他進入未知的領域，給予他無法想像的閱歷與經驗，讓他一頭栽進北極海浮冰危險而血腥的工作。面對前所未見的艱困環境，他更努力地工作。他與同船水手辯論哲學與宗教，不只一次與死亡擦肩而過。他說，這趟旅程是「我人生第一次親身經歷的冒險犯難之旅」。

「事情是這麼發生的，」許多年後他在自傳《回憶與冒險》（*Memories and Adventures*）中解釋：

> 愛丁堡一個溼冷的下午，我正坐在桌前努力準備考試，每個醫學院學生都被這些考試搞得焦頭爛額，此時有個叫居里（Claud Currie）的人走進來，他也是醫學院的學生，我跟他稍有交情。接下來他問的荒唐問題讓我的心思無法專注在書本上。
>
> 「你想不想下星期跟著捕鯨船出海？」他說，「你可以擔任船醫，一個月兩英鎊十先令，獲得的鯨魚油每噸以三先令

亞瑟．柯南．道爾，攝於一八八〇年代初，他在樸茨茅斯南海城執業期間。
（圖片鳴謝：Conan Doyle Estate Ltd.）

計算。」

「你怎麼知道我上得了船？」我毫不思索地反問他。

「因為我自己在船上有個鋪位。我是上個月找到這份差事，但現在我沒辦法去，所以我要找個人頂替我。」

「到北極的服裝配備呢？」

「你可以用我的。」

這件事當下就搞定了，不到幾分鐘，我的人生突然轉了大彎，往全新的航道駛去。[1]

柯南．道爾此時只有二十歲，是愛丁堡大學醫學系三年級的學生。「說到我的大學成績，」他回憶說，「我總是屬於人數最多的那一群，既不是最好的，也不是最差的，我的考試成績大概可以贏六成的人。」他典型的自謙之詞，總是輕描淡寫自己在面對困難時的努力與成就。數年後，他以慣有的振奮語氣表示，他是在「刻苦自勵的貧困生活中」長大的，但這段話顯然掩蓋了「家中的混亂與艱難，亞瑟十歲前，道爾家至少搬了五次。然而他們家雖然貧困，卻還是重視教養，亞瑟的父親查爾斯．道爾（Charles Doyle）長年染病酗酒，勉強靠著測量員的薪水度日，直到他丟了這份工作為止，當時他才只有四十四歲。

無論如何，家裡還是籌足了錢，讓年輕的亞瑟到斯托尼赫斯特（Stonyhurst）——英格蘭傑出的耶穌會寄宿學校——接

1 "Whaling in the Arctic Ocean," *Memories and Adventures* (London: Hodder & Stoughton, 1924), ch. 4,〈前言〉隨後引用時將不再註明出處。

受第一流的教育。畢業後，亞瑟覺得自己必須分攤一些父親的責任，並且設法改善一大家子的生活。「日子艱難對我來說或許是好事，」他寫道，「因為我桀驁不馴、精力充沛而且容易闖禍，但家裡的狀況需要我費心與投入精力，這樣才能解決家庭困境。我的母親努力持家，所以我們不能讓她失望。很早我就決定當醫生，主要是因為我認為愛丁堡是個醫學研究重鎮。」

而就在這個時期，夏洛克·福爾摩斯（Sherlock Holmes）故事最初的種子也開始播下。柯南·道爾小時候讀過「世上最原創的短篇小說家」埃德加·愛倫·坡（Edgar Allan Poe）的作品，還大聲朗讀他的小說，有時「會把全家人嚇得魂不附體」。在愛丁堡大學，柯南·道爾有幸擔任約瑟夫·貝爾醫生（Joseph Bell）的助理，貝爾的觀察與診斷技巧是極具魅力。只要簡單看一下病人，貝爾就能看出病人染上什麼病，以及病人詳細的背景與職業資訊。「對喜愛華生（Watson）的讀者來說，」柯南·道爾晚年開玩笑說，「一切似乎是如此的不可思議，但在解釋之後，卻又變得如此簡單。」這位夏洛克·福爾摩斯的未來創作者，早在二十歲時就已出版了一本推理小說，因而讓他賺到了三基尼（guineas），令當時經常為了花兩便士買舊書而不吃午飯的他興奮不已。

柯南·道爾簽約參加北極捕鯨，這個決定在勤奮而節儉的母親看來，無疑是冒險而莽撞的，但這也給予柯南·道爾難得的機會。他可以滿足心中的探險欲，而且這麼做還有錢可拿。此外，在船上的六個月也讓他有機會磨練文筆，滿足他成為作家的野心。在前往蘇格蘭港口彼得赫德（Peterhead）登上捕鯨船「希望」號（Hope）之前，柯南·道爾把克勞德·居里給他的航海裝備再加以擴充，他增添了幾本書，包括詩、哲學與文學，以及幾本空白的日記本，用來記錄旅途上的所見所聞。[2] 這些日記本將成為這名年輕人在遭遇前所未有的試煉下的深刻個人紀錄。

可惜的是，柯南．道爾一直到了「希望」號從彼得赫德出航時，才開始記錄，但大家其實很想知道出發前幾天發生了什麼事。如果有相關紀錄記下柯南．道爾辛苦工作的母親，對於二十歲的兒子中斷醫學學業從事這趟危險的旅程作何感想，應該會是件有趣的事。「幾乎沒有人知道捕鯨船在北極海會面臨什麼樣的危險，」自然學家法蘭西斯．巴克蘭（Francis Buckland）於一八七六年寫道：「他們從事的工作十分凶險。」他說，他們的船有時甚至要像攻城鎚一樣，靠著蠻力在冰上「撞出一條航道」，否則的話，浮冰「一合圍，船隻被凍住無法動彈，屆時全船的人都將困在北極過冬」。[3]

柯南．道爾如果寫下他對於船長與船員，以及往後七個月他要待的「希望」號的第一印象，那麼想必內容應該會非常有趣。「希望」號是在一八七三年由亞伯丁的亞力山大霍爾公司（Alexander Hall & Co.）建造完成，長四十五英尺五英寸，寬二十八英尺一英寸，深十七英尺。一八八二年，『希望』號奉命執行一項危險的北極救援任務，因為這艘船「在各方面都很適合探險工作。它的結構堅固，吃水線下敷設了雙層木板，內部以鋼鐵支架加固，船頭蒙上鐵皮。與其他捕鯨船相比，『希望』號的破冰能力更加傑出；凡是駕駛『希望』號的船員都相信，這艘船可以協助他們完成任何任務」。[4]

柯南．道爾提到，「希望」號可以搭載五十六名人員。『希望』號的船員名單現已不存，但是與「希望」號大小差不多的捕鯨船，也就是來自鄧迪（Dundee）的「北極」號，則是可搭載五十八名船員：船長、大副與二副（兼任魚叉手）、

2 柯南．道爾的日誌包括了兩本筆記本，內容將近兩萬五千字，以及七十幅附文字說明的鋼筆畫，其中一些手工上色的圖片描繪了「希望」號從一八八〇年二月二十八日到八月十一日的航程見聞。我們對日記的抄本做了註解，使其更為清楚易懂，同時也賦予讀者可理解的脈絡。我們另外附上了柯南．道爾在旅途中寄回家的兩封信，第一封是從昔德蘭群島（Shetland Islands）的首府勒維克（Lerwick）寄的，第二封是在海上交由經過的船隻帶回。

3 Francis Trevelyan Buckland, *Log-Book of a Fisherman and Zoologist* (London: Chapman & Hall, 1876), p. 290.

4 "Experiences of a Naval Officer in Search of the *Eira*", *Blackwood's Magazine*, November 1882, p. 599.

「希望」號示意圖。「希望」號由亞伯丁的亞力山大霍爾公司建造，「當時公司的事業正處於巔峰時期，或許可以說是世界上最成功的快速帆船建造商。」（引自 Basil Lubbock's *The Arctic Whalers*, Glasgow, 1937.）

一名船醫、一名勤務員、一名輪機長、一名大管輪與鐵匠、三名火伕、一名木匠與一名木匠助手、一名負責切除鯨魚油脂的「鯨油手」（兼任魚叉手）、兩名「資深」魚叉手與兩名「見習魚叉手」、一名桶匠（兼任魚叉手）、八名纜繩手（他們纏繞纜繩的技巧攸關全船的生死）、六名小艇舵手、一名水手長、一名負責將鯨魚油脂儲藏在船的儲藏槽的「儲藏長」（水手長與儲藏長也兼任舵手）、一名船舶看守員、一名廚師與一名廚師助手、十名一等水手、五名二等水手與三名船上服務員。[5]「希望」號的船員，來自彼得赫德與來自昔德蘭群島的人數比例大約是二比一。

「希望」號是依照彼得赫德的約翰·格雷船長（John Gray）的訂單建造的，此次出航他正好五十歲。「我看見船長，」多年後，柯南·道爾回憶說，「他有著紅潤的臉龐，鬚髮都已斑白，他的眼珠是淺藍色的，

5 Albert Hastings Markham, *A Whaling Cruise to Baffin's Bay and the Gulf of Boothia* (London: Sampson Low, 1874), p. 11.

總是望著遠方，全身充滿肌肉，總是站得直挺挺的。沉默寡言、冷嘲熱諷，必要時相當嚴厲，但終究來說他是個正直的好人。」約翰·格雷與他的哥哥大衛（David）和弟弟亞歷山大（Alexander）是彼得赫德捕鯨家族的後裔，他們在此發展已歷三代。「不可擊敗的格雷家族」建立的捕鯨事業在十九世紀中葉達到巔峰，現在則因鯨魚數量減少而沒落。為了回應挑戰，格雷家族除了採取前瞻性的保育措施，也在帆船上裝設蒸汽引擎，好讓船隻能深入北極海域。一八八〇年代，捕鯨業終於步入衰途，但彼得赫德當地的捕鯨業，如研究當地的史家所言，「由於格雷家族的堅持，因而比其他地區持續更久。有人說，捕鯨業的消亡不是因為產業本身的衰微，而是因為格雷家族的人年老體衰所致，這話恐怕不假。」[6] 約翰與大衛·格雷在一八九一年賣掉他們的船隻，就此退休。

一八八〇年，當格雷與他的船員準備航行時，誰也沒想到捕鯨事業未來將畫上句點。柯南·道爾馬上就對船長產生好感，但船長先前不知道柯南·道爾是什麼樣的人物，等到他們見面之後，他覺得這名新船醫跟他的想像有點差異。「我很快就發現到，」柯南·道爾寫道，「船醫的主要任務是陪伴船長，由於行規的關係，船長與其他船員只能進行非常簡短而技術性的交談，因此幾乎找不到人可以聊天。如果船長是個惡劣的傢伙，我應該會無法忍受，但『希望』號的約翰·格雷是個傑出人物、了不起的水手，同時也是熱心的蘇格蘭人，因此他跟我成了朋友，長期相處下來，我們從未起過爭執。」

柯南·道爾雖然在彼得赫德待的時間很短，但他發現這座城鎮非常殷切地盼望日漸減少的捕鯨船隊能獲得成功。

6 Alexander R. Buchan, *The Peterhead Whaling Trade* (Peterhead: Buchan Field Club, 1999), p. 52.

「這群傑出而誠實的海上男兒，個個精神煥發，健壯無比」。一八八〇年，「希望」號船員攝於彼得赫德凱斯島（Keith Inch）的鯨油處理場。

一九〇二年，愛丁堡報紙《蘇格蘭人》（*The Scotsman*）的一篇文章回顧過去那段「光輝而偉大的產業」榮景。

> 現在住在鎮上的居民想必都還記得，當時出港捕鯨的船隻不下三十一艘，而商人從捕鯨船運回的珍貴貨物獲得了大量財富。不難想像，那是彼得赫德人的輝煌時光。在上個世紀的四〇與五〇年代，鎮上很少有人與捕鯨業無關，鎮民要不是捕鯨船的船主或船員，就是在鯨油處理場（把「鯨油」製造成可販售的商品的地方）工作。當春天來臨時，鎮民總是成群前往港口，向北航的船隊致予「祝福」；到了夏末，鎮民急切地等候捕鯨船捎來豐收的佳音，當被暴風雨摧殘的船隻終於拖著沉重的船身進港時——這是當時常見的場景——民眾開始歡喜慶祝。[7]

對英國捕鯨業的一項研究估計，在捕鯨業存在的三個世紀裡，至少從三十五個港口出發了六千趟船次前往北極地區，要不是到「格陵蘭漁場」——介於格陵蘭東部海岸與挪威之間的海域，向外延伸到斯匹茲卑爾根島（Spitzbergen）——就是前往格陵蘭西邊的戴維斯海峽（Davis Strait），包括哈德遜灣（Hudson Bay）與巴芬灣（Baffin Bay）。「希望」號在格陵蘭漁場作業，先是在冰島北方揚馬延島（Jan Mayen Island）外的菱紋海豹漁場，然後再往北到捕鯨海域。「主要獵捕的鯨魚是『格陵蘭鯨』、『格陵蘭露脊鯨』或『弓頭鯨』（Baeaena mysticetus）……此外還獵捕白鯨（Delphinapterus leucas）、一角鯨（Monodon monoceros）、北瓶鼻鯨（Hyperoodon ampullatus）、海象（Odobenus rosmarus）與數種海豹。」[8] 捕鯨人每年有六到七個月的時間在海上，從年輕到退休乃至於死亡全在海上，在北極圈的他們，完全不知道一般夏天是什麼樣子。

一八八〇年，當船隻啟航，柯南．道爾站在後甲板，接受盛大慶祝與傳統的洗禮。「我查了一下日誌，發現那是二月二十八日下午兩點，我們在群眾的歡呼聲中從彼得赫德出發，」他回憶說。[9] 海上生活的現實很快就讓他們受夠了。當「希望」號往北朝勒維克駛去，也就是昔德蘭的主要港口，船遭遇了不良的天候與暴風。「我們趕在暴風雨來臨前進入勒維克港，」柯南．道爾在自傳裡回憶說，「風勢極為強勁，船隻停泊時我們僅靠幾根柱子固定，而在缺乏遮蔽下，每個人的身

7 "The Peterhead Whalers," *The Scotsman* (Edinburgh), November 19, 1902.

8 見 Sidney Brown, Arthur Credlund, Ann Savours and Bernard Stonehouse, "British Arctic whaling logbooks and journals: a provisional listing," in *Polar Record*, January 2008, pp. 311-12。

9 事實上，柯南．道爾這裡說的日誌，可能是他的個人日記（他稱為他的日誌），也可能是由他保管的官方航海日誌。捕鯨船的船醫「經常受船長囑託，負責留意航海日誌是否逐日記載，」布坎（Buchan）的 *The Peterhead Whaling Trade* 第五十六頁說道，柯南．道爾也如此表示。一九三七年之後，這份航海日誌就消失無蹤了，盧伯克（Basil Lubbock）的 *The Arctic Whalers* (Glasgow: Brown, Son & Ferguson Ltd.) 說這本日誌寫滿了「柯南．道爾整齊的字跡」，並且引用八月四日的條目，認為上面的紀錄比柯南．道爾在自己的日記上寫的更為切合實際，關於這點，我們接下來將會看到。

約翰．格雷船長（一八三〇～一八九二），「希望」號的船主。「他是傑出人物、了不起的水手，同時也是熱心的蘇格蘭人。」（圖片鳴謝：Conan Doyle Estate Ltd.）

子都彎成極尖銳的角度。如果暴風早幾個小時到來，我們鐵定會損失幾艘小艇——而這些小艇是捕鯨人的命。」

在天氣好轉前，恐怕要等待一個星期以上。在這段時間，柯南．道爾逐漸喜歡上昔德蘭群島的遺世獨立。「我與當地一名老人說話，他向我問起一些新聞，」他寫道。「我說，『泰河橋（Tay bridge）[10]倒塌了。』這件事其實已是舊聞。他說，『喔，那麼他們在泰河上蓋新橋了嗎？』」柯南．道爾對於勒維克並沒有太大興趣，但他在當地待了十一天，正值三月初該鎮最熱鬧喧騰的時候，那是現在已不復見的蘇格蘭捕鯨熱季。一九二三年，研究勒維克的史家問道：

有多少人記得在二月與三月初，勒維克港裡許多格陵蘭捕鯨船爭奇鬥豔的景象？——雙桅橫帆船、三桅帆船、前桅橫帆三桅船，這些船絕大多數是三桅；蒸汽船與帆船，有些在船身漆上炮

10 編註：泰河橋建於一八七一年，於一八七九年十二月二十八日在暴風雨中倒塌，當時正有一列火車行駛其中，導致所有乘客罹難。

眼，看起來就像戰艦一樣；船隻的旗幟在微風中飄揚著；充滿活力的船員到了岸上，立即加入狂歡的行列，然後把自己搞得累到半死；全國各地對捕鯨充滿熱情的人紛紛雲集於這個城鎮；船公司辦公室日夜擠滿了人，許多簽約上船的船員在這裡採買航往北極所需的各項裝備與補給。[11]

三月十一日，惡劣的天氣好轉。「希望」號離開勒維克，繼續往北前進，柯南．道爾的船醫工作也正式開始。「由於我的醫學知識只有醫科生大三的程度，」他寫道，「我常想，船上應該不會出現太嚴重的病症吧。」[12] 然而，多年後的輕鬆回憶，掩蓋了他醫療事業上的一個重大悲劇：他第一次遭遇病人死亡。這名病人染上嚴重的腸胃疾病，在海上，年輕醫生沒有辦法治好他。

柯南．道爾有處理傷口的經驗，他自己弄傷的部位都是自己處理。「我念書的時候，拳擊是我最喜歡的消遣活動，」他回憶說，「我發現，為了爭取時間念書，必須尋找一種能將最多運動量壓縮在最短時間完成的運動。因此，我隨身帶了兩副打扁而且褪色的拳套。剛好勤務員也有點喜歡打鬥，於是等我行李一放好，他就馬上拿起拳套，提議兩人打一場。」

勤務員的身材矮小，但體格強壯，他後來成為柯南．道爾最喜愛的船員之一。「我看見他，」他日後寫道，「碧眼黃鬚，個子矮小，胸膛厚實，肌肉發達，雙腿外八。」柯南．道爾剛戴上拳套，勤務員就舉起雙拳壓上來。「我們的比賽不

11 Thomas Manson, *Lerwick During the Last Half Century* (Lerwick: T. & J. Manson, *Shetland News Offices*, 1923), p. 141.
12 "Life on a Greenland Whaler," *The Strand Magazine*, January 1897 (reprinted in the volume).

勒維克，昔德蘭群島的首府，從港口觀看的景象：「骯髒的小鎮，居民單純好客。」（圖片鳴謝：Shetland Museum）

太公平，」他說，「因為他比我矮了數寸，手臂比我短得多，而且他對拳擊一無所知，不過我毫不懷疑如果我們是在街頭打鬥，他會是一個可怕的對手。他一直衝過來，我只好用拳頭頂著他，最後，我發現他執意想找到空隙出拳，於是我只好狠狠給他一下。」

但之後：

大概過了一個鐘頭，當我在大廳讀書時，聽見隔壁大副房間傳來低語的聲音，突然我聽見勤務員用確信的語調大聲地說：「幫幫我吧，柯林，他是我們手邊所能找到最好的醫生了！他把我的眼睛打青了！」

把勤務員的眼睛打青這件事，使柯南．道爾成了「希望」號最好的醫生，而這件事也「考驗著我（柯南．道爾）的醫術，但我想這點傷沒什麼大礙」（柯南．道爾起初對於紅鬍子大個兒柯林．麥克林（Colin McLean）感到疑惑，船長為什麼任命「一個度量狹小、衰老、失意的傢伙擔任大副，這實在是一件奇怪的事，他顯然無法履行他的職務」，而且麥克林簽的約還是廚師助手的工作。船一離港，大副與廚師助手馬上交換位子：強壯的麥克林扛起大副的職責，而那位身形單薄的船員則消失在廚房裡。但麥克林不識字，不具備擔任大副的資格）。

從勒維克出發後不到一個星期，「希望」號駛抵開闊的冰原地帶。「北極地區最讓我驚訝的一點，」柯南．道爾寫道，「是你很快就能抵達這個地區。我過去從不知道北極幾乎就在我們的家門口。」他在日記裡記錄抵達的日期是三月十七日。「有天早晨我被浮冰碰撞船身的巨大聲響吵醒，」他回憶說，「走到甲板一看，整片海都被冰塊覆蓋了，一直相連到天際。這些浮冰不算巨大，但相當厚實，人可以在冰塊與冰塊之間跳躍，毫無問題。浮冰白得令人目眩，相對之下，大海顯得更藍了，還有頭頂上的藍天，以及穿過鼻腔的冷冽北極空氣，這是個令人難忘的早晨。」

英國與挪威已訂定協議，在三月海豹繁殖期結束前，不許獵捕海豹，因此船員紛紛利用這個時間追蹤小群的海豹，以找出牠們的主要群落。「當你真的來到此地，那景象真是美麗，」柯南．道爾寫道。「從主桅頂端的瞭望台望去，完全看不到盡頭。在肉眼可見的最遠處，只見冰上散布著像胡椒粉般的黑點。」然而，惡劣的天氣再度阻礙了他們的計畫。「『希望』號是那年最早發現海豹群的船隻，」柯南．道爾說，「但在准許獵捕那天到來之前，我們遭遇一連串的暴風，起伏的波浪使浮冰劇烈搖晃，許多小海豹因此提早入海。因此，等到解禁之時，大自然已讓我們無事可做。」

即使如此，四月三日，船員們還是手持木棒四向而出，在冰上進行搜尋。柯南．道爾也想跟著去獵捕海豹，但當他準備加入獵捕行列時，卻被格雷船長叫住——他認為冰上的狀況對新手來說太危險了。「我的抗議無效，」他說，「我悶悶不樂地坐在舷牆邊，兩隻腳在船側晃蕩著。我一口氣吞不下，整個身體隨著船身的搖動而上下起伏。然而，我坐的木頭上

勒維克港中的「希望」號：「幾天前，我們換了停泊的位置，現在我們離其他船隻有一段距離，與『上風』號（Windward）停靠在一起。」（圖片鳴謝：Shetland Museum）

剛好結了一層薄冰，冰隆起之後產生了傾斜，我一不留心，整個人滑下船，從兩塊浮冰之間跌入海裡。」柯南．道爾掙扎著爬回船上，卻發現他的厄運為他帶來意想不到的好處：「船長說，反正我無論如何都會摔進海裡，那麼在冰上或在船上都一樣。」

柯南．道爾頭一次在冰上行走，曾摔進海裡兩次以上，回到船上後他只能待在床上結束這一天，因為他的衣物必須拿到引擎室烘乾。「此後很長一段時間，大家都戲稱我是『偉大的北方跳水員』，」他笑道。

儘管一開始不太順利，但柯南．道爾還是逐漸習慣在冰上行走，甚至可以跟其他船員一樣獨自出去打獵。有天下午，當他蹲伏在剛殺死的海豹旁時，突然往後一滑，從冰緣跌進海裡。「我和其他人有一段距離，」他說，「沒有人看見我出事。冰的表面非常光滑，我找不到任何可施力的地方讓自己爬上來，而在寒凍的海水裡，我的身體很快就變得僵硬。」如果他無法爬回冰上，不消幾分鐘，就有可能喪命。他有幾次緊攀著光滑的冰緣，直到最後，他奮力抓住剛剛剝皮的海豹尾端的鰭狀肢。有幾次緊張的時刻，就像「噩夢般進行著拉鋸戰」，柯南．道爾靠著冰塊，試著讓自己放鬆一點，以免海豹也跟著他滑進海裡。最後，他終於將一個膝蓋抬出水面，然後奮力起身讓自己落在冰上，剛好摔在死去的海豹旁邊。這位「偉大的北方跳水員」再度待在床上結束了這一天：「當我回到船上時，身上的衣服硬得跟盔甲一樣，我必須先烤融這一身發出爆裂聲的冰衣裳，才能換上新的衣物。」

柯南．道爾日後坦承，他對於獵殺海豹充滿不安。「那是一件殘忍的差事，」他寫道，「雖然比不上為了供應國內民眾餐桌上的菜餚所做的事來得殘忍。然而深紅的池子映照著雪白的冰原，在寧靜安詳的湛藍天空下，確實予人深刻的恐怖感受。然而，無可抵擋的需求創造出無可抵擋的供給，海豹的死，養活了一長串的人：水手、碼頭工人、製革工人、醃製工、食品檢驗者、蠟燭商、皮革商與油商。一端是專門宰殺動物的人，另一端則是穿著海豹皮製成的軟皮靴、過著優雅生活的人，或者是使用海豹油脂作為鑽研哲學的利器的學者。」

六月，「希望」號繼續往北航行，捕鯨行動開始。「真正了解弓頭鯨價值的人並不多見，」柯南．道爾日後寫道：「鯨鬚優良的大鯨魚在今日價值可達兩千到三千英鎊。昂貴的價格主要來自於鯨鬚，這是非常罕有的商品，但某些商業卻是以鯨鬚作為核心。」由於獲利他也能分一杯羹，因此他自然就對獵鯨的成功與否特別在意。「希望」號上有八艘捕鯨艇，只要船上有人留守——所謂的「遊手好閒者」，但他們其實身負其他任務——那麼通常只會派七艘出去，留下一艘在船上。在這次航行中，也許是出於柯南．道爾的煽動，這些遊手好閒者自願搭乘剩下的一艘小艇出航。他們很快就捕到鯨魚，一如他的估算，而且是所有船隻中最有效率的。「我們都很年輕、強壯而且很積極，」[13] 他日後對訪談者說，「我認為我們的小

早期的捕鯨船，「上方是沉重如屋椽般的桅杆，下方則是隆起的冰丘」，一八六九年。（來自 William Bradford, John L. Dunmore and George Critcherson, *The Arctic Regions*, London: Sampson Low, 1973.）

艇跟其他小艇相比，毫不遜色。」[14]

「捕鯨是件令人興奮的工作，」柯南．道爾寫道：

你背對著鯨魚，你想知道鯨魚的一舉一動，必須從舵手的臉才能看出。舵手越過你的頭頂凝視前方，看著生物在水中緩慢穿梭。當他發現鯨魚的眼神起了變化，他會舉手做出停止划船的信號，而在快接觸鯨魚的時候，他會要求大家安靜。這裡有許多浮冰，只要船槳不發出聲響，那麼就算船隻靠近也不會讓鯨魚潛入海中。所以要慢慢前進，

13 在他的日誌裡記著，甭提那艘「烏合之眾小艇」了，上面坐的都是「希望」號上年紀最大的人。

14 訪談者——文章見一九〇七年七月二十八日的《紐約世界》（*New York World*）——是盎格魯愛爾蘭劇場經理與小說家布萊姆．斯托克（Bram Stoker），他在十年前出版了《德古拉》（*Dracula*）。這篇訪談 "Sir Arthur Conan Doyle Tells of his Career and Work, his Sentiments towards America, and his Approaching Marriage," 收入 *Sir Arthur Conan Doyle: Interviews and Recollections*，Harold Orel 編輯（London: Macmillan, 1991）。在《德古拉》第六章，伯爵抵達惠特比（Whitby，英國早期捕鯨業的重鎮），登上一艘從黑海來的俄國船。在此之前的一則由古代水手斯威爾斯（Swales）告訴蜜娜．莫瑞（Mina Murray）與露西．韋斯騰拉（Lucy Westenra）的北極捕鯨故事，成了這則故事的先聲。

等到距離夠近時，舵手知道可以趕在鯨魚潛水前採取行動——因為這麼龐大的身軀需要一點時間才能做出反應。你看見舵手的眼睛一亮，臉色一變，他喊道，「兄弟們，划槳，快，用力划！」巨大魚叉槍的扳機一扣，船槳在海中打出大量的泡沫。大概划了六下左右，在沉重的油脂擠壓聲中，船頭撞上某件柔軟的東西，把船上的人與船槳震得東倒西歪。但你沒有時間理會這種事，因為當你碰撞到鯨魚時，魚叉槍也發出爆裂聲，你知道魚叉已經射進鯨魚巨大而呈鉛色的曲線身體裡。鯨魚就像石頭一樣下沉，船頭再度往下敲擊水面，此時座位底下的纜繩颼地快速往前拉扯，從你張開的雙腿之間直直朝船頭奔去。

此時正是最危險的時刻——因為在這種狀況下，很少有鯨魚會回頭來攻擊船隻。纜繩早已由專門的纜繩手纏好，確保鯨魚拉扯時不會糾纏打結。然而，如果發生打結，如果繩圈剛好圈住某個船員的四肢，那麼這個人會一下子就死於非命，速度可能快到連他的同伴都不知道他是怎麼死的。此時割斷纜繩已無濟於事，反而白白損失一頭鯨魚，因為受害者恐怕已被拉到水下幾百噚[15]的深處。

「住手，」魚叉手叫道，一名水手正打算拿刀割斷繩子。「這條魚對逝者來說可是好東西。」聽起來很無情，卻不無道理。

柯南．道爾成了一名經驗豐富的捕鯨人，他的技術熟練到讓格雷船長邀請他隔年再來捕鯨，除了擔任船醫，也擔任魚叉手。「我當然拒絕了，」他說，「因為這個行業雖然吸引人，卻太危險。」即使如此，這趟漫長的海上探險卻賦予他筆下人物愛好冒險的性格。「釣鮭魚是個莊嚴的活動，」柯南．道爾表示，「但是，當你的魚比一棟郊區別墅還貴重，而且

15 譯註：一噚約一點八三公尺。

價值高達兩千英鎊；當你的釣線是一條拇指粗的馬尼拉麻繩，由五十條小細繩編成，每條細繩可承重三十六磅時，我想任何經驗都會相形見絀。」

然而，與屠殺海豹一樣，柯南．道爾也對自己在捕鯨漁場目擊到的「殺戮豐收」感到不安：「在興奮中──唯有親身參與其中，才能感受那股難以言喻的興奮──人們不可避免對這個遭受獵殺的可憐生物感到同情。鯨魚的眼睛很小，只不過比公牛的眼睛稍微大一點；但我無法輕易忘記我在一頭鯨魚眼中看見的無言抗議，我只要一伸手就能觸摸到牠，而牠的眼睛隨著死亡的逼近而漸漸黯淡無光。」

有一次，柯南．道爾記錄著，有一頭鯨魚差點成功復仇。他與一群船員用魚叉刺一頭已經被射中的鯨魚。槳手試圖把船划向安全的地點，以免被鯨魚的尾鰭打中，此時這頭受傷的鯨魚巨大的「前鰭」突然從水中舉起，拍打他們的船。「光這麼一拍就足以讓我們沉入海底，」柯南．道爾回憶說。「我永遠不會忘記，我們努力從下方衝出，每個人都伸手要趕走那片巨大而充滿威脅的魚鰭──彷佛我們可以阻止鯨魚潛入水中。」

「希望」號於八月初返航，帶回「數量不多」的貨物，包括兩頭鯨魚、三千六百隻海豹與各種北極熊、獨角鯨及北極鳥類。對船員來說，這次的漁獲量不怎麼理想，顯示這次出海並不成功，但柯南．道爾卻從不同的角度判斷這是一次成功的航行。「我上船時還只是個浮誇、渙散的年輕人，」他在自己的回憶錄裡表示，但「我下船時已是個強壯、成熟的男人。我這輩子身體一直相當健康，無疑是受到北極新鮮空氣的影響，而我的精力充沛，也應該是在北極捕鯨時鍛鍊出來的」。

柯南．道爾從未忘記他與其他船員長達數月與世隔絕而產生的孤立感。「我們在令人興奮的時期離開，」他回憶說，尤其當時英國似乎即將與俄國發生戰爭。孤立也讓人產生不同的感受。柯南．道爾回憶說，當「希望」號繞經蘇格蘭北部時，看見有個女人出現在岸邊燈塔上，船員們紛紛低聲而興奮地說：「是女人！」「要欣賞女人，必須六個月沒看過女人才行，」柯南．道爾評論說。「每個人都緊盯著她。那個女人顯然已年過五十，穿著短裙與防水長靴——但她是個『女人』。『戴著老婦帽的人一定是女人！』水手們習慣這麼說，而當時我也這麼想。」

柯南．道爾在彼得赫德與船上的同伴道別，然後回到愛丁堡，與母親團圓。令人更高興的是，他的薪水與分得的鯨魚油錢，總共為家裡補貼了五十英鎊。「之後我開始準備我的期末考，」他說，「一八八一年冬季學期末，我順利通過考試，但成績不是非常突出。我成了一名醫學士與外科醫學碩士，然後開始我的執業生涯。」

當時，他已忘記他曾寫下北極日記，但北極的經驗已滲透到他的骨子裡。一百三十年後，柯南．道爾在「希望」號的日記提供我們一個遙望過去的窗口。他的日記不只是一個男孩如何成為男人的故事，它也是北極探險與如今已不復見的海上生活故事。晚年的柯南．道爾在回顧這段過程時仍充滿敬畏。「你站在未知的懸崖邊，」他說，「你射下的每一隻鴨子，砂囊裡留存的小石子，都來自地圖尚未繪出的地方。那是我人生中一段奇異而美妙的篇章。」

強．雷能柏格（Jon Lellenberg）與丹尼爾．史塔蕭爾（Daniel Stashower）

亞瑟・柯南・道爾

航海日誌註解謄本

強・雷能柏格與丹尼爾・史塔蕭爾謄寫註解

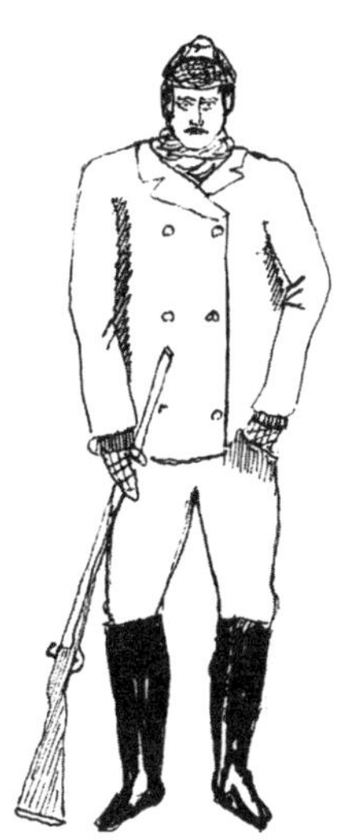

「希望」號航海日誌（一八八〇年）

獵捕弓頭鯨與海豹

〔〕內為航海日誌摹本頁碼

二月二十八日 星期六〔D005〕

兩點鐘，在群眾歡呼聲中，船隻出航。[1] 「上風」號船長穆雷[2]在我們前頭出港，只見他像巴珊公牛（Bull of Bashan）[3]一樣吼著「左舷」與「右舷」。與「上風」號相比，我們比較安靜，也比較有執行職務的樣子。我們的船跟紳士的遊艇一樣乾淨，黃銅擦拭得光亮，甲板也雪白無垢。[4] 我看見一位別人介紹認識的年輕女士，但我已想不起她的芳名，她就站在碼頭末端揮舞手帕。雖然我想不起來她是誰，但我還是站在「希望」號後甲板向她脱帽致意。外頭的天氣相當惡劣，氣壓計下降得很快。船在港灣來回繞了幾個鐘頭，然後在晚宴中以香檳向巴克斯特[5]與登船貴客表示敬意。最後，引水船把這群客人接下船，一名躲在甲板間隙的偷渡客運氣不佳，也被揪出來送下了船。[6] 在暴風中航往昔德蘭群島，氣壓計就像牡蠣一樣[7]直線下墜。[8] 雖然風勢很大，但我仍想繼續待在甲板上。

三月一日 星期日[9]（D005）

下午七點三十分，進入勒維克。此時吹起了八級風，我們的運氣不錯，如果我們再晚一點靠岸，恐怕就會失去幾艘小艇與舷牆。我們原本感到很不安，直到下午五點三十分看到布雷塞燈塔[10]的燈光才放下心來。船長很高興我們比「上風」號早抵達勒維克，雖然「上風」號其實比我們早了五小時出發。

1 捕鯨人迷信星期五出航會遭遇厄運，因此延後到星期六出航。

2 亞歷山大·穆雷船長（Alexander Murray, 1838-1894）多年來一直是彼得赫德螺槳三桅帆船「上風」號的船長。一八九三年，「上風」號成了彼得赫德最後一艘捕鯨船，當時的船長是大衛·格雷，也就是「希望」號船長的哥哥。

3 詩篇二二12（欽定版）：「有許多公牛圍繞我；巴珊大力的公牛四面困住我。他們向我張口，好像抓撕吼叫的獅子。」羅伯特·格雷夫斯（Robert Graves）在他的詩〈我猜想溺水是什麼感覺〉中寫道，「如雷鳴般的可怕呼吼，／是巴珊公牛的叫聲。／海水高漲，船隻應聲碎裂……」

4 「跟我對捕鯨船的印象不太一樣，」柯南·道爾在《回憶與冒險》（一九二四）中坦承。

5 威廉·巴克斯特（William Baxter）是「上風」號的船主。一九〇二年十一月十九日《蘇格蘭人》刊載的〈彼得赫德捕鯨人〉（The Peterhead Whalers）在回顧時提到，「彼得赫德捕鯨船隊的資助者與管理者，絕大多數是住在彼得赫德的商人。這些人精明、謹慎，但當他們對船長與船員充滿信心時，他們絕不會懼於投入大筆金錢。他們當中有許多人在捕鯨業的全盛期賺了大錢。」另一位是羅伯特·基德（Robert Kidd），根據紀錄，他是「希望」號的老船主，當初是透過「希望海豹與鯨魚獵捕公司」取得這艘船。

6 根據一八八〇年三月六日《昔德蘭日報》（*Shetland Times*）的報導，這幾年捕鯨船數量已到達歷史低點，在勒維克，受僱的船員數量也同樣大減——大約二百四十四名，其中十九名受僱於「希望」號，與彼得赫德的船員一起工作。報紙說，「他們通常只收有經驗的人」，其他想出海的人則是找不到船可以上。

7 編註：牡蠣肉質嫩滑，人可不費力氣吞食，故拿來形容氣壓計下墜速度之快。

8 船上的氣壓計讀數下降，表示天氣轉壞。

9 這邊柯南·道爾搞錯了：一八八〇年是閏年，因此星期日是二月二十九日。

10 布雷塞燈塔（Bressay）位於勒維克東南方二點五英里。

三月一日　星期一〔D006〕

暴風雨來襲。「上風」號在凌晨兩點入港，剛好來得及避風。整座港口就像覆上一層泡沫一樣。在船上感到非常舒適。窩在僅容一人的小艙房裡。從此地到彼得赫德的電報故障。狹小的監獄。

三月二日　星期二〔D006〕

氣壓計降到二八．三七五。船長從未看過這麼低的讀數。[11]外頭的強風宛如棍棒。填寫購襪的單子。[12]泰特看起來像個虔信者，但有時又像無神論者。他是我們在昔德蘭的仲介，看起來一副精明能幹的樣子。[13]

三月三日　星期三〔D006〕

天氣晴朗。氣壓計讀數依然很低。早餐後跟船長上岸，準備招募幾名昔德蘭船員。泰特的小辦公室裡人聲鼎沸。「揚馬延」號[14]與「勝利者」號（Victor）進來了。「上風」號的穆雷船長看起來是個不錯的人。格雷船長和我走出泰特的辦公室時，一名喝醉的昔德蘭人一把拉住他。「船長，我要（打嗝聲）跟你一起去。我還沒有機會參加捕鯨！（打嗝聲）讓我去吧，三百五十噸，先生，我會帶來好運的。」格雷轉身回到裡頭的房間，看起來不太高興。我說，「船長，需要我把他趕出去嗎？」他說，「你拿他沒辦法，醫生！我自己回絕他就行了，只不過他一定還會繼續纏著我。」我們把房門鎖上，然而房門上半部起霧的玻璃窗突然浮現鬼魅般的手與手臂。砰！在碎裂聲中，木頭與玻璃四散飛進房內，這位不死心的昔德蘭人，手被割傷流血，他的頭還伸到破洞前望進來。「不管是木門還是鐵門都擋不了我的，格雷船長。我一定要去。」船長從頭到尾都安閒地抽著他的菸斗，站在火爐旁寸步不離。這名男子被拉走了，他被人又捶又踹地帶往監獄，不過我認為他該去的其實是醫院。什麼叫酒精中毒引發的震顫性譫妄（DT）[15]，我算是見識到了。邀請「上風」號的穆雷船長與泰特共進晚餐，聊起了石造建築、捕鯨等話題。與穆雷爭論藥物的療效問題。喝了許多好酒。這一晚跟格雷船長談話，感到很愉快。[16]順帶一提，另一名偷渡者在今日出現，一個外表極其悽慘的生物。船長起初嚇他，說要送他回去，但後來還是讓他簽約。[17]

11 「我記得這是我在海上四處漫遊所見過最低的讀數，」柯南·道爾在四十三年後寫道（《回憶與冒險》，〈北極海捕鯨〉〔Whaling in the Arctic Ocean〕）。

12 「在船上，船醫的工作是最輕鬆的，」布坎在 *The Peterhead Whaling Trade*（Peterhead: Buchan Field Club, 1999），第五十六頁說道：「除了某些時候他必須用上他那貧乏的醫學知識……其他時候他最重要的工作就是辦事員，」填寫購襪單就是柯南·道爾的工作之一。

13 喬治·泰特（George Reid Tait）「擔任布商、服裝商與船主的仲介工作，他所接的工作各色各樣，但都非常成功」，湯瑪斯·曼森（Thomas Manson）在 *Lerwick During the Last Half Century*（Lerwick: T. & J. Manson, Shetland New Offices, 1923）第八十九頁說道：「泰特先生對於捕鯨與捕海豹船很感興趣，他同時擔任好幾艘船的仲介。在獵捕季，一大堆人跑來找他，他的辦公室總是門庭若市」——柯南·道爾在下個條目就提到這點。

14 這艘彼得赫德的船隻以北角西邊的北極火山島命名，這座島嶼在十七世紀由荷蘭與英格蘭的捕鯨人發現，現屬挪威王國所有。

15 震顫性譫妄（delirium tremens）。醫學博士，同時也是諮詢病理學家的羅伯特·卡茲（Robert S. Katz），他對柯南·道爾一直有濃厚的興趣。卡茲指出柯南·道爾在診斷上出現的矛盾：如果這位昔德蘭人當時已經喝醉了，那麼他不可能同時出現震顫性譫妄，「因為震顫性譫妄是酒精戒斷症候群的一種；如果患者喝酒了，就不可能出現酒精戒斷症候群。」無庸置疑的是，這個人已經醉了，他當時有沒有喝酒其實不是重點。「他的行為，」卡茲博士說道，「聽起來比較像是單純喝醉。」

16 柯南·道爾發現他的主要職責「是陪伴船長」，蓋文·蘇瑟蘭（Gavin Sutherland）的 *The Whaling Years: Peterhead, 1788-1893*（Centre for Scottish Studies, University of Aberdeen, 1993）第二十七頁提到，因為「船長與船員的社會地位差異很大」。船上必須嚴守階級分野，高級船員共進晚餐，「船長講著笑話，滔滔不絕地說話，大家夥聊著當天發生的事，」皇家海軍指揮官馬克罕（Albert Hastings Markham）在本書先前引用過的日記裡第二十頁，提到他在「北極」號捕鯨船上的觀察。當然，甲板下的景象就完全不同了，蘇瑟蘭說：「船員區裡菸味瀰漫，大家狂飲著杜松子酒。在昔德蘭小提琴的伴奏下，船員熱情而高聲地唱著淫穢下流的歌曲。」他們許多人跟柯南·道爾一樣，只有十幾二十歲，但只有柯南·道爾可以來往於甲板上下，通觀兩個世界的生活方式。

17 工作合約載明水手的職責與船上的責任。

三月四日　星期四 D008

早上，分發菸草給船員。[18]上午，睡回籠覺。晚間上岸。先跟二副與勤務員[19]到女王飯店[20]，買些他所謂需要的東西。然後到布朗太太的店[21]，接著他們就不見人影。對方很殷勤地招待我，要我不要見外。沿著商業街[22]走著，路旁聚集著閒暇輕鬆的人群[23]。我聽到一些美妙的歌曲並且唱了〈傑克的冒險故事〉（Jack's Yarn）。[24]與船長聊到哲羅姆親王[25]與其他的事。

三月五日　星期五 D009

船長與我受邀到泰特家吃晚餐。我們都認為這頓晚餐會很無聊。我們到女王飯店打撞球。然後散步到泰特家。我們見到「上風」號的穆雷與蓋洛維，蓋洛維是個小律師，但傲慢得讓人難以忍受——我討厭這傢伙。[26]乏味的晚餐，配上劣質的香檳。老泰特聽到我說，我是理查．道爾（Richard Doyle）的姪子時，感到很驚訝[27]——這個老傢伙，我後來才知道船長早在之前就已經告訴他這件事。他養了一隻狗，被訓練成特別喜愛拿破崙這個名字，如果你說要槍斃拿破崙，那麼這隻狗會朝你衝過來，或許還會把你身上某件東西叼走，可能是你身上的肉、衣服與物品。穆雷談到把三個人丟到冰層下，看見暴民抗爭時有十個人被射殺，以及其他奇怪的事。我們在晚上九點上了小艇，很高興自己又回到船上來，可以平靜地伸直我們的雙腿。起風了。我看到船長說的那地方，他說那是過去羅馬人的營地，但我認為那是過去皮克特人[28]蓋的圓塔。

三月六日 星期六 〔D010〕

下起大雨，風勢也變大了。一整天無事可做。柯林·麥克林[29]與幾個人晚間上岸，他需要使用小艇，不過風勢實在太大了，我們花了一番工夫才搞定這件事。開始閱讀包斯威爾寫的約翰生傳記。[30]

18 這是身為船醫的他所從事的另一項類似辦事員的工作。

19 日誌上拼成 Stewart（原該拼成 Steward），這是蘇格蘭當地的拼法。柯南·道爾從未在日記裡提到勤務員的姓名，但他確實知道並且記得這個人的姓名：傑克·蘭姆（Jack Lamb），這名好鬥的夥伴，就在上船的第一天，柯南·道爾就把他的眼睛打青了。一八九七年一月，柯南·道爾在《河濱雜誌》（*The Strand Magazine*）回憶這段插曲，「我不知道傑克·蘭姆是不是還在人世，如果他還在，我想他一定還記得這件事。」傑克·蘭姆在捕鯨當時是二十七歲，他在一八九七年時還活著：「我親愛的老夥伴，」他向柯南·道爾致意，「當我看到你在《河濱雜誌》上的文章時，十七年前的事彷彿昨日才發生一樣。事情被你描述得栩栩如生，讓我覺得言猶在耳。還有你形容我的樣子，我的同事一看見就知道說的是我。我已經把鬍子刮了，但我的體格跟外八還是一樣。」若說此時的柯南·道爾已是世界知名的作家，那麼蘭姆也不遑多讓。他於一八八一年結束捕鯨工作，進入巴爾莫羅（Balmoral）皇家城堡工作，此時他已是溫莎城堡的女王烘焙師。

20 女王飯店（Queen's Hotel）建於一八六〇年代初，地點位於勒維克港旁，至今仍持續營業。

21 也許是家庭式旅館，但不是旅社，根據昔德蘭圖書館管理員嘉登（Douglas Garden）的調查，一八七九年與一八八二年的勒維克年鑑上並沒有一個由名叫布朗太太的人開設供船員住宿的地方。也許這裡指的是妓院，因為柯南·道爾不見他們的人影。布坎的 *The Peterhead Whaling Trade* 第六十四頁提到，在勒維克，旅舍、算命攤與妓女戶的生意絕大多數都靠「南方少年維持，這個榮景一直維持到捕鯨業衰頹為止」。羅伯特·史密斯（Robert Smith）的 *The Whale Hunters*（Edinburgh: John Donald Publishers, 1993）第五十一頁提到：「勒維克的街道狹窄，到處都是垃圾，店鋪也相當簡陋。這裡的酒商與妓女惡名在外。」

22 今日的格蘭德飯店（Grand Hotel）就位在商業街一四九號，從這裡可以俯瞰勒維克港。

23 人群聚集在酒吧與其他場所喝酒唱歌。

24 一首海上歌曲，讚頌皇家海軍於十九世紀反對奴隸貿易，由路易斯·迪爾（Louis Diehl）譜曲，弗雷德里克·衛勒禮（Frederic Weatherly）作詞。衛勒禮也是〈丹尼少年〉（Danny Boy）的作詞者。

25 哲羅姆·波拿巴（Jerome Bonaparte, 1784-1860），拿破崙的幼弟。

26 蓋洛維（James K. Galloway）是勒維克當地的律師，三十四歲，顯然是穆雷的資助者。

27 理查·道爾（一八二四—一八八三）是柯南·道爾的伯伯，住在倫敦。他為《笨拙》（*Punch*）雜誌畫插圖，此外還畫了其他許多作品，包括在〈英國人的風俗與習慣〉（Manners and Customs of ye Englyshe）上的諷刺系列。

28 編註：皮克特人為先於蘇格蘭人居住在福斯河以北的皮克塔維亞的族群。

29 希望號四十歲的大副，他以廚師助手的身分上岸，其實是因為少了一紙證書。柯南·道爾對於他的領導能力感到印象深刻，他說他是個「天生的高階船員，遠比商業局給的證書更來得令人信任」。

30 最早的傑出英國人傳記《薩繆爾·約翰生》（*Samuel Johnson*），由約翰生的朋友詹姆斯·包斯威爾（James Boswell）撰寫，出版於一七九一年。在日誌中，柯南·道爾不只一次提到他在空閒時閱讀這本傳記。

三月七日　星期日〔D010〕

無事可做，除了郵船「聖馬格努斯」（St Magnus）號靠岸時，帶來一封從家裡寄來的信，以及一封蕾蒂（Letty）[31]寄來的信，此外還有一星期份的蘇格蘭人。[32]令人滿意的消息。我們最近更換了停泊處，與其他船隻分開，停在「上風」號旁邊。大副柯林昨晚待在女王飯店，旁邊有一群鄧迪人，他們提到那兩個該死的彼得赫德人垂頭喪氣離去的事。柯林聽了隨即起身，並且自稱是「希望」號人，他殺氣騰騰地衝進那群人裡，打倒一名鄧迪[33]醫生。今天早上，當我拿東西給他提神時，他對我說，「醫生，我運氣很好，所以現在我還清醒著，否則我很可能照例跟人大吵一頓。」我搞不懂柯林說的照例大吵一頓是什麼意思。勒維克是座骯髒的小鎮，居民單純好客。大街的設計者恐怕有斜視的毛病，街道不是呈直線，而是螺旋狀的。[34]今天我注意到，港裡有幾艘船隻掛著共濟會的旗子，[35]穆雷升起了皇家方舟旗，藍底的羅盤圖案。〔三角旗的插圖〕

漁夫每英擔[36]鱈魚賣五先令，一個晚上最多能捕到二十五英擔的鱈魚。順帶一提，昨天「上風」號的管輪，兩根食指被機器弄傷了，我必須在早餐之前過去幫他包紮。港灣裡一共有二十艘捕鯨船。

三月八日　星期一〔D011〕

沒有任何東西比用來寫日記的羽毛筆來得重要，然而我手上這支筆實在難寫透頂。今日上岸，閒逛一陣子之後，跑去看奧克尼（Orkney）與昔德蘭的足球賽——踢得相當糟。遇見「揚馬延」號（船長鄧查斯〔Denchars〕）、「新地島」（Nova Zembla）[37]號與「艾瑞克」（Erik）號三艘船的船長，以及倫敦人布朗，他是「艾瑞克」號的船醫。比賽結束後，我們一行六人前往女王飯店，一開始先喝了劣質的威士忌，然後喝咖啡。布朗點了一瓶香檳，穆雷與我也跟著一起點。雪茄與菸斗。我想我們大家酒喝多了。

布朗去年在「拉文斯克雷格」號[38]上遭遇船難。他說他射擊很準確。[39]船長與我大約在九點半回船。

31 也許他指的是法蘭西絲·蕾提夏·佛利（Frances Letitia Foley），她是柯南·道爾在愛爾蘭沃特佛德郡（Waterford）的遠親，柯南·道爾喜歡這個遠親。一八八〇年十一月，也就是結束捕鯨的幾個月後，柯南·道爾寫信給母親，詢問蕾蒂的住址以及他的妹妹安妮特（Annette）與洛蒂（Lottie）的住址。一八八九年，蕾蒂與其他家族成員與朋友都接到柯南·道爾的請託，希望他們能建議自己居住地附近的圖書館收藏他的小說，以提升他的知名度。見 *Arthur Conan Doyle: A Life in Letters*, eds. Jon Lellenberg, Daniel Stashower and Charles Foley (Harper Press, 2007)。蕾蒂的父親尼爾森·佛利（Nelson Trafalgar Foley）是利斯摩爾（Lismore）巴里加利（Bally gally）家族的成員，直到死前數年，他一直是佛利家族的大家長，也是柯南·道爾母親瑪麗·佛利（亦為利斯摩爾人）的表親。

32 指《蘇格蘭人》，愛丁堡的主要日報。

33 鄧迪是彼得赫德在蘇格蘭的競爭港口，柯南·道爾從未喜歡過這個城市——他在一九〇〇年寫給母親的信上提到，鄧迪是個「可憎的地方，沒有半點可取之處」。

34 該鎮出生的史家湯瑪斯·曼森同意這個說法（*Lerwick During the Last Half Century*，第八十四頁）：「勒維克是一座設計得相當古怪的城鎮，這點無庸置疑，它的大街也是個大笑話——從街道的角度來說是如此。如果把它當成迷宮的話，那就太完美了。」如果說柯南·道爾對勒維克的評價不高，那麼比他早二十年的另一名年輕船醫，「上風」號的塔普林（J. F. Taplin）的說法也不太好聽：「這是個小鎮，只有三千名居民，這裡的街道非常狹窄，車子無法通過，依我所見，我認為他們大概只能使用瘦小的迷你馬吧……在貼妥郵資之後，我離岸上船，我想我應該不會在乎是不是能再見到這座小鎮。」塔普林醫生的日記見蘇格蘭亞伯丁郡的東北民俗網站（North East Folklore Archive）。

35 「愛馬的人通常富有同情心，而且謹守共濟會的規範，」這是一八九一年小說〈波希米亞的醜聞〉（A Scandal in Bohemia）中福爾摩斯說的話，而柯南·道爾也在許多船長身上看到這項特質。彼得赫德是共濟會皇家方舟水手（Royal Ark Mariners）五十六號基斯集會所（Keith Lodge）的所在地，它建立於一七三九年，曼森的 *Lerwick During the Past Half Century* 曾清楚提到共濟會對當地的深刻影響。柯南·道爾自己也在一八八七年加入共濟會，不過他不是終身都是共濟會會員。

36 譯註：一英擔約合五十點八公斤。

37 Nova Zembla，這是 Novaya Zemyla 的荷蘭名，指兩座多山的北極島嶼，這兩座島嶼是俄國烏拉山的延伸。

38 對來自鄧迪的捕鯨船「拉文斯克雷格」號來說，一八七九年是禍不單行的一年。五月，在前往戴維斯海峽途中遭遇強風，船隻進水超過了警戒線，有些船員堅持船隻必須返航。五月十三日，《蘇格蘭人》報導，當「拉文斯克雷格」號駛近泰河（Tay River）河口時，「船長才剛下令收捲船帆，讓引水人上船，就突然從船橋摔入海中，甚至連跟大副『道別』的機會都沒有，就無預警地消失。船員立刻降下兩艘小艇前去救援，十五分鐘後找到船長，但已回天乏術。」同年稍晚，在新船長的帶領下，「拉文斯克雷格」號再次遭遇強風，最後觸礁沉沒。

39 他的這項技能比身為船醫的醫術更受人看重，因為船隻的任務是獵海豹。布坎的 *The Peterhead Whaling Trade* 第五十六頁曾提到一八七六年某艘捕鯨船的招募廣告：「年輕學生亦可，重點是射擊準確」——「儘管商業局要求捕鯨船上需要有一名具備資格的醫療從業人員」，但實際上這些人多半是亞伯丁、格拉斯哥與愛丁堡大學的醫學系學生。

當天寫給他母親的信，柯南．道爾的母親是瑪麗．佛利．道爾，住在愛丁堡。

「希望」號

勒維克

星期一

最親愛的媽媽：

靠著手邊的筆墨，我要將北方的事一五一十說給妳聽：郵船昨天靠岸，除了捎來妳的信，也帶來親愛的女孩蕾蒂的一紙關心，她似乎不太清楚我在做什麼，她以為我大概是到格陵蘭接受一場考試，還是面對醫學委員會的口試之類的，因為她在信裡提到希望我一切順利，還談到我回來之後就是一名合格的醫生了。多麼和善的女孩啊！總之，我來到這個地方，連鑷子鉗子都帶來了。接下來，我會盡可能詳細回答妳在信上提到的問題。

一．我已經收到妳的信件、包裹與其他物品。

二．我還沒收到我的「？」，我現在還是需要這件東西。

三．我沒有生病。

四．我已經回信給霍爾太太了。[40]

五．我像個聽話的孩子一樣去拜訪羅傑家。我也看到了嬰兒，至少我看到一對水汪汪的大眼從襁褓中直盯著我，就像包在餃子裡的章魚似的伸出四個觸手。嬰兒雖然不是沒有聲音，但「Son et oculi et prosterea nihil」，[41] 此外還帶著一點嘔吐物的味道。喔，是的，鬼王別西卜（Beelzebub）是個乖孩子——真是抱歉——克莉絲塔貝爾（Christabel）。[42] 現在，既然我已經一一回答這些問題，安撫了妳不安的情緒，那麼接著讓我說說別的事，看能不能引起妳的興趣。首先，妳會高興聽到我這麼說，我這輩子從未像現在這麼快樂。恐怕我的個性裡帶有強烈的波希米亞元素，船上的生活真的很適合我。[43] 這群傑出而誠實的海上男兒，個個精神煥發，健壯無比。妳無法想像他們當中有人非常努力自學。輪機長昨晚從煤炭投入口爬出來，在月光下，在甲板上與我辯論達爾文主義。我駁得他無話可說，但他接著又跟我討論柯倫索反對摩西五經的說詞，[44] 這一回他占了上風。船長自己也是個知識淵博之人。現在，在勒維克灣裡，有將近三十艘捕鯨船停泊著。當中只有兩艘彼得赫德的船，

40 艾米·霍爾（Amy Hoare），伯明罕的雷吉諾德·霍爾博士（Reginald Ratcliffe Hoare）的妻子。柯南·道爾攻讀醫學時曾接受過霍爾博士的指導，當時他是在校外實習的醫學系學生。霍爾夫婦對柯南·道爾來說猶如第二父母，他們的情誼維繫了多年之久。

41 有瑕疵的拉丁文，意思是「除了聲音與眼睛，什麼都沒有」。

42 羅傑家是柯南·道爾的母親在亞伯丁的朋友。「克莉絲塔貝爾十九歲了！」柯南·道爾在一八九九年再度造訪時禁不住大叫：「上回我看到她，她還在搖籃裡呢。」

43 柯南·道爾（儘管事實恰恰相反）深信自己的個性帶有波希米亞的色彩，他在《回憶與冒險》中說道，他在十五歲時第一次到倫敦拜訪伯父伯母，「對他們來說，我太波希米亞，而對我來說，他們太傳統。」他把這個主題寫入一八八三年的首部小說《約翰·史密斯的告白》（*The Narrative of John Smith*, eds. Jon Lellenberg, Daniel Stashower and Rachel Foss; British Library, 2011）之中，而且也如此形容福爾摩斯，華生醫生說，福爾摩斯的「波希米亞靈魂，無論哪一種社會形式都令他感到厭惡」。

44 約翰·柯倫索（John William Colenso, 1814-83），一名具爭議性的聖公會神學家：令神職人員與俗人沮喪的是，他竟質疑摩西五經（舊約的前五卷）的歷史真實性。

那就是「上風」號與「希望」號；鄧迪與彼得赫德的捕鯨船存在嫌隙，格雷與穆雷被人當成貴族一樣看待。[45] 我們的大副柯林・麥克林星期六在女王飯店聽見六個鄧迪高級船員詆毀「希望」號。柯林是個高大的紅鬍子蘇格蘭人，沉默寡言的他慢慢站直了身子說道，「我就是『希望』號的船員，」話剛說完就朝這群鄧迪人衝過去。他把一名醫生打倒在地，又打殘了一名船長，最後以勝利之姿離去。隔天早上他對我說，「醫生，我運氣不錯，還保持清醒，否則很可能就要跟人吵架了。」我搞不懂柯林的吵架是什麼意思。勒維克這個城鎮，街道彎彎曲曲，人不分男女都長得難看。最令人失望的是，這裡只有兩家飯店與一張撞球台。郊外的鄉村則是貧瘠而醜陋。島上連棵樹也沒有。星期五到我們的仲介泰特家吃晚飯，我們吃得很飽，喝了香檳與其他的酒，但氣氛很無聊。我們順道帶了上好的香檳與葡萄酒上船，我們就像上等的豬隻一樣被餵了好多東西。我已經有一段時間一直沒胃口吃東西，我想我需要加強運動，這才是我需要的。我稍微練習一下拳擊，[46] 光是能做點運動就能帶來許多好處。我們先前剛好及時在吹起八級風前進港。船長說，如果我們當時還在海上，很可能會失去小艇與舷牆，甚至連桅杆都會不保。現在天氣好多了，我想我們星期四就能啟程。

親愛的媽媽，這就是這些日子以來發生的所有事情。願我離家這段期間，上帝一直保佑妳。接下來大約要等兩個多月的時間，妳才會收到我的信。國會立法禁止我們在四月二日前獵捕海豹，所以現在我們只能繼續待在這裡。我愛你們，請代我向格林希爾街[47] 致意。

愛妳的兒子

亞瑟・柯南・道爾

我今天已經跟船長請假，跟幾個塊頭最大的高級船員到女王飯店去，看看誰敢跟我們吵架。

妳從德拉蒙太太[48]那裡聽來的名字是錯的。

洛蒂的信非常聰明伶俐而且有趣。[49]

信件到此結束，接下來是日記。

45 大衛·格雷（David Gray, 1828-96），「蝕缺」（*Eclipse*）號船長，人稱「捕鯨王子」，但現在彼得赫德在捕鯨上面已經落後鄧迪，因為鄧迪有較大的港口可以容納更多與更大的捕鯨船。盧伯克的 *Arctic Whalers* 第四〇一頁表示，「彼得赫德在一八七一年時還有十一艘捕鯨船，但是，除了格雷的『蝕缺』號，沒有任何一艘船能比得上鄧迪性能優良的輔助汽船，而就捕鯨來說，彼得赫德在一八七〇年代與八〇年代的收益幾乎全仰賴格雷兄弟。」（根據盧伯克，第四〇九頁的說法，到了一八八〇年，彼得赫德的捕鯨船只剩七艘，其中一艘甚至到了捕撈季也未出海。）布坎的 *The Peterhead Whaling Trade* 第三十五頁指出，格雷家族「決定投資建造現代汽船，企圖反轉漁獲減少與財務損失的劣勢」。

46 其實，柯南·道爾在「希望」號上練拳擊的時間相當長。他日誌後期的條目上寫著，「這對我的捕鯨工作幫助很大」，他在《回憶與冒險》中也提到這點。

47 愛丁堡的格林希爾街（Greenhill Place），指的是他們的好友萊恩（Ryan）家。喪夫的萊恩太太對柯南·道爾的照顧也如同他的母親，而萊恩太太的兒子詹姆斯與柯南·道爾從小就認識，他們是一輩子的好友。

48 愛丁堡的夏洛特·德拉蒙（Charlotte Thwaites Drummond），她也很照顧柯南·道爾。

49 他最疼愛的妹妹，比他小六歲：卡洛蘭·瑪麗·伯頓·道爾（Caroline Mary Burton Doyle）。

三月九日　星期二〔D012〕

晚餐前與船長上岸。傑克．韋布斯特[50]喝醉酒，在街上鬧事。船長一把抓住他，讓引水船送他回「希望」號，但船開到半途，他跳進水中，又游回岸上。之後，必須仰賴康恩（Cane）與小艇船員，才把他抓了回來。早上，逛了幾間店鋪，依然覺得無聊。如果明天天氣轉好，我們就會出海。之後，泰特上船，我們聊得很愉快。他是個明理的人，但就是有點無趣。閱讀斯科斯比的作品。[51]船長告訴我一些關於捕鯨的趣事。鯨魚很遠就聽得見汽船的聲音，因此很容易就會嚇跑牠們。[52]鯨魚油一噸約五十英鎊，而骨頭約八百英鎊。[53]所有的鯨魚骨全銷往歐陸。海中獨角獸[54]很常見，鯊魚和海豚數量也很多，但真正有趣的地方是鯨魚其實是靠食用微小的生物維生。

三月十日　星期三〔D013〕

強勁的北風打亂了我們的出海計畫。老舊的「蝕缺」號清晨四點盛大出港，所經之處，每艘船都予以歡呼祝福。[55]上船，看到大衛船長、[56]阿雷克（Alec）與克拉布（Crabbe）。晚上上岸，玩船長遊戲，[57]有幸能在撞球桌上擊敗克拉布。克拉布在勒維克有著很高的聲望。我把海泡石菸斗與手套忘在吸菸室裡。

三月十一日　星期四 〔D013〕

利斯（Leith）的大日子。[58] 早餐過後，船隻紛紛駛離勒維克港灣。在如此晴朗寧靜的日子裡，聽見港口裡到處有人歌唱，呼應著起錨的噹啷聲響，真是讓人心情舒爽。每艘船經過時，所有的船都會為他們高聲歡呼三次。船長與我上岸，船員跟我一起尋找傑克・韋布斯特特。我們終於找到他，我們總共五人架著他，一邊咒罵著，一邊沿著勒維克大街走向小艇，

50　我們不清楚傑克・韋布斯特特（Jack Webster）這個船員擔任什麼職位，也不知道格雷船長為什麼堅持讓這個闖禍鬼繼續待在船上。我們努力想找出一八八〇年「希望」號完整的船員名單，但未能成功；也許這份名單已在最近幾年被公共檔案局（現在的國家檔案局，位於丘區〔Kew〕）銷毀了。

51　小威廉・斯科斯比（William Scoresby the Younger, 1789-1857），柯南・道爾在〈北極的魅力〉（The Glamour of the Arctic）中稱他是「最後一位偉大的英國船長」。斯科斯比的父親是英格蘭惠特比的極為成功的捕鯨船船長，因此他在十歲時就已經乘船抵達過北極海。一八一〇年，二十一歲的斯科斯比在結束愛丁堡大學的科學研究之後，接掌了父親的船隻「決心」號（Resolution），往後進行了十次北極航行。第一任妻子去世後，斯科斯比成為一名教士。十年前，斯科斯比作品的編輯傑克森（C. Ian Jackson）在哈克路伊特會（Hakluyt Society）版寫下導言，他提到斯科斯比的日誌與日記不僅是前往北極海域與陸地的重要指南，也包括了「社會軼聞、宗教信仰、幽默話語與科學研究。」格陵蘭的斯科斯比峽灣便是因小威廉・斯科斯比而得名，月球上的某個隕石坑也以他的名字命名。

52　十九世紀初期，以蒸汽引擎作為輔助動力曾在捕鯨業裡引起不小的爭議，雖然現在已成為業界的標準配備，但部分人士認為蒸汽引擎就是造成捕鯨數量減少的元凶。

53　編註：一八八一年，警察一年的名目工資（以現時的幣值計算）為七十六點七三英鎊、礦工為五十九點五八英鎊、務農工人為四十一點五二英鎊。資料來源：www.wirksworth.org.uk/A04VALUE.htm#1264

54　獨角鯨。

55　「蝕缺」號被公認是彼得赫德最好的捕鯨船。「造價近一萬兩千英鎊，」蘇瑟蘭的 *Whaling Years* 第七十頁表示，「船身使用堅硬的橡木，船上各項設備一應俱全，堅固如堡壘一般，足以擔負起冰洋任務。船的引擎超過六十匹馬力，可以攜帶八艘捕鯨艇，與五十五名船員。」「蝕缺」號建於一八六六年，由格雷家族出資興建，之後建成的則是她的姊妹船「希望」號，建成時間是一八七二年到一八七三年。

56　大衛・格雷也是個重要的自然學家與北極地區權威。格雷家族中最年輕的亞歷山大（一八三九－一九一〇），這個時期在大衛底下做事，可能就是這裡指的阿雷克。一八八三年，大衛接掌「艾瑞克」號，柯南・道爾在日誌中曾多次提到這艘捕鯨船（通常是拼寫成 Eric）——根據布坎的 *The Peterhead Whaling Trade*，第二十二頁的說法，「艾瑞克」號是彼得赫德有史以來最大的捕鯨船。

57　這種酒館遊戲或許又叫船長情婦，類似今日的四子棋，庫克（Cook）船長在他的史詩航行中曾與船上的科學家玩過這種遊戲。一八八七年版的《霍伊爾的遊戲》（*Hoyle's Games*）並未提到這種名叫船長的紙牌遊戲。

58　不清楚是什麼節日，利斯是愛丁堡的港口，有悠久的捕鯨歷史。

我必須抓著他，以免他又跳海。我們大約一點出發，穿過島嶼，直到七點左右在一處小峽灣下錨，同在此地的還有「揚馬延」號、「艾瑞克」號與「奮進」（Active）號。[59]我們從勒維克出發時就與「揚馬延」號競速，而且一路領先，最後在離「艾瑞克」號約一個擲石的距離停船下錨。晚間，與麥克勞[60]和船長談到前往北極的事。無疑地，每個人都想錯了。[61]敞開在我們面前的是一片廣闊的海洋，我們必須從中尋出一條通往北極的路。但我們走的可不是一條越來越狹窄的水道，浮冰在上頭自然流動著，這是戴維斯海峽的狀況，但通往北極的路可不是如此。[62]

三月十二日　星期五

{D014}

我擔心我們可能必須在這裡停留一整天，雖然氣壓計讀數很高，但風勢應該已經達到四級風的標準。整天無事可做。島上迤邐著低矮的山嶺，表面的泥炭呈現出縱橫交錯的切痕，上面零星散布著古怪的小茅草屋。晚間，船長到「艾瑞克」號船上。他們似乎想抓魚，但我們沒有適當的魚餌，所以船副與我連同另一名船員上岸撿拾一些蛤蜊充當魚餌。由於天色幾乎全黑，我們很難找到蛤蜊，所以只好到那些小屋討求一點。這些簡陋的小屋，連愛斯基摩人的房子也比他們強。每間屋子的天花板都開了一個方形小洞，讓房間中間燃燒泥炭產生的煙霧能飄出去。這些屋主都很客氣有禮。即使在這處看似未開化的地區，我們仍看見一名美麗而怕生的少女。[63]我抓了幾尾剃刀魚當餌，因而得以體面地離開。上岸時，泥濘淹到了大腿，此時離開小島，又得再忍受一次。晚間，緝私艇搭載我們，上尉僅靠著那一根菸草鎮定心神。我則擔心柯林會把我們的餌全吃光了。船長則是擔心我們會一直困在這裡。氣壓計的讀數仍高。

三月十三日 星期六（D015）

風大雨急。「奮進」號與「揚馬延」號已經出發。我們也隨即跟著出發。他們起錨，唱著「再會了，事事順心，再會了，事事順心」。這也是一首好聽的曲子。[64] 海面上波濤看起來並不洶湧。我們穿過島嶼，全速前進，昔德蘭群島最北端從我們右手邊通過，我們看見海中出現幾個奇岩怪石，這些岩石又稱為蘭納礁石（Ramna Stacks）。[65]

〔插圖，「蘭納礁石」〕

59 這裡指的峽灣，其實是昔德蘭人口中的港灣。昔德蘭圖書館的嘉登提到，「所有船隻一口氣離開勒維克，在比較靠北的小港灣停泊，這已經是長年的習慣。各船可以在此排定船員的工作輪班，準備橫越大西洋。」馬克罕一八七四年日記第十七頁打趣地說了另一個理由：「一般來說，捕鯨船剛出發時所有的船員都會手忙腳亂，因為他們啟程前多半會跟朋友與熟人辦惜別宴，往往為了預祝成功而喝得酩酊大醉。」

60 約翰·麥克勞（John McLeod），四十歲，「希望」號的輪機長。

61 如何抵達北極，在當時是個大挑戰。「當探險家從格陵蘭與斯匹茲卑爾根島之間北上時，阻擋他們去路的，」柯南·道爾在〈北極的魅力〉中說道，「是巨大的漂浮冰礁，科學探險家稱之為『古凍海』，至於捕鯨人則是簡單明瞭地稱之為『障礙』。」之後有人針對柯南·道爾的陳述加以評論，如大衛·格雷船長、艾伯特·馬克罕他當時是海軍少將，曾指揮英國的「警戒」號（Alert）於一八七五年到一八七六年進行北極探險）與姪子克雷門茲·馬克罕（Clements Markham，他是皇家地理學會榮譽祕書，於一八七三年出版《跨入不可知的領域》〔*Threshold of the Unknown Region*〕一書）。三人都同意柯南·道爾的說法，但對於障礙的難度與如何抵達北極有不同的看法。儘管許多人嘗試前往北極，但一直等到三十年後，也就是一九〇九年，才由海軍上將羅伯特·皮里（Robert Peary）與幾名夥伴乘雪橇完成抵達北極的壯舉。一九一〇年五月，柯南·道爾在午餐會上向羅伯特·皮里致敬。「羅曼史作家總是對探險家滿腹牢騷，」報紙報導柯南·道爾用自嘲而遺憾的語氣說道：「過去，世界上充滿了未知之地，讓擁有想像力之人自由馳騁自己的幻想。然而，由於一群訪客誤用了自己的精力，以及另一群有著類似傾向的紳士們，使這些空間霎時被填滿了；往後，這些羅曼史作家該何去何從。」

62 戴維斯海峽位於格陵蘭西岸與加拿大巴芬島之間。一八八三年十一月四日，柯南·道爾公開發表這個觀點，當時他為樸資茅斯文學與科學學會演講〈北極海〉。柯南·道爾指出，對北極海的認識，有部分（根據《漢普夏電訊報》〔*Hampshire Telegraph*〕的報導）歸功於「畢生在這片海洋航行的捕鯨船長」。

63 「奇異的、未開化的、和善的居民，他們對外在世界一無所知，」柯南·道爾在《回憶與冒險》中說道。「一名狂野、長髮的少女手持火把引領我回到船上，因為這裡滿布著泥炭坑洞，夜裡在這裡行走相當危險。我看見她，她有著一頭烏黑的鬈髮，赤裸的雙腿，沾染茜草汁的裙子，以及在火光下搖曳不定的狂野輪廓。」

64 有一首水手一邊工作時唱的歌，歌詞說著水手到利物浦尋歡作樂的事，歌詞一開頭是這麼唱的：「我們就要返國，回到利物浦城，／再會了，事事順心，再會了，事事順心，／那些利物浦姑娘，想必會搶著迎接我們，／歡呼吧，水手們，我們就要回家！」

65 這些是位於昔德蘭群島北端的礁石群，今日已成為野鳥生態保護區。

整天下著大雨。我們與「艾瑞克」號競賽，全速前進。完全沒有暈船。看見大不列顛最北端的布拉費歐德沙洲（Burrafiord Holms），[66] 下午四點，已經完全不見陸地的蹤影。船隻整夜在強風中航行，引擎有四分之三徹夜發動著。夢見被大猩猩痛打以及被拉上牛津的小艇。[67] 一百六十七英里。

三月十四日　星期日〔D016〕

「艾瑞克」已經遙遙領先我們，而且偶爾才出現在我們眼前。洶湧的大西洋，讓我們向北前進，嘿！[68] 一整天同時使用風帆與蒸汽引擎。

〔插圖，「洶湧的大西洋」〕

向北前進，嘿！前進了約一百五十英里。就要進入北極圈，灣流往北流經斯匹茲卑爾根島，[69] 當然，我們要順著灣流北上。這是歷史上最容易讓人上當的幻覺，許多船隻一艘接一艘地開進死胡同裡，戴維斯海峽也有相同的陷阱。閱讀包斯威爾的作品。我不同意麥考利[70] 的說法，他認為包斯威爾是個不聰明的人。如果說有人得了所謂的「包斯威爾病」（morbus Boswellianus），那麼在沉默者威廉（Willy the Silent）[71] 的例子裡，這個人就是麥考利勳爵自己。

三月十五日 星期一 〔D017〕

起初同時使用風帆與蒸汽引擎，之後就只用風帆。今天應該可以經過航程的中點。整天都待在船艙裡，直到晚上。閱讀包斯威爾。我喜歡約翰生這個老頑童自大浮誇的行徑。一個十足的老頭，我在心裡頭想像著。他在普利茅斯，幾天的時間，市民與碼頭工人之間產生極大的惡感。約翰生與這件事完全扯不上關係，大家卻經常聽見他大喊，「我恨碼頭工人。」我喜歡這類的事。晚上，天空看起來就像冰一樣。一天之內，氣溫就從華氏四十四度降到三十八度。[72]

66 昔德蘭群島北方另一個礁石群，現在礁石上立有馬柯弗魯加燈塔（Muckle Flugga Lighthouse），當時稱為北安斯特燈塔（North Unst light）。

67 或許是指源於一八二九年的牛津劍橋划船比賽用的牛津小船。柯南・道爾一生參加過許多運動競賽，但我們不知道他是否曾參加過划船比賽。

68 可能是指精力充沛的馬克罕寫的另一本跟北極有關的書，出版於前一年，書名叫《向北前進，嘿！》（*Northward Ho!*, London: Macmillan）。但也有可能是指一八七五年的一首流行歌，這首歌提到英國的北極探險，歌名叫〈向北前進，嘿！或不畏挫折〉（Northward Ho! Or Baffled Not Beaten），作詞者是薛尼（Cdr. John P. Cheyne, RN），作曲人是巴瑞（Odoardi Barri）。

69 挪威的斯瓦巴群島（Svalbard），位於北極圈內，該群島的最大島就是斯匹茲卑爾根島。

70 儘管柯南・道爾在這裡批評了麥考利（Macauley），但他在一九〇七年討論文學與作家的作品《穿過魔法之門》（*Through the Magic Door*）中，卻大為誇讚他在此次航行中隨身帶著的麥考利作品：「如果我必須從書堆中選出一本我認為讀來最愉快也最有益的作品，那麼我一定會指著遠處那本外表已經有點髒污的麥考利《隨筆》（*Essays*）。回想起來，這本書幾乎與我的人生結合在一起。它陪伴我度過學生歲月，跟我一起熬過黃金海岸的炎熱氣候，當我帶著簡單的個人物品前往北極捕鯨時，這本書也在其中。率直的蘇格蘭魚叉手被這本書搞得頭昏腦脹，而且你仍可看見大管輪在腓特烈大帝那個篇章留下的油漬。雖然這本書已變得破爛、骯髒與磨損，但就算你拿著鑲金邊以摩洛哥羊皮革製成的書籍來跟我換這本書，我也不會答應。」

71 奧倫治親王威廉一世（William I, Prince of Orange, 1533-84）曾領導荷蘭人革命，反對西班牙統治。麥考利的《英格蘭史》（*History of England*）對威廉一世沒有好感。威廉一世的曾孫奧倫治的威廉在斯圖亞特（Stuart）王朝被推翻後，於一六八九年當上英格蘭與蘇格蘭的國王。

72 譯註：大約是攝氏七度降到攝氏三度。

三月十六日 星期二 D017

繼續使用風帆，依然順風。看來我真的帶來好運。早上有兩頭瓶鼻鯨繞著船玩耍，但我沒看見。我們可能正經過鯨魚喜愛的覓食地點。預計明天會看到浮冰。我們昨天前進了一百五十九英里。大約在冰島北方數百英里處，揚馬延島東南方六十英里處。老經驗的船員說，他們航行從來沒這麼順利過，然而我們不能太沾沾自喜，因為隨時有可能遭遇麻煩。水溫從十二點後降了兩度，看起來像冰一樣。天空出現白線。每個人都認為也許今天我們就能看見浮冰。在無風狀態下，我們可以看出，好像有一層冰原覆蓋在我們上方。船長告訴我，他做了幾個有趣的夢，其中比較特別的是與德國人有關，以及幾頭黑色的小母牛。

三月十七日 星期三 D018

Dies creta notanda。[73] 大約五點左右，我聽見二副對船長說，我們已經在浮冰之中。船長隨即起身，但我實在懶得起床。大約八點左右，我們從一艘挪威船旁經過。九點，我終於起床，凜冽的新鮮空氣提醒了我外頭一定相當寒凍。我走到甲板上，一眼就看見浮冰。這些海冰並不是如床單般連續不斷地延伸，但整個洋面上確實滿滿覆蓋著冰，只是間或分布著隆起的冰丘，隨著波浪起伏，層層疊疊的浮冰也不規則地上下搖晃著，上頭是純白色，底下則是美麗的綠色。[74] 每塊浮冰高出水面不過四到六英尺，但形狀各異。沒看見海豹。早上，建造瞭望台。

〔插圖，「彼得赫德捕鯨船」，副標題「背景是浮冰與『希望』號的約翰．格雷船長」〕

〔插圖，「獵捕海豹的服裝」〕

我們整天以蒸汽驅動，更多的時候則是使用風帆。我們穿過海上四散的大塊浮冰，有些浮冰很結實，你可以從這一塊跳到另一塊，藉著這個方式可以一路跳到離船數百碼的地方，但也有一些浮冰只有少許部分露出水面。冰原似乎在我們的左方。看見在我們後頭約五英里處有一艘船，可能是「揚馬延」號，在我們前方則看不清楚有什麼東西。康恩說，他在桅頂看見了九艘船。

三月十八日　星期四

D019

昨晚史都華（Stewart）夢見他置身在一大群豬之中，因此我們確信今天一定能看見海豹。如果有人夢見任何跟農業有關的事，便表示海豹就在附近。一個難以理解的事實。大塊大塊的冰跟昨天一樣，靜靜地浮在水面上。史都華的夢似乎

73 「克里特島愉快的一天，」引自賀拉斯（Horace）的頌歌。

74 一八八三年，在樸資茅斯文學與科學學會的演說中，柯南．道爾邀請他的聽眾一起想像這趟旅程，《樸資茅斯時報》（*Portsmouth Times*）報導提到，「經過四天的航行之後，他們已經將安斯特燈塔拋在後頭，那是他們唯一可見最後一處文明的蹤跡……往後二十四小時的航行，帶著他們來到與冰島相同的緯度，然後船員看見如溪流般的浮冰，這些都是從主冰帽斷裂漂浮過來的，對於從未見過這個景象的旅人來說，總是想寫實地描繪這場變化。過了北緯七十六度線之後，船隻進入浮冰之中，這些巨大的冰平原，面積廣如英國的一個郡，絕不小於一個南海公園（Southsea Common）。柯南．道爾提到在浮冰間的狹窄水道航行的危險，並且引領聽眾進入捕鯨的漁場。漁場的海水就像豌豆濃湯一樣濃稠，裡面有數百萬微生物，牠們是龐大鯨魚的食糧。在經歷許多令人沮喪的事件之後，捕鯨船終於來到北緯八十度與八十一度之間，船員們發現由東到西橫亙著一道巨大的冰牆，毫無間隙，一直從斯匹茲卑爾根島的北端延伸到格陵蘭的東岸。他們大可掉轉船頭打道回府，就算這麼做，也沒有人敢笑他們，因為他們距離北極點已不到一百二十英里，這已經創下歐洲船隻的紀錄。」

應驗了，因為我們在早上十一點左右看見了第一隻冠海豹。牠身上長著黑白斑點，當船經過時，牠仍安閒地躺在冰上，與我們只有十二碼的距離。我靜靜地看著海豹，可憐的動物，如果牠們是這麼溫馴，獵殺牠們似乎是一件羞恥的事。

〔「我們的第一隻海豹」插圖〕

船長看到幾百碼外有一隻帶著斑點的巨大貓頭鷹，以及幾隻羅區鳥和海鳩，[75]但這裡離陸地太遠了，因此這些生物的數量不多。我們現在位於「揚馬延」號北方更遠之處。經過另一隻冠海豹，隨後又經過一隻豎琴海豹。之後看到水中有幾隻海豹。最宜人的早晨，但晚上開始起霧。與「艾瑞克」號船員說話，對此次航行順利互道恭喜。順帶一提，在勒維克時，沃克曾對我說，「先生，要是去年我就認識你的話，事情可能便不一樣了。」我覺得心情好多了，但我沒告訴他。[76]

三月十九日　星期五〔D020〕

在濃霧中，隱約看見大塊浮冰。每個方向的能見度大約一百碼。經過兩隻巨大的冠海豹，一公一母，牠們在一小塊浮冰上。〔摺頁插圖，「一八八〇年三月十六日，『希望』號四周全是稀疏的浮冰」〕

我們試著鳴汽笛，顯然那隻公海豹愣住了，牠聽著聲音，母海豹沒那麼敏感，但牠立刻掉轉了方向。我估計公海豹體長約十英尺，母海豹七到八英尺。我希望霧能早點散去。開始下起毛毛雨。霧氣籠罩了一整天，於是我們夜裡停船。晚上，康恩與史都華兩人打拳擊。與船長聊起文學，他認為與薩克利（Thackery）相比，狄更斯（Dickens）根本不算什麼。巴克蘭[77]則是個可愛的小夥子。

三月二十日 星期六 D021

離開昔德蘭才一星期，我們已經深入冰原之中。這確實是一趟很棒的旅程。天氣很好，萬里無雲。舉目所及，雪白的冰原覆蓋在深藍的海水上。我們破冰前進，展現出雄壯宏偉的氣勢。視野內可以看見五艘船，其中一艘是「艾瑞克」號。史都華堅持要我收下一個愛斯基摩小菸袋；我想他是想用這個作為我給他菸斗的回禮。尚未看見海豹。晚間，在厚冰旁停船。有幾隻冠海豹在船旁嬉戲。從瞭望台上可以看見數百隻海豹，所以我們應該已經很接近海豹的主要群落。看見十一艘船。亞當·卡納[78]看見冰上有熊的足跡。

三月二十一日 星期日 D024

由於濃霧的關係，停船一整天。十幾隻冠海豹圍繞著船。有幾隻豎琴海豹。船長認為主群落應該就在我們前方二十英

75 編註：羅區鳥——此處原文為「roach」，應是一種魚類「擬鯉」或蟑螂的名稱，但就內容來推斷柯南·道爾似乎指的是某種鳥類，故只能取音譯。海鳩，海鳥的一種。

76 「蝕缺」號的羅伯特·沃克（Robert Walker）醫生——在岸上執業——可能是柯南·道爾於一八七九年曾向他申請校外實習，但未錄取。

77 法蘭西斯·巴克蘭（一八二六—一八八〇），英國醫生與自然學家。「四點五英尺高，但胸圍似乎更大於此數，」一個熟識他的人說，他的作品——如《一名漁夫兼動物學家的日誌》（*Log Book of a Fisherman and Zoologist*, 1876）——充滿了活力，使他在一八六〇與一八七〇年代成為廣受歡迎的作者與演講者。他是個肉食主義者，主張食用異國的動物、爬蟲類、禽鳥類等等，而且他在倫敦的家中豢養了可觀的動物，以供庖廚之需。一八七〇年代，巴克蘭擔任漁業督察，因而得以認識格雷家族，特別是大衛船長；根據蘇瑟蘭的 *Whaling Years*，第九十一至九十二頁所言，隨後頒布的每年四月三日前禁獵海豹的規定，絕大部分是他們為了保育所制定的。巴克蘭在他死後出版的 *Notes and Jottings from Animal Life*（一八八二）中，對格雷大為讚賞。

78 雖然柯南·道爾在日誌裡一直叫他卡納（Carner），但我們認為這個人其實是亞當·卡德諾（Adam Cardno），一名生於一八三三年的彼得赫德人。他先前在格雷船長的另一艘船上做事，一八七一年之前他已經升任為資深魚叉手，現在他則擔任水手長。

里處。強尼[79]晚上有個聚會，歌唱的聲音從甲板傳了過來。[80]晚餐後，大家分享波特酒。船長告訴我，他打算把裝有氫氰酸的圓錐體裝置在魚叉前端。他會利用蒸汽設備將魚叉射進鯨魚體內。鯨魚游動的速度非常快，在拖拉的過程中很可能讓長繩因摩擦生熱而起火燃燒。繩子燒斷，鯨魚逃脫，但鯨魚似乎是死了，因為往後幾天海邊不見狗鯊的蹤影。許多鯨魚的長度可以達到一百英尺。順帶一提，卡納教我一些愛斯基摩語，如amalang（是的）、piou（非常好）、piou smali（壞的）、kisi-micky（冰狗，也就是熊）。

三月二十二日　星期一 〔D025〕

再度起霧，一些豎琴海豹與牠們生下的圓滾滾毛色呈黃色的小海豹在船附近游著。推出船尾小艇，拿出步槍。不過要用到這些東西還有一段時間，必須要等到四月三日星期六。濃霧籠罩一整天，因此我們只能停船。晚上練習拳擊。讀完包斯威爾第一卷。夢見G．P。[81]

三月二十三日　星期二 〔D025〕

早上，霧氣散去，看見幾隻海豹。

〔插圖，「公海豹、母海豹與小海豹」〕

「蝕缺」號終於來了，船長在晚餐前登上「蝕缺」號。繼續前進數英里。整天颳著八級風。零下十一度。[82] 風非常寒冷。索具全覆蓋著一層冰。在下午茶之前爬上瞭望台，但當我正要爬上去時，卻被船長叫住，他認為我可能會凍傷。從康恩那裡拿到一個好菸草袋。卡納告訴我，在戰前的紐奧良，一名碼頭工人一天可以賺一英鎊。現在，他們一天賺一美元。船長在戰時看見封鎖突破船[83] 離開利物浦，如長腳蜘蛛般的高速汽船，船身全漆成海的顏色。貨物絕大多數是奎寧，幾乎不需要任何船員。氣壓計讀數再度升高。

三月二十四日 星期三〔D026〕

另一個利斯的大日子。我們看見海豹群，而且是巨大的海豹群。我尚未從瞭望台上觀看海豹群的樣子，但已可見到一

79 輪機長約翰·麥克勞。

80 柯南·道爾先前未提到教會儀式的事，但蘇瑟蘭的 *Whaling Years* 第二十七頁提到：「這群『捕鯨的小夥子』是一群粗人，他們非常迷信，而且敬畏上帝。每到星期日，船員們絕不會忘了禮拜禱告，儀式完全依照聖公會的『船員祈禱書』來進行。雖然船員很少信奉聖公會，但儀式進行時並未有所偏重，無論是長老教會還是羅馬天主教信眾，全一視同仁。有些船隻早上與下午各祈禱一次，晚上還有讀經會。有時儀式會因為鯨魚『噴水』而突然中斷，這時間就看到船員直接拿著聖經跳入小艇前去捕鯨，等到殺死這頭可憐的生物之後，船員再回來唱詩歌與祈禱。」

81 不清楚指的是誰；或許是他喜歡的某個女孩的姓名首字母簡寫，但也可能是柯南·道爾想著自己未來成為合格醫生開始執業的景象。

82 譯註：約攝氏零下二十四度。

83 美國南北戰爭（一八六一—六五）時南方邦聯的船隻：這些船隻建造時故意把重點放在速度，試圖藉此突破北軍對南方港口的封鎖，將重要的戰略物資如奎寧送進南方。

大片從地平線一端連綿到另一端，彷彿無邊無際。我們離海豹群越近，越能感受到數量之龐大。柯林說，他這輩子還沒看過這麼多的海豹。這肯定是世界上數量最龐大的大型動物群落，至少我不知道還有哪種動物會數百萬隻地聚集在一起，其所覆蓋的區域大約長十五英里，寬八英里。我們這一趟應該滿載而歸了，還是一樣，靠著我帶來的運氣。所有的船全停在附近，各自選好停泊的位置。「上風」號從我們旁邊經過，船首飄揚著旗幟，「上風」號略微降下旗子，向我們致意。還要再等十天。屆時就可自由捕獵。

三月二十五日 星期四 〔D027〕

為羽毛筆歡呼！今晚降到零下十九度[84]。我們各就崗位，整天都在準備小艇與清理槍枝。從艦橋已可清楚看見每個海豹群。船隻附近有許多落單的海豹。我在寫東西時可以聽見小海豹的叫聲。牠們的聲音介於貓的喵聲與羔羊的咩聲之間。海豹看起來就像羔羊與巨大蛞蝓的混種。我們現在只擔心一些粗魯的挪威人或鄧迪人會闖入海豹群裡。如果我們捕到的海豹少於五十噸，我會感到沮喪，如果少於一百噸，我會很驚訝。船長準備教我如何測量經度與緯度。想到巧妙的對句

「Till Silence, like a poultice comes,
To heal the blows of Sound.」
「沉默，就像熱敷的膏藥，／

撫療了聲音的擊打。」

我想這應該是霍姆斯的對句。[85] 炫耀我的防水長靴。

三月二十六日　星期五〔D027〕

依然寒凍，白天零下十七度，夜間零下二十度。這是我們要的，可以讓冰原的縫隙凍結起來，使我們可以安全行走。船隻緩緩前進。船副說，海豹躺在幾乎已完全固結的地方。他說這次的數量比一八五五年多，[86] 當年有五十艘船，每艘船都滿載而歸。我們現在有二十三艘船，每一艘船都認為前景大好。等到禁令一解除，我們就要大顯身手。等待的過程特別煎熬，不過禁令設定的時間是個相當好的條款。過去這些可憐的動物會在生育子女前遭到獵殺。「蝕缺」號殺死了一頭熊，我們看見船邊的雪地上留下了熊的足跡。熊是怯懦的野獸，但絕不能將牠逼到無路可走。船長曾經用小艇的魚鉤殺死一頭熊。管輪告訴我，曾經有一頭熊追逐一名船員幾英里遠，以及船員如何把身上的衣物一件一件脫下來以轉移牠的注意力，

84 譯註：約攝氏零下二十八度。

85 奧利佛·霍姆斯（Oliver Wendell Holmes, 1841-1935）是柯南·道爾喜歡的作家，他這裡想起的對句是〈音樂花園〉（The Music-Garden, 1836）裡的句子：「And Silence, like a poultice, comes/ to heal the blows of sound.」

86 一八五五年是蘇格蘭海豹產業的巔峰期，根據《蘇格蘭人》的說法（The Peterhead Whalers, 1902.11.19），二十七艘彼得赫德船共獵捕了十三萬一千零四十九隻海豹。

等到他上船時，全身已經近乎赤裸，而且凍得全身發紫。英國任何一座博物館都沒有露脊鯨的標本，只有露脊鯨的胎兒。看見小海豹在喝奶。與史都華練拳，我的手受傷了。為老基斯補牙，治好了小基斯的 collywobbles。[87] 今天似乎成了基斯家的休假日。

三月二十七日　星期六 [D028]

一星期後的今天，就是解禁的日子。領取我的刀子與磨具，請卡納幫我處理棍棒。

〔插圖，「刀子」〕

天氣晴朗，依然停泊於海豹群的邊緣地帶，船員們似乎都很滿意目前的狀況，只有船長發了一點牢騷，但我想他只是在開玩笑。看見另一頭熊留下的足跡。

〔插圖，「熊的足跡」〕

「蝕缺」號已經殺死兩頭熊，但我們連一頭都沒看見。他們告訴我，熊總是二、三十頭成群行動。晚上，分配步槍。船隻緩緩前進。哈吉．米爾納（Haggie Milne）晚上感覺舒服一點了。沒有新的消息。撰寫我的〈現代寓言〉。[88]

三月二十八日　星期日 [D029]

哈吉又覺得不舒服，所以我給他一點利眠寧（Chlorodyne）。[89] 船長登上「蝕缺」號，不一會兒，又派了小船接我過去吃晚餐。令人愉快的一餐，餐後又有美酒。[90]話題轉到了戰爭、[91]政治、北極點、達爾文主義、科學怪人、[92]自由貿易、捕鯨與地方事務。大衛船長似乎對於我們可能的漁獲量相當悲觀。他說，我們能捕到二十噸已經是萬幸；話是這麼說，但我不認為他心裡真這麼想。看見他穿著熊皮。順帶一提，船長告訴我們一些奇怪的故事，我試著把他講的故事寫下來。

「我年輕的時候，」他說，「恰好在倫敦，手上戴著金錶，腰纏萬貫。有一晚，我在萊西姆劇院（Lyceum）[93]，想回到位於霍爾本（Holborn）[94]的住處，但我左繞右繞就是找不到回家的路。最後，我看見一個外表體面的先生，於是向他問路，並且告訴他我是外地人。他說他也要去霍爾本，並且自我介紹，他是第十七騎兵團[95]的伯頓上尉（Captain Burton）。我們並肩而行，伯頓上尉提到在倫敦時身上帶太多錢是件危險的事，他看到我手上戴的錶與黃金，特別提醒我一聲。不久，我們轉進一扇開啟的門，上尉說，「我們喝點什麼吧，我想喝點干邑白蘭地。」我說，「咖啡對我來說就夠

87 十九世紀用來表示腹痛或腹瀉的口語體。

88 已亡佚。前一年，柯南．道爾曾在《錢伯斯週刊》（*Chambers's Journal*）發表一篇小說。〈薩撒颯谷之謎〉（The Mystery of Sasassa Valley）未受到重視，因此他下一篇小說便遭到退稿，然而「失敗並不要緊。重要的是我已經做了，而我很樂於再做一次」。

89 藥名念起來類似 cure-of-kill，牛津大學字典提到：「一種常用的止痛劑，成分有氯仿、嗎啡、印度大麻、氫氰酸等等。」

90 蘇瑟蘭的 *Whaling Years* 第二十七頁提到，「即使在高緯度的極地地區，在船長的餐桌上，維多利亞禮儀的嚴格規定仍受到一絲不苟地遵守，而在此同時，賓客享用著剛射下來的海鳥，通常是絨鴨與潛鳥，然後搭配上好的紅葡萄酒。接著是白蘭地、聊天，或許還會玩三戰兩勝制的惠斯特紙牌。」

91 第二次阿富汗戰爭（一八七八－八〇）：「我們在令人興奮的時期離開，」柯南．道爾在《回憶與冒險》中回想時表示。「阿富汗戰事已經如火如荼地進行中，與俄國的戰爭似乎一觸即發。我們（在八月）回到波羅的海的出口，渾然不知可能會有巡洋艦攻擊我們，就像我們獵殺鯨魚一樣。」

92 瑪麗．雪萊（Mary Shelley）的《科學怪人》（*Frankenstein*, 1818）開始而且結束在一艘北極探險船上，敘事者是一名先前曾在格陵蘭捕鯨船服務的船長。雪萊在嫁給詩人之前，曾在一八一三年到一八一四年待過鄧迪。她在當地聽聞許多捕鯨業的事。她運用自己的見聞在小說的第二十四章描述船隻被北極浮冰圍住，差一點船身就破損，全船的人可能因此喪命，包括那位垂死的維克多．弗蘭肯斯坦博士，他的怪獸就潛伏在附近。

93 維多利亞時代，倫敦主要劇院之一，位於河岸地區的威靈頓街上。在《四簽名》（*The Sign of Four*）中——這是福爾摩斯第二部小說（一八八九）——福爾摩斯與華生醫生在萊西姆劇院與瑪麗．莫斯坦小姐見面，同時也與她神祕的捐助者會面，而後便開啟一段冒險歷程。

94 牛津街從倫敦西區到倫敦市的延伸。它的歷史與文學意義使它成為柯南．道爾兩部福爾摩斯小說的場景。

95 劍橋公爵騎兵團的格言是「死亡或光榮」，這句格言體現在一八五四年克里米亞戰爭期間輕騎兵衝鋒造成的重大死傷上。

了。」端酒進來的服務生一臉凶相，我從未見過如此凶惡的面容。我看見他的舌頭頂著自己的臉頰，向上尉使了個臉色。頓時覺得自己中了圈套。

我丟了半英鎊金幣到櫃台上，起身要走，但那名服務生用背擋著門，說道，「我們不許我們的客人這樣離去。」上尉說，「來吧，先生，今晚我們就痛快一下；嘿，從三號櫃子裡拿雪利酒過來。」服務生喊著「珍妮」，一名少女現身，她看起來美麗但臉色蒼白。他說，「三號櫃。」少女說道，「可是今天晚上你用不到這個櫃子。」他說，「妳照做就是。」當她拿酒過來時，她低聲對我說，「你要假裝睡著。」我只喝了一點酒，絕大多數全灑在地上。然後我倒下閉上眼睛。不久，兩名惡棍過來，他們低聲交談，其中一名用燭光照著我的眼睛，「他睡著了。」他們又開始低聲說話，其中一人說，「死人是不會說話的。」另一個人說，「那麼我們最後把床準備好。」於是兩人離開房間。我立刻跳起來打開窗戶，像顆子彈一樣跳到街上，然後跑了半英里路，直到看到警察為止。然而我對倫敦實在太不熟悉，因此無法找到那間屋子。我從此再也沒聽說類似的事。再來一瓶波特酒吧，醫生。」這個故事的結尾相當完美。[96]船長又告訴我們另一個故事，他在波耳[97]服役時曾擔任間諜，他趁著對方睡覺時，殺死了三名卡菲爾人（Kaffir）[98]，並且射穿了一名德國人。

他曾看過一次海象吃掉獨角鯨的景象。他是個不錯的人，而沃克醫生看起來也非常正派。船長認為在晚間可以捕獲更多鯨魚，因此當他來到北極，進入微明之地時，他會在晚上十點吃早餐，凌晨兩點再吃一餐，早上七點吃晚餐。然後白天睡覺。他說鯨魚會留下非常獨特的味道，你在看見鯨魚之前，通常會先聞到牠們的味道。

三月二十九日 星期一（D032）

解禁的時間快到了。出現濃霧，而且下起大雪。沒有特別的事。晚上，在船副的房間玩得很開心。我們不停地唱歌，唱著〈傑克的冒險故事〉、〈美人魚〉（The Mermaid）與〈蒸汽手臂〉。[99]太有趣了。順帶一提，柯林大副今天一直誇我。他說，「開始獵捕海豹之後，我會要求每個人努力工作。我不擔心你，醫生。如果有需要人手的地方，儘管吩咐。你跟我很合得來，我第一天看到你就欣賞你的作風。本來我是討厭你們這種不蹚混水的紳士，但你不一樣。」柯林向來沉默寡言，所以他能這麼說算是很大的讚美。

96 這個故事讓人想起羅伯特·路易斯·史帝文森（Robert Louis Stevenson）的《自殺俱樂部》（*Suicide Club*, 1878）三部曲，這本書連同其他故事，構成了他的《新天方夜譚》（*New Arabian Nights*）。這個故事也引發柯南·道爾的興趣，因為他也不熟悉倫敦，但對倫敦的黑暗面感到好奇。一八七四年，柯南·道爾曾到倫敦探望親戚，當時他十五歲。他曾寫信回家開心地提到他到貝克街杜莎夫人蠟像博物館裡的恐怖室；而大衛船長的故事也產生了影響，六年後，柯南·道爾創作福爾摩斯時，他的冒險故事也以「倫敦最底層與最骯髒的巷弄」為場景。

97 波耳人（Boer）：南非的荷蘭移民，他們建立川斯瓦共和國（Transvaal Republic）與奧倫治自由邦（Orange Free State）與英國的開普殖民地（Cape Colony）對抗。第一次波耳戰爭爆發於一八八〇年十二月，在一八八一年三月結束，但事情仍未解決。一八九九年年底，第二次或大波耳戰爭爆發，慘烈的戰事持續了好幾年，柯南·道爾曾自願前往當地六個月擔任陸軍軍醫。

98 南非原住民的蔑稱。

99 水手的歌曲有太多與美人魚有關，因此我們很難確定是哪一首。但〈蒸汽手臂〉（Steam Arm）是史密斯（H. V. Smith）於十九世紀初作的歌曲，歌裡提到一名士兵失去了一條手臂，從滑鐵盧返國，他製造了一條機械蒸汽動力手臂，來對付他那潑辣的妻子。

三月三十日 星期二〔D033〕

沒有什麼事可做。「上風」號來到我們旁邊，穆雷上船。他的想法似乎不太樂觀，他認為十噸已經超出他的預期。穆雷告訴我們，約翰．羅斯爵士曾經開槍射穿房子的窗戶，因為他的船副在裡頭，而他要他的船副上船。穆雷曾是弗蘭克林搜尋隊的成員。羅斯說，「年輕人，向前的每一步都代表著榮譽與光榮。不要背負恥辱而死，」然後他們開始乘坐雪橇。[100]與柯林及史都華打拳擊。

三月三十一日 星期三〔D034〕

一整天沒什麼事可做。海面開始變得洶湧，我們對於這種現象可能造成的結果感到不安。如果這種情況一直持續到星期六，一定會讓我們的獵捕工作變得困難而且危險。這些海冰不是一整塊固體的冰層，而是由數千塊大小不等緊密相鄰的浮冰所構成。現在海面起伏不定，將使這些浮冰在強大力量下拉扯碰撞。如果有哪個可憐蟲不小心掉進浮冰的縫隙裡（這種事很容易發生），那麼他很可能在浮冰一開一闔之際被切成兩半，事實上，確實有幾個鄧迪人遭遇這種慘事。[101]船員在大塊浮冰上玩起蛙跳遊戲。我開始撰寫〈北極之旅〉（A Journey to the Pole），我想這會是個好故事。當鄧迪人回家時，我們會寫信給格萊斯頓與迪斯雷利。[102]

四月一日 星期四 〔D034〕

波濤依然洶湧，事情看起來不太妙。白天，我們稍稍前進一點。三年來，這是第一次我在這一天沒有考試。[103] 叫輪機長去找船長，讓他講了難以置信的窗簾掛環故事。強尼的自尊心嚴重受創。順帶一提，昨天我爬上桅頂，也走到冰上。晚上七點三十分，向金髮王「哈拉爾」號（Harald Haarfager）[104] 致意。海浪還是很大。

〔摺頁插圖，「船隻在海豹間就定位」〕

四月二日 星期五 〔D038〕

波濤依然洶湧，浮冰越來越分散。我擔心我們無法達成預期的漁獲量。然而，每個人都必須盡全力，如果成績仍不理想就無話可說。熬夜到十二點，想清醒地撐到解禁時間。

100 海軍少將約翰·羅斯爵士（John Ross, 1777-1856），蘇格蘭探險家，他尋找西北航道的探險行動失敗，卻蒐集了許多珍貴的科學資訊。一八五〇年，他嘗試救援海軍將領約翰·弗蘭克林爵士（John Franklin），後者於一八四五年前往加拿大的北極海域探險卻全員罹難。羅斯與他的船員曾經困在北極地區長達四年。

101 「上風」號的塔普林（J. F. Taplin）曾在日記裡（一八六〇年四月十五日）提到他親眼看到的狀況：「這個可憐的傢伙掉進冰縫裡，當他試圖爬上來時，一陣強風吹來，把另一塊浮冰推送過來，當場把這個人撞成兩截。」

102 班傑明·迪斯雷利（Benjamin Disraeli）是保守黨員，他在一八七四年年初擔任英國首相，但不到一個月就被自由黨的威廉·格萊斯頓（William Ewart Gladstone）接替。柯南·道爾這裡的意思或許是想要求這兩名政治家壓制鄧迪的捕鯨船。

103 指愛丁堡大學的醫學院考試。

104 挪威船，金髮王哈拉爾是維京酋長。八七二年，他統一挪威全境，成為挪威國王。

四月三日 星期六〔D038〕

凌晨兩點三十分。浪還是很大，作業難以進行。四點三十分，把小艇降到小浮冰上。但船長不顧我的要求，命令我待在船上，負責將海豹皮拉上來。[105]成年的海豹會游泳，所以用步槍射殺，至於無法逃走的可憐小海豹就用棍子敲碎牠們的頭骨。

這是件血腥的工作，當這些可憐的小傢伙用牠們又大又黑的眼睛看著你的臉時，你必須敲碎牠的腦子。我們快速將小艇拉上來，開始裝運。所有的人都要下船，跳過一塊塊的浮冰，殺死眼前看見的所有海豹，然後船發動引擎，把海豹皮運上去。要知道哪塊浮冰可以承載你的重量，哪塊不行，需要一點訣竅。我興致勃勃地開始，但一下船，馬上就掉進兩塊浮冰之間，然後被鉤竿拉上來。[106]我換了衣服，重新開始。我順利殺死了幾隻海豹，在剝皮之後，將牠們拖到船邊。我們今天獵了七百六十隻海豹。我想這個成績不理想，但我們希望越來越好。畢竟，捕鯨才是真正獲利的來源。

〔插圖，「用來打海豹的棍子」〕

四月四日 星期日〔D039〕

整天都在工作。我掉進北極海三次，但我很幸運，每次附近都有人把我拉上來。掉進海裡相當危險，因為像今天這種海浪比較大的天氣，你可能會被兩塊浮冰夾住，硬生生切成兩半。我被救了幾次，晚上我只能一直待在床上，因為我所有的衣服都放在引擎室裡烘乾。順帶提一下我心不在焉的例子，今天，在剝了一隻海豹的皮之後，我手裡拖著兩個後鰭狀肢，把我的連指手套忘在冰上。我們有些船員工作非常認真，但有些船員——絕大多數是昔德蘭人，但當中還是有例外——卻很偷懶，令人厭惡。[107] 它顯示了一個人的人品，這份工作需要到遠離船隻與船長視線以外的地方作業，殺死海豹之後，往往需要拖行數英里回船，在這種狀況下，如果有人想偷懶，你也無法阻止他。大副柯林孔武有力而且工作努力。我今天聽見他說，如果某人不好好工作，他會拿棍子揍他。我看見柯林口中說的那個傢伙，他從一隻肥美的海豹旁走過，卻宰了一隻可憐的小「托比」，新生的小海豹，他這麼做是為了減輕自己拖行的重量。船長整天都待在桅頂的瞭望台，透過望遠鏡尋找哪邊的海豹最密集。今天獵到四百六十隻海豹。

105 本書的〈前言〉提過，柯南·道爾數年後寫〈格陵蘭捕鯨船上的生活〉（Life on a Greenland Whaler）時，提起此事仍憤憤不平，但他也坦承：「我想船長的謹慎是有道理的，因為光是那天，我就摔進海裡兩次。當我的衣服放在引擎室裡烘乾時，我必須可恥地一直待在床上。」

106 掉進接近冰點的海水裡，這可不是件小事。「看這裡，」柯南·道爾一八八二年的故事〈「北極星」船長〉裡的某個人物說道，「即使一切看來安好，但這裡是個危險的地方——一個變幻莫測、危險的地方。我知道有人就像這樣，突然就死在冰下。有時只要稍一失足——摔進浮冰的縫隙，大家只能藉由綠色海水中的氣泡來找出你摔落的地方。」在本條目後過了兩天，柯南·道爾差點因為相同的原因失去性命。

107 柯南·道爾後來說得稍微公允一點。十六年後，在〈格陵蘭捕鯨船上的生活〉一文中，他說道：「在船上有五十個人，其中一半是蘇格蘭人，一半是昔德蘭人，昔德蘭人是我們經過勒維克時僱用的。昔德蘭人較為穩重、順從、安靜、規矩而且溫和；反觀蘇格蘭船員則很容易惹麻煩，但也較為壯健剛強。高級船員與魚叉手都是蘇格蘭人，但一般船員，特別是船工，昔德蘭人的表現完全能符合要求。全部船員有五十五人，其中有六名只有十九歲，全是昔德蘭人。」

四月六日【五日】 星期一〔D040〕

今天早上與柯林一起出去從事例行的粗活，但才剛開始作業，我就掉進海裡。當我從冰緣掉下去時，才剛殺死一隻躺在大浮冰上的海豹。沒有人在我附近，而海水實在冰冷透頂。我抓住冰緣，以免我往下沉，但冰面實在太滑，我沒辦法爬上去。最後，我抓住了海豹尾部的鰭狀肢，努力讓自己爬上來。這隻可憐的老海豹居然不計前嫌救了我。[108] 與史都華一起下船，做點好差事。[109] 又獵到四百多隻海豹。

四月六日 星期二〔D041〕

早上，跟柯林下船到浮冰上，這次沒掉進海裡了。船長叫我「偉大的北方跳水員」。我們獵了相當多年輕與年老的海豹，然後把船開出去，看是否能找到別的獵物。射殺兩隻體型相當大的冠海豹，從七十碼左右射擊算是相當簡單的事，但輪到我射魚叉時卻沒有射中，我太高估自己了。這兩隻海豹是龐然大物，我保留了其中一隻的骨頭，足足有十一英尺長。牠們又稱為象海豹。牠們在口鼻部有個布滿血管的肉袋，在憤怒時會充血擴大。看見「揚馬延」號與其他船隻，它們的小艇都在獵殺老海豹。獵到兩百七十隻年輕海豹與五十八隻老海豹。

四月七日 星期三 〔D042〕

今天的成績不佳，海豹很少，我們只獵到一百三十三隻。米爾納的狀況很糟，我擔心他可能會死。他出現了腸套疊[110]的現象，不斷嘔糞與疼痛。這不是疝氣。注射肥皂與海狸油。[111]

四月八日 星期四 〔D042〕

把我們的信件送到「奮進」號上。[112]拿到簡短的便條，只寫了一封信，其實我是想多寫一點。今日收穫不佳，只獵到三十隻海豹。然而，絕大多數的船成績都比我們差，對方可是有八十名船員，而我們只有五十六名。晚間，起風。

108 一八六〇年，塔普林醫生也遭遇類似的不幸，雖然被附近的船副拉上岸，但他必須趕緊回船，這可是攸關生死的大事：「我必須疾速奔跑，以免我的腿被凍僵。冰面相當難走，但我還是在四十分鐘內回到船上。我立刻衝到船艙換衣服，但要這麼做得花上一點時間，因為我的褲子連同靴子已經冰凍住了，而我的外套也與我的背心及長褲凍結在一起。我無法想像我是怎麼回到船上的……當我抵達船旁，我的腿整個僵直無法彎曲，因此我無法爬梯子登上甲板，只好用繩索圈在我的腋下，然後吊上甲板。」

109 柯南·道爾年輕、有活力而且幸運。艾伯特·馬克罕（七十七頁）提到有個北極船員掉進海裡，狀況跟柯南·道爾類似：雖然「被帶回船上做了治療……但他還是花了好幾天才得以從冰寒中康復」。

110 一種腸子疾病，部分的腸段凹陷到其他部分的腸段中，使食物或液體無法前進，並且阻塞於某個腸段，造成組織缺血壞死。如果沒有立即治療——開刀是最後手段——可能會致命，但對於一八八〇年一名待在船上毫無開刀器械與助手的大三醫學生來說，這樣的手術是不可能進行的。

111 根據卡茲醫生的說法，「診斷出腸套疊的話，或許可以試試灌腸器。然而，腸套疊很難藉由身體檢查看出。就連使用X光也不容易確診，通常只能透過手術的方式來確認。此外，這種病症比較常見於孩子身上，但這名患者卻是個老人。『米爾納已經七十歲。』聽起來米爾納似乎有腸阻塞的毛病，而且有長期的腸供血不足（包括腸沾黏）或腫瘤（這比較可能在成人身上看到）的問題。在現代，病人可以接受靜脈注射供給養分，直到病好為止。」

112 根據布坎的 *The Peterhead Whaling Trade* 第五十四頁，「奮進」號是約翰·格雷首次擔任船長時指揮的船隻——當時他只有二十二歲。

給他在愛丁堡母親的信

北緯七十三度十分，東經二度

「希望」號

格陵蘭，一八八〇年四月七日

最親愛的媽媽

我還是跟以前一樣健康、強壯與難看，我們現在位於北極圈內，在揚馬延島的外海。我們三月十日從昔德蘭出發，航行途中天氣良好，萬里無雲，十六日，我們看到浮冰。我們上床睡覺，腦子裡還縈繞著一望無際的藍色海面。早晨，當我們走到甲板，發現海上全是大片浮冰，上面是白色，底下是藍綠色，隨著海面起伏而上下擺盪。我們從浮冰當中開過去，經過一天，沒有看見任何海豹的蹤影。第二天，我們看到冰上有一隻年輕的象海豹，有幾群海豹朝西北游去。我們跟著這些海豹，十八日，看到六艘汽船的黑煙，它們全開往同一方向，想找到主要的海豹群。隔天早晨，從甲板上可以看見十一艘船，以及大量的象海豹或冠海豹，於是我們充滿希望。妳必須了解，在四月三日之前，北極圈內不許有任何流血的活動。[113]三月二十日，我們看到真正的海豹群。牠們躺在堅硬的冰層上，分布的範圍長約十五英里，寬約八英里，估計有數百萬隻。二十二日，我們在浮冰邊緣下錨，然後等待。視野所及的二十五艘船全做著相同的事。二十九日，開始吹起八級風，令人扼腕的是，海豹群紛紛四散，幾個笨拙的挪威水手穿過海豹群，驚擾了那些即將分娩的母海豹。四月三日，血腥的工作從這天開始。母海豹被射殺，小海豹則以帶尖刺的棍棒將牠的頭打碎。然後就地將海豹剝皮，然後將海豹皮連同附在上面的油脂拖回船邊。這是相當辛苦的工作，因為通常要走上好幾英里的路，我今天就是如此，在找到獵物之前，必須跳過一塊又一塊的浮冰，然後獵殺之後又要拖著沉重的豹皮回船。船員們一定以為我對於辛苦的工作有特殊的愛好，特別是他們覺得最疲憊的任務，但我認為這麼做可以激勵他們。我的肩膀被拖繩磨破了。[114]順帶一提，過去四天以來，我一共掉進海裡五次，遠遠高於平均。第一次，我試圖跳到另一塊看起來相當牢固的浮冰上，當我正打算順著繩索扭動身子跳過去時，船的螺旋槳打轉，一下子把浮冰推遠，我於是掉進華氏四度[115]的海水中。船上的人用船竿勾住我的外套，把我拉了上來，我換了一件衣服，再度回到冰上，這回沒出什麼事。第二天我就沒那麼幸運了，因為我掉進海裡三次，我帶來的所有衣物全放在引擎室晾乾。第三天，我只掉進海裡一次。現在，我已有兩天沒掉進海裡。必須經過多次的嘗試才會了解哪些浮冰是安全的，而哪些浮冰是不穩定的。我們在船附近的雪地上發現熊的足跡，但我一頭也沒獵到。我昨天獵到一頭象海豹，體長十一英尺，跟海象一樣大。牠們的體型非常巨大，恐怕連熊也招架不住。我們獵捕年輕海豹的行動已經結束，相對來說是失敗的，我們只捕到二十五頓，但我們接下來將尾隨老海豹往北航行，我們會經過斯匹茲卑爾根島，並且到北緯八十度以北的地區捕鯨，希望在那裡能取得好成績。

113 根據一八七七年英國與挪威的協定，英國方面推動保育措施的是大衛．格雷船長與漁業督察巴克蘭（Frank Buckland）。

114 柯南．道爾在這裡把困難描述得過於輕描淡寫。一八八三年，《樸資茅斯時報》報導他的談話，柯南．道爾告訴讀者：「你們可以想像從樸資茅斯走到倫敦，每隔三到四步就會出現一道深刻崎嶇的裂縫，而且裂開的口子極寬，根本不可能跳過去；你們可以想像在這些裂縫之間與頂端散布著數百萬塊與房子一般大小的巨石；在某些地方，傾斜的冰面如玻璃一樣滑溜；在另一些地方，積雪厚達人的脖子；此外，再加上北極地區的氣候，哪怕是短暫暴露一下，就有可能凍傷；而且，我們是拖著一百到一百五十英磅的重物來這趟旅程，我們不僅要從裂縫的一邊拖到另一邊，還要拖著東西爬上巨石；在抵達倫敦之前，你很清楚，在北極海，距離不是用英里來計算的。一個人從倫敦走到君士坦丁堡，所花的力氣要比我們突破這六十英里的重重險阻輕鬆得多。

115 譯註：約攝氏零下十五點六度。

親愛的媽媽，我很高興能參與這次航行，希望妳也能為我感到開心。我想，現在走進船艙的我，模樣恐怕連妳也不認得。船長說，我是他所見過樣子最可怕野蠻的人。我的頭髮全豎起來，臉上滿是塵土與汗水，手上也沾滿血跡。我穿著最舊的衣服，我的防水長靴外頭凍著一層海水，看起來閃閃發亮，靴口則積滿了雪。我的外套圍了一條皮帶，上面繫著刀鞘，裡頭插著刀子，另外我也在腰際插了一根鋼條，這些物品上頭全結著血塊。我的肩膀繞著一捆繩索，手裡拿著沾滿血污的長斧。親愛的夫人，這就是妳天真無邪的孩子現在的樣子。我的身體從未像現在這麼健康過，我覺得自己彷彿可以到任何地方或做任何事。我相信自己可以到任何地方，想吃什麼就吃什麼。親愛的媽媽，接下來這一兩個月妳完全不用擔心。我在這裡是如魚得水。代我向格林希爾街、沃勒太太與沃勒醫生[116]，以及向尼爾森太太（Neilson）與所有在倫敦的親友[117]問好。我已經寫過信給格林希爾街與倫敦，但此時剛好有一艘船等著收我們的信，我想一件好消息抵得上三件壞消息，因此還是麻煩妳幫我向他們轉達一聲。

代我向巴德夫婦致上所有的問候。[118]別弄丟了他的地址。

妳的愛兒

亞瑟·柯南·道爾

船長要我代他向妳致上問候之意，他說，我是一條骯髒的破布；但他拒絕解釋這句難聽話的意思。他也叫我「偉大的北方跳水員」，暗指我最近頻頻跌入海中的窘樣。我從離開愛丁堡之後，一直未曾暈船。代我向父親請安以及向瑪麗、洛蒂與康妮[119]問好。

信件到此結束，接下來是日記

四月九日 星期五 〔D042〕

八級風持續吹襲，我們完全無法工作。波濤洶湧。到海岬的背風處尋找庇護。悲慘的一天。無事可做，只能睡覺與寫寫日誌。

他們開始從海豹皮取下脂肪。我擔心明天的天氣會跟今天一樣壞。

〔八幅小插圖，分別是「拖著海豹皮」、「等待母海豹」、「隊伍」、「用棍子打小海豹」、「一大串海豹」、「我出了意外」、「危險的一刻」與「剝海豹皮」〕

116 布萊安·查爾斯·沃勒醫生（Bryan Charles Waller）比柯南·道爾大六歲，他對柯南·道爾的求學與醫學生涯有著重要但有時混亂的影響；或許文學上的影響也是，因為沃勒也是曾經出版過詩作的詩人。雖然兩人偶有不和，但柯南·道爾於一八八五年結婚時，還是請沃勒當他的男儐相。

117 「所有在倫敦的親友」指的大概是他的叔伯與姑媽，但尼爾森太太是誰，我們不得而知。

118 喬治·特恩艾文·巴德醫生（George Turnavine Budd）是比柯南·道爾高一個年級的醫學院學長。儘管他的脾氣暴躁而且作風頗有爭議，柯南·道爾還是排除眾議，於一八八二年到普利茅斯（Plymouth）擔任他的助理。「巴德醫生的前途充滿光明，除了曾在世上最重視實務經驗的醫學院習得高深的醫學知識，他那言語難以形容的作風馬上就贏得病人的信任。」這是柯南·道爾在半自傳短篇小說〈克拉布的執業〉（Crabbe's Practice）裡對他的形容。在普利茅斯，柯南·道爾發現巴德的醫療事業搞得有聲有色，但他使用的方法卻有違職業倫理。兩人的合作關係維持了六個星期。柯南·道爾搬到樸資茅斯的南海城自行開業。在日後的小說《斯塔克·蒙羅的書信》（*The Stark Munro Letters*）以及《回憶與冒險》中，柯南·道爾寫下兩人緊張的合作關係（他們經營的診所叫巴德柯林沃斯〔Budd Cullingworth〕）。巴德只活了三十四歲，顯然是腦部病變奪去了他的性命，而這個疾病也影響了他的行為。

119 他的妹妹洛蒂，之前曾經提過；康妮（Connie）也是他的妹妹，此時十二歲。瑪麗（Mary）是愛爾蘭人，十六歲，在道爾家幫傭，她的全名是瑪麗·基爾派崔克（Mary Kilpatrick）。

四月十日 星期六〔D044〕

可憐的安德魯．米爾納幾乎是沒救了。以他的年邁，再加上這樣的病症，復元的可能性很渺茫。間斷地出現陣風，浪大。整天無事可做。開始閱讀卡萊爾的《英雄崇拜》。[120] 這是一本很棒的書。

四月十一日 星期日〔D044〕

出航以來黑暗的一日。早上，可憐的安德魯心情非常愉快，而且病情改善很多，但他晚餐吃了一點梅子布丁之後，突然急速惡化。我立刻下到船艙，不到十分鐘，他就死在我的懷裡。[121] 可憐的老頭。在他生病期間，大家都悉心照顧他，當然，我也盡了全力診治他。[122] 當晚，製作安德魯的遺產清冊。屍體、燈籠、四周圍繞著毫不矯飾的面孔，構成生動的畫面。我們明日埋葬他。一整天在大片浮冰上獵海豹，冰面融化，感覺像走在融雪上，我想我們獵到的海豹大約有六十隻。

四月十二日 星期一〔D045〕

今天早晨，我們為可憐的老安德魯舉行葬禮。桅杆降半旗表示哀悼之意。他被捆綁起來放在帆布袋裡，腳上綁著一袋鐵塊，海葬前先誦念亡者禱文。然後載著屍體的擔架開始傾斜，老人腳前頭後地落入海中，一點水花也沒有。只看到幾個氣泡與微弱的水流聲，老安德魯就這樣走完人生最後一程。他現在已經知曉最不為人知的祕密。我想，他在抵達海底之前，整個人恐怕已被壓成扁平狀。或許，他永遠到不了海底，在下沉的過程中，鐵塊的重量可能漸漸被抵消。他也許會像穆罕默德的棺材一樣在海裡懸浮著。[123]船長與我都同意，在棺材消失的那一刻，大家齊聲歡呼三次。這麼做不是輕佻簡慢，而是發自內心的道別。足足幹了一天的活兒，我想應該獵了有六十隻海豹。晚上，想起安德魯的事。「冰穴」號（Polynia）到目前為止捕到兩千零五十隻海豹，比我們少。

四月十三日　星期二（D046）

又到了水煮牛肉日（Tuesday — Teugh-day — Tough-day — Boiled Beef day）。[124]一個星期當中，除了星期五，就屬今天的晚餐菜色最差。由於風勢太大的關係，船隻整天停駛。把拳套放在鍋爐口烘了一下，痛快地打了幾場拳擊。一隻海豹

120 蘇格蘭歷史學家湯瑪斯·卡萊爾（Thomas Carlyle, 1795-1881）對年輕時的柯南·道爾有很大的影響，儘管他並不完全贊同卡萊爾的說法——隔年，柯南·道爾再度出海，他在航海日記中寫著，卡萊爾是個「偉大而嚴苛的思想家，我想詩文、藝術與一切令生活愜意之物，在他眼中恐怕都是無用的東西」。卡萊爾的《論英雄、英雄崇拜與歷史上的英雄》（*On Heroes, Hero-Worship, and the Heroic in History*, 1841）提到幾個不同類型的人物，如克倫威爾、莎士比亞、拿破崙、約翰生、馬丁·路德與穆罕默德。柯南·道爾或許會同意卡萊爾說的這兩句話，「人類的行為、思想、成就或本質，全神奇地保存在書本裡」，以及「除了老師的教導之外，我們只能靠自己閱讀。世界最棒的大學就是書本」——柯南·道爾一九〇七年的作品《穿過魔法之門》（*Through the Magic Door*）也顯現出大致相同的觀點。柯南·道爾一八八三年首次嘗試寫作的小說《約翰·史密斯的告白》並未提及卡萊爾，但內容明顯深受卡萊爾的影響。

121 梅子布丁是腸套疊患者最不能吃的東西，但它卻是長期航行海上的捕鯨船與其他船隻最常做的甜點，這種硬布丁是用水、麵粉、糖蜜與葡萄乾製成（名稱叫「梅子」其實添入的是葡萄乾），即使是有一副強健胃腸的人，吃了梅子布丁也會感到有點吃不消。當船員把梅子布丁拿給可憐的米爾納吃的時候，柯南·道爾並不在場，對他來說這似乎是不幸中的大幸，因為沒有人認為米爾納的死是柯南·道爾的錯。

122 羅伯特·卡茲醫生說：「這個時候，米爾納或許腸子已經出現不可回復的損壞（梗塞），而且伴隨出現了腸穿孔，腸的內容物已經滲漏到腹腔（腹膜炎）。一盤梅子布丁足以加重米爾納的病情，不久就死去，並不令人驚訝。這種狀況絕大多數都需要動手術，但在汪洋大海中，在捕鯨船上，柯南·道爾根本無計可施。無論診斷結果如何，柯南·道爾都救不了這個可憐的傢伙。」

123 譯註：據說穆罕默德的棺材由天然磁石或磁鐵打造，因此能在墓室裡懸空飄浮。

124 譯註：Teugh-day 是蘇格蘭英語，也就是 Tough-day，倒楣的日子。

也沒獵到。

〔插圖，「懷念安德魯．米爾納，一八八〇年四月十一日」〕

四月十四日 星期三 〔D047〕

揚帆，一面在浮冰間前進，一面獵捕海豹。今天的天氣很適合獵捕，大約獵到八十隻海豹，總計獵到的海豹數來到兩千四百五十隻左右。整天站在艏艛回報行進狀況。雖然寒冷，但還是射殺了一兩隻海豹。有人告訴我，在南海，如果有人死了，那麼第一個趕到的人可以獲得他的財產。因此，一旦有人從船上落水，你會看到好幾個人站在艙門口，準備等人一溺死就衝進去搶奪錢財。

四月十五日 星期四 〔D047〕

天氣晴朗，但我們的收穫不多，大概只獵到四十六隻海豹。我在其他船員協助下射殺了兩隻冠海豹。這兩隻海豹各自中了五槍。看到一隻美麗的小鳥，頭上長了一簇紅毛，體型不過比麻雀稍大一些，牠飛到我們的小艇附近，不斷地振翅飛舞。船上沒有人看過這種鳥。這隻鳥的嘴喙稍長，腳上無蹼，腹部是白色的，發出「皮—皮—」的愉快叫聲。牠屬於雪鵐（Snowflake）的一種。[125] 傍晚，喬吉．格蘭特（Georgey Grant）的褲子被一頭年輕象海豹咬破。

四月十六日　星期五〔D048〕

加足馬力往西北方航行，如此持續了一整天，試圖尋找海豹的蹤影。但成效不彰，我們只捕到六隻海豹。傍晚，傑克・布坎（Jack Buchan）射中一隻老鷹，船長用他銳利的眼睛辨識出冰丘上有東西，而且隔著遙遠的距離居然看出那是一隻老鷹。這隻鷹高十八英寸，美麗的羽毛點綴著斑紋。

〔三張插圖，「我心中浮現的老鷹模樣」，「船長心中浮現的老鷹模樣」與「船長看到的老鷹正在尋找的獵物」〕

四月十七日　星期六〔D048〕

整天無事可做。還是一樣，只獵到六隻海豹。我們與挪威船「冰山」號（Iceberg）一起往南航行。現在哪怕是只捕到三十頓，我都感到心滿意足。我們現在總計大約捕了二十八頓。今日氣溫華氏四度。[126] 傍晚在船副的艙房唱歌。

〔插圖，「星期六夜晚，在海上，一八八〇年四月十七日」〕

125 一種小型的北極鳥類，比較常見的稱呼是Snow Bunting。

126 譯註：約攝氏零下十五點五度。

我以菸草為題，開始作詩，我覺得寫得還不賴。我一直未能把詩寫完。Ce n’est que la derniére pas qui coute.[127]

四月十八日　星期日〔D049〕

下著細雪，天氣看起來霧濛濛的。早上，從船頭射殺了一隻海豹；當時牠的頭才剛伸出海面。看到兩隻大海鳥，這種鳥稱為「北極鷗」（Burgomaster）。傍晚，參加管輪麥克勞舉行的衛理宗聚會，他朗讀福音雜誌上的布道文，然後大夥兒齊唱讚美詩。之後，我跟麥克勞起了爭執。

四月十九日　星期一〔D050〕

早上，開始製作老鷹的標本，或者應該說是剝皮，在沒有金屬線的狀況下，我只能這麼做。我打開鳥腹，先設法從鳥的體內逆著拉出鳥的腿、膝蓋乃至於肱骨，然後將整隻鳥由內而外翻出來，清理鳥的腦子，只剩下空殼的頭骨。結果令人滿意。我們今天獵到幾隻冠海豹，並且往北航行，尋找老海豹群的蹤跡。船長似乎不大滿意浮冰的狀況。

〔插圖，「迅速開了一槍」〕

四月二十日 星期二（D051）

整天無事可做。一隻海豹也沒獵著。往東北方航行。今日，抵達北緯七十二度三十分。清理幾隻海豹的鰭狀肢，用來製作菸草袋。用明礬摩擦老鷹的皮。

四月二十一日 星期三（D051）

除了發發牢騷，我們實在無事可做。我們經歷過不少次狂風巨浪，不過今天是最糟糕的一次。沒有獵到任何海豹，要說我們有什麼收穫，那麼只能說是悲慘。一整天心情跌到了谷底。凌晨一點被人從被窩裡叫起來，去診斷某人的心悸毛病。我的情緒沒有因此轉好。

四月二十二日 星期四（D051）

持續昨天的大浪。大約捕到十三隻海豹，其中兩隻是我射殺的。成績不好，但至少優於昨天。濃霧。捕到一隻新生的

127「只有最後的結果才算數。」

海豹，就季節來說，這隻海豹出生的時間似乎太晚了。到目前為止，我射殺了十五隻海豹。今後，我會開始計算自己獵殺的海豹數量。

四月二十三日　星期五 〔D051〕

今天好多了，一共獵到三十六隻海豹。其中十一隻是我獵的，因此到目前為止，我總共獵到二十六隻海豹。今晚看起來應該會吹起八級風。船長又看到一隻老鷹。到目前為止，我們連一頭熊也沒看見，這是很稀罕的事。船長曾經看過流星墜落到離船不到一百碼的海面上。磁北極位於北緯六十九度的威廉王島（King William's Land）上。[128] 此外還有一個磁南極，這是我過去不知道的。

〔插圖，「我們的夜間運動」〕

四月二十四日　星期六 〔D052〕

我們一整天持續朝西北航行。我們看見一大群絨鴨，雄鴨的羽毛黑白相間，雌鴨身體呈青銅色，頭部是綠色。獵到十七隻以上的年輕海豹。我想，我們離老海豹群不遠了。晚上，在船副的艙房消磨時間。今日一槍未發。早上，我們打了幾場拳擊。學到一些祕訣可以教導吉米。[129]

與技術最高超的魚叉手赫爾頓（Andrew Hulton）聊到一些珍奇動物。他說，在往返魁北克與利物浦途中，曾經遭遇八級風吹襲，他看見兩條魚躺在水面上。這兩條魚長約六十英尺，上面布滿斑點，就像豹紋一樣。魚的種類不明。船長曾在北緯六十八度附近看過另一種魚，外皮非常厚，連魚叉都無法刺穿。以下我列出幾種北方的鯨魚。

露脊鯨：格陵蘭鯨。身上有十到二十噸的油脂。鯨骨每噸賣價一千英鎊。一頭鯨魚可賣一千五百到兩千英鎊。出現在極北的冰原之間。

長鬚鯨：各大洋均可見牠們的蹤影，往往數百頭為一群。體形比露脊鯨來的龐大強壯，但價值很低。有些長鬚鯨長度可達一百二十英尺。背部如剃刀。有兩個噴氣孔，但一般鯨魚只有一個。

瓶鼻鯨：分布在浮冰區以南，冰島附近。體長只有三十英尺。每頭可以生產一噸鯨油（八十英鎊）。皮的價值很高。

白鯨（貝魯加鯨）：到處可見牠們的蹤跡，包括西敏水族館（Westminster Aquarium）。主要分布在美洲河口。油脂很有價值。體長約十六英尺。

黑鯨：相當稀有的鯨魚。船長只看過一頭。價值很高。美國人有時會在北角（North Cape）外捕到這種鯨魚。

赫爾頓的鯨魚（Hulton's Whale）：（Balaena variagatum）

格雷船長的鯨魚（Capt Gray's Whale）：（Balaena ironsidum）

128 位於加拿大的極地地區。

129 可能是指他在愛丁堡的朋友詹姆斯・萊恩。

四月二十五日 星期日〔D054〕

早上，發現一群年輕海豹，獵到二十二隻。晚餐前，我獲得了豐碩的成果，我站在船頭射了八槍，打中七隻海豹。但在晚餐後，我只打中一隻，另外兩槍全落空了。現在我們總共捕到兩千五百零二隻海豹。看見一隻老海豹。與史都華打拳擊，與強尼一起唱讚美詩。畫了我們獵捕年輕海豹的插圖。看到一篇有趣的戲仿詩。130

喔，他寫下的狂野同韻詞，
有些詩人驚訝地看見
〈輕騎兵〉裡的
「百名」（Hundred）與「雷轟」（Thundered）

四月二十六日 星期一〔D054〕

整日往北北西航行，尋找老海豹。有些冰層結得很厚，而且往海中突出延伸，形成海岬，許多老海豹就躺臥在海岬之上。然而我們無法得知這些海豹會在什麼地方出現；你只能沿著格陵蘭的厚冰航行，才能發現牠們。今天，我們位於北緯七十四度。昨天，獵到一隻年輕海豹，看到幾隻年輕海豹。我們想到更好的獵物。晚上打拳擊。與史都華賽跑一百碼。現在我終於徹底了解捕海豹這份工作是怎麼回事了。

〔摺頁插圖，「所有人手全下船去獵捕年輕海豹。一八八〇年」〕

〔插圖，「格陵蘭海豹獵捕地圖」〕

四月二十七日　星期二 〔D058〕

整日往北北西航行。我們經過剛形成的海灣浮冰，試圖開往冰層較厚的地區，並且預期那裡會有海豹棲息。快到傍晚時，我們覺得離目標已經不遠。整天無事可做。我的老鷹的皮損壞了。因為米爾納的兄弟上船了，所以我們重新舉行一次米爾納的喪禮。

四月二十八日　星期三 〔D058〕

早上，抵達格陵蘭的厚冰區。早餐後，我走到甲板上，看到冰層一直延伸到遠方的地平線上。我從未見過這麼厚的冰層。極地區的折射效果令人嘖嘖稱奇。一英里外的景物與近處的景物，看起來不太一樣。

〔兩張插圖，「近處的厚冰層」與「一英里外的厚冰層」〕

130 戲謔地模仿丁尼生（Tennyson）的〈輕騎兵的衝鋒〉（The Charge of the Light Brigade, 1854）。

看見浮冰上留有大批海豹的痕跡。海中有少數海豹往北游。傍晚，靠近來自鄧迪的「勝利者」號。只會依賴別人的人沒有權利待在這裡。我們期待明天時來運轉。

四月二十九日 星期四 〔D059〕

我們的期望並未實現，雖然我們看見海中有幾個海豹群，而且我們一整天不斷往北航行，但還是未能發現海豹的主要棲地。早上，「勝利者」號船長戴維德森（Davidson）登上我們的船——這個人相當粗鄙，全身毛茸茸的。他曾是我們的船副，而且以脾氣暴躁著稱。今晚，折射現象特別明顯，許多浮冰懸浮在半空中。「勝利者」號整天跟在我們後面。我打賭，我們離海豹不遠了。看到許多雪鳥，這是個好預兆。我們來到北緯七十五度十一分。

四月三十日 星期五 〔D060〕

早上，吹起了南風，開始起霧，這是不祥的預兆。在這種天候開始獵捕海豹，大家都感到有點沮喪。我們在霧中往東北航行，水面看起來像是漂浮著灣冰的湖泊，上面棲息著無數潛鳥與海燕。就在喝下午茶之前，我們看見前方有個厚冰結成的海岬，我們祈求海岬的另一面會出現海豹。我心裡滿是狐疑，因為海面上根本沒有海豹的蹤影。夜裡，天色明亮如同白晝，我可以在半夜輕鬆閱讀《錢伯斯週刊》。晚上，大家一起喝起烈酒，因為明天是五月一日。浮冰的狀況似乎頗適合捕鯨。晚上十點。我想到冰上完全沒有海豹的蹤跡，我們於是認定，我們可能位於海豹的北方。「我也這麼想，媽咪。」船員一般都在五月一日這天刮新船員的鬍子，一名小艇舵手晚上告訴我，我將是受害者，但我告訴他，他們必須叫兩名值班的船員來做這件事。[131]〔此處的筆跡相當潦草：我相信，如果我真的遭到攻擊，那麼我會把值班的船員趕出甲板〔？〕，我覺得吵架是理所當然。我會等到午夜，看看他們會做出什麼事來。〕

131 這是個考驗，蘇瑟蘭的 *Whaling Years* 第四十一頁說：「五月的前幾個小時，新人要被帶到甲板上，接受難熬的入會儀式。資深船員戴上面具披上古怪的海豹皮袍子，他們將新人的雙眼蒙上，刮擦他們的臉直到流血為止，然後再用生鏽且看似鋸子的剃刀為他們刮鬍子。強灌新人骯髒的雞尾酒，美其名是向『海神』敬酒。整個古怪的儀式到此結束，通過考驗的新人將成為『格陵蘭自由民兄弟會』與『冠海豹獵人榮譽兄弟會』的成員。」布坎的 *The Peterhead Whaling Trade* 有同樣可怕的描述。柯南·道爾雖然在此未多加說明，但福爾摩斯的讀者應該會想起《恐怖谷》（*The Valley of Fear*）中死酷黨人（Scowrer）的入會儀式。

五月一日 星期六〔D061〕

早上，風浪襲來，我們的前景黯淡到了極點。但到了晚餐前，情況有了變化，因為我們看見冰上有一隻年輕的冠海豹，之後不久，我們看到一大群海豹在水中順風前進。晚餐時，船長跟所有的船員都感到心情鬱悶，但晚餐後，船長爬上瞭望台，下來之後他開心地大叫，「全員集合。」我坐上二副的小艇，下午四點三十分左右，降下小艇。七艘長條形的捕鯨小艇掠過藍色水面，往冰面前進，這真是美好的景象。這些海豹似乎比我上次看見牠們時變得更白。船副開槍，但沒有打中，我則是找不到機會開槍。船副拿著棒子走到舵手的位置，他讓我自行走上浮冰，於是我努力用槍托測試冰面是否牢固。這真是一件討人厭的工作。在冰上行走是很危險的事，我有兩次差點因為落水而喪命，而且在我的四周完全沒人。事實上，依照當時的情形，我其實是活不了的。這比獵捕年輕海豹危險得多，因為厚冰的底部已被海水融蝕，你以為自己站在大塊浮冰上很安全，其實整塊浮冰很可能突然間瓦解崩散。一直找不到機會開槍。船副殺死一隻海豹。真是悲慘，我們這個小艇是成績最差的。如果船副的槍法跟我一樣準，或者我能跟船副一樣在冰上健步如飛，那麼結果一定大不相同。然而，能下船工作畢竟是件愉快的事。海豹因為受到驚嚇，很快就離開冰上。往西邊游去。以下是我們今天的戰果

布坎的小艇	14
蘭尼（Rennie）的小艇	13
卡納的小艇	10
柯林的小艇	10

馬提森（Mathieson）的小艇	10
赫爾頓的小艇	9
麥肯吉（McKenzie）的小艇	2
康恩的小艇	1
總計	69

五月二日　星期日〔D063〕

陣雨、厚冰、雪與風，似乎串通好要毀了我們。我們發動引擎頂著八級風向北航行，這風一整天都沒停過，一股勁地朝我們吹來。傍晚，船長從桅頂下來，臉上帶著絕望的表情。他指著天上的冰映光，表示船的前方有厚冰。「如果那裡沒有海豹，」他說，「我必須再度往南走。」我們繼續往北航行，令人高興的是，在下午茶之後，船長突然召集「所有船員」。發現了大批海豹，不過這些海豹朝海冰而去，因此有人認為今晚先按兵不動，等到明天再獵捕牠們。最好是能在「勝利者」號發現我們要做什麼之前，就能採取行動，進行獵捕。「勝利者」號是視野內唯一一艘來自鄧迪的船，該船船長是個 sumph。[132] 今晚早點上床睡覺，明日早點起床。

132 這是蘇格蘭的詞彙，「傻瓜」或「笨蛋」的意思。

五月三日 星期一〔D064〕

早上六點左右，我們降下小艇。小艇才剛放下去，五英里外的「勝利者」號就開始加足馬力朝我們這裡駛來。我與彼得．麥肯吉同船，因為魚叉手只剩下他一個。我們把我們的小艇稱為「烏合之眾」，因為坐我們這個小艇的船員在船上都屬於最底層的人物，但我認為他們與其他船員相比毫不遜色。我們有魚叉手彼得、舵手傑克．庫爾、[133]醫生、勤務員、大管輪，以及基斯，他是船上年紀最大的人。小艇分別降落在不同的地點，而我們是最後一艘降下的小艇。浮冰很厚實，看起來相當穩定。起初，我們停泊的地點不好，只射中兩隻海豹，但我們努力在冰上探索前進，並且來到一處聚集了許多海豹的水灣。彼得與我提著槍衝了出去，並且在冰上匍匐前進，其他船員則是趴在我們身後，我們獵到的海豹，由他們負責剝皮。我看見彼得射中兩隻，然後我打中一隻。接著我躲藏在冰丘後方，開槍射中九隻，有五隻排成一排倒在浮冰邊緣。我腦子剛想著今天可能會大豐收，並且又射中一隻，此時我聽見一百碼外彼得的槍聲響起。「勝利者」號的小艇來了，他們就在我們後面，匆匆忙忙地趕來。這些人只是不斷地往前跑，越過冰面，還沒瞄準就開槍。他們跳上冰丘，大吼大叫，這群人簡直糟糕透頂。他們嚇跑了海豹，不僅壞了我們的工作，連他們自己也得不到好處。我認為這些人連五十隻海豹都獵不到。我們的小艇獵到二十七隻，總計整個早上我們一共獵到二百三十四隻，赫爾頓的小艇一馬當先，獵到六十八隻，康恩的小艇只獵到八隻。船長降旗三次向「勝利者」號致意，諷刺地向對方說，「多謝承讓」。小艇才剛吊上船，船長又看到更大群的海豹，於是我們趕緊出發。此時是下午兩點，我們只簡單吃了幾口晚餐。當我們吃完晚餐來到甲板，發現「勝利者」號的小艇已經降下，於是我們只好另尋地點。海豹的數量非常多，但很容易受驚，所以我們只好待在遠處射擊。我們這次射中了二十八隻，總數來到了二百八十七隻左右。今天我們總共獵到五百四十隻，成果豐碩的一天，大約有十一噸的海豹油。我感到疲累，因為今天一整天我不是划船就是趴在地上匍匐前進。船長發現另一群海豹，等明天再採取行動。

五月四日　星期二〔D066〕

跟昨天一樣，早上六點，小艇降下，然後如同往常將小艇投放在不同地點。彼得與我躲在冰丘後頭，我們各自射殺了七隻海豹，此時船長發現這裡不是海豹聚集最多的地方，於是他在船首升起了旗幟，通知小艇返航。船長將先到的五艘拉上來，剩下的小艇，例如我們的小艇，則是改用拖曳的方式。接下來船長全速前進，經過「勝利者」號的小艇，並且在適合的地點降下小艇。這是個積極而合理的決定。我想我們大約拖行了十五英里左右。我們利用這個機會，努力射擊。「烏

133 在〈格陵蘭捕鯨船上的生活〉中，柯南．道爾描述了庫爾（Jack Coull）的軼事，而且稱呼他「我們英俊的亡命之徒」，他提到庫爾擔任小艇舵手的職務：「在船上，只有一個人既非蘇格蘭人，亦非昔德蘭人，他的出身是個謎。他是個皮膚黝黑、黑眼珠的高大男人，頭髮與鬍子都是藍黑色，外型出眾，走路時會搖晃肩膀，流露出狂放不羈的性格。據說他來自英格蘭南方，因為犯法而遠走他鄉。他沒有朋友，沉默寡言，但他是船上最聰明的船員之一。我從他的外表推斷，他的脾氣可能相當殘暴，而他犯的罪也許非常血腥。我們只有一次從他的眼神中看出他隱藏的怒火。船上的廚師——一名孔武有力的男子，矮小的船副只是他的助手——自己儲藏了一些蘭姆酒，他過於放縱自己喝酒，結果造成船員們連續三天沒晚餐可吃。到了第三天，我們這位沉默寡言的亡命之徒走到廚子旁邊，手裡拿著黃銅製的平底深鍋。他不發一語，只是拿著鍋子猛力朝廚子砸下去，由於用力過猛，廚子的頭穿透了鍋底，整個鍋身就這樣套在廚子的脖子上左右晃蕩。半醉半驚的廚子嚷著要打架，但他很快就發現船上的人都反對他，只好乖乖回去煮飯，但他嘴裡還是氣不過，不住地嘟囔。至於那個報復者，則是又回到原來鬱鬱寡歡的樣子，對一切視而不見。之後，我們再也沒聽過誰抱怨廚子的問題。」這個人應該就是約翰．庫爾，一八八〇年時四十一歲，彼得赫德的格陵蘭捕鯨船船員——不過，根據蘇格蘭的戶政資料，庫爾是在彼得赫德出生的。

合之眾」表現出眾，殺死了四十一隻海豹。布坎表現最好，七十五隻，然後是柯林的五十一隻，卡納的四十二隻，我們的四十一隻，其他小艇則表現欠佳。我們捕到兩百七十五隻海豹，之後未再放下小艇。挪威船「黛安娜」號（Diana）來到我們的側面，但捕獲的海豹不多。他們的一艘小艇來到我們的小艇旁，我們問他們，是否曾在北方海面看見「蝕缺」號，他們說有，但我懷疑他們是否真的聽懂我們在說什麼。「勝利者」號的船員昨晚一整晚都在外頭作業——非常短視的做法。

五月五日　星期三（D067）

往東北方前進。四周全是開闊的水域。應該是不可能看到海豹的蹤影。

〔插圖，「二百碼外的五隻海豹」〕

然而，就在晚餐前，船長又要求大家集合。「黛安娜」號已經搶在我們前面，在海豹群最密集的地方降下所有小艇。海豹躺臥在範圍不大的冰面上，看起來非常緊密。我們的船員這回把事情給搞砸了，每艘小艇都急著搶占最好的位置，因此陷入彼此爭奪的狀態。我們捕了七十一隻，其他海豹全嚇跑了。船長很不高興，他確實有理由不高興。

69
540
275
71
119
32
———
1106
2502
———
3608

	麥肯吉	馬提森	蘭尼	布坎	赫爾頓	卡納	康恩	柯林	五月
69	2	10	13	14	9	10	1	10	一日
540	55	47	68	87	112	61	36	35	三日
275	41	10	26	75	11	42	20	51	四日
71	8	11	7	18	6	11	2	8	五日
63	5	2	2	20	12	2	13	7	十四日
32					14			16	十五日

攻擊剩餘部分 ↙（指向十四日 63）
56

一八八〇年「希望」號捕獲數量

		我捕獲的數量
四月三日	760年輕海豹　57老海豹	1老海豹
四日	450年輕海豹　10老海豹	
五日	400年輕海豹	
六日	270年輕海豹　6冠海豹　57老海豹	2冠海豹
七日	133年輕海豹	
八日	30年輕海豹	
九日	50年輕海豹	
十日	72年輕海豹	2海豹
十一日		
十二日		
十三日		
十四日	80年輕海豹	2海豹
十五日	46年輕海豹　2冠海豹	2海豹　1冠海豹

十六日	6年輕海豹	1鷹
十七日	10年輕海豹	2海豹
十八日	10年輕海豹	1海豹
十九日	6年輕海豹	
二十日		
二十一日		
二十二日	13年輕海豹	2海豹
二十三日	36年輕海豹	11海豹
二十四日	17年輕海豹	
二十五日	22年輕海豹	8海豹
二十六日		
二十七日		
二十八日		
二十九日		
三十日		

日期		
五月一日	69老海豹	
二日		
三日	540老海豹	27海豹
四日	275老海豹	10海豹
五日	71老海豹	
六日		
七日		
八日		
九日		
十日		
十一日		
十二日		
十三日		
十四日	119老海豹	
十五日	32老海豹	
十六日		

十七日　6老海豹

十八日

十九日

二十日

二十一日

二十二日

二十三日

二十四日

二十五日

二十六日

二十七日

二十八日

二十九日

三十日　2地海豹

三十一日　1浮冰鼠

六月一日 1冠海豹
二日 4羅區鳥 7潛鳥
三日
四日
五日 1冠海豹
六日 1獨角鯨 2罕見的鴨子
七日
八日 1羅區鳥 1潛鳥
九日 1羅區鳥 6雪鳥
十日 1三趾鷗 1北極海燕 3潛鳥
十一日 1牙鱈
十二日 1熊
十三日
十四日
十五日
十六日

十七日

十八日　1熊與 2小熊

十九日

二十日　1熊

二十一日

二十二日

二十三日

二十四日

二十五日

二十六日　1格陵蘭鯨

二十七日

二十八日

二十九日

三十日　1北極鷗—雪鳥—5潛鳥　1浮冰鼠（Flaw Rat）[134]

134 或 floe rat：在日誌裡，柯南·道爾總是 flaw 與 floe 彼此代換。浮冰鼠是體型最小的一種海豹，柯南·道爾在五月十二日的條目中做了解釋。

五月六日　星期四〔D077〕

船長認為，我們最好稍微往南去尋找海豹，至於「黛安娜」號與「勝利者」號就任由他們往北航行。我們今天的位置是在北緯七十七度二十分，預料將會看見斯匹茲卑爾根島的西岸。所有船員都急著出發，這裡的風強浪急，不太可能有海豹。

〔摺頁插圖，「划呀，小夥子們，用力划！」〕

全日往西南方航行，但沒有發現海豹。我們現在捕獲了約五十噸。

〔插圖，「準備獵捕海豹」〕

五月七日　星期五〔D080〕

「黛安娜」號看見我們昨天夜裡停船，以為我們發現了漁獲，於是全速朝我們這裡趕來，想分一杯羹。挪威船拚命加煤，來到此地才發現整件事是個「騙局」。他們在氣憤下離開，我們相信他們是往冰島駛去。我們揚帆朝東北行駛。看見海中有幾群海豹。

五月八日　星期六〔D080〕

加足馬力朝西北前進。「勝利者」號出現在視線之內，他們也朝相同的方向行駛。冰上全是海豹。今天是風和日麗的一天。傍晚，發放菸草與糖。舉行了十分有趣的拍賣會。昔德蘭人曼森・特維爾是拍賣官，他仗著一張能言善道的嘴，打算哄騙大家買下他手上那件破爛不堪的舊大衣。「從五捲菸草開始喊價，五捲！沒有人再加價嗎？這件大衣保證可以抵禦華氏負一百九十度[135]的低溫——沒有人要加價嗎？先生們！先生們！五捲半的菸草。感謝你，先生！五捲半！襯裡的一面有海狸的圖案，另一面有響尾蛇的圖案，這不另外加價，完全半買半送！喊價吧，再不喊就沒機會了。先生們，最後一次了。好，五捲半賣出。」我向亨利・波森[136]買了一件海豹皮褲。

〔插圖，「不加價，半買半送。」〕

五月九日　星期日〔D082〕

為什麼海豹（seal）是最神聖的動物？因為在啟示錄中曾經提到，當末日來臨時，天使將在天上揭開六個封印（seal）。但這些印今日還無從得見。不過，正如馬克・吐溫所言，當他在煙囪底下寫詩時，如果牛從煙囪掉下來，第一次會讓他驚訝，

135 譯註：相當於攝氏零下一百二十三度。
136 曼森・特維爾（Manson Turville）身分不明；亨利・波森（Henry Polson）是一名中年的魚叉手與桶匠。

但到了第三次，恐怕就讓人無聊。[137]多雲的一天。讀了斯科斯比有關捕鯨的作品。一些軼事相當冗長，無法囫圇呑棗讀完，必須細細加以咀嚼。他看見一頭鯨魚被一條呈U字形的繩子纏住，而這條繩子先前已經牢牢纏住另一頭鯨魚。他看見一名男子攀在一頭活鯨魚背上，在海中載浮載沉了四分之一英里。然而，整體而言，這是一本相當可讀的作品，就我的判斷，它的內容也很精確！整日無事。傍晚，下到魚叉手的艙房，跟大家聊到動物學、謀殺、處決與鐵甲船。朝西北航行。

五月十日　星期一 D082

我們往南來到北緯七十三度二十分的位置，大約就在我們先前獵捕年輕海豹的地點略微靠北一點。我很高興地說，我們又往北航行了。沒有海豹。早上持續喝咖啡與喝茶。下午茶後，氣壓計大幅下降，開始風雨交加。我希望能颳點暴風雨，讓我們清醒一點。一條鱈魚經由一道大裂縫被幫浦吸了進來。

五月十一日　星期二 D083

夜裡海浪極大，而且持續了一整天。但我們幾乎感受不到風力，因為浮冰構成了天然港口。整日往北行駛。這麼做實在太糟了——因為我們獵捕老海豹才開始漸入佳境。然而，時好時壞是這個行業的常態，我們只能等待時來運轉的一日。今晚，老彼得被繩子割到眼睛，傷得頗嚴重，他似乎認為自己會瞎掉，但我順利處理好他的傷口。這傢伙真是愛發牢騷。

五月十二日　星期三〔D083〕

最美好的一天。晴空萬里，跟往常那種如豌豆湯般綠濛濛的一片大不相同。海中有許多海豹，但牠們全不在冰上。到了午夜，視野仍跟白日一樣清晰。晚餐後，有人看見一頭長鬚鯨在船旁噴水，但此時的我已感到昏昏欲睡。我希望我也能親眼看到那幅景象。Balaena Physalis 是長鬚鯨的科學分類名稱。而牠是鯨魚當中游得最快、最強壯、體型最大卻最沒價值的一種，因此獵捕長鬚鯨是白費力氣。然而，還是有人固定地獵捕長鬚鯨。長鬚鯨每頭一百二十英鎊，而我們的鯨魚每頭大約一千五百英鎊，所以我們捕的不是廉價品。在船副的艙房玩紙牌遊戲「Catch the Ten」。[138] 我上回玩牌是在格林希爾街。今天，看見一隻「浮冰鼠」繞著船游。這是體型最小的一種海豹。船長想到一種治禿頭的祕方。從另一個人頭上連根拔起頭髮。然後在禿頭上鑽個洞，把頭髮種上去。他在做夢。

五月十三日　星期四〔D084〕

我聽到引擎室傳來的說法，麥克勞先生，也就是我們的大管輪，他很榮幸每天早上能閱讀我的私人日誌，並且在餐桌

137 出自馬克．吐溫《傻子國外旅行記》（*The Innocents Abroad*, 1869）。

138 又叫「Scratch the Ten」，馬克罕在第七十三頁描述這種遊戲是「相當吵鬧的遊戲……玩家的目標是搶到十這張王牌」。捕鯨船的船員經常玩這種遊戲，但馬克罕相信，這種遊戲應該十分受歡迎，因為這種遊戲又稱為 Scotch Whist（柯南．道爾隨後的評論證實了他在勒維克玩的「船長」遊戲不是紙牌遊戲，而是另一種類似「船長情婦」的遊戲）。

上當著火伕的面做出嘲諷的評論。我寧可他讀我的私人信件，也不希望他讀我的日記，因為那是我唯一無法容忍的事。如果有人干涉我私人的事，我知道該怎麼對付他。我只是驚訝於一個宣稱自己抱持宗教原則的人，居然會有這樣的行為，我不會說他欠缺紳士的自重，但他顯然缺乏基本的誠實。如果在警告後他還一意孤行，那麼他就要為自己的行為付出代價。講道理的人值得信任，但在引擎室談論我對水煮牛肉的喜好，這樣的人必須加以譴責。我希望明天早上他能好好看看我寫的這幾句話。

今天看見一頭長鬚鯨。我對這種生物的大小與形狀毫無概念。牠噴氣時，看起來就像一道白色煙霧。牠離我們的船約四分之一英里遠，但當牠潛入水中時，我依然能看到牠根根分明的長鬚。這是我見過最龐大的生物。早上，今日的天光似乎較為明亮，看見海豹在冰上，水中也有許多。晚間十一點，康恩跑來告知，說他看見冰上有一大群海豹。

五月十四日 星期五 〔D085〕

早上九點左右，降下小艇。但海豹已不在冰上。牠們游往拉布拉多（Labrador）海岸，在經過一個月的旅行之後，牠們身上已經沒有油脂，只剩下皮毛。我們的小艇獵到五隻，算是成績最好的小艇之一。各小艇總計獵到六十三隻海豹，之後將海豹運上船。魚叉手全被叫到船頭，攻擊剩餘的海豹群，又殺死五十六隻海豹，今天的漁獲總計達一百一十九隻。很高興又有大展身手的機會。康恩正在浮冰上flinching[139]一隻海豹，結果旁邊突然衝出一頭海象，牠的頭像水桶一樣大，把康恩嚇了一大跳。康恩對牠射了四槍，但牠似乎不痛不癢，只是轉身游泳離開。

〔插圖，「推著『烏合之眾』的小艇穿過厚冰。一八八〇年五月十四日。」〕

五月十五日　星期六〔D086〕

早上，派出兩艘小艇，分別是柯林與赫爾頓的小艇，讓他們去獵捕一小群海豹。捕到三十二隻。之後，我們加足馬力揚起風帆全速朝北前進，但看不到任何鯨魚。時間越來越緊迫了，我們必須收起捕鯨繩，往北行駛。

如果往後兩天我們找不到海豹，那麼我們就應該放棄。我們認為「蝕缺」號與「上風」號應該已在北方，我們上次看到他們已是一個多月前的事，當時他們正前往冰島獵捕瓶鼻鯨。閱讀斯科斯比在北緯六十九度到七十四度的格陵蘭東岸探索時寫的日記。丹麥人在這個區域建立的最後一個屯墾地位於何處，成了耐人尋味的問題。斯科斯比一直找不到這些開拓地的遺跡。[140]

139 割下海豹或鯨魚屍體上的皮與脂肪。

140 「這是歷史上最浪漫的問題，」柯南．道爾在《穿過魔法之門》中表示：「我睜大眼睛努力在古老的艾爾比吉亞（Eyrbyggia）可能的地點，也就是格陵蘭岸邊的浮冰處搜尋……艾爾比吉亞這座斯堪地那維亞城市，是冰島人來此建立的，這座城市逐漸繁盛，甚至需要派人到丹麥，要對方派遣一名主教前來。主教準備前來這個新教區，卻因為氣候變遷的關係無法抵達，因為格陵蘭與冰島之間被重重的浮冰阻絕。此後，沒有人知道那群老斯堪地那維亞居民過得如何……如果南森（Fridtjof Nansen）與皮里在偶然間發現老殖民地的遺址，並且在防腐的冷空氣中找到昔日文明完整未朽壞的遺留物，那將是件奇妙的事」。柯南．道爾在樸資茅斯文學與科學學會的討論上談到這件事，《漢普夏郵報》（*Hampshire Post*）表示：「這些擁有高度文化的人是否與當地的野蠻人通婚（這種狀況不太可能發生），他們是否已經滅絕（這也不太可能發生，因為他們是一群吃苦耐勞的人），他們是否成為與世隔絕的人，保留著古老世界的風俗與知識，這些問題只能停留在推測階段。」九年後，柯南．道爾又在〈北極的魅力〉中說，這是「有趣的歷史問題，就像被貝利撒留（Belisarius）趕入非洲內陸的汪達爾人一樣，他們後來的發展成了不傳之祕。隨著我們對世界的一切越來越明瞭，有關他們的羅曼史與詩歌也將遭到抹除。就像薄霧一樣，所有藝術的想像終將消散不見」。

五月十六日　星期日 {D087}

沒有海豹。正午，來到北緯七十六度三十三分。我們傾盡全力往北方前進。波特酒。老庫伯（Cooper）在艙門口跌倒，差點把手臂摔斷。

五月十七日　星期一 {D087}

天氣晴朗的日子。全天朝北前進。北緯七十七度，東經五度。大約在斯匹茲卑爾根島西方一百英里處。晚餐後，從一小群海豹中獵捕到六隻海豹。這些海豹變得非常瘦。最近捕到的海豹，我們認為不是格陵蘭海豹，而是來自拉布拉多海岸的海豹，這些海豹經過一個月的旅行，身上幾乎已經沒有什麼油脂。早上，我們匆忙地搭起魚叉槍。這件笨重的東西必須放在支架上才能運作，它的拉力有二十八磅。

〔插圖，魚叉槍〕

必須拉扯繩子才能發射。大約三十碼內的目標可以精準命中。底座大約一又二分之一英寸。

〔插圖，裝在小艇上，已經上膛的魚叉槍，有「Capt. J G.」（格雷船長）的簽名〕

五月十八日　星期二〔D088〕

把小艇清空，準備用來捕鯨。晚飯時間，看到西北方有一艘船，仔細一瞧原來是「上風」號，我們認為「上風」號與「蝕缺」號正往南去獵捕瓶鼻鯨。我們放慢速度，等待「上風」號。穆雷上船，告訴我們一些壞消息。在獵捕年輕海豹之後，他一心只想著獲取更大的漁獲，不想跟我們一樣只獵捕海豹。他一天只獵捕半噸左右的海豹，其他時間都放在全速北上到斯匹茲卑爾根島獵捕鯨魚，連一隻老海豹也沒獵到。他的野心帶來的結果，是我們現在已捕到五十二噸的海豹，而他只有二十八噸。他來這裡已有三個星期，但完全沒看見鯨魚。他對整件事感到沮喪，我想，此時的他如果看到冠海豹一定會毫不考慮追逐過去。傍晚，西南方吹來九級風，讓我們窮於應付。

五月十九日與二十日　星期三與星期四〔D089〕

連續兩天吹著九級風。我們在浮冰與斯匹茲卑爾根島之間搶風前進。當風暫時停止時，我們可以辨識出「上風」號的位置，他們有時在我們前方，有時落在我們後面。浪高，天色陰暗。星期三，船上打進不少海水，值班船員拚了命地舀水。我的老毛病，牙痛，從蘇格蘭就一直緊跟著我，出海之後，似乎就隱身在船上的某個角落，未再出現。昨天，它突然從隱匿的地方現身，說道，「啊，我的敵人，我找到你了嗎？」於是它一把揪住我的門牙，疼得我臉都扭曲了。（艾迪生）[141]。星

141 儘管這裡指的似乎是約瑟夫・艾迪生（Joseph Addison, 1672-1719），但柯南・道爾引用的句子其實應該是列王記上二一20：「亞哈對以利亞說，我仇敵阿，你找到我麼？他回答說，我找到你了，因為你賣了自己，行耶和華眼中看為惡的事。」

期四，我們看見斯匹茲卑爾根島的蠻荒海岸，暴風雨席捲的巨浪，打在嶙峋怪石上，瞬時破碎。岸邊聳立著一排高數千英尺的黑色峭壁，黑如煤炭，裂縫覆蓋著白色霜雪。這是一幅令人望而生畏的景象。我們打算駛近岸邊，停泊在國王灣（King's Bay），但海圖的標示似乎有誤。牙痛。

五月二十一日　星期五〔D090〕

斯匹茲卑爾根島仍在視線之內，大約位於東北方五十英里的位置。完全無風，但天色陰暗，浪依然很大，我們因此推測風向可能即將改變。「上風」號往南航行，傍晚時，我們看見「蝕缺」號從遠處趕來。我們已經有一個月沒看見他們，因此我們急於知道這段時間他們做了些什麼。船長登上「蝕缺」號，三個小時後回來，他得知「蝕缺」號這段期間去了冰島，而且捕獲三十二頭瓶鼻鯨，成果相當豐碩。平均每頭鯨魚重約一噸，此外，大衛船長捕獲的年輕與老海豹數量也與我們相當，因此他的漁獲遙遙領先我們。我相信他們總共捕了九十噸。這陣強風對我們造成可怕的傷害，因為所有的浮冰全在強風吹襲下朝我們逼近，浮冰形成的港灣也因為擠壓而消失，鯨魚在這裡找不到可棲息的水灣，就會另覓他處，這對我們獵捕極為不利。然而，我們必須振作精神（keep up our peckers），[142]希望能得到最好的結果。

五月二十二日 星期六〔D091〕

整日風浪很大。我今天成年。[143] 在這樣的地方過生日的確是很新奇的體驗，離北極只有六百英里左右。

〔摺頁插圖，「在斯匹茲卑爾根島外海受八級風吹襲的『希望』號」〕

度過相當悲慘的生日傍晚，不知為何，我感到一陣噁心。船長好心地讓我吞下兩大塊芥末，幫我催吐，我覺得自己好像嚥下一座維蘇威火山，吐了之後，我感覺舒服多了。「蝕缺」號今天一直在我們附近。冰灣一個接一個遭到破壞。

五月二十三日 星期日〔D094〕

又到了梅子布丁日——天氣晴朗，海面上風平浪靜。再度往西前進，穿過緊密的浮冰。船長與我拙劣地改編吉恩・英格婁的〈麻雀築巢〉[144]

當麻雀築巢，而樹葉

142 十九世紀英國的慣用說法，跟 keep your chin up 的意思類似。

143 柯南・道爾於一八五九年五月二十二日出生於愛丁堡。

144 第一句來自吉恩・英格婁（Jean Ingelow, 1820~97）的〈麻雀築巢〉（Sparrows Build）。吉恩・英格婁是相當受歡迎的英國詩人，這首詩的第一句受到格雷船長與柯南・道爾的青睞：「當麻雀築巢，葉子萌芽，／我埋藏已久的悲傷再度甦醒哀哭，／我知道曙光在遙遠、遙遠的北方出現，／鮮紅的旭日終將升起；／緋紅的羊毛在雪地上延展，／冰凍的泉源自由奔流，／冷峻的冰山終於低頭，／下水的船隻，揚帆駛向海洋。」

當「波吉鷗（Burgies）」在格陵蘭築巢，
我的精神受苦而憔悴
因為我心知海豹在遙遠的北北西
卻不得不「收起我們的繩索。」
往南來到「冠海豹」棲息之處
但厄運緊跟著我，
「獨角鯨」的長角直指天際
而後鑽入海中，快樂嬉戲

合唱

喔，鯨魚，露脊鯨啊，露脊鯨！
我們都愛鯨魚
格陵蘭「緊密」的海冰是否找不到任何水灣
讓十二英尺長的鯨魚有地方可以噴氣。
你們確實上了船，過起海上生活

前往那悲慼寒冷而孤寂的海岸，
你們為海豹悲傷，因為殺死牠們全為了毛皮，
牠們來自拉布拉多。
牠長得巨大，卻見人就跑，
足足逃了二十多英里，
我們怎麼知道「海豹」棲身何處，
東邊有一處浮冰構成的大海灣。

合唱

我們絕不可能像過去一樣
再度在五月返航
除非我們一天之內捕到四千隻「年輕海豹」
而且有辦法載著兩百噸回家，
我們絕不可能光靠海豹就能滿載豐收
儘管再怎麼辛勤工作也不可能，
然而就算鯨魚瘦到只剩皮包骨，
「冠海豹」身上剝不出半點油脂，

我們也絕不輕言放棄。

合唱

五月二十四日 星期一〔D096〕

又是晴朗的一天。我希望我們最終能擁有一點運氣。晚上六點。不，我們的運氣還是很差。我們今年的運氣顯然糟透了。東邊吹來的七級風把即將形成的小水灣給破壞了，我們完全看不到希望。柯林說，我們船上有個約拿（Jonah）。「蝕缺」號在我們附近。讓魚叉槍保持直立。

五月二十五日 星期二〔D096〕

越來越糟了。東方繼續吹來強風，破壞了浮冰。船員們心情都很不好。「蝕缺」號揚帆往南航行，但似乎認為原來的主意比較好，於是又回來。恐怖！

五月二十六日 星期三〔D096〕

天氣晴朗，但浮冰毀了。我們努力迂迴穿越浮冰。下午，我在後甲板抽菸，此時突然傳來喊叫聲，「有一頭熊——就在船附近。」船長在桅頂，他馬上下令，「降下船尾小艇」。我跑下艙房，拿了我的手槍，[145] 然後成功在小艇裡找到一個座位。我看見那頭熊——一頭巨獸——在雪地裡，牠的毛顯得格外棕黃，而且順著與船同樣的方向快速奔跑。牠在跑了數百碼後，蹲伏在一個水坑裡，只將鼻子露出水面。馬提森是小艇的魚叉手，我們開始划船，但必須繞上一圈才能越過冰面。我們看不見牠了，當我們再次看見牠時，牠站了起來，前掌挨著冰丘，牠的頭高聳著，凝視著我們，用力吸著氣。牠在射程之內，但我們覺得牠有可能讓我們更靠近一點，於是我們繼續划船。但小艇似乎讓牠愚鈍的腦袋想起什麼，只見牠突然爬下冰丘，消失在我們的視線之外。然後我們看見船上打了小艇返航的信號，我們看見那頭棕熊在冰上快速奔跑，離我們越來越遠，於是我們只好放棄獵捕的念頭。依然吹著東風。

145 柯南·道爾小時候讀過英裔美國小說家梅恩·雷德（Mayne Reid）的作品，其作品充滿了美利堅主義色彩；柯南·道爾十分喜愛這種美國西部故事的題材，因此運用在他的第一本福爾摩斯小說《血字的研究》（*A Study of Scarlet*）裡。

獵捕到老海豹的平均數量

姓名	數量	合計
布坎	14 + 87 + 75 + 18 + 20	214
柯林	10 + 85 + 51 + 8 + 7	161
赫爾頓	9 + 112 + 11 + 6 + 12	150
卡納	10 + 61 + 42 + 11 + 2	126
麥肯吉	2 + 55 + 41 + 8 + 5	111（烏合之眾）
蘭尼	13 + 68 + 26 + 7 + 2	116
馬提森	10 + 47 + 10 + 11 + 2	80
康恩	1 + 36 + 20 + 2 + 13	72
攻擊剩餘部分		55
獵捕年輕海豹		141
總計		**1,216**（老海豹）

〔插圖，「我們未射擊的熊」〕

五月二十七日 星期四〔D099〕

早晨，浮冰開始圍繞著我們，越來越近，我們必須盡快駛離到開放海域，以免被浮冰凍住而動彈不得。但要脫離包圍不是件容易的事。「蝕缺」號緊跟在我們後頭。船長到「蝕缺」號上吃晚餐，待到八點才回來。船長不在這段期間，我畫畫、睡覺、玩跳棋與打拳擊。我們將前往北緯八十度看看是否有鯨魚可捕，簡言之，我們要前往北方界線。[146]這裡的海域的恐怖之處，在於這裡有一種稱為劍魚的生物，但事實上牠並不是劍魚。這種動物是鯨魚的一種，長長的口鼻看起來類似鯖魚，擁有尖齒與長顎。牠的體長達到二十五英尺，長著高聳而帶有曲線的背鰭。牠以最大型的鯊魚、海豹與鯨魚為食。幾年前，「愛斯基摩」號（Esquimeaux）的尤爾（Yule）在海峽捕到六頭鯨魚，事實上，這六頭鯨魚是自己跑到他的船底下尋求保護，因為前述的怪獸就在附近。船長告訴我，有一次他在桅頂瞭望台看見船的前方出現一陣騷動。他用望遠鏡仔細一看，一頭巨大的象海豹坐在一塊只比牠的身軀略大一點的浮冰上。在浮冰周圍，有六頭前述的嗜血大魚圍繞著，牠們用長鰭拍打這隻可憐的生物，試圖將牠打落浮冰，好將牠吞吃下肚。當船靠近時，船長說他永遠不會忘記那頭可憐的海豹瞪大雙眼看著船的模樣，牠突然奮力躍離浮冰，幾乎是貼著水面游泳，然後從水中跳上船側，牠的頭已經越過船尾欄杆，幾乎就要跳上甲板。一艘小艇降下，這頭長十二英尺的龐然大物於是爬進小艇，牠的頭遭到敲擊。船員開槍防止那些魚攻

146 到了北方界線，這裡的冰橫亙在前，使人無法前往北極。

擊小艇，牠們對於獵物不翼而飛感到憤怒。[147]

〔插圖，「格陵蘭劍魚」，有「Capt. J G.」（格雷船長）的簽名〕

五月二十八日　星期五〔D101〕

與「蝕缺」號一起朝北方與東北方航行。顯然，五月我們不可能捕到任何鯨魚，我們只能期盼六月的到來。傍晚飄起了濃霧，我們必須每隔幾個小時鳴放汽笛與鳴槍示警，以確定我們與「蝕缺」號保持一定距離，同樣地，「蝕缺」號也出聲示警。反正需要鳴槍，於是我用步槍遠距離射擊潛鳥，不過我只打中白雪，什麼鳥也沒射中。

五月二十九日　星期六〔D101〕

〔插圖，「潛鳥或小海雀」〕

星期六，不提還比較不煩心。忘了星期六吧。無事可做。傍晚起霧。正午在北緯七十九度十分。傍晚玩牌。

五月三十日 星期日〔D102〕

大衛船長早上登船，他對於浮冰的狀況感到不滿，事實上，他說他從沒看過這麼糟的狀況。沃克醫生之後上船，帶航海日誌給我，這是大衛船長好心叫他拿來的。早上，我們發現有兩個物體在浮冰附近游泳，船長認出是兩隻地海豹，一種非常罕見的品種，幾乎跟冠海豹一樣大。我們降下一艘小艇，在經過一陣興奮的追逐，以及魚叉手展現出丟盡臉面的槍法之後，我們終於射中這兩隻海豹。其中一隻是母海豹，另一隻是年輕海豹，前者體長約八英尺六英寸。順帶一提，提到冠海豹，柯林曾經殺過一隻體長達十四英尺的海豹。牠把小艇完全塞滿了，而且還中了兩發魚叉。我們希望這是個好兆頭，能一舉扭轉我們的厄運。另外，在北極的動物分布中有一件非常耐人尋味的事，去年，大衛船長曾在北緯八十度的地方捕到一隻大型的信天翁。牠是從哪裡來的？難道北極成了副熱帶氣候？

147 柯南·道爾返家後不久，《蘇格蘭人》就爆發一場有關劍魚（orca gladiator，虎鯨或殺人鯨）的論戰。九月十五日，最近剛從魁北克橫越大西洋返國的坎貝爾勳爵（Archibald Campbell）表示，他曾在海上目睹一頭鯨魚遭受一隻長尾鮫與一隻看似劍魚的生物攻擊。第二天，愛丁堡的T·G雖然無法確認鯨魚的種類，但他自信地表示，即使像長尾鮫與劍魚這類大型肉食動物，也不可能勝過鯨魚，除非後者生病了。柯南·道爾接著發文，他認為T·G把劍魚誤認為別的生物：「這個可怕的生物，『劍魚』，北方海洋之鞭，與T·G誤認的可憐的『長鼻』生物大不相同。Orca gladiator或殺人鯨是一種生性殘暴的鯨魚物種，過去格陵蘭捕鯨人由於牠長形的背鰭，而為牠取了『劍魚』的綽號。這種魚有著數排巨大的牙齒，在水中的速度極快，體型遠大於任何一種鯊魚，牠很有資格稱為深海中最令人畏懼的生物」。他舉了一兩個例子說明這種魚類力量足以對抗鯨魚，並且認出其中一種鯨魚是座頭鯨，「一種經常出現在這個緯度的鯨魚……我在揚馬延島南方看見這種鯨魚出現在鯡魚群裡，而且數量還不少。」（T·G對於自己遭到指正，感到很不高興，但西敏水族館的自然學家阿伯拉罕〔J. Abrahams〕於二十二日根據他的所學表示，這種鯨魚很可能是塞鯨〔Rorqualis borealis〕）。

五月三十一日　星期一〔D103〕

夢見鯨魚出現在卡利多尼安運河（Caledonian Canal）[148]裡，在夢中，我們很擔心平底船與馬匹嚇跑牠們。總共有十七頭，全是瓶鼻鯨，牠們躲在橋底下。一個非常耐人尋味的夢。今天早上的風向是西北西，很完美，水的顏色是淺綠色，更是完美。

〔摺頁插圖，「劍魚追逐海豹群」〕

〔插圖，「捕捉」〕

我的夢還沒說到一半。當我們捕殺運河橋下的鯨魚時，我聽到鐘敲了兩聲，我突然想起，我的醫學院期末考在一點鐘開始。在恐慌之下，我丟下鯨魚，急忙趕往大學。守門人不讓我進去考試，我一時情急，跟他扭打起來，最後他把我轟了出去。即使在這個時候，我依然未醒，我夢見某人遞給我一張紙，上面似乎寫著考題的樣子。有四題，我忘了中間兩題。第一個問題是，「柏林附近有什麼地方水深十英里？」最後一題，標題寫著航海，以下是一字不漏的問題內容，「如果一個男人與他的妻子與一匹馬在一艘小艇上，妻子如何讓男人與馬離開小艇而不使小艇進水沉沒？」我抱怨這個問題不適切，醫學院的考試怎麼能考航海的問題。於是我決定把試卷寄給格雷船長，讓他解答，最後我終於醒了。顯然這是我做過最具連貫性的夢，也是最生動的夢。[149]

傍晚，我們的前桅樓因為鉤環斷裂而掉落下來，砸壞了吊索。我們利用備用的圓木，在四小時內將一切恢復元狀，不得不說我們有一群訓練有素的船員。船長爬上瞭望台，我則在艙房裡與大家狂歡時寫下這件事。我聽見甲板上傳來修理前桅樓的敲打聲，而在艙門外，我聽見勤務員用他美妙的男高音唱道，「午夜，在搖晃不定的甲板上，我不動如山——她明媚的笑容仍在我腦海中繚繞著。」[150]午夜，他似乎腦子裡一直想著這件事，於是他用剩餘的二十三個小時不斷地談論這件事。大衛船長傍晚登船，他借我一本有關鯨魚的小書。[151]傍晚，我對「北極海燕」做實驗。我拿了四塊麵包，分別將它們浸泡在番木鱉鹼、苯酚、硫酸鋅與松節油裡。然後我將麵包丟向鳥群，想知道哪塊麵包效果最快，但令我驚訝的是，鳥群中的年長領袖向前吃了這四塊麵包，奇怪的是，牠似乎完全無恙。

148 卡利多尼安運河成於一八二二年，連接英格蘭東岸的因佛內斯（Inverness）與西岸的寇帕奇（Corpach），不過這條運河只有三分之一是人工開鑿的。

149 先前（四月一日），這位年輕的醫學院學生曾說這是他三年來第一次在這天沒有參加考試。他由於金錢拮据，因此一直想努力早點結束醫學院學業。現在，他暫時休學，參加這次為期七個月的捕鯨冒險，這一點很可能成為他潛意識裡焦慮的原因。「我不只一次從夢中獲得重要訊息，」他在未來的恐怖小說〈皮革漏斗〉（The Leather Funnel）中，讓某個角色如此說道。

150 萊頓（W. T. Wrigton）和喬治亞州馬孔（Macon）的卡本特（J. E. Carpenter）於一八六四年的音樂作品。「他有著美妙動人的男高音，」柯南·道爾在〈格陵蘭捕鯨船上的生活〉提到，「有好幾個鐘頭，我一直聽著他的歌聲，其間伴奏著他在餐具室洗碗盤的聲響。他知道許多悲愴傷感的歌曲，當你有六個月的時間未能看見女人的臉孔時，你才知道真正的傷感是什麼。當傑克用顫音唱著，『她明媚的笑容仍在我腦海中繚繞著』，或『甜美的貝兒·瑪紅，請在天堂門前等我』，他歌聲中那種朦朧甜蜜的缺憾打動了我們，現在的我回想起來，那感覺彷彿又回來了。而說到拳擊，他每天跟我練習，終於變成一個不可輕視的勁敵——特別是在風浪不平靜的時候，他的雙腿在搖晃的地板上不動如山。就算船已經傾斜一邊，他還是能猛衝攻擊。」

151 可能是他與約翰·格雷於一八七四年合寫的作品，《南海新捕鯨漁場報告》（*Report on New Whaling Grounds in the South Seas*, Aberdeen: D. Chalmers），裡面提到南極洲羅斯海（Ross Sea）與威德爾海（Weddell Sea）的露脊鯨，因而引起人們注意，最終於一八九二年組成探險隊前往調查。

六月一日 星期二 〔D108〕

我相信這個月我們的運氣會比上個月好。我們可以看見整個地平線橫亙著北方界線，「蝕缺」號逐漸加快速度，我想我們將會看見北緯七十八度的海灣，我們之前就是從那裡被海冰硬生生趕出來的。如果一切順利，我們將啟程前往利物浦海岸的斯科斯比灣（Scoresby Sound）。[152]海水中充滿了微生物，泛著橄欖綠。

弓頭鯨啊！

弓頭鯨！

如果我們是微生物

你馬上會把我們吃掉。

船長說他看見鯨群噴出一道又一道的水柱，看起來就像大型城鎮的煙霧。非常生動的描述。順帶一提，水溫昨天升高了八度，我們想是因為我們身處在灣流之中。看到水面上漂過一棵樅樹。它可能來自數千英里之外，從西伯利亞的鄂畢河（Obi）或葉尼塞河（Yenesei）沖入海洋，然後順著西北洋流漂到北極海。

晚上，看見兩隻冠海豹，但因為技術不佳，只射中一隻。希望在晚上能射到幾尾羅區鳥，不過連一尾都沒看到。布坎在早上射中四尾。

六月二日 星期三 〔D109〕

揚起風帆，往西與往南行駛。船長為了獵不到冠海豹而發愁。天氣非常寒冷，簡直跟四月時一樣冷。我身上的毛髮變得濃密了，我好像未老先衰。讀了一篇好故事，一名醫生埋葬在教堂大墓園的正中央，一名同為醫生的弟兄建議寫下這樣的墓誌銘，「Si monumentum quaeris, circumspice.」。[153] 非常幽默。被浮冰阻隔，離鯨魚群越來越遠，令人心灰意冷。如史都華所言，「這讓血氣方剛的年輕人心神不寧，靜不下來」。席德尼‧史密斯提到傑弗瑞（Jeffrey）時說到，「他的身體太小，包不住他的心靈。傑弗瑞的才智總是大剌剌地展示在大家面前。」[154] 非常絕妙的一句話。傍晚，看見大熊的蹤跡，在水中也看見了冠海豹。今天傍晚，似乎出現了一線希望，我們往西行駛了一大段路程，拉近了與鯨魚群的距離。

152 這裡的利物浦不是英格蘭的利物浦，而是冰島北方格陵蘭的東岸。

153 「如果你要尋找他的豐功偉業，看看四周就好了。」

154 法蘭西斯‧傑弗瑞（Francis Jeffrey, 1773-1850）因為評論拜倫的詩「不行」，而在文學批評史上留下一席之地。柯南‧道爾在他首度嘗試寫作的小說《約翰‧史密斯的告白》裡，以傑弗瑞為例來說明文學批評裡判斷錯誤的例證。席德尼‧史密斯（Sydney Smith, 1771-1845）與傑弗瑞一起創立了《愛丁堡評論》（*The Edinburgh Review*）。

六月三日　星期四〔D110〕

還是很冷，灰白色的大霧逼近過來。從北方吹來七級風。我們來到目前為止最有利的位置，如果風向固定不變，我們應該可以捕到一些米諾魚。傍晚，開始起霧。我使用鱈魚線，以豬肉做餌，將魚線掛在船邊，但一直沒有咬餌。這個月大約有五十艘俄國船到斯匹茲卑爾根島捕鱈魚，因此這裡肯定有一些鱈魚巡游。晚間，拋下袋網進行拖曳，看看能不能捕到一點食物。收網時撈上來一個美麗的海螺，大約幾英寸長，看起來像是某種奇特的小仙子。我把牠塞進醃菜瓶裡，並且為牠取名為「約翰．湯瑪斯」（John Thomas）。我希望牠能活下去，我們放了一些奶油與豬肉到瓶子裡。看到許多獨角鯨在附近漫游，其中有一頭體型特別大，幾乎是雪白色的，體長有十五英尺。牠跳躍著越過了船尾，當牠們躍起時，發出了獨特的呼嚕聲。另外還看到幾隻美麗的medusae。155

六月四日　星期五〔D111〕

約翰．湯姆斯極為亢奮。我們把裝著牠的醃菜瓶放到離火稍遠一點的地方，由於氣溫只有華氏十一度，156 瓶子因此結凍了，約翰也受了風寒。牠坐在角落，嘴裡含著牠的尾巴，看起來就像耍性子的嬰兒把拇指插進自己的嘴裡。為了轉移約翰的注意力，我丟了奶油與豬肉進去當牠的早餐，而牠馬上狼吞虎嚥地吃個精光，但牠似乎還是喜歡待在瓶底。牠或許想著

牠的外殼被彎流沖到何處，
小海螺嬉戲著，
牠們的母親如變形蟲，而身為父親的牠
恐怕要被宰來慶祝鯨魚假期。

（插圖，「約翰·湯瑪斯浮上來吃牠的早餐（表示牠還活著）」與「約翰的小巧玲瓏的朋友」）

剛過一點，我站在甲板上與安德魯·赫爾頓談到漁獲慘澹的事。赫爾頓是船上數一數二的魚叉手。我不經意地問他，「安德魯，順便問你一下，你們看見鯨魚的時候，我想應該不會真的像書裡說的那樣，會大喊『她噴氣了』，是吧？」他說，「喔，他們會大叫『有魚』或者當時腦子裡想到什麼就喊什麼。等一下，柯林好像要到桅頂上，我必須去船橋一趟。」赫爾頓一上到船橋，就大聲喊道，「有魚！」值班船員火速衝往小艇，但船長叫住他們。「動作輕一點，」他說，「等我下令，大家就上小艇。」我們可以看見前面浮冰之間噴出兩道氣柱，我在龐然大物潛入水中時瞥見牠的背部。我們先降下值班船員的小艇，然後再降下四艘，我們一共降下六艘小艇。我們心裡充滿希望，但最終免不了沮喪。出現另外兩頭鯨魚，這四頭鯨魚往西北西方向離去。小艇一直注意牠們（厚冰）達四個小時，但無法更進一步，大家似乎都有所顧忌。然而鯨魚一

155 一種水母，在北極海域數量極為豐富。
156 譯註：約攝氏零下十一度。

定留下了一些蹤跡。我們看見前面有一些縫隙，[157]我們希望有機會捕到鯨魚。「蝕缺」號也追逐兩頭鯨魚，但因為二副的技術不佳而追丟，他因此丟了職位。

六月六日【五日】　星期六〔D113〕

約翰健康而精力充沛。今天看見許多獨角鯨，但這不是我們想捕的。從早餐到晚餐，持續在船橋瞭望。正午時分，我們看到冰上有一頭巨大的象海豹，安德魯・赫爾頓與我離開船橋，射殺了這頭海豹。牠大約有九英尺長，非常肥胖。我們剖開牠的胃，發現裡頭裝著大大小小一堆烏賊。船長傍晚登上「蝕缺」號。這裡的鳥糞是血紅色的，而且有奇怪的效果。船的周圍圍繞著許多鳥。風轉向南吹。這是最令人興奮的時刻，整個人神經都繃緊了。

六月六日　星期日〔D114〕

約翰比我早起，而且吃了豐盛的早餐。牠現在繞著瓶頂轉圈，顯然正在探索牠的王國，並且打算繪製地圖。每天傍晚，我會把牠放在水桶裡，牠可以自由地在裡頭遨遊一兩個鐘頭。風轉向西南，我很高興地說，昨天吹的是南南西風。我們很可能隨時能看到鯨魚，海水呈現特殊的深灰綠色。我認為我昨天在甲板上聞到了魚的味道。你可以在還沒看見鯨魚之前，就能在很遠的地方聞到鯨魚的油脂味。亞倫（Aaron），我們的昔德蘭男孩，他是預言者老彼得的兒子，昨天曾搭小艇到「蝕

缺」號訪問。當他回到船上，我聽見他直接去找他父親，劈頭就說

「父親，彼得·尚（Peter Shane）做夢了！」

（彼得·尚是「蝕缺」號上的預言者）

「是，孩子，怎麼啦？」

「彼得·尚做夢了，父親。」

「他夢到什麼了呢？孩子。」

「他在夢裡看見他們在『希望』號上殺牛。」

「喔，這是個好夢，孩子，是個好夢。這表示『希望』號會先捕到鯨魚。這是非常好的夢。」

因此我們還懷抱希望。

看見海水表面下有一隻大型烏賊，還有許多水母與海螺。大約下午三點左右有消息傳來，「蝕缺」號已經降下小艇。他們追捕魚群幾個鐘頭，最後還是升起吊桶將小艇召回。[158] 傍晚六點左右，亞當·卡納在桅頂看見遠處出現氣柱。降下四

157 因為冰的裂縫而產生的開闊水面。

158 一種用好幾個圓箍交錯構成的球狀物，上面覆著帆布，用來通知捕鯨小艇返航。

艘小艇前去追逐，但連鯨魚的影子也沒看見。傑克．布坎下床沒換衣服，只穿著汗衫與褲子就跑去獵鯨，他射中了一頭獨角鯨，身長十三英尺，角長兩英尺。魚叉漂亮地切開牠的喉嚨。這頭獨角鯨由四艘小艇拖回船，然後吊到船上。牠的身上有許多黑色與灰色的斑點。在除去脂肪與皮之後，我們剖開胃部，發現裡面裝了一隻非常巨大的蝦子，我將牠稱為「江湖郎中」蝦，此外還有許多烏賊。鯨魚身上有兩種寄生蟲，一隻就像細長的蟲子一樣躲在耳朵的鼓膜裡，一隻像種子一樣埋在角的根部。

晚上，在船後頭看見兩隻非常罕見的鴨子。船長親自搭乘小艇，用左右槍管獵殺了這兩隻鴨子。船上沒有人看過這種品種的鴨子。牠們長著黃色的鳥喙，喙的底部長出了橙色的胼胝，並且像曲線一樣朝眼部延伸。牠們比我們知道的鴨子更大一些，頭部呈深褐色，脖子是白色，背部是深褐色，胸部是淺銀褐色。全身羽毛非常柔軟而纖細。

〔插圖，「把獨角鯨拖回船上」〕

〔插圖，「獨角鯨」〕

六月七日　星期一〔D118〕

今天沒看到鯨魚，不過晚上船長認為他瞥見了一頭鯨魚。下午茶後，我前往「蝕缺」號去拿一些砷皂來保存我們的鴨子。大衛船長說，他認為這些是王絨鴨（King Eider duck），一種非常罕見的鳥類。大衛船長與我一起回船，並且待了一個小時。昨天，他追逐三頭鯨魚，但一條頭也沒捕到。我捉到一隻海燕，我在鉛塊綁上細繩，然後投擲鉛塊，當細繩纏住海燕時，我便把牠拉回來。海燕看起來相當驚恐。我再度放牠離去。吹北風與東北風。早上颳起強風。

六月八日 星期二 〔D118〕

早上，稍微增加馬力前進。陽光普照。把錨下在一塊浮冰上固定船隻，用哨子示意風向改變。派出三支遠征隊追捕獨角鯨，但一無所獲。我們轉而獵鳥，但只中了兩發，殺死一隻羅區鳥與重傷一隻潛鳥。追捕一隻浮冰鼠，但被牠跑掉了。格蘭特看見冰上有北極狐的足跡。整體來說，今天是愉快的一天。船長說，如果我把自己的彈匣裝滿，就可以快速地連續射擊，直到大家臉色發青為止。晚上，再度揚帆航行。在引擎室玩「拿普」（Nap）。[159]幾乎是一片死寂。

六月九日 星期三 〔D119〕

因為浮冰出現變化，因此今天我們不得不離開浮冰，再度駛向開闊的海面。傍晚，我們與「蝕缺」號停泊在一塊浮冰旁。大衛船長與沃克醫生在晚上十點來我們船上，一直待到凌晨兩點。今天，他們在冰上射殺了一頭非常巨大的熊。牠當時坐著，津津有味地嚼著牠拖到冰上的獨角鯨頭部，反觀另一頭，一條大鯊魚緊緊咬住獨角鯨垂落水中的尾巴。這頭熊是

159 根據霍伊爾的說法，「拿普」或「拿破崙」是一種紙牌遊戲，玩家二到六人，衍生出各種不同的玩法，其中一種玩法叫作「威靈頓與布呂歇爾」（Wellington and Blucher）。

怎麼將獨角鯨拖到冰上的，我們不得而知。凌晨兩點離船獵鳥。然而，幾乎很難發現鳥的蹤影，我只獵到一隻羅區鳥與六隻雪鳥。看見一隻龐大的冠海豹，但我無法射中牠。下午四點回船。

六月十日　星期四〔D120〕

我們仍努力嘗試前往我們所知的鯨魚棲息地。發動引擎，我們稍有進展，然後與「蝕缺」號一起在冰山旁下錨。在甲板外射中一隻三趾鷗與一隻潛鳥，然後在撿拾第一隻潛鳥時又射中兩隻潛鳥。下午，我在鉛塊上綁上細繩，然後將鉛塊往海燕頭部上方丟擲，讓細繩纏住牠們的翅膀，這種東西就像南美的「流星錘」，我樂在其中。順帶一提，另一天我射中一隻羅區鳥，一隻體型龐大的北極海燕趁著牠落下時將牠銜走，完全不理會一旁小艇船員的怒吼。我大聲咆哮著，但牠還是繼續叼走獵物，我只好拿起小艇的橫木，揮舞著將牠趕走。

〔插圖，「北極海燕偷走我們的羅區鳥」〕

約翰．湯瑪斯

死於六月八日，牠的朋友們咸感遺憾

牠是個思慮正確心靈高尚的海螺，與牠的兄弟海蝸牛相比，牠的心智與身體都臻於完美。牠從未因為自己可以自稱屬於等級較高的棘皮動物或環棘動物，而瞧不起體型較小的原生動物夥伴。牠從未嘲笑牠們沒有水管系統，也不會在牠們面前炫耀牠的雙重神經節。牠是個謙遜低調的原生質，牠一天能吃掉的肥豬肉，比其他自命高等的生物來得多。牠的父母在牠小時候就被鯨魚吃掉，因此牠所受的教育可以說完全是靠著自己的勤勉與觀察得來。牠已享盡天年，願牠的分子安息。

捕鯨航行的動物清單

無脊椎動物

一・原生動物

　　鯨魚的食物

二・纖毛蟲

　　稻米食物

三・環棘動物

　　蝨子（在昔德蘭人身上）　振翅海蝸牛

　　蝦（一般常見的蝦子）　獨角鯨角上的蝨子

裸海蝶（約翰．湯瑪斯）獨角鯨耳朵裡的蝨子

蝦「江湖郎中」　鯨蝨（歐西納）

四．棘皮動物

水母 gulius　北緯78度40分

水母——？　北緯78度40分

瓶狀水母　北緯78度5分

五．軟體動物

烏賊——北緯78度40分

脊椎動物

一．鳥

北極海燕

愚海鳩或潛鳥

羅區鳥

綠鴿

北極鷗

三趾鷗

雪鳥

雪鵐

紅頂雀 北緯75度

北極海鸚 北緯78度

賊鷗 北緯78度12分

冰島鷹 北緯73度40分

雪鴞 北緯71度

普通燕鷗 北緯78度18分

黑雁 北緯78度

絨鴨

海鷗

鸕鶿（勒維克）

鴨（卡爾佛〔Calvo〕？）非常罕見。王絨鴨。 北緯78度50分

北極椋鳥 北緯78度6分

鷸 北緯75度30分

北極海鷗 北緯69度

魚

浮冰魚（相當類似牙鱈） 北緯78度40分
銀魚 北緯78度12分
鯡魚 北緯69度
格陵蘭鯊

哺乳動物

馬鞍海豹（港海豹）
冠海豹
浮冰鼠
地海豹 北緯79度
海象 北緯77度30分
白面海豹
淡水海豹 （北緯78度）
格陵蘭劍魚 北緯69度
瓶鼻鯨 北緯63度
長鬚鯨

獨角鯨

露脊鯨

座頭鯨　　北緯68度

北極熊

北極狐

其他航行時看見的鳥類

北方塘鵝

史丁恰克（Stienchuck）

海燕

黑背海鷗

松雀鷹

馬雷特鳥（Mallet）

六月十一日　星期五〔D129〕

我們朝計畫的方向行駛了數英里。今天早上，「蝕缺」號射殺了兩頭熊。大約一點左右，有一頭鯨魚出現在「蝕缺」

號附近，但並未捕獲。傍晚，我們在冰山旁下錨。今天捕到一隻奇怪的魚，這是我在格陵蘭首次看見的魚。牠看起來很像牙鱈，但不是牙鱈。船員傑克．威廉森（Jack Williamson）遭到舵輪重擊。他裸露出約五英寸的頭骨。我縫合他的傷口，並且讓他上床休息。傍晚，勤務員（小艇舵手）與我走在冰上，我們都清楚看見浮冰外約半英里的地方有鯨魚噴出氣柱。然而，我無法搭小艇接近牠。

六月十二日　星期六〔D129〕

浮冰正在閉合而非敞開。諸事不順令人煩心。大約八點左右，有人射殺了船側外的一頭熊。我感到昏昏欲睡，希望找點有趣的事來做。胃裝滿了海豹油，但他非常瘦〔有幾個字難以辨識〕。晚餐時與船長一起到「蝕缺」號上。度過一段愉快的用餐與聊天的時光。大衛船長似乎完全沒有沮喪的樣子。從西方與西南方吹來七級風——應該對我們有好處。浮冰開始快速地朝我們靠攏，我們必須行駛三十英里左右，以避免被浮冰圍困。要脫離浮冰的包圍並不容易。今天早上，海面上出現許多獨角鯨。

六月十三日　星期日〔D130〕

往西找到一處不錯的開闊海域，往西與西南方全速前進。這段時間只看到一隻海豹。還需要往北二十英里左右才能抵達鯨魚的棲地。「你是如此近，又是如此遠。」這的確是很困難的事，我們穿過了不可穿越的浮冰，在我們與大海之間還有四十英里不斷移動的厚冰，我們暴露在風暴與滿潮的危險之中，有可能失去這艘船，搞不好連自己的命都得賠上去，要是被圍起來，我們就要在這裡過冬了。我們有就像半弔子的乞丐，只能放下大批漁獲不管，往南去追逐少量的魚群。這是羞恥也是罪過，我們不能這樣下去。「蝕缺」號與我們是賡續十代的勇敢北極海員的最後一代，這個血統越來越凋零，我們是在北緯八十度到七十二度之間的格陵蘭捕鯨的唯一倖存者，而我們在這裡陷入泥淖與無助。這種狀況就連聖人也會罵髒話。

六月十四日 星期一 〔D131〕

早上，出現濃霧。吹霧笛，但沒有聽見「蝕缺」號回應。傑克・威廉森的頭恢復得不錯。狀況就跟看起來一樣糟糕，也許實際上還更糟一點。我希望我們可以去獵冠海豹，那會比在這兒堅持來得好。鯨魚群就在二十英里外，但中間橫亙著無法穿越的冰層，而風向也把這些浮冰聚攏在一起，結成一整塊厚冰，而不是將它們吹散。我們希望能吹西風、西北風或西北西風，而現在吹的全是南風。ο ποτοι ποτοι![160] 五十三噸！這就是人生！

160「喔，奇怪！喔，可恥！」——在荷馬《伊利亞德》與其他希臘文學中的表達痛苦的方式。

六月十五日 星期二〔D132〕

天氣唯一的差別是霧變濃了，而風變得更令人討厭而邪惡。然而，我們已經處於最糟的狀況，因為沒有任何事能讓我們的狀況更糟，所以正如老山姆．約翰生（即薩繆爾．約翰生）所言，「事情就是如此」。船長在晚餐時間登上「蝕缺」號。我真希望我們能殺死冠海豹或瓶鼻鯨或任何長著獨特鼻子的動物，並且把動物身上的油脂帶回來。一整天都在看包斯威爾的書。

六月十六日 星期三〔D132〕

早上八點左右，「蝕缺」號降下小艇追捕一頭鯨魚，直到中午，但並未捕獲。事實上，我們到達的地方並不是鯨魚的棲地，因此我們看到的鯨魚只是鯨魚群行進時落單的一兩頭鯨魚，鯨魚群並未停下來在此覓食。吹西風，目前這個狀況還不錯。晚上，風停了，海面看起來就像水銀一樣，到處都是獨角鯨，這些巨獸長約十五到十六英尺。你可以聽到四面八方傳來牠們獨特的噴氣聲。我看見一頭獨角鯨像光影搖曳的巨大白色鬼魂，從船底下穿過去。閱讀《項狄傳》（*Tristram Shandy*），一部拙劣的作品，但也妙趣橫生。[161]

六月十七日 星期四 〔D133〕

一個重大的日子——無論如何，對「蝕缺」號來說是如此。早上十點左右，柯林在瞭望台看見五英里外有一頭鯨魚，此時，「蝕缺」號已經放下小艇追逐另一頭鯨魚。我們揚帆開往柯林看到的鯨魚所在地，但失去牠的蹤影，直到下午一點左右，牠突然出現在離船不到五十碼的地方，旁邊還有一頭鯨魚。這兩頭鯨魚像小羊一樣在海裡翻滾嬉戲。我們降下四艘小艇，分別是柯林、卡納、蘭尼與彼得。他們在浮冰旁停下，認為鯨魚可能再度在此處出現。牠們在蘭尼的小艇附近現身，但可惜蘭尼不是個有決斷力的人，他擔心射擊最近的那頭鯨魚可能會嚇跑另一頭眼睛盯著他直看的鯨魚。這兩頭鯨魚分散了，一頭消失了，其他的小艇於是追捕另一頭，並且在迎風下展開一段驚心動魄的追逐。我從甲板上可以清楚看見鯨魚的氣柱就在小艇前面噴出，鯨魚的尾巴在空中揮舞著，但我們的船員卻一直無法駛近到射擊範圍內。「蝕缺」號看著鯨魚前進的方向，於是預先來到鯨魚的前方，降下兩艘小艇。鯨魚來到其中一艘小艇面前，也就是二副的小艇，此時，我們看到小艇的船員驚惶失措的樣子，讓人顏面無光，但這也顯示他們已經牢牢盯住了鯨魚。要讓一千英磅的大魚從眼前逃脫，我想這是很困難的事。他們在晚餐時間殺死了那頭鯨魚，在晚上八點前將牠運上船。蘭尼上船時，被船長狠狠教訓了一頓。

〔插圖，上述故事的圖示〕

161 勞倫斯・斯特恩（Lawrence Sterne）於一七六七年寫成的《項狄傳》（*The Life and Opinions of Tristam Shandy, Gentleman*），以充斥著猥褻幽默聞名於世。柯南・道爾讀了薩繆爾・約翰生的傳記後說道，「譁眾取寵無法長久。《項狄傳》只會流行一陣子。」——這句話促使叔本華評論說，「斯特恩抵得上一千名學究與約翰生博士這類尋常人。」

晚餐後，我們看見冰岬上有一頭大熊，牠顯然處於極興奮的狀態，或許是因為聞到鯨魚血的緣故。我跟馬提森下了小艇，打算去捕獵這頭熊。我們上到冰上，上頭有延綿好幾哩長一道巨大的裂縫。[162]我們拿著步槍，可以看見離我們四十碼外，那頭熊正在冰丘之間四處探索。突然間，牠看見我們，而且在冰上快速向我們衝來，牠高舉前足，動作就像貓一樣敏捷。馬提森與我跪在冰上，我打算等到那頭巨獸來到我們頭頂上時再射擊。然而，馬提森在十五碼外就射擊了，但只是稍微傷到牠的頭。牠轉身，開始小跑步遠離我們，由於牠背對著我們，我想機不可失，就開槍射擊。那頭熊受傷了，但還是快速穿過冰面，我們再也沒看到牠。

看到一隻賊鷗。晚間，在船副的艙房裡喧鬧。

六月十八日　星期五〔D136〕

「蝕缺」號夜裡發現另一頭鯨魚，在早餐前將牠獵捕上船。真是好狗運。布坎在夜裡獵到一頭熊與兩隻小熊。順道一提，昨天那頭熊，牠逃到一段距離外，用後腳站立著杵在冰丘上，像隻跳舞的熊一樣一直盯著我們。

〔插圖，「我們的熊」〕

我不知道在自然環境下，熊也會這麼做。巡航一整天，連一隻冠海豹也沒看到。夜裡，[163]我們與「蝕缺」號的小艇追捕一頭鯨魚，他們並未占上風。浮冰逐漸包圍我們，我們與外圍的海洋斷絕聯繫，除非風向轉變，否則我們很可能會被困住。大家都感到沮喪。

六月十九日 星期六 〔D136〕

海面平靜得像座魚池，海水就像水銀一樣。附近有許多獨角鯨。浮冰還是靜止不動或原地漂浮。今天完全沒看到鯨魚，只看見一隻鯊魚跟在船邊，牠躍出水面獵到一隻北極海燕。如果其他船跟我們一樣未能捕到魚，那麼我們還好受一點，但偏偏「蝕缺」號捕到了約三千英鎊的漁產，而我們連一便士也沒賺到，我們快被逼瘋了。在前往格陵蘭捕魚的漁夫中，我們的船長算是箇中好手，這點，船上的船員全都同意。他的技術跟他的兄弟大衛不相上下，但不知為何，他的運氣就是沒大衛好。對方從開始到最後，總共看見約十四頭鯨魚，而我們只看見五頭。

六月二十日 星期日 〔D137〕

早餐時看見一頭大鯨魚，但在短暫追逐之後，牠躲進浮冰之間，我們只好放棄追捕。牠曾經一度非常接近射程範圍內。

162 巨大的浮冰島從海岸線的冰棚斷裂，然後受到洋流的推送。在《格陵蘭、鄰近海域與通往太平洋的西北通道》（*Greenland, the Adjacent Seas, and the North West Passage to the Pacific Ocean*, New York: James Eastburn, 1818, pp. 144-47）中，貝爾納德·歐雷利（Bernard O'Reilly）描述浮冰時表示，「有時廣達數里格（譯註：一里格約三英里〔陸上〕或三海里〔海上〕），上面是一成不變的平坦地面，雪深約十英寸。」他說，船隻必須留意浮冰前進的方向，以免遭到巨大浮冰夾擊，造成船身損毀。

163 雖然是夜裡，但在高緯度地區太陽並不西沉。「跟白天比起來，夜晚帶了點橙色，光線比較柔和，但整體來說跟白天沒什麼差別，」柯南·道爾在〈格陵蘭捕鯨船上的生活〉提到：「有些船長會任意地調整時鐘，把早餐時間定在半夜，把晚餐時間定在早上十點。這是屬於你的二十四小時，你可以任意規定作息。等一兩個月過去之後，你的眼睛就會開始厭倦永晝的世界，並且開始懷念起黑暗。」

明明看到鯨魚，卻捕不到，這種感覺實在糟透了。[164]沒有實際經歷過的人，無法體會捕鯨的興奮。這種動物的稀罕，牠的棲地難以接近，牠有著極高的價值，牠的力量、聰明與龐大，這一切都令人傾心不已。深夜射殺了一頭大熊。

白晝，浮冰逐漸朝我們聚攏，但到了夜裡又散開。大衛船長白天來我們船上，我們的船長過去他們的船上，與大衛船長共進晚餐。大衛船長底下的一名魚叉手前幾天在小艇上被一頭熊攻擊，他沒有帶步槍，於是他用魚叉槍射牠，這倒是個好方法。然而，與我們的魚叉手幾年前做的事比起來，簡直是小巫見大巫，如果我不知道確有其事，我還以為他是在吹牛。[165]布坎被派去獵殺冰上的一頭熊與兩隻小熊，但他還沒抵達，熊已經跳進水裡。他把套索丟到這三隻一邊游泳一邊對著他咆哮的熊的頭上，並且將三條繩索的另一端綁在小艇的橫木上。布坎不划船，只掌著舵，他站在船頭，當他想改變方向時，就用船竿打熊的頭，就這樣讓熊把小艇拖回船邊。史都華看見這個情況便說，熊的叫聲一英里外都聽得見。希望明天能有所收穫。

六月二十一日 星期一〔D139〕

還是一樣，希望破滅了。我們被困在一小片水塘裡，放眼望去全是巨大的冰原。如果繼續這樣下去，我們會被冰層圍住，那麼我們就會徹底失敗。柯林因喉嚨痛而感到不適。附近都沒有魚。昨天抓到一隻漂浮在水面的海檸檬，[166]但捕上船後不久就死了。午夜，看見非常奇妙的景象，就算你每年都來北極，也不一定能看到。有三個太陽同時在天上閃耀著，而且三個太陽周圍都圍繞著美麗的彩虹，在太陽的上方，還出現了倒轉過來的彩虹。這真是令人難忘的奇景。

〔插圖，「家族宴會」〕

六月二十二日　星期二〔D140〕

一日無事。我們依然困在這個小水塘裡。傍晚，捕到一隻難以用言語形容的水母（Medusa Doilea Octostipata）。悲慘而孤寂。

六月二十三日　星期三〔D140〕

發動引擎，透過巧妙的操控，我們終於脫離了這片水塘。我們穿越厚冰約六十英里左右，其中哪怕是最小的浮冰，也

164 這大概是柯南．道爾在《格陵蘭捕鯨船上的生活》說的，有關大副柯林．麥克林的軼事的起源：「他唯一的缺點是過於熱血，一點小事就會讓他異常亢奮。我印象很清楚，某天晚上，我花了很大的力氣把他與勤務員拉開。勤務員相當魯莽地批評柯林的捕鯨方式造成鯨魚逃走。兩個人都喝了蘭姆酒，這使得其中一人變得好逞口舌，另一人變得非常暴力，而當我們三人坐在長七英尺寬四英尺的空間時，流血衝突顯然是免不了的。每一次，當我以為危險已經過去，勤務員又會愚蠢地說道，『我不是要冒犯，柯林，我只是想說，如果你捕魚時動作能快一……』我不知道這樣的話重複了多少遍，但勤務員沒有一次能把話說完；因為講到『快一』的時候，柯林就已經衝上前去勒住他的脖子，而我只能死命地抱住柯林的腰，直到我們精疲力竭為止。然後，等勤務員休息夠了，他又會重複那個可悲的句子，『快一』就成了另一場衝突的發起信號。我確信如果我不在那裡，大副一定會打傷勤務員，因為大副是我所見過脾氣最暴躁的人」。麥克林曾經寫信向《河濱雜誌》的出版者喬治．紐恩斯爵士（George Newnes）提出反對。柯南．道爾於一八九七年一月十五日告訴編輯格林霍．史密斯（H. Greenhough Smith）：「我很遺憾柯林．麥克林認為我的文章有誤，因為他是個經驗老到的船副，而我非常尊敬他。因此，我也親自致函給他。我告訴他，雖然他否認有這件事，但他確實記錯了。我與勤務員傑克．蘭姆聯絡過，也就是事件裡另一名主角，他肯定確有其事。我保留了我在『希望』號上的日記。這本日記已經收起來了，但我很肯定我可以在當天找到相關的紀錄。蘭姆似乎很高興我提到他的名字。我很遺憾喬治爵士被這樣的事所驚擾。」在二十一號：「我剛剛收到勤務員的信，他再次確認我的說法不假——因此，如果你想做出任何修正，千萬別讓人對你說話的可信度產生質疑。」

165 這些日子以來，柯南．道爾見識了不少奇事，回想五月九日那天，他看到斯科斯比的北極日誌，對於裡面的記載還有所質疑。那些事與他現在聽到的事比起來，其實還算比較可信的。

166 色彩鮮豔的海蛞蝓。

可能像敲蛋殼一樣把我們撞沉。我們幾乎是慢慢地從浮冰之間擠過去，因此船身的兩側不斷地與冰塊摩擦著。發動引擎，往南方與東方前進。「蝕缺」號追捕一頭鯨魚，但並未成功。氣壓計急速下降。

六月二十四日　星期四〔D140〕

早上六點，船長與我被船副叫醒，他把黃褐色的頭伸進船艙裡，像唱歌似地喊著「有魚，先生」，然後就像點燈的街伕一樣[167]從船艙的樓梯消失。當我們抵達甲板時，船副與彼得的小艇已經來到先前看到鯨魚的位置，準備採取行動。

〔摺頁插圖，「『蝕缺』號與『希望』號的小艇追捕兩頭鯨魚」〕

他們看到一英里外的背風處還有一頭鯨魚，於是轉而朝那頭鯨魚駛去，但最後失去牠的蹤影。在此同時，又有一頭非常不錯的鯨魚出現在船尾，離船很近，於是降下赫爾頓與蘭尼的小艇前去獵捕。四艘小艇追了幾個小時，之後開始吹起強風，海面波濤洶湧，小艇的前端都已經泡入水中。我們只好收起小艇，任由那頭鯨魚離去。一整天吹著強勁的東北風，風速九級。

六月二十五日　星期五〔D144〕

風還是很大，但比昨天緩多了。一整天只看到一頭龐大的長鬚鯨，這是個壞徵兆。長鬚鯨對我們沒有用處，而且有牠的地方，露脊鯨就不會出現。晚上，玩紙牌遊戲拿普。現在吹的是五級風，開始發動引擎跟著「蝕缺」號北上。

六月二十六日 星期六（D144）

一整天無事可做，令人感到沮喪，但突然間有了轉機。我大約在十點時下到船艙，此時聽見甲板上一陣慌亂。然後我聽見船長在桅頂上喊著，「把左舷兩艘二副艇降下去！」我衝到船副的艙房通知，柯林趕緊著裝，但二副只是穿著襯衫手裡拿著褲子便衝上甲板。當我從艙口探頭出去，首先看見的是已經露出水面的鯨魚頭部，牠在浮冰突起的大「燭台」[168]另一側躍出水面。那是個美麗的夜晚，風平浪靜，深綠色的水平靜無波。船員們跳進小艇，值班的人已經弄好魚叉槍，然後他們推開這兩艘長捕鯨艇，船員們努力划船，兩艘小艇分別沿浮冰的兩側前進。卡納幾乎無法接近浮冰，那頭鯨魚再度出現在小艇前方四十碼處，整個軀體躍出水面，浪花四濺。此時船上的人急切地異口同聲喊著，「現在，亞當，機會來了！」但滿頭灰髮的亞當·卡納是個經驗老到的魚叉手，他知道怎麼做才是最好的。鯨魚的小眼朝著他看，而小艇就跟它後頭的浮冰一樣靜止不動。但現在，「鯨魚轉身了，牠的尾巴正對著他們打過去——划呀，小子們，快划呀！」從浮冰到鯨魚的距離，還在射程之外，卡納是否能在鯨魚深潛之前獵到牠呢？每個人心中都存有相同的疑問。他慢慢靠近牠，依然是無聲無息地——越來越近，越來越近。然後，卡納站起來放下槳，站到魚叉槍旁——「連划三下，小子們！」他一邊說著，一邊撥弄著嘴裡的菸草塊，接下來是一聲槍響，海面上泛起了泡沫與喊叫聲，卡納的小艇豎起一根小紅旗，捕鯨的魚繩也愉快地奔騰而出。

167「像點燈的街伕一樣」（To run like a lamplighter），這是當時的慣用語，起源於上個世紀。

168 對海員來說，這裡的燭台指的是被海水沖刷而成的小冰山。

然而，光是中一根魚叉還不能說已經捕到鯨魚。傑克出現在小艇上的同時，船上也傳來「降下小艇」的指令。於是其他六艘小艇也一併降下，協助「射中鯨魚」的小艇，準備等鯨魚再度露出水面，一起發動攻擊。我搭乘船副的小艇，努力往前划。當然，鯨魚可能出現在魚繩的半徑範圍內，魚繩的長度大約三到四英里左右，因此我們七艘小艇必須分散在相當廣大的區域。五分鐘過去了，十分鐘，十五分鐘，二十分鐘，然後，二十五分鐘過後，這頭巨獸出現在二副與蘭尼的小艇之間，他們發射魚叉，終於殺死這頭鯨魚。我們發現這頭鯨魚相當小，體長約四十英尺，尾鰭寬約四英尺一英寸，價值約兩百到三百英鎊。我們歡呼三聲，然後將鯨魚拖上船。我們發現牠的身體上長滿了龐大的蟹蝨，這解釋了為什麼這頭鯨魚在水中的行動有些古怪。到了凌晨三點，油脂已經取好，鯨魚已做好儲藏。而在眾人處理鯨魚時，我爬上瞭望台，觀察是否還有其他鯨魚，但一無所獲。早上六點上床睡覺，十二點起床。

〔插圖，鯨魚尾鰭上標了「四英尺一英寸」，下面寫著「亞當．卡納」〕

六月二十七日　星期日〔D148〕

一整天海上毫無動靜，但凌晨四點左右，柯林看見遠處有一頭大鯨魚。「蝕缺」號降下兩艘小艇，我們也一樣，原本掌握了機會，但最後還是失去了魚蹤。這頭大鯨魚似乎是個龐然大物。

六月二十八日 星期一〔D148〕

一日無事。

六月二十九日 星期二〔D148〕

資深魚叉手昨晚到「蝕缺」號上，凌晨兩點才回來。整天風平浪靜，迎風停船——無事可做。等待吹北風的時機，但浮冰的狀況不佳。午夜離船打獵，下午四點返回船上。獵到一隻波吉鷗、一隻雪鳥與五隻潛鳥。我認為波吉鷗應該是體型僅次於信天翁的海鷗。牠們翼展大約有五英尺。

六月三十日 星期三〔D148〕

昨晚出去打獵，今天睡了一整天。到「蝕缺」號上，相談甚歡。在「蝕缺」號上使用顯微鏡。布坎獵到一隻浮冰鼠。赫爾頓把我獵到的鳥剝了皮。

七月一日與二日　星期四與星期五 {D149}

從上星期一以來，我們一直陷在濃霧中無法動彈。沒有值得記錄的事，除了柯林在星期四清晨獵到一頭大獨角鯨。我們忙了半天，花了一整捆魚繩（一百二十噚，約兩百二十公尺）才殺死牠。一頭獨角鯨大約值十英鎊。牠的皮很值錢。到目前為止，我的北極博物館已經稍有收藏，包括許多有趣的物品。我收藏的有

一．一條愛斯基摩海豹皮褲
二．一隻冰島鷹
三．我的獵海豹的刀子與磨刀鋼棒
四．冠海豹的骨頭——我自己獵到的
五．兩隻老海豹的骨頭
六．年輕冠海豹的兩隻前鰭肢
七．地海豹的兩隻前鰭肢
八．一顆熊頭
九．冠海豹的鬃毛
十．一隻北極鷗

十一・鯨魚的鼓膜

十二・兩隻王絨鴨

〔四張插圖，統一的標題是「我們捕到的第一頭鯨魚」，以下依序是四張插圖的標題：「開槍」、「射中鯨魚的小艇」、「等待小艇拖回鯨魚」、「鯨魚死了，萬歲！」〕

十三・在王絨鴨身上發現的些許熔岩

十四・（？）獨角鯨的角　　增補：兩個愛斯基摩菸草袋

一隻三趾鷗

一隻熊掌

七月三日　星期六〔D151〕

天氣晴朗，我們出發前往快樂的漁場。整日往北與西北航行。什麼也沒看見，倒是看見冰上有一隻小得出奇的海豹，大約就像兔子一般大小。牠看見我們的船，就跟我們看見牠一樣，雙方同樣露出驚異的神色。大家的心情都很低落。史都華細心地將木屑塞進我的地海豹的鰭狀肢裡。

七月四日 星期日 〔D151〕

往北航行，之後又再度往南航行。一切看起來毫無希望，令人沮喪。不要說鯨魚，就連鯨魚的食物也不見蹤影。看見冰上有一隻冠海豹。一隻看起來像椋鳥或鶇鳥的小鳥，繞著船飛行。看到一隻海鸚。沒有心思寫日誌。閱讀莫特利《荷蘭共和國的興起》，[169] 一本好歷史書。

七月五日 星期一 〔D151〕

駛進一處裂隙水，晚間加速前進。看到幾頭長鬚鯨。「蝕缺」號誤以為看見了鯨魚，於是降下小艇，但隨即收回。這一天沒看到什麼令人感興趣的東西。從海冰中取得一些淡水，好喝極了。

七月六日 星期二 〔D152〕

一片死寂。雖然氣溫只有華氏三十六度，[170] 但陽光給人的灼熱感彷彿到了熱帶。浮冰反射出刺眼的光芒。早上，到「蝕缺」號上。下船打獵，獵到七隻潛鳥、一隻羅區鳥、一隻三趾鷗、一隻雪鳥與一隻浮冰鼠。光用槍沒辦法打死浮冰鼠，我們興致高昂地追逐了至少一個半鐘頭，最後當牠打算潛入水中時，我們用小艇的魚叉射中牠。我們將牠帶上船時，牠還活著，船長起了憐憫心，殺死牠讓牠免受痛苦。晚間，再次下船打獵，但找不到獵物。看到兩隻海燕[171]繞著船玩耍。看到幾頭長鬚鯨。非常愉快的一天！

七月七日　星期三 〔D152〕

發動引擎，往南移動二十到三十英里，看到鯨魚的蹤影，改用風帆。傍晚，大衛船長與管輪來我們船上，他們抓到一隻罕見的蝦子。昨日外出打獵，今日想起來，仍覺得心情不錯。晚餐吃的是以非常科學的方式烹煮的紅鯡魚。

七月八日　星期四 〔D153〕

又是令人難忘的一日。「蝕缺」號在前，我們沿著巨大的冰縫邊緣，在碧藍的海水中航行。大約一點左右，星期日以來首次見到的鯨魚出現在大衛船長的船附近；他降下三艘小艇追捕鯨魚，到了下午四點十五分，他成功射中鯨魚，晚上八

169 約翰·洛思羅普·莫特利（John Lothrop Motley, 1814-77），美國史家與外交家，他在一八五六年完成的作品《荷蘭共和國的興起》（*The Rise of the Dutch Republic*）被譯為多種文字，在歐洲興起風潮。

170 譯註：相當於攝氏二度。

171 一種北極燕鷗。

點，將鯨魚拖回船上，午夜時，順利取下魚油。我們刻意與他們保持距離，希望對方的鯨魚能朝我們這裡游過來，這樣的話，我們就能順理成章地捕捉這頭鯨魚，但到了四點左右，從桅頂傳來歡呼聲，「先生，船頭背風面還有一頭鯨魚！」馬提森與鮑伯．康恩降下小艇追捕牠，而船員們也都擠到甲板的一側等候著，但他們不久就在浮冰間失去牠的蹤影。然後我們聽到一陣呻吟聲，一頭大長鬚鯨在船的附近浮出水面，由於長鬚鯨與露脊鯨是死敵，我們擔心可能驚動了獵物。我下了甲板，進到船艙，抽個菸紓解心中的沮喪，此時我聽到船長在桅頂喊叫，「倒下了！倒下了！」這個信號表示船員射中鯨魚了。我們把船員們全叫起來，他們許多人還半裸著身子，然後我們派了五艘綠色的長型捕鯨艇去支援「射中鯨魚」的小艇與另一艘小艇。我搭上彼得．麥肯吉的小艇。我們遲遲無法駛離船邊，小艇舵手說鯨魚浮上來了，用鰭與尾巴猛烈拍擊著。然後我們知道這個工作再適合我們不過了，因為鯨魚被射中後只會在水裡待上短暫的時間，牠會保存力氣與小艇一搏。如果鯨魚潛入水中半個小時，那麼牠在回到水面時會極為疲倦，這時要獵捕鯨魚極為容易。小艇停下來，赫爾頓與卡納向鯨魚發射魚叉，而且牢牢射中了。接下來是我們這艘小艇，我們來到鯨魚的頭部，朝牠的頸部深深刺進去。鯨魚顫抖了一下，然後開始在水面快速前進。當鯨魚前進時，布坎讓小艇朝鯨魚頭部前進，這個莫名其妙的舉動使小艇的艇首被抬了起來，斜向空中，最後，在船員的吶喊與槳的敲擊聲中，整艘小艇落在鯨魚的背上。布坎叫嚷著，「划啊！用力划！往後！撐住！划！你們在怕什麼！」我對彼得說，「準備好把他們救上小艇！」但他們努力划離鯨魚，沒有發生意外。鯨魚游向浮冰，躲在浮冰下面，但不久牠又浮上水面，布坎與蘭尼又向牠發射魚叉。牠又潛入水中，但又再次浮上水面，而且就位於我們三艘小艇之間，有趣的事開始了。我們朝著牠，將魚叉刺進牠的體內，大約五英尺深，我們三艘小艇試著維持在牠的側面，但鯨魚一直旋轉身體想用牠巨大的尾鰭拍擊我們。鯨魚鑽到我們的小艇下方，差點害我們翻船，但我們設法讓小艇不偏斜。然後，鯨魚開始進入臨死前的掙扎，在水中來回抽打著，產生了大量的泡沫，然後鯨魚肚朝天的浮出水面，牠死了。我們站在小艇上，齊聲歡呼三次。我們拖回鯨魚，下午一點，我們已經把鯨魚運上船。這是一頭上好的鯨魚，每一片鯨魚骨板有九英尺六英寸長，魚油約十二噸。價值約一千英鎊，這已經能確保我們此次出航不賠本。一隻體型龐大長相醜陋的鯊魚靠了過來，窺伺我們取魚油的過程，牠似乎不擔心眾多船員的刀子從牠身上砍下去。我請求船長允許史都華與我降下小艇去獵殺鯊魚，但船長不答應。

〔插圖，鯨魚尾鰭上標了九英尺六英寸，下面寫著鮑伯·康恩〕

〔跨頁插圖，「鯨魚在水中拖著兩艘射中牠的小艇」〕

〔插圖，「布坎的小艇在鯨魚的背上」〕

七月九日 星期五（D157）

無事可做。昨日捕鯨之後，今日每個人都呈現精疲力竭的狀態。[172]船長說，鮑伯·康恩在捕鯨行動中表現非常好。白

172 許多年後，柯南·道爾撰寫自傳時，他記得「希望」號獵到的是三頭而不是兩頭鯨魚，而且在〈回憶幾件冒險犯難的往事〉（Some Recollections of Sport）中，說了一則捕鯨的故事。「我曾經跟人比賽看誰說的捕魚故事精采，結果我贏了，然而大家褒揚的恐怕不是我的誠實。事情發生在伯明罕的一間小客棧裡，一個做生意的旅人誇耀著他的成功事蹟。我大膽地用上次捕到的那三頭鯨魚的重量跟他打賭，我相信他一輩子都不可能捕到那麼大的魚。大家下好注之後，那人說他捕過一次巨大的漁獲，重達一百磅以上。『現在，先生，』他說道，一副勝券在握的樣子，『你那三條魚多重？』『只比兩百噸多一點，』我回道。『鯨魚？』『是的，三頭格陵蘭鯨。』『你贏了，』他叫道；但我是以漁夫的身分，還是以說捕魚故事的人的身分贏的，這我就不確定了」。

天，看到幾頭長鬚鯨。美麗的陽光。

「蝕缺」號捕到的鯨魚只有一隻眼睛，令大夥嘖嘖稱奇。這頭鯨魚跟我們捕到的鯨魚一樣，有食物攝取不足的問題。牠的眼窩完全是空的。也許格陵蘭鯨裡有著獨眼的物種。

七月十日 星期六 D160

我想，我們往北航行可能是個錯誤。我覺得南方也許比較容易捕到鯨魚。降下小艇去獵捕冠海豹，但一無所獲。晚上，在引擎室玩紙牌遊戲尤克（Euchre）[173]玩了四個小時。問大家，亞當與夏娃的孩子和誰結婚？

七月十一日 星期日 D160

起床的時間晚了，但還想繼續賴床，全身提不起勁。早上，「蝕缺」號捕到一隻冠海豹。傍晚，與「蝕缺」號一同開往東方，行進時我們驚嚇到一頭鯨魚。看見許多長鬚鯨。晚上七點左右，據報有一艘蒸汽船出現在東邊約二十英里的位置。這是五月初以來，我們看見的第一艘船。我們加速前進，很快就認出那是李·史密斯的新探索船「艾拉」號。[174]如果冰況良好的話，史密斯打算試著航向北極，不過實際上冰況並不理想，[175]而無論如何，他想探索法蘭士約瑟夫地群島（Franz Joseph Land），在上頭獵鹿。史密斯是個紳士，年收入八千英鎊，未婚，他把斯匹茲卑爾根島當成自己的妻子。當我們的船接近時，我們升起旗幟並且歡呼三聲，向「小艾拉」號致意，而「艾拉」號也向我們回禮。史密斯的船員穿著海軍後備

「我今天會寫信給『艾拉』號的李·史密斯，跟他要我的寶貴照片，」柯南·道爾在當年十一月寫給母親的信上說道：「妳知道的，後甲板的這群傑出船員深深吸引了我。」格蘭特拍攝的這張照片，可以看見柯南·道爾旁邊是大衛·格雷船長、班傑明·李·史密斯、約翰·格雷船長、「蝕缺」號的船醫羅伯特·沃克、「艾拉」號的船醫威廉·亨利·尼爾，以及「艾拉」號的冰區領航員。（圖片鳴謝：Hull Museums and Art Gallery.）

173 這是美國的紙牌遊戲，一共有四個玩家。一八七四年，艾伯特·馬克罕第一次知道這種紙牌遊戲，當時「北極圈」號（Polaris）搭救了遭遇船難的探索船「北極星」號上的美國船員，而馬克罕在他的日誌上記錄了這件事，頁二二二：「尤克這種遊戲正在流行，每張桌子都在玩這種牌。」

174 如柯南·道爾以下所言，班傑明·李·史密斯（Benjamin Leigh Smith, 1828-1913）是一名頗具資財的紳士，他在一八七一年到一八八二年間致力進行北極探險。裝設螺旋槳的三桅帆船「艾拉」（Eira）號，是在彼得赫德建造的，格雷船長曾給予不少建議。

175 「七月十一日，『艾拉』號偶然遇見彼得赫德的捕鯨船『蝕缺』號與『希望』號，這兩艘船是由大名鼎鼎深具進取心的船長大衛與約翰·格雷領導，」馬克罕在報告裡表示。"The Voyage of the *Eira* and Mr. Leigh Smith's Arctic Discoveries in 1880," *Proceedings of the Royal Geographical Society*，一八八一年三月，第一百三十頁：「這些經驗豐富的船員報告說，浮冰往南漂到了斯匹茲卑爾根島的海岸邊，如果往那個方向航行，成功越過的機會微乎其微……『艾拉』號於七月十四日看見斯匹茲卑爾根島，格雷兄弟關於浮冰的報告獲得確認。」

役制服，高級船員的制服繡著金飾線。船長登上「艾拉」號，而對方的船醫尼爾、攝影師、[176]管輪與兩名船副登上我們的船。船長大約在下午一點回船，他與我還有「艾拉」號的攝影師與船醫喝了一整晚的香檳與雪利酒。[177]早上五點，我們吃了罐頭鮭魚，六點半就寢。

七月十二日 星期一 〔D161〕

與「蝕缺」號及「艾拉」號在浮冰旁下錨。[178]我們的舵因為跟冰碰撞而損壞，因此我們只能將舵拆卸下來。此外，我們從「艾拉」號得知到六月十八日為止的家鄉消息。沒有收到愛丁堡寄來的信，但洛蒂倒是有個令人愉快的消息傳來。得知自由黨勝利的事，感到驚訝，但也感到噁心。[179]受邀登上「蝕缺」號，與李．史密斯及他的船員共進晚餐。享用了假海龜湯，[180]新鮮的烤牛肉佐馬鈴薯，四季豆與醬汁，竹竿布丁，薄煎餅抹上果醬，最後以喝葡萄酒抽雪茄結尾。非常豐盛的捕鯨人食物。之後，登上「艾拉」號。這艘船的船尾十分美麗。享用了更多的雪茄與葡萄酒。與眾人合照之後，十二點回到船上。「艾拉」號繼續往北航行，遇見了「揚馬延」號，並且在北緯七十二度三十分看見數百萬隻冠海豹，我希望我們往南航行時也能看到那麼多的海豹。

七月十三日 星期二 {D162}

往南行駛二十英里之後，突然停船，我不知道為什麼。我幻想如果我們朝著海豹群而去，我們的船可能滿載而歸，但我們必須立即啟程。我認為，我們在這裡遲疑太久了，但一切還是要交給船長來決定。我們這次出航是否成功，就看接下來這幾天，這是我們成功的最後機會。「蝕缺」號追逐一頭熊，最後在我們船附近的水面殺死牠。早上，揮別「艾拉」號，希望他們一切順利。這是一艘令人愉快的船，上面載著令人愉快的船員。這艘船是黑色的，船身漆了一道金線，載重約兩百噸，擁有五十匹馬力的引擎。我認為我會想搭這艘船出航，不過目前返鄉的念頭更吸引我。他們把要寄的信交給我們。[181] 傍晚起霧。

176 攝影師是格蘭特（W. J. A. Grant），他的作品為北極探險留下珍貴的視覺紀錄。見 Willem F. J. Mörzer Bruyns, "Photography in the Arctic, 1876-84: the work of W. J. A. Grant," *Polar Record*, 2003。

177 與柯南·道爾同為船醫的威廉·亨利·尼爾（William Henry Neale）在「艾拉」號上服務，他比柯南·道爾年長三歲，於一八七九年取得醫學士學位。他在隔年參與了「艾拉」號多災多難的前往法蘭士約瑟夫地島的航程（詳見註181），而且寫下生動的紀錄，"Castaways in the Frozen North," for *Wide Word Magazine*, April, 1898。從他在船上記錄的事情來看，尼爾醫生很可能是華生醫生的原型人物；而且跟華生醫生一樣，兩個人都是倫敦大學醫學院畢業的（「一八七八年，我在倫敦大學獲得醫學博士學位，」華生在《血字的研究》中說道）。

178 當天下午三點，在航行一段距離之後，格蘭特在「艾拉」號一八八〇年航行的日記中寫道，「正午，三艘船稍微往北航行一段距離。」他的日記可以跟馬克罕的描述合起來看，見註175。

179 或許——但這要到一八八〇年代中期才是如此——柯南·道爾是積極的自由統一黨員，該黨因為不滿首相格萊斯頓（Gladstone）的愛爾蘭自治政策而與自由黨分裂。

180 編註：用小牛的腦、腿肉煮成的牛雜碎湯，以模擬海龜的肉質和口感。此湯發明於十八世紀的英國。

181 「艾拉」號於六月十九日離開彼得赫德，直到十月十二日才返回。如柯南·道爾所言，浮冰的狀況不利他們前往北極，因此「艾拉」號轉而深入探索法蘭士約瑟夫地島，然後再沿挪威海岸南下，中間甚至還擱淺了數日（"An Arctic Exploring Voyage," *The Scotsman*, October 12, 1880）。一八八一年，「艾拉」號的運氣不佳：八月，在法蘭士約瑟夫地島的海岸遇難，史密斯與船員艱難地度過十個月，才在一八八二年六月搭上長艇向外求援。一八八三年，柯南·道爾在樸資茅斯文學與科學學會的演說中向史密斯這群人致敬，《樸資茅斯時報》報導說：「我們無法想像比史密斯與他的船員更孤立無援的狀況——在荒涼的北極島嶼遭遇船難，求援困難，漫長的冬天緩慢地襲來，完全沒有逃離的可能……他們搭了一間小屋，仔細保存武器彈藥，射殺了一些熊與海象作為過冬的食物。他們明智地安排各種活動，保持樂觀的情緒，所有人都健康地撐過永夜的六個月，直到春天冰融，他們終於搭上小艇，最後才被艾倫·楊爵士（Allen Young）派來的『希望』號救起。」

七月十四日　星期三〔D163〕

發動引擎搭配風帆往南與西南行駛。「蝕缺」號在傍晚降下小艇，但他們把長鬚鯨誤認為露脊鯨。幾乎整天起霧。沒有任何消息傳來。整天讀報

七月十五日　星期四〔D163〕

又是無所事事的一天。斜躺著抽菸。完全無事可做。濃霧，天候非常糟糕。看了歌德《浮士德》裡的一個小場景，大概是我讀過的作品中最生動而詭異的，比莎士比亞筆下的女巫還要來得陰森。[182]

夜——廣闊的原野

浮士德、梅菲斯特騎黑馬飛奔而來

浮士德—這些女人繞著烏鴉石[183]做什麼？

梅菲斯特—我不知道她們在搞什麼準備什麼。

浮士德—她們往上揮舞—往下揮舞。她們俯身—她們彎腰。

梅菲斯特——一群女巫。

浮士德—她們灑東西並且念咒。

梅菲斯特—繼續走吧！別停下來！

這真是恐怖，我覺得。

七月十六日 星期五 〔D164〕

依然多霧。「蝕缺」號夜裡降下四艘小艇，但一無所獲。我們不知道，他們是否真的看到鯨魚。傍晚登上「蝕缺」號，發現對方很確定他們看見的是一頭鯨魚，而且他們也差點獵到牠。當鯨魚潛入水中時，小艇已經近到可以發射魚叉。大衛船長似乎還是對前景感到樂觀。我們儲備的糧食有些已開始短缺，我們從「艾拉」號拿了一些馬鈴薯。在「蝕缺」號一直待到凌晨兩點。拿到更多報紙。白天，看到水中有許多海豹。

182 歌德的悲劇分成兩部分，講述一名學者出賣靈魂給魔鬼（梅菲斯特）以換取超越世俗知識之物。這段文字是第一部分的倒數第二個場景。這部作品的最後形式直到歌德於一八三二年死後才出現。以下，兩天後，柯南·道爾與大衛·格雷船長討論歌德與莎士比亞。

183 譯註：指刑場。

七月十七日 星期六〔D165〕

完全無事可做。今天依然起霧，總計過去的這一個星期以來，我們一直籠罩在大霧裡。往南方與東方前進約二十英里。夜裡，大衛船長登上我們的船。我們接下來想前往格陵蘭西部[184]的利物浦海岸，也就是北緯七十三度的位置碰碰運氣。大衛船長曾在捕魚季末尾在當地捕獲許多大噸位的鯨魚，其中比較知名的是一八六九年，他捕到十二頭鯨魚，他在七月十六日捕到第一頭，八月四日捕到最後一頭。我記得我以前一直以為捕鯨船只要一看見鯨魚，通常都能成功捕獲，但事實上平均值卻是每追捕二十次只能捕獲一頭。

七月十八日 星期日〔D165〕

今天視野比較清楚，但霧還是很大。傍晚，稍強的南南西六級風突然轉強成為九級風。一整天，包括晚上，強風不斷吹襲。進入浮冰裂縫避風。我想著李·史密斯的船是否也遭遇了強風。順帶一提，我在「艾拉」號的後甲板與該船的傑出船員合照，但我在拍照時抽著雪茄，我擔心煙霧會不會遮了我的臉。

七月十九日星期一〔D166〕

整日吹著九級風。無事可做，但我們還是找事情做。

七月二十日　星期二〔D166〕

霧又散去一些，我們整天沿著大片的冰原之間航行，大約往西南方航行了四十英里。如果天氣能保持這個樣子，我們還可以做更多事。今年，陸地邊緣累積了大量的冰，數量遠超過以往。我們現在離這些陸冰約兩百四十英里，冰原幾乎是連綿不絕。我擔心我們可能無法到達。

七月二十一日　星期三〔D166〕

濃霧再起，我們動彈不得。我們在黑暗中摸索前進。傍晚，停泊在冰縫間，船長與我登上「蝕缺」號。

〔插圖，「取下鯨魚油脂。一八八〇年七月十八日」〕

184 編註：利物浦台地位於格陵蘭東岸，但原文如此。

從八點到凌晨兩點，吟唱著〈夜之女神安波羅修〉。[185] 已故的普羅克特先生。[186] 大衛船長告訴我，他曾經捕到一頭鯨魚，這頭鯨魚的尾鰭上長了一團東西，大小形狀就像蜂窩一樣。大衛船長批判分析了歌德的《浮士德》，而且拿《浮士德》與莎士比亞的著作做比較，指出前者借用了後者。看來捕鯨船上並不是每個人都粗鄙無文。

七月二十二日 星期四 D168

依然起霧，我們繼續停泊在冰縫。早上，在半甲板討論消失的「亞特蘭大」號（Atlanta）。[187] 看見兩隻「賊鷗」，非常罕見的鳥類，牠們以非常快的速度飛過冰縫。我們打算獵捕牠們，卻讓牠們跑了。打中五十碼外在水中的浮冰鼠的頭，牠的頭被子彈打飛了。可惜的是身體沉到水裡去了。

七月二十三日 星期五 D168

霧消散一些，我們發動引擎往南和西南方前進。整晚使用風帆朝相同方向前進，穿過非常厚的冰原。風向轉而向西。

七月二十四日 星期六 〔D169〕

再度發動引擎往西南方航行，就這樣維持一整天。穿過一些讓喬治・那爾斯爵士[188]與整個北極委員會翻白眼的浮冰。回頭看，整片海洋直到海平面的盡頭，似乎全成了堅硬的地面，你幾乎無法想像兩艘船能緩慢地穿越這片冰原。船上有一兩個膽小鬼感到害怕；他們說，進去跟出來是兩回事，我們只剩下兩星期的存糧。如果我們被困住，一定會陷入缺糧的狀態。在我們與大海之間，還隔著兩百英里的厚冰。

七月二十五日 星期日 〔D169〕

晴朗的一天，偶爾出現一點薄霧。發動引擎往西航行四十英里。傍晚使用風帆。看見許多「賊鷗」。過去幾天，我們

185 一夜狂歡，伴隨著大衛・歐斯伯恩（David McEwen Osbourne）的詩〈夜之女神安波羅修〉（Nox Ambrosiana）的開頭幾句：「燈已亮，火在跳躍，／魚與肉齊邀上船，／你與我，當全城進入夢鄉，／一起啜飲，整夜不眠。／斟滿你的酒杯！不至天明誓不散，／英雄把酒言歡，不醉不歸。」（譯註：似乎是一種文學的對話形式，幾個人在一起不斷地銜接對方的句子）。

186 多產的詩人布萊恩・普羅克特（Bryan Waller Procter, 1787~1874，又名巴瑞・康瓦爾〔Barry Cornwall〕），他做的歌〈海〉（The Sea）與〈暴風雨中的海燕〉（The Stormy Petrel），當中都提到了鯨魚，而且都適合在「希望」號上進行 Nox Ambrosiana。普羅克特是柯南・道爾在愛丁堡的導師布萊恩・魏勒醫生（Bryan Charles Waller）的叔叔。魏勒醫生於一八九三年將他的韻文集 *Perseus with the Hesperides* 獻給他的叔叔以及他的堂妹阿德蕾得・普羅克特（Adelaide Anne Procter），後者在一八六四年去世，得年三十八歲。布萊恩・普羅克特就算在英國不是最具影響力的詩人，但至少他的名字家喻戶曉。他的妻子是倫敦著名的女主人：「凡是認識她的人，沒有不喜愛與讚美她，」查爾斯・沃倫（Charles Dudley Warren）的《世界最佳文學圖書館》（*Library of the World's Best Literature*, 1896）寫道；「她家是倫敦藝文界最喜歡的聚會處。」

187 一八八〇年一月三十一日，皇家海軍訓練船「亞特蘭大」號搭載三百名船員與見習軍官從百慕達航向英格蘭的法爾茅斯（Falmouth），卻從此音信全無。

188 皇家海軍上校（後晉升為海軍中將爵士）喬治・那爾斯（George Nares, 1831-1915）是北極與南極的探險家。一八五二年到一八五四年，他還是一名資淺的軍官，試圖尋找消失的弗蘭克林船長及其船員。一八七二年到一八七五年，他率領「挑戰者」（Challenger）號到大西洋與印度洋進行科學航行，而且首度越過南極圈，而後於一八七五年到一八七六年的著名探險中回到北極，寫下《航向北極海》（*Narrative of a Voyage to the Polar Sea*, 1878）。成為皇家學會成員，服務於海軍部北極委員會（Arctic Committee）。

心情一直不錯，因為我們很順利地往西航行，不過現在我們的前方似乎出現了大片的冰隙水道，我們希望能順利通過。

七月二十六日 星期一〔D170〕

往西與西南航行。測量所在位置為西經六又四分之一度，北緯七十三度五十六分。傍晚，船長前往「蝕缺」號。海水充滿食物，但看不見任何水中生物，只看到九隻北極海燕與一群港海豹（Phoca Vitulina）。[189]寫了一首關於海泡石菸斗的詩

菸斗放在皮革縫製的盒子裡
經過許多年，
值得信賴的朋友與同志經久不變，
就像老菸斗與我。

從年輕就形影不離，
度過放浪不羈的夜晚，
大學生狂飲、抽菸、歌唱，
我的菸斗依然潔白如新。

幾乎不帶一點褐色

我第一次離開家鄉與朋友，
航往俄羅斯的凶險海岸，
我把菸斗放在胸前。

來到沾滿血跡的地面，
許多人來此，卻少有人平安返鄉，
死亡與瘟疫到處流竄，
就在此地，我將菸斗抽成了黑色。

上校陣亡的那天，
我們衝鋒攻下馬拉科夫，[190]
一顆俄軍子彈從我側身擦過，
打掉了菸斗上的琥珀。

189 即 Harbour 或 common seals。
190 一八五五年九月七日，馬拉科夫高地之役，這場勝仗結束了克里米亞戰爭中的塞瓦斯托波爾圍城戰。

現在的我頭髮斑白，彎腰駝背，
死神的鐮刀已近——他的莊稼已經成熟，
我毫無懼意，只是滿足地等待，
一邊等待，一邊抽著我的海泡石菸斗

A
C
D

七月二十七日 星期二 〔D172〕

揚帆往南南西航行。正午時我們的位置在北緯七十三度二十九分。一頭巨大的長鬚鯨——此時離我們此行第一次看到長鬚鯨已有一段時間——在船尾掛艇的下方出現。長鬚鯨的出現引發了討論，有人說這是好兆頭，也有人說這代表厄運。絕大多數船員認為是後者，但大衛．格雷船長獨排眾議，認為這會為我們帶來好運。從我的經驗來看，我必須說，長鬚鯨的出現跟厄運一點關係也沒有。

〔插圖，「取下鯨魚油脂，『蝕缺』號大衛船長草繪」〕

傍晚吹起五級風，浮冰快速移動。在半甲板上待了一段時間。「艾瑞克」號在戴維斯海峽搭了一間屋子作為補給站。某個捕鯨季，當他們返航時，發現有一頭北極熊在屋內的一張床上睡覺，牠就躺在毛毯上。閱讀莫里的《海洋的自然地理學》。[191]他解釋了馬尾藻海（位於維德角〔Cape de Verdes〕、亞速群島〔Azores〕與加那利群島〔Canaries〕之間的三角地帶）的海草，提到它位於灣流漩渦的中心，就像你在洗臉盆裡轉出一個水渦，擺在漩渦中心的軟木塞可以維持不動一樣。他也提到火車無論往北還是往南行進，總是會往右手邊出軌。

七月二十八日 星期三〔D173〕

又是令人討厭的一天。東南方吹來強風，這幾乎是大家最不想遭遇的風向。這是我們度過最長最難熬的一段時間。從七月八日之後，船上再也沒有獵到東西，勉強能算的就是我獵到的一隻浮冰鼠。傍晚吹起東風。霧像豌豆湯一樣濃，浮冰快速地朝我們接近。我們希望往南能看到開闊的海域，因為我們看見海豹成群從南方游過來。我也認為從南方有浪打來，而這能解決我們的問題。

〔插圖，「潛鳥，左邊與右邊各打下一隻」〕

191 作者是馬修·莫里（Matthew F. Maury, 1806-73），他是美國海軍軍官與海洋科學家，是美國海軍氣象台的第一任台長，但他後來支持南軍。他最後任職於維吉尼亞軍事研究所，他的榮譽包括了有三艘美國軍艦以他的名字命名。《海洋的自然地理學》（*The Physical Geography of the Sea*, 1855），是當時的重要作品，其中有一章是〈北極海的開放海域〉（The Open Sea in the Arctic Ocean），提到有一天可以抵達北極的可能性。柯南·道爾也許從莫里導論裡的這麼一段話看到了自己：「一名非常聰明的英國船長〔羅伯特·梅斯倫（Robert Methren），《商船海員日誌》（*Log of a Merchant Officer*, 1854）〕最近提到航海對教育的有利影響，他說：『對於一個有教養的小夥子來說，首次出海航行會為他開啟一個全新的世界。如果他受過適當的教育，那麼他會有能力看出，隨著歲月的累積，他的專業會讓他熟悉嶄新而具啟發性的事物。他的智能使他有能力欣賞每個國家在整體、風俗習慣、生產、航行模式上的不同，同時也能適應各國海岸、氣候與河流的特性。他會興致勃勃地探索海洋，無論是在暴風、無風還是微風的時候，他會尋找這當中有無解釋的原則。這會使他認真地看待自己的工作，此時新手必須負擔的各種令人厭煩乃至於讓人感到冒犯的職務，對他來說也就算不上什麼了。』」

令全體船員焦慮與憂心的一晚，船身撞擊的力道猛烈，濃霧，到處都是浮冰。船長與我直到早上四點才回船。

七月二十九日　星期四〔D176〕

該死的混蛋濃霧讓我們什麼都看不清。在浮冰縫隙停船，等待霧氣散去。帶著我們的紐芬蘭犬桑普森（Sampson）到冰上走走。我們一直走到看不見船的地方，心情似乎跟著愉快起來。發現一座極不尋常的自然雪屋，大約十二英尺高，形狀像蜂窩，有扇門，裡頭有個不錯的房間，我在裡頭坐了下來。旅行了這麼長的距離，差點就到了北極，但現在的我火柴卻用光了，沒法抽菸。隔著很遠的距離射擊賊鷗，但沒有射中。霧散了，發動引擎往東南航行，但又開始起霧，我們不得不再次停船下錨。「蝕缺」號朝一隻冠海豹射擊，但沒射中。在冰上發現一個奇怪的蕈類。晚上喝琴酒抽菸。

〔插圖，「自然冰屋。北緯七十三度十五分，西經六度」〕

七月三十日　星期五〔D177〕

喝了太多琴酒，而且抽了太多菸，身體很不舒服。最美好的一天。北緯七十二度五十二分。揚馬延島位於西南方約一百英里處，目前還無法看見島的蹤影。發動引擎往南南東行駛，航速六節。沒吃晚餐，我寧可爬到桅頂抽菸，曬曬太陽。看到兩隻小冠海豹，我們射了兩槍，一隻被我擊中，另一隻則完全暴露出我過去從沒見過的低劣射擊技術。我把彈藥全射光了，但距離太遠，我完全沒射中，此時兩名魚叉手代勞，他們各射了三槍，或者總共射了七槍，那隻不幸的海豹頭被打掉了。

七月三十一日 星期六〔D178〕

來到開闊的海面，船身劇烈搖晃，朝西南西航行前往瓶鼻鯨岸（Bottlenose Bank）。我們在那裡是否能捕到鯨魚，我感到非常懷疑，我認為這些鯨魚就跟其他動物一樣，也會改變棲身的地點。不可能因為大衛船長四月在那裡看到鯨魚，我們在八月還能在那裡看到。完全看不到浮冰。我再也看不見巨大的格陵蘭冰原，再也看不到我曾在上面抽菸的小島。我曾在那些小島上獵捕狡猾的鯨魚與致命的瓶鼻鯨。可憐的冰原，誰說你冷酷而不好客呢？我曾在無風時以及颳著風暴時看著你，我認為你是溫和而仁慈的。你那奇形怪狀的冰山，充滿了詭異而陰森的幽默。你的浮冰潔白宛如處子，但即便如此，她們仍不請自來，隨意阻擋我們的去路。是的，你是文靜的少女，充滿吸引力，只是霧氣經常遮蔽了你的容顏，讓人難以一窺全貌。

我大可省略冰原不提，但唯有談到冰原，我才有理由提及斯匹茲卑爾根島，斯堪地那維亞神話的約頓海姆，[192] 我曾在八級風中看到它，也在八級風中離開它，那是一個貧瘠崎嶇的隆起地面。揚起風帆，整日朝西和西南方向前進。傍晚無風，

192 在北歐神話中，約頓海姆（Jotunheim）是冰霜巨人與石頭巨人的家，他們不僅威脅凡人，也威脅諸神。「斯匹茲卑爾根的黑色峭壁與白色冰河」，柯南・道爾在〈格陵蘭捕鯨船上的生活〉中回憶說，「是個令人望之生畏的地方……我在狂風的吹襲下，從短暫出現的浮冰罅縫中首次也是最後一次瞥見了那個險惡之處，對我來說，那是既可怕又美麗的地方，足以震懾你的心靈。」

平緩的長浪推著我們前進，我們的帆拍動著，此時濃霧又圍了上來。

八月一日 星期日〔D179〕

「蝕缺」號脫離視線之外——或許他們一整晚發動引擎，在濃霧中離去。我們也發動引擎，在平靜無波以及濃霧中朝西和西南前進。我們希望我們也許能在揚馬延島東南方八十英里處發現瓶鼻鯨，並且從那裡前往冰島的朗加尼斯（Langaness）。[193]我們振作精神。今日，我們看到一些漂流木。傍晚，把我們所在的經緯度寫好放進瓶子裡，然後丟入海中，我們在信裡要求撿到的人能載明拾獲地點的經緯度。至今仍未捕到瓶鼻鯨，有好幾艘船獵捕，不過大家都心不甘情不願的樣子，到最後一隻也沒捕到。「揚馬延」號六個星期之內捕到九隻瓶鼻鯨，但本益未能相抵。大衛船長今年在這個月就捕到三十二隻，已經收回成本。夜裡，來到充滿油脂的水域，散發出大批鯡魚的氣味，而且出現了許多海蝸牛，我抓了約一百多隻各種種類的海蝸牛。有人可能以為瓶鼻鯨會受到這些食物的吸引。在霧裡，聽見遠處長鬚鯨的噴氣聲，彷彿是空啤酒桶的聲音。北緯七十度五十九分，東經零度十五分。漂過兩隻死亡的北極海燕以及另一批從西伯利亞來的漂流木。看見幾頭長鬚鯨。

八月二日　星期一〔D180〕

海面平靜無波，一點風也沒有。貝倫火山（Mount Beerenberg）[194]的山巔隱約可見，位於西北西方八十英里處可看到幾隻海鸚、海燕與絨鴨，這些鳥只會出現在鄰近陸地的地方。大約兩點左右，看見四頭瓶鼻鯨，兩頭年老的，兩頭年輕的，降下兩艘小艇去獵捕。牠們直接朝著康恩的船游過來，但當牠們進入射程時，卻突然潛進水裡。雖然我們追捕了兩個小時，卻找不到第二次機會。大約五點左右，又有兩隻瓶鼻鯨出現，派柯林去追捕牠們，但還是讓牠們跑了。看見「蝕缺」號，他們也降下小艇去追捕鯨魚，同樣沒有得手。瓶鼻鯨是長相滑稽的海中生物，牠們的背鰭高聳，就像長鬚鯨一樣。瓶鼻鯨每頭值六十英鎊。天氣變暖和了，我們把身上的法蘭絨脫了下來。

〔插圖，「水中的瓶鼻鯨」〕

八月三日　星期二〔D181〕

今天早上的狀況不是很好，因為風勢轉強，而且鳥群變少了，顯示水中的食物不像昨天那麼多。揚帆往西航行。一整天都沒看見獵物。

193 冰島東北部海岸的一處人口稀少的半島，以大量海鳥棲息聞名。

194 世界最北的火山，在揚馬延島。

八月四日 星期三〔D181〕

今天早上來到比較好的漁場，這裡有許多鳥群，海中油脂也較多。看到賊鷗——牠們是一群非常惡劣的捕魚者——追逐可憐的老三趾鷗，直到三趾鷗吐出上次吃的一餐為止，這群惡霸就這樣狼吞虎嚥地吃光已經消化一半的食物。大約正午左右，海中出現了鯨魚群，於是我們趕緊降下兩艘小艇。我們以為牠們是瓶鼻鯨，但牠們原來是年輕的長鬚鯨，不僅毫無價值，而且孔武有力，牠們有能力耗盡我們的魚繩，所以我們只能召回小艇。船長射殺了一隻賊鷗。看見許多絨鴨。也看見一些劍魚。一隻劍魚繞著「蝕鈌」號追著一頭長鬚鯨。這頭可憐的鯨魚躍出水面，發出可怕而吵鬧的聲音。康納用步槍打中了一頭長四十英尺的年輕鯨魚，牠快速逃離找母親訴苦去了。從揚馬延島到冰島的這片海域，也許可以稱為羽毛海。海面上確實覆蓋著大量的鳥類羽毛。獵捕瓶鼻鯨是一種可怕的狂歡活動。

〔插圖，「平靜海域上的『希望』號，附近全是鯨群。一八八〇年八月四日」〕

晚上十一點左右，船長召集大家觀看一個不可思議的景象。你不可能期望自己再看到第二次。大海因為出現了大批座頭鯨群而整個活躍起來，而座頭鯨是相當罕見的鯨魚。牠們離船很近，你幾乎可以在船上朝這兩百多頭鯨魚扔餅乾，而舉目所及，你只見到陣陣噴出的水氣與巨大的尾鰭翻出水面。有些鯨魚在船首斜桅底下噴氣，把水噴進了船首的水手艙裡，我們的紐芬蘭犬被逗得異常興奮。牠們有六十到八十英尺長，奇異的頭部與下垂的眼袋，從下頷望去就像蟾蜍一樣。座頭鯨身上大約有三噸非常劣質的油脂，而且很難捕捉，牠們是不值得獵殺的鯨魚。我們降下一艘小艇，並且朝一頭鯨魚射了老舊而未用魚繩固定的魚叉，那頭鯨魚很快鑽入水中逃走。座頭鯨與長鬚鯨不同的地方，在於牠的鰭的底面是白色的。有些座頭鯨在噴氣時會發出汽笛般的聲響，在幾英里外都聽得到。[195]

〔插圖，「揚馬延島南方的座頭鯨群」〕

八月五日　星期四（D183）

今日一無所獲。到了傍晚吹起了六級風，船身搖晃得有點劇烈。我們認為「蝕缺」號已經返鄉了。往西南行駛。

八月六日　星期五（D184）

連日來毫無收穫，決定放棄，往東南東行駛，前往昔德蘭群島。濃霧、大雨，但風勢微弱。令人討厭的天氣。所有船員都對我們的漁獲如此寡少感到沮喪，就這樣返鄉實在令人汗顏，但我們又能如何？我們已經盡可能做好準備上船，但今年實在是不利捕鯨的一年，因為去年冬天嚴寒，使格陵蘭的浮冰往東擴大，將鯨魚群覓食的地點圍在裡面，形成船隻無

195 在「希望」號的官方日誌中，柯南·道爾只寫了以下這幾句話：「看見數量龐大的座頭鯨。數百頭在船的附近覓食與噴氣，有些甚至待在船首斜桅的下方。座頭鯨沒有商業價值。」（Lubbock's *Arctic Whalers*, p. 409.）與柯南·道爾自己的日記相比，可以看出他確實具有寫作才華。

法進入的巨大藩籬。以下是我們在這個捕鯨季捕獲的清單（根據我的統計）

2 格陵蘭鯨
2400 年輕海豹
1200 老海豹
5 北極熊
2 獨角鯨
12 冠海豹
3 浮冰鼠
1 冰島鷹
2 地海豹
2 王絨鴨
2 絨鴨
1 賊鷗
7 羅區鳥
23 潛鳥
1 北極鷗

8 雪鳥

3 三趾鷗

〔插圖，「桑普森與座頭鯨」〕

八月七日　星期六〔D187〕

起了濃霧，站在船邊，看不見水面，我們引擎與風帆並用，摸索著朝回家的路前進。看到兩艘有煙囪的船。我們有幾天的時間未曾估算船的所在位置，因為我們為了追逐瓶鼻鯨，而不斷地曲折前行，因此航位不太容易估算。在北海海域遇到大霧時，一味地發動引擎往前行駛並非明智之舉，因為這附近有冰島與法羅群島（Faeroe Islands），稍不注意就有擱淺撞擊的危險。看到幾隻海鸚與陸地鳥類。

八月八日　星期日〔D187〕

霧稍微散了一點，但幾乎整天都在下雨。傍晚開始放置鯖魚線，但一無所獲。晚間八點左右，看見陸地，之後確認是法羅群島的北端。如果我們是在一片陰暗中來到這裡，那可就不妙了。[196]看見一艘雙桅縱帆船在半夜往北方行駛，或許是

196 譯註：以當時的季節來說，晚間八九點還是天亮的狀況。

從丹麥前往冰島的船隻。船員忙著晾乾鯨魚繩。

八月九日　星期一〔D187〕

天氣晴朗的一天，看得見藍天與明亮的太陽。吹起了六級的東北風，正好與我們返鄉的方向一致，於是我們展開所有風帆，船頭劃開淺綠色的海浪，發出嘶聲與泡沫。還是看不到鯖魚。船上掛滿了鯨魚繩，準備晾乾。預計今日深夜會靠岸。看見一隻北方塘鵝與一種名叫史丁恰克的小鳥，此外還看到一些海燕。我覺得這裡的三趾鷗體型比北方的三趾鷗小。所有的船員都仔細看著陸地的蹤影。

八月十日　星期日〔D188〕

早上快八點的時候，在船首右舷西南西的方位看見陸地。吹起五級風，老舊的「希望」號發動引擎，直接迎著海浪前進，船身劇烈搖晃。因此我的字跡變得極為潦草。六個月不見，岸上的綠草看起來令人心曠神怡，但房子卻讓人看了討厭。我憎惡這些粗俗的人，我寧可再回到看得見浮冰的地方。

「遺世獨立，闃無人聲

海中樂音，自在喧騰！」[197]

經過成群的礁石，來到勒維克，但我們沒有進港，因為我們想直接開回彼得赫德，於是岸上的人將大批我的信件、報紙與其他物品送到船上來。我們看見燈塔上有個女孩揮舞著手帕，所有的船員全跑出來看她。這是半年來我們看見的第一個女人。我們的昔德蘭船員搭乘四艘小艇上岸，在離開「希望」號時，他們歡呼三聲，然後小艇由我們的船員開回來。燈塔管理員留下上星期的《蘇格蘭人》週報給我們，我們才得知英國在阿富汗戰敗的消息。這真是太可怕了。[198] 此外，「勝利者」號漁獲達到一百五十噸，這個混帳東西。[199] 我們收起小艇，往彼得赫德全速前進。從船尾看去，位於海岬的桑波

197 「There is society, where none intrudes, /By the deep sea, and music in its roar.」引自拜倫《恰爾德．哈羅德遊記》（*Childe Harold*），出版於一八一二到一八一八年。但柯南．道爾以船醫身分航往西非時，他在船上寫的日記卻引用拜倫的下一句詩，可以看出他的心境已然不同：「拜倫說，『捲入深刻陰暗的海中』，這深刻陰暗帶有報復的意思。我對大海已不感到敬畏，對我來說，大海似乎已無意義。如果你仔細想想，會發現大海不過是由兩個氫分子與一個氧分子反覆組成的，鹽是當中的懸浮物。」

198 「恐怖且最令人不想看見的災難降臨在阿富汗的英軍身上，」一八八〇年七月二十九日的《蘇格蘭人》如此描述，它的標題是「阿富汗的災難／布洛旅的慘敗／撤往坎達哈」。約三千名英軍差點在邁萬德（Maiwand）遭帕坦人（Pathan tribesmen）殲滅。柯南．道爾對此留下了難以磨滅的印象。六年後，他開始撰寫小說《血字的研究》，場景是一八八一年的倫敦，敘事者是前軍醫華生醫生：

「我被派到第五諾森伯蘭火槍團擔任助理醫生。該團當時駐紮在印度，在我加入之前，第二次阿富汗戰爭已經爆發。當我在孟買上岸時，我聽說我的部隊已經過了隘口，深入敵境。然而，我還是跟著其他和我一樣掉隊的軍官……

「這場戰役為許多人帶來勳章與晉陞，但對我來說，這無疑是一場不幸與災難。我被調離我所屬的旅，派到伯克夏旅去，因此參與了邁萬德這場要命的戰事。我的肩膀被傑撒伊步槍的子彈擊中，骨頭碎裂，而且擦傷了鎖骨下動脈。要不是我的醫護兵莫瑞奮勇將我抬上馬背，成功將我安全送回英軍防線，恐怕我就要死在加齊人的手裡。」

返國之後，華生不知自己接下來該做什麼，他想找人合住。有人介紹合住的人給他，這個人被形容成「想法有點古怪──對科學的某些內容相當熱心」。「您好嗎？」華生在聖巴托羅繆醫院的實驗室裡遇到這個人，那人劈頭就說：「我看得出，您到過阿富汗」。這個人是夏洛克．福爾摩斯，他與華生的夥伴關係就此開始，也為柯南．道爾帶來了文學聲望與財富。

199 隔年，「希望」號的狀況遠優於「勝利者」號。根據盧伯克的 *Arctic Whalers* 第四一〇頁說法，一八八一年，「希望」號獵得九頭鯨魚、四頭瓶鼻鯨、五千隻海豹、十三頭北極熊與兩隻北極狐。反觀「勝利者」號，根據布坎的 *The Peterhead Whaling Trade* 第三十二頁指出，他們在北極浮冰中迷失。

（Sumburgh）燈塔的燈光[200]明滅閃爍，就像星星一樣。鯡魚捕得不少。看到一條巨大的逆戟鯨。

八月十一日　星期三〔D189〕

一片死寂，日照十分強烈，讓人吃不消。下午四點，看見拉特雷（Rattray）海岬。[201]海面上密密麻麻都是漁船。為返鄉而歡呼！下午六點，引水船過來了，我們於是等待漲潮，直到早上四點。在我們周圍有數百艘捕鯡魚的船隻。[202]船員們換上上岸的服裝。好了，我們已到了「希望」號日誌的尾聲，無論在平靜無風，還是暴風雨來襲，無論是豐收，還是失敗，這本日誌都完好地保存下來；每天，我都虔敬地寫下我的印象，任何讓我感到奇妙的事物我都記錄下來，並且試著把我看見的景物繪製下來。那麼，這就是

「希望」號日誌的末尾。

我們的插圖

新鮮的肉[203]

共濟會的旗子

蘭納礁石

彼得赫德捕鯨船

獵捕海豹的服裝

「希望」號四周全是稀疏的浮冰

海豹家庭

用來殺海豹的刀子

熊的足跡

船隻在海豹間就定位

用來打海豹的棍子

年輕海豹的素描

米爾納的葬禮

我們的老鷹

200 一八二一年建立的燈塔，是昔德蘭群島最古老的燈塔，位於主島南端。

201 位於亞伯丁海岸的海岬，表示「希望」號已經順利回到蘇格蘭。離彼得赫德已不到十英里。

202 事實上，鮭魚業是彼得赫德另一項重要產業。根據紀錄，在漁獲量最多的那年，在捕魚季（七月中旬到九月第一個星期）期間，總共有七百艘以上的漁船出海，在岸上則有五十多處處理漁獲的地點。那年的漁獲量是前一年的兩倍以上。

203 這些插圖，與其他柯南・道爾未列在這裡的插圖，都可以在他的日誌裡找到，但第一幅（「新鮮的肉」）卻不在日誌裡。第二幅插圖（「共濟會的旗子」）出現在第九個條目中，日期是三月七日。從手稿的內容來看，「新鮮的肉」似乎不可能代表前八個條目。而從清單的順序來看，它似乎早在描述捕鯨與捕海豹之前就已出現。或許它是某種卷頭插畫——這種標題似乎是一種悲慘的自我描述——之後他基於某種理由而故意將其去除。

星期六夜晚，在海上
迅速開了一槍
我們的夜間運動
所有船員全下船
獵海豹的地圖
折射的效果
一百碼外的五隻海豹

第二卷

獵捕老海豹
取下海豹的脂肪
不加價半買半送
推著烏合之眾的小艇
魚叉槍
在斯匹茲皐爾根島外海受八級風吹襲的「希望」號

我們未射擊的熊

格陵蘭劍魚

潛鳥或小海雀

劍魚追逐海豹群

捕捉

約翰・湯瑪斯與牠的朋友

把獨角鯨拖回船上

獨角鯨

北極海燕偷走我們的羅區鳥

第三卷

「蝕缺」號小艇的捕捉

我們的熊

熊與鯊魚吃掉獨角鯨

小艇追捕兩頭鯨魚

我們的第一頭鯨魚

鯨魚與射中牠的兩艘小艇

布坎的小艇

取下鯨魚油脂（約翰．格雷船長）

同上（大衛．格雷船長）

左邊與右邊各打下一隻潛鳥

自然冰屋

瓶鼻鯨

鯨群中的「希望」號

座頭鯨

桑普森與鯨魚

希望號的捕獲數量（續前）

七月一日　1　獨角鯨

二日

三日

四日

五日

六日　1浮冰鼠　7潛鳥　1羅區鳥　1三趾鷗　2雪鳥

七日

八日　1格陵蘭鯨

九日

十日

十一日

十二日

十三日

十四日

十五日

十六日

十七日

十八日

十九日

二十日

二十一日

二十二日

二十三日

二十四日

二十五日

二十六日

二十七日

二十八日

二十九日

三十日

三十一日

2 冠海豹

八月一日

二日

三日

四日　1　賊鷗

五日　2　絨鴨

我的捕獲數量

年輕海豹與年輕冠海豹　XXXXXXXXX．XXXXXXXXXXXXXXXX
XXXXX．XXXXXXXX

老海豹　XXXXXXXXXX．XXXXXXXXXX．XXXXXXXXX

冠海豹　XXX

潛鳥　XXXXXXXXXX．

羅區鳥　XXX

北極海燕　X

雪鳥　XX

三趾鷗　XXXX

浮冰鼠　XX

「這是一場極受歡迎的演說」柯南・道爾重臨北極

六個月結束，我們再度停泊，
小夥子全上了岸，
懷裡有錢，手中摟著美女
嗯，咱們要在酒館裡熱鬧一晚！

斟滿酒，敬格陵蘭海岸一杯，
那是我們最親近的地方；
穿過無垠的冰原，再度來到捕鯨漁場，
咱們明年再來！

〈前往格陵蘭〉（Greenland Bound，傳統船歌）

Licensed to kill

圖片鳴謝：Conan Doyle Estate Ltd.

圖片鳴謝：Surgeon's Hall Museum, Edinburgh.

柯南．道爾在船上維護船員的健康，也從事獵捕的工作。他的表現非常出色，船長格雷希望他隔年能再次參與捕鯨，他願意付他兩份薪水，也就是魚叉手加上船醫。「我這輩子從沒這麼快樂過，」柯南．道爾提到「希望」號時這麼說，但他還是選擇留在愛丁堡。一八八一年五月，他獲得第一個醫學學位——醫學士與外科碩士。完整的醫學博士需要撰寫一篇論文，這要等到一八八五年才完成，但醫學士與外科碩士的學歷已經足以讓他開始執業。他戴上學士帽，穿上學士服，煞有介事地拍了一張高貴的照片，但他也畫了一張表現自己歡欣鼓舞的素描，只見他揮舞著自己的文憑，下面的標題寫著「殺人執照」。此時，二十二歲的柯南．道爾面對人海茫茫的世界，還不知道自己要做什麼，但他至少可以靠行醫養活自己，並且改善家人的生活。

「一個二十出頭的人，一般人不會真的拿他當醫生看，」柯南．道爾在往後幾年逐漸領悟這一點，「雖然我的外表看起來比較老成，但顯然我還需要用別的方式來彌補我年齡的不足。」畢業後過了幾個月，柯南．道爾考慮了幾個職業，包括到皇家海軍服役當醫官。他也參與了另一次航行，同樣也是擔任船醫。他登上的是客輪「馬永巴」號（Mayumba），從利物浦前往西非，然後返回，時間從一八八一年十月到一八八二年一月。「我可以利用這個機會看看世界，」他寫道，「還能賺點小錢，為了開業，我非常需要這筆錢。」但到了最後，柯南．道爾變得不願意從事這方面的工作。他在寫給家人的簡單便箋裡說道，「我在非洲得了熱病，最終雖沒事，但之後又差點被鯊魚吃了。到末了，船從馬德拉（Madeira）開回英格蘭時突然起火，當時我們很可能被迫搭上救生艇划到里斯本。」

這時，他希望在大城市的醫院裡爭取到外科醫生的職位，最好是在倫敦，但競爭實在太激烈。於是，他決定到巴德醫生（也就是他在愛丁堡大學的學長，見註118）那裡碰碰運氣。巴德的事業做得有聲有色，但柯南．道爾對他不是完全沒有

一八八〇年代中葉，柯南．道爾站在他的房子前面，地址是南海城布希住宅一號（站在窗子後頭的是僕役以及他的弟弟英尼斯〔Innes〕）。從一八八二年六月到一八九〇年年底，柯南．道爾一直住在這裡，而這裡也是他執業的地方。一八八六年，他也在這裡完成第一本福爾摩斯故事。（圖片鳴謝：Conan Doyle Estate Ltd.）

疑慮。在普利茅斯，巴德宣稱他一年能賺三千英鎊；巴德說的是真的，柯南．道爾加入他的診所成為他的助理之後，也證實了這一點——但他能賺這麼多錢，也跟他從事違背醫學倫理的行為有關。柯南．道爾與巴德的合作關係只維持了六個星期，最後是在巴德的強詞奪理下結束。柯南．道爾離開後，在別的地方開了自己的診所。

柯南．道爾年輕、無經驗，在樸資茅斯也沒有認識的人，但這裡畢竟是英吉利海峽沿岸最大的城市。一八八二年六月，他搭船到樸資茅斯，在南海城住宅區租了一間房子，除了用來開業，也充當住家。「明天，我搬進我的房子，地址是厄姆格羅夫布希住宅一號，」柯南．道爾把住址告訴母親：「我身上還剩幾先令可以撐個幾天，另外要預留五英鎊當作房租。」他在寫給愛丁堡的家族朋友夏洛特．德拉蒙太太的信上，以自嘲的口吻總結了自己目前的處境：

我找了最接近市中心的屋子，抱定了破釜沉舟的決心，我為診療室購置了價值三英鎊的家具，此外，我買了一張床，一個罐頭鹹牛肉與兩個大黃銅牌子，牌子上寫了我的名字。然後，我坐在床邊，吃著罐頭鹹牛肉，就這樣過了六天。六天後，有人上門來接種疫苗。我必須付六分之二英鎊向倫敦購買疫苗，卻只能向接種疫苗的女子索求六分之一英鎊，因此我的結論是，如果我的病人越來越多，我就得賣家具了……我必須利用刷洗地板、擦皮鞋與其他勞動時間的空檔撰寫論文——偶爾偷偷地從百葉簾的細縫望出去，看看有沒有人看著我的診所門牌。

他在沒辦法填飽肚子的時候，只能避免外出：「我每晚總是熬到半夜才外出去擦亮我那兩面門牌，這樣就可以避免讓人看見，」他對他的母親說。「沒有煤氣燈——只能使用蠟燭。」儘管如此，柯南．道爾還是決心獲得成功，為了彌補他微薄的診療收入，只好靠寫作賺點錢。

不久，家人為他寄來了書籍與個人物品，剛好可以用來裝飾他的診療室。「我才剛打開箱子，頓覺這輩子從未如此驚訝，」他對母親說。「如果妳現在來看我的診療室，相信妳會感到吃驚。它看起來美輪美奐。妳寄這些東西來真是太好了。跟北極有關的物品尤其管用。」這些是從「希望」號帶下來的紀念品，在他的一八八〇年七月一日到二日的航海日誌中，曾列出這些物品。柯南．道爾可能是英格蘭南部唯一一位在診療室裡展示冠海豹骨頭的醫生。但這些與北極主題有關的物品，確實在他等待病人上門的時間裡，對他的文學創作產生了一些激勵作用，特別是在初期他的寫作遭遇瓶頸時——「我孵化了許多文學小雞，牠們到處奔走跳躍，但就是不願回巢安安靜靜地棲息下來」——結果，他在海上的經驗反而成為他文學事業首次獲得成功的關鍵。

這些創作當中，柯南．道爾的首部作品完成於一八八二年下半年，這是一部與心理學相關的靈異故事，題為〈「北極星」船長〉（The Captain of the Pole-Star），背景設在北極海上航行的一艘鬼船。以當時他的年紀來說，能寫出這樣的作品是相當了不起的。一八八三年一月，柯南．道爾在給德拉蒙太太的信上寫道：「近來，文學也為我帶來一些好處。我在一月份《聖殿闕》（*Temple Bar*）上有一篇鬼故事〈「北極星」船長〉，希望妳能給我一些意見。對方匯了十基尼與一本當月雜誌給我，我想他們應該是喜歡我的故事。」這部作品的成功，使柯南．道爾開始以非小說的方式撰寫以北極為主題的作品。「我現在正為《每日電訊報》（*Daily Telegraph*）撰寫一篇指揮船員獵捕海豹的領導者的故事——如果受歡迎的話，我會再寫一篇關於捕鯨的故事，」這回他把這件事告訴他的母親。然而，他這次的作品並不受歡迎，於是他重新回到以小說形式表現他的航海經驗，這一次他著重於汲取第二次的航海經驗，也就是西非之旅。「我把我的〈哈巴庫克．傑弗森的證言〉（Statement of J. Habakuk Jephson M. D.）寄到《康希爾》（*The Cornhill*）雜誌——祝我好運！」他在一八八三年六月十五日寫信給母親時如此說道，這天剛好是他抵達樸資茅斯滿一年的日子。經過審查之後，這篇小說——受到「瑪麗．塞勒斯特」號（Mary Celeste）的激勵，這艘船於一八七二年在東大西洋神祕地遭到遺棄，成為一艘鬼船——獲得《康希爾》採用。《康希爾》是英國最知名的文學雜誌，而雜誌編輯詹姆斯．佩恩（James Payn）也是柯南．道爾的偶像。

這部作品大獲好評，使柯南．道爾在同年秋天得以受邀參加倫敦文學界為認識《康希爾》投稿人而舉辦的盛裝晚宴，地點在格林威治的一家酒館裡，而酒館的店名剛剛好就叫作「船」。「我還記得我恭恭敬敬走到詹姆斯．佩恩面前的樣子，對我來説，他就像是聖殿門口的守護者，」柯南．道爾在《回憶與冒險》中説道——而且「我回家時腳步輕飄飄，彷佛漫步在雲端」一樣。從他返家後立即回報的語氣也可以看出這一點：「每個人都充滿魅力，我們相處得十分愉快。每個人看起來都容光煥發，可憐的我是當中的例外。」而這更激勵了柯南．道爾想在這些人當中求得一席之地的野心，他不久就表示：「今年冬天，我將在樸資茅斯文學與科學學會宣讀一篇文章——為此，我打算學習美國幽默作家的説法，但我還沒下定決心要這麼做。」

柯南．道爾住在樸資茅斯的八年半期間，當地提供了許多機會，其中尤以文學與科學學會對他意義最大，使他成為樸資茅斯的知識分子，而且引領他走向更寬廣的思想視野，使他結識來自不同階層的新朋友，甚至於讓他獲得更多的患者。柯南．道爾認識的一個新朋友是學會主席，退役少將阿弗雷德．德雷森（Alfred Drayson）。他是一名業餘的天文學家，柯南．道爾喜歡把他形容成哥白尼。德雷森也鼓勵年輕的柯南．道爾持續對通靈研究的興趣，而這將成為柯南．道爾晚年的重心。「學會給了我許多愉快與滑稽的回憶，」柯南．道爾在《回憶與冒險》中説道：

我們讓舊城的神聖火焰保持不滅，每年整個漫長的冬日，我們每週都撰寫文件進行討論。在那裡，我學會面對聽眾，而這對我這輩子的作品有著最大的影響。我天生容易緊張、膽怯、自我懷疑，當我被告知，我即將參與討論的對象是我坐的那段長凳上所有的人時，我不禁動搖了。但是，一旦起身，我學著大聲演説，隱藏我的不安，並且慎選我的措詞。

一八八三年十二月四日是柯南．道爾首次上台演説的日子，但他決定不採用美國幽默作家的路數，而是以自己的個人

Portsmouth

Literary and Scientific Society,

SESSION, 1883-4.

PENNY STREET LECTURE HALL, PORTSMOUTH.

SECOND ORDINARY MEETING

WILL BE HELD

On TUESDAY, DEC. 4th, 1883, at 7.45 p.m.

Paper by

ARTHUR CONAN DOYLE, Esq., M.B.C.M.:—

"THE ARCTIC SEAS."

SYNOPSIS.

What has been done there.—What remains to be done.—The Expedition of 1876.—Leigh Smith's Expedition.—The Commercial Aspect of the Question.—The Seal Fishery.—The Whale Fishery.—Life in the Arctic Circle.

The favour of your attendance is much desired.
Ladies are invited to attend.

J. WARD COUSINS, Hon. Sec.

「這應該會是一場精采的演說，」這張告示上列的大綱，顯示柯南．道爾如何組織他的想法：「我們在那兒做了什麼—我們還應該做什麼—一八七六年的探險—李．史密斯的探險—問題的商業面向—捕海豹業—捕鯨業—北極圈的生活。」照片是柯南．道爾自己保留的告示複本。（圖片鳴謝：Conan Doyle Estate Ltd.）

經驗來選擇主題。他在《回憶與冒險》中說道，考慮了一段時間：

> 我寫了三篇文章，一篇是談北極海，一篇是談卡萊爾，最後一篇是談吉朋（Gibbon）。第一篇使我得到名實不符的讚賞，人們把我當成了不起的冒險家。因為我從樸資茅斯專門製作標本的師傅那裡，借來了各種在北極圈出現的鳥類與野獸標本。我把這些標本擺滿講桌，聽眾可能以為這些全是我獵到的，因此紛紛用尊敬的眼神看著我。第二天早上，這些人又為了看這些標本而來聽第二次演說。

「這應該會是一場精采的演說，」柯南．道爾在此之前對德拉蒙太太表示，而德拉蒙太太也從遙遠的地方給予支援，她寄了一套像樣的服裝給柯南．道爾，讓他穿著這套衣服上台，給聽者留下好印象。柯南．

道爾對結果感到很高興。「如果我不回信告訴妳，我穿這件襯衫上台會令我多高興，那我簡直是個惡棍，」他在演說前一兩天回信給德拉蒙太太：

但妳知道的，我一直是個性格乖僻的通信者，事實上，過去一個多星期以來，我一直埋首工作，對一切充耳不聞。這件襯衫也是個傑作。我有一根黑檀木與白銀製成的手杖，這是我贏得的戰利品，現在搭配上襯衫，讓我覺得自己不只是一個調情求愛的輕浮之輩——而是個講究儀表的人。

演說已經準備就緒……我的確希望它能成功。若能如此，我的名字將在那些有頭有臉的人物之間流傳。我有一群強悍的單身朋友，他們全副武裝，堅守陣地，準備在最後給予我最熱烈的掌聲。

柯南．道爾〈北極海〉的主旨是抵達北極的渴望，以及柯南．道爾認為怎麼做才能抵達北極。在樸資茅斯文學與科學學會一八八三年的紀錄簿中——現保存於樸資茅斯中央圖書館——有三份報紙提到柯南．道爾十二月四日在便士街演講廳（Penny Street Lecture Hall）發表的演說，其中報導得最全面的是八日的《漢普夏電訊報》：

〈北極海〉

柯南．道爾醫生宣讀了這份以北極海為主題的稿子。一開始，講者提到，雖然上個世紀我們對世界的認識有很大的進展，但未來的旅人與地理學家還有很多工作要做。環繞著北極有兩百五十萬平方英里的土地人跡未至，而在南極地區，這片

退役少將阿弗雷德·德雷森。（圖片鳴謝：Morgan Family History Blog.）

廣大神祕的南方大陸仍覆蓋在冰層之下。從西藏高原到澳洲內陸的礫石平原，從非洲大湖到中美洲疏林草原，地圖上這些尚未探索的空白地帶，成了科學界的恥辱，並且對人類的冒險心構成挑戰。逐漸地，在經過一段時間後，「未知之地」的疆界不斷萎縮後撤，也許是因為商業與文明的緩慢推進，也許是憑藉一些大膽的旅人，他們的足跡如流星般劃進了毫無人跡的黑暗地帶。然而，這個探索的過程是緩慢的，他們將會把自己的發現傳承給子孫，然而待解的自然之謎並不比已解開的部分來得少。不過，由於設備的進步與交通工具的進展，後人終能突破先人的局限，解開各種謎團。在所有漫長而驚心動魄的旅行紀錄與發現史中，最具戲劇性的就是人類前往北極的奮鬥過程。過去這兩百年來，許多人前仆後繼地投入這項冒險事業，其中的艱辛困難，即使是鐵石心腸也會為之動容。這則故事讀來並不令人感到愉快。它是希望落空、行動失敗的真實紀錄；沉沒的船隻、饑餓、壞血病、物資缺乏，最後成為極北昏暗之地的一座孤墳。然而，這當中也有光明的一面，因為這份紀錄不也表彰著不屈不撓的意志，完美的自我克制與投入，激發出人性中崇高與神聖的特質？人們接二連三競相前往，他們為了公眾的利益而犧牲小我，為了科學的進展而甘冒生命危險，這充分顯示人性遠比悲觀主義者所想的來得高貴許多。道爾醫生描述了北極海，其中絕大部分來自他的親身體驗。他也依序介紹了戴維斯、巴芬、哈德遜、帕里（Parry）與其他人努力前往北極的故事，並且描述這一連串探險中最精采的部分。

談到英國在一八七五年的探險，道爾表示這個世代的英國船員，不僅將他們的船開到大西洋對岸與歐陸的船隻尚未抵達的地方，也超越了自己祖先的成績。有人喜歡說「一代不如一代」，但這一代的英國船員充分證明，與老一輩相比，他們毫不遜色，即使是最一味「憧憬過去年代」的人，也無法忽視一個鐵一般的事實，那就是新一代的船員已經來到過去的船員從未到達過的緯度。近年來，已經有某個文明開化之人前進到離北極三百九十九又二分之一英里內的範圍。他是否能抵達北極呢？他沒有理由懷疑；問題在於接下來三百九十英里的路程是否跟他先前橫越的海況一樣嚴酷貧瘠。他傾向於認為不是如此，而且堅信在過了某一點後，隨著他們越接近北極，氣溫將會回升。他知道這個想法會遭受許多偉大的北極權威的嘲弄，但在此同時，也有許多一輩子都在這個海域捕鯨的船長支持這個論點。在支持他的論點中，有個說法是莫頓提出的，[1] 他親眼看到開闊的洋面，即使海面出現浮冰，也因為季節而有所變化，時而縮減，時而擴大。然後浮冰會一致地往南方漂移，因此在北極正中央一定會出現無冰的空間，而且地球並非完美的球體，在兩極稍微平坦一點，因此兩極離地心的距離會比其他地表近，這個

1 威廉．莫頓（William Morton）曾經參與兩次（一八五〇年與一八五三年）由亨利．格林內爾（Henry Grinnell）贊助的美國探險隊，前去解救約翰．弗蘭克林爵士船長。他於一八五七年出版了《康恩醫生的北極航行》（*Dr. Kane's Arctic Voyage: Explanatory of a pictorial illustration of the second Grinnell expedition*）（格林內爾贊助的第二次探險是由康恩醫生〔Elisha Kent Kane〕帶領的）。

差異應該不難察覺出來。越接近地心——例如在煤礦坑或其他地方——溫度越高，因此，不難推知極地附近應該會獲得較多地心的熱能，因此補足了日光溫度的不足。道爾醫生在描述了捕鯨與其他有關北極海的軼聞之後，他問道，他最初提的想法是否正確，而事情照他的說法來進行是不是最有可能成功？這些問題當然都可以討論，但從事實來看，北極海所有的浮冰都往南移動，如果檢視這些海域的地理，那麼我們首先會發現史密斯海峽（Smith's Sound）與甘迺迪海峽（Kennedy Channel）都極不適合充當通往高緯度地區的通道。為什麼寧可選擇它們，而不願選擇格陵蘭與斯匹茲卑爾根島之間的廣闊海域呢？這裡明明有寬敞的航道，浮冰之間也有足夠的空隙可以通過。然而道爾醫生坦承，如果冬天嚴寒，而夏天僅是微溫，那麼幾乎不可能有成功的機會，然而要是情況相反，他認為這條水道絕對是較佳的選擇。倘若政府希望抵達北極，那麼他們必須不惜經費，委託適合的本國船隻，僱用充滿豪情壯志的那些退休領半薪的軍官前往。讓船隻每年出航，在六月中出發，往北走到浮冰構成的障礙時，改用蒸汽引擎繼續前進，並且避免船隻陷入浮冰之中。兩個月後，他們可能無功而返，但讓他們來年繼續出航，下一年也是。遲早他們總會遇到暖和的季節，或強烈的北風吹襲，讓浮冰四散漂移。此時就有機會，在浮冰之間出現水道，這時候只要以連續兩天使用蒸汽引擎往北行駛，應該就能到達北極。他認為政府至少應提供三萬英鎊作為發現北極的獎金，[2] 而雖然有人質疑抵達北極的好處，但他的回應是，這是一種褊狹的想法，因為抵達北極可以提振國家的精神與自尊。經濟學家與功利主義者愛怎麼說是他們的事，但道爾醫生認為，當那天到來時（他相信終有這麼一天），當他們所愛的旗幟在地球極北的端點升起時，自豪與歡欣的光輝將會填滿偉大盎格魯撒克遜民族的心靈。

2 「政府提供的五千英鎊獎金對捕鯨人來說完全沒有誘惑力，」他說，根據《漢普夏郵報》十二月七日的描述，「每捕到一頭鯨魚可以賣一千英鎊。他認為獎金應提高到三萬英鎊。」

學會主席[3]投票感謝講者，並且表示讓他印象深刻的是道爾醫生說的，有個通往北極的廣闊水域。他自己也有相同的想法。他不太同意兩極因為離地心較近所以溫度較高的說法，他認為越接近地心溫度越高只是過去理論家提出的假設性說法。主席也想知道講者對一些問題的看法，例如靜態氣球是否有用，他認為利用氣球或許會比現在這種盲目尋找路線的做法更能早日發現水道。另一個有趣的思考是如果發現北極，那麼能帶來什麼好處？嗯，關於這點，恐怕只有真正發現北極之後才能揭曉吧！（眾人同意。）主席也認同講者說的，每年都進行嘗試的做法。——榮譽祕書[4]也投道爾醫生一票，他說，很少有人到北極探險，但每年卻有兩、三百人致力於尋找西北航道。尋找北極的人之所以數量如此稀少，原因就在於是否具有商業利益。他支持主席的意見，認為探險確實能帶來巨大的好處。（眾人同意。）知識就是力量，生理學特別能從這類探險中獲益。有一項重要事實已經獲得證明，那就是在北極海的嚴寒氣候下，即使不靠酒精也能忍受得了低溫（眾人同意），因此戒酒的人不能再拿天氣冷作為無法戒酒的理由。——牧師科爾本博士（Colbourne）表示，他相信在高緯度的極地地區有煤礦的存在，若是如此，在過去的某個年代，當地的氣溫一定比現在高得多，才能讓構成煤礦的植物得以生長。同樣地，格陵蘭當地的住民又是從什麼地方來的？——他們是殘存的原住民嗎？——這些問題在當時就獲得了解答。道爾醫生回應說，格陵蘭與斯匹茲卑爾根島發現了煤礦，而且也有證據顯示過去當地的氣溫曾經非常高，但科學家的研究成果仍無法對這個主題提出非常堅實而無可動搖的結論。至於原住民的問題，道爾醫生認為科學界已有共識，認為幾千年前全歐洲都居住著愛斯基摩人。

3 阿弗雷德．德雷森少將。

4 考辛斯醫生（J. Ward Cousins），皇家外科醫生學會會員。

但愛斯基摩人逐漸受到更高等文明的壓迫，而慢慢遭到征服。至於利用靜態氣球觀測的問題，他認為這是個很棒的點子[5]（眾人同意）。——會議於是結束。

「演說結束——謝天謝地！這是個令人承受不起的驚人成功，」柯南．道爾在給母親的信上寫道：「演說受歡迎的程度，遠超過我的夢想或我大膽希求的狀況。從第一個字到最後一個字，聽眾（現場座無虛席，可以說擠得水泄不通[6]）緊緊跟隨著，每個字都不願聽漏了，而且我經常在中途被聽眾的歡呼聲打斷。當演說結束時，現場響起如雷的掌聲——無異議地投票通過，表示感謝之意，其他講者也一一評論，這是他們聽過『最精采的演說』、『最棒的演說』、『文字最優美的演說』。這是一場極受歡迎的演說。」

這場演說是柯南．道爾在南海生活的轉捩點，使他重獲自信，且再度燃起了事業的野心。相隔了一個月，柯南．道爾出版了〈哈巴庫克．傑弗森的證言〉，這部作品相當受到好評。雖然作品依照《康希爾》雜誌的慣例並未署名，但稿酬令他相當滿意，一共是二十九基尼。這篇小說得到許多人的注意，有批評家認為這是出自羅伯特．路易斯．史帝文森的手筆，還有人認為這部作品可以媲美埃德加．愛倫．坡的《亞瑟．戈登．皮姆的故事》（*Narrative of Arthur Gordon Pym*）。「好日子就要到來了，」他向

5　事實上，根據十二月五日《樸資茅斯時報》的報導，道爾最後講了一個哄堂大笑的笑話，為演說畫下完美的句點：「他完全同意可以使用氣球，而且認為人可以坐在氣球上越過北極，然後再由船隻從海中將他救起。然而，他建議這樣的探險家事前最好先買保險（眾人笑）。」這則笑話講得恰到好處；在當時，「他為了賺外快，因此在格雷沙姆人壽保險公司（Gresham Life Assurance Company）擔任醫檢員，他甚至偶爾會為這家公司撰寫廣告文宣。*Arthur Conan Doyle: A Life in Letters* 第一九九－二〇一頁。

6　根據已故的斯塔弗特（Geoffrey Stavert）的作品 *A Study in Southsea: The Unrevealed Life of Doctor Arthur Conan Doyle* (Portsmouth: Milestone Publication, 1987) 第四十五頁的說法，蒞臨現場的有兩百五十名女士與先生。

母親保證。「我們獲得每個人的讚譽、尊敬與喜愛，而且就我所知，並沒有人討厭我們，因此我們一定會成功。」

柯南．道爾在這個時期完成的最有名小說——〈「北極星」船長〉與〈哈巴庫克．傑弗森的證言〉——結合了他的海上經驗與愛倫．坡的說故事技巧。閱讀他這個時期的作品，不難看出夏洛克．福爾摩斯的出現只是時間的問題。四年後，柯南．道爾依然同時兼顧醫療與文學事業，他開始撰寫偵探小說《血字的研究》，故事中的華生醫生與福爾摩斯很快就成為讀者心目中不朽的角色。然而，柯南．道爾前兩部以福爾摩斯為主角的中篇小說並未引起當時讀者的興趣，因此身為作家與醫生的他，眼前還有很長一段路要走。而他在結婚組成家庭之後，開始撰寫歷史小說《麥卡．克拉格》（*Micah Clarke*）與《白色軍隊》（*The White Company*）。

一八九一年，柯南．道爾搬到倫敦，成為眼科的執業醫生，在此之前，他曾到維也納與巴黎進行短期進修。柯南．道爾仍想在醫療上開創出自己的事業，而即便他努力鑽研成為一名合格的專科醫生時，他也仍持續撰寫小說。他又給了福爾摩斯一次機會，這回是以短篇小說的形式呈現。他的前兩篇福爾摩斯小說分別在七月與八月號的《河濱雜誌》刊出，突然間，柯南．道爾成為家喻戶曉的作家，而這也使他決定棄醫從文。然而，即使獲得這個新的名聲，柯南．道爾依然對北極地帶念念不忘。「那個地方的氣候實在太特別了！」訪談這位文學新星的人興致盎然地記下他說的話：「我們不了解北極。我指的不是它的寒冷——而是它的衛生。我相信，未來幾年，北極地區會成為世界知名的療養院。在這個遠離煙霧數千英里之處，擁有全世界最清新的空氣，傷殘病弱之人可以在這裡呼吸到其他地方沒有的空氣，並且在極地的大氣之下重新恢復精力。」

柯南．道爾利用他剛獲得的名聲地位宣揚他的理念。一八九二年七月，〈北極的魅力〉刊登在《遊手好閒》（*The Idler*）雜誌上，內容賡續他在樸資茅斯文學與科學學會宣讀的文章，提到前往北極的方法，並且獲得挪威探險家斯提芬森

（Vilhjalmur Stefansson）的讚揚，兩人還結為終身好友。「柯南·道爾不只是比較強壯的華生與比較仁慈的福爾摩斯。他也是比較溫和的奈傑爾爵士（Nigel），而且是他筆下所有高貴人物的綜合體，」斯提芬森於一九二三年五月三日在《展望》（*The Outlook*）雜誌上寫下這些頌詞。「親愛的斯提芬森，」一九二〇年，柯南·道爾結束在澳洲的心靈主義演說後寫道，「我們的任務真是古怪！你講的是馴鹿，我講的是無實體的精神，兩者都是巨大整體的一部分。」我們不清楚斯提芬森是否分享了柯南·道爾的心靈主義，不過他發表於《展望》的文章倒是顯示出支持的看法；無論如何，兩人都承認彼此是有決心、敢於探索未知地帶的探險家。

五年後，柯南·道爾在一八九七年一月號的《河濱雜誌》上發表了一篇個人經歷的描述——〈格陵蘭捕鯨船上的生活〉。他在文章中提到與勤務員傑克·蘭姆打拳的故事，而蘭姆告訴大副柯林·麥克林，柯南·道爾是「希望」號歷來最好的醫生，因為他把蘭姆的眼睛打青了。這篇文章受到整個英語世界的歡迎，一九二四年，柯南·道爾重新修改這篇文章，成為他的自傳《回憶與冒險》的一章。在家鄉的《彼得赫德前哨》（*Peterhead Sentinel*）寫道：

> 無疑地，柯南·道爾醫生一定有興趣知道，柯林·麥克林與傑克·蘭姆都尚在人世。前者一如以往在十一月時結束捕鯨返港，他現在在一艘鄧迪捕鯨船上擔任船副。他跟過去一樣健壯，但他談到將會放棄捕鯨，在彼得赫德定居，因為他的眼睛已不像一八八〇年那樣銳利。他依然記得一八八〇年「希望」號上打拳的船醫；當我們把《河濱雜誌》刊出的照片拿給他看時，他可以毫無困難地指出道爾醫生與其他船員。此外，他對醫生的體格讚譽有加，正如醫生讚美他的體格一樣，但柯林對於醫生在冰原上步行的能力則是評價甚低。關於傑克·蘭姆，這位擁有優美歌喉、強健胸膛與愛打拳的勤務員，道

爾醫生的猜測完全正確。無疑地，格陵蘭對他而言就跟過去那位「希望」號船醫一樣，是一個夢想；他現在已經回到自己的本行，成為女王重要的烘焙師傅，無論女王到哪裡，他都必須隨行。如果道爾醫生在秋天偶然造訪迪賽德高地（Deeside Highlands），或者更好的是，如果他能花一兩個小時到溫莎看看，傑克．蘭姆與他的妻子家人住在這裡，他可以來此跟老朋友敘舊。傑克的傷感小曲肯定又增加了不少，但面對老友，搞不好他會開心得忘了「她明媚的笑容仍在我腦海中繚繞著」或「甜美的貝兒．瑪紅，請在天堂門前等我」該怎麼唱。他們也許又會戴起拳套，一起較量一番。

柯南．道爾經常在公開場合提到他搭乘「希望」號進行的北極之旅，偶爾，他會從讀者或聽眾口中得到一些消息。一九〇〇年一月二十三日，即使《每日郵報》（*Daily Mail*）報導作家俱樂部為他餞行——柯南．道爾將以志願軍醫的身分前往南非治療波耳戰爭的傷兵——當時完全未提到北極航行的事，他還是發現有人留意到這件事。倫敦皇家艾伯特碼頭船運協會的詹姆斯．布朗（James Brown）說：

> 雖然你不認識我，但我可是聽聞與閱讀了很多關於你的報導。我過去曾是彼得赫德的船長，我認識約翰．格雷船長、柯林．坎貝爾〔（Colin Campbell）原文如此〕船副，以及當你在「希望」號上擔任船醫時船上所有的船員。而且我擔任船副時，也跟這些人共事過。我讀到今天的《每日郵報》，知道你昨晚在作者俱樂部的餞行晚宴上致詞，我特別寫信給你，祝你一帆風順，旅途平安。

柯南．道爾想起來他是「上風」號的船長，他曾於一八九六年在南森嘗試前往北極失敗後，帶南森平安返回挪威。柯南．道爾將這封信，連同傑克．蘭姆寄給他的信，小心保存在文件裡。

北極探險的經驗也影響了福爾摩斯的故事。柯南．道爾的日誌倒數第二個條目提到了邁萬德戰爭，他從第一篇小說開始就把華生派到當地，此外，在其他小說裡也提到了水手與船隻的外觀，以及各式各樣的航海主題。「除了雜要人員或水手，沒有人能攀上那條敲鐘索，除了水手，沒有人能打出那樣的繩結，」福爾摩斯曾在一件案子裡說出這句名言。「他的臉瘦削、黝黑，看起來詭計多端，」華生在另一篇小說裡記錄著，「他的手滿是皺紋，那是水手才有的手。」在《黑彼得懸案》（*The Adventure of Black Peter*）中，一個名叫彼得．凱瑞（Peter Carey）的捕鯨船長死狀極慘，他的胸部遭魚叉貫穿——「就像釘在紙板上的甲蟲一樣」。在描述凱瑞的惡形惡狀時，柯南．道爾不僅援引了自己的捕鯨知識，也微妙地呼應了他過去認識的彼得赫德船副，以及他們與鄧迪人的對抗：我們得知，可憎的凱瑞原來是鄧迪人。

就連柯南．道爾的詩也回憶著他年輕時的冒險經驗。〈給年輕作者的忠告〉（Advice to a Young Author）這首輕鬆活潑的詩作發表於一九一一年，裡面以航海的方式來表現：

一開始
先收集。
貨囤好，
運上船，
多思考

再下筆。
腦袋空空，
多寫無益！

這段忠告用來與布倫（Frank Thomas Bullen）交好與惕厲是再適合不過的了，布倫年輕時到處漂泊，曾經在麻州新貝德福德（New Bedford）一艘捕鯨船上長期航行——他把這段經驗寫下來，成為一八九八年的暢銷作品——《抹香鯨的巡遊》（*The Cruise of the Cachelot*），這是布倫描述海上生活的第一部作品。布倫把他一九〇一年完成的小說獻給柯南．道爾，而柯南．道爾則是在《穿過魔法之門》讚賞《抹香鯨》及其作者，「獵捕抹香鯨，在廣闊的洋面作業，與我擔任七個月學徒期間在格陵蘭的浮冰中摸索出路，感覺完全不同。描寫這段經驗的是最具活力的作家，他刻畫的是真正的海上生活」。一九一四年，他為布倫編輯的船歌集寫序，他說：

> 跟你一樣，我聽過這些歌曲無數次，我們總是和著歌曲的旋律，努力划著沉重的捕鯨艇朝吊柱而去。悠揚的歌曲幫了我們大忙，只要隨著主旋律划，不知不覺地感到輕鬆許多。近日來，我對於蒸汽絞盤的出現感到憂心，以後恐怕再也看不到十名船員同心協力拉繩放下小艇的景象。但是，你的作品將協助保存這個景象，對於那些知道與親身經歷此事的人來說，從你的粗魯而充滿活力的每一行韻文裡，彷彿都能聞到那一道道帶著鹹味的水氣柱。[7]

7 引自 Frank T. Bullen, F. R. G. S., and W. F. Arnold, *Songs of Sea Labour* (London: Orpheus, 1914)。

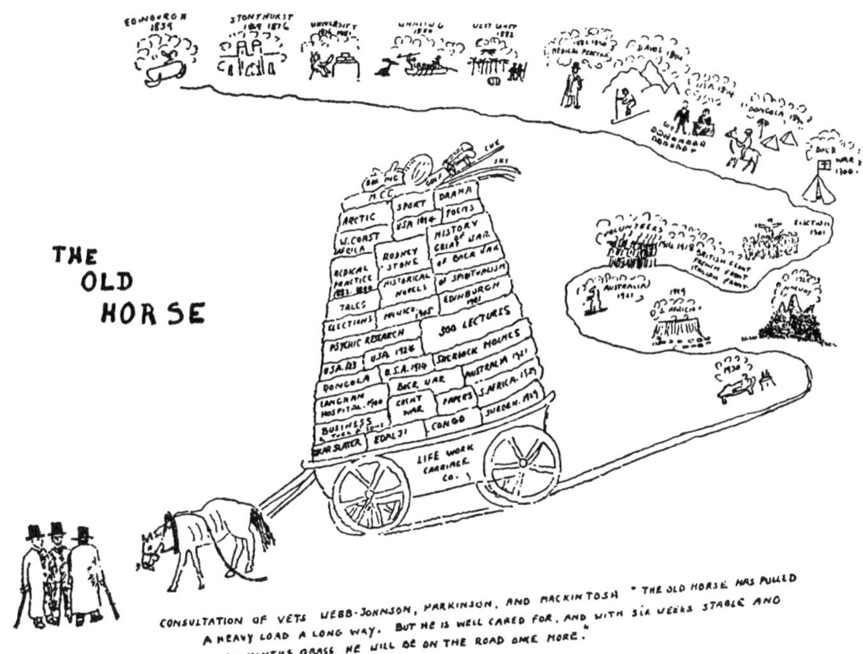

圖片鳴謝：Conan Doyle Estate Ltd.

布倫「是我所聽過最棒的船歌歌手」，柯南．道爾在一九二一年的旅行文學《心靈主義者的漂泊》（*The Wanderings of a Spiritualist*）中如此說道，而他也描述自己在海上看見矢嘲鶇與抹香鯨時，「又喚醒了內心那股捕鯨的悸動。」

新貝德福德捕鯨博物館（New Bedford Whaling Museum）館長史都華．弗蘭克（Stuart Frank）提醒我們，柯南．道爾與赫曼．梅爾維爾（Herman Melville）是唯一兩位親身捕過鯨的偉大作家，他們描述的十九世紀捕鯨故事，是貨真價實的一手經驗。直到一九三〇年過世為止，北極航行的經驗一直是柯南．道爾回憶時最念念不忘與記憶鮮明的部分。他在去世前幾年寫道：「極地地區有一股魅力，凡是進入其中的人莫不受其感染影響。我的心一直惦記著那位頭髮斑白的老船長，他在臨終前，突然自己下床，穿著睡衣蹣跚地走著，最後被護士發現他走到屋外很遠的地方，嘴裡念念有詞，『往北走』。」柯南．道爾死前不久曾畫了一張奇怪的素描，稱為「老馬」。他把自己描繪成一匹疲憊不堪的馬，這匹馬身後拉的貨車，上面裝著他忙碌而進取的人生所累積的貨物——「醫療工作」、「福爾摩斯」、「歷史小說」以及更多更多，而在這堆貨物的最頂端則是「北極地區」。在背景裡，沿著蜿蜒的小徑，他描繪了其他的里程碑，其中包括一船魚叉手獵捕著鯨魚。

一九三〇年七月七日，柯南．道爾在家人陪伴下於家中去世。最後，他也「不斷地朝北方走去」。

強．雷能柏格與丹尼爾．史塔蕭爾

亞瑟·柯南·道爾

關於北極的作品

北極的魅力

編輯說明：柯南·道爾這篇文章刊登在一八九二年七月號的《遊手好閒》雜誌上。這本暢銷雜誌是由他的朋友羅伯特·巴爾（Robert Barr）與傑洛姆（Jerome K. Jerome）創立的，柯南·道爾投稿時，該雜誌正值創刊第一年。之後，一八九四年三月，本文又刊載於美國的《麥克魯爾雜誌》（*McClure's Magazine*，柯南·道爾自己也是這家出版社的股東）。一八八三年十二月，柯南·道爾在樸資茅斯文學與科學學會演說時，提到北極以及前往北極的過程，當時他還是個為錢所苦的醫生，文學事業也尚未開展。但到了一八九〇年代，柯南·道爾已因為創作了福爾摩斯這個角色而成為著名作家。名氣所及，他撰寫過的北極作品也重獲大眾關注。這篇文章提到的一些細節，日後在他一九二四年寫成的自傳《回憶與冒險》中又加以引用。

在大不列顛，如果有這麼一群人，他們絕大多數從孩提時期開始，就未曾見過田裡的穀物，那麼我們一定認為這是件怪事。然而，彼得赫德的捕鯨人就是如此。他們很早，也許從他們還是個男孩開始，就像一般船員一樣過著艱困的生活。

而從那時起，他們會在每年二月底離家，那時田野上的作物還沒開始萌芽，然後他們會在九月時返鄉，那時田地上只剩收割過的殘株。我曾經見過許多老捕鯨人，也跟他們說過話，對這些人來說，麥穗竟是件不可思議的東西，值得讓他們悉心收藏。

這些人從事的行業，既古老又值得榮耀。曾有一段時期，格陵蘭附近的洋面有多國船隻交相侵擾著，巴斯克人（Basque）與比斯開人（Biscayan）是技術非凡的捕鯨人，荷蘭人、漢薩城邦（Hansatown）的漁民、西班牙人與不列顛人，全加入這場鯨魚大獵殺。然後，隨著民族能量或工業資本的減退，各國的實力一個接一個減弱，一直到本世紀初，才由赫爾（Hull）、普爾（Poole）與利物浦成為三大捕鯨港。但是捕鯨業的重心不久又開始轉移。斯科斯比是英國最後一位偉大的船長，從他開始，捕鯨業就逐漸往北轉移，直到格陵蘭洋面的捕鯨業完全被彼得赫德獨占為止。彼得赫德唯有在獵捕海豹方面與鄧迪平分秋色，而且也使用挪威的船隊捕鯨。但現在，唉！捕鯨業已經日薄西山，彼得赫德的船到南極海洋尋找新的出路，而在歷史上以勇敢與耐勞著稱的彼得赫德漁民也將成為歷史。

之所以如此，並不是因為彼得赫德的年輕一代比上一代不願吃苦或技術較差，也不是因為格陵蘭鯨面臨滅絕的危險。真正的理由是自然，這些鯨魚雖然手無寸鐵，但老天卻給了牠們聰明的腦袋。鯨魚無疑了解人類是用什麼方法獵捕牠們。鯨魚在被魚叉射中之後，普遍會潛到浮冰下方，前後來回地游動，利用浮冰尖銳的邊緣來切斷魚繩。然而，就某種程度來說，鯨魚也了解牠的敵人力量有限，藉由藏身於遙遠的冰原之中，即使是最大無畏的追捕者也無能為力。逐漸地，鯨魚遠離了開闊的海洋，越來越深居於浮冰界線以北的區域。現在，終於，鯨魚只出現在遙不可及的覓食地帶，桅杆的瞭望者再也看不到噴得高高的氣柱，以及令人怦然心動的巨大黑色尾鰭在海面上揮動的樣子。

然而，如果一個人運氣夠好，剛好在他面前出現了一頭「衰落」的鯨魚，更重要的是，如果這個人——我曾經有這樣的經驗——剛好在魚叉與長矛小艇上時，那麼此時他會產生非獵到不可的心態，這樣的決心可不是鯨魚所能輕易擺脫的。釣鮭魚是件高尚的活動，但如果你的魚重量超過一棟市郊別墅，價值足足有兩千英鎊，此外你手上的魚繩有一根拇指粗，是用五十條馬尼拉繩纏起來的，每一條馬尼拉繩都能承重三十六英磅，那麼與這樣的經驗相比，其他的釣魚活動根本算不了什麼。長矛也是，當鯨魚筋疲力盡的時候，你把小艇划近一點，用冰冷的鋼鐵給牠最後一擊，那是令人興奮的一刻！重達一百噸充滿絕望的生物在水中攪拌出紅色的泡沫，兩片巨大的鰭高舉又落下，宛如風車的巨大翼板，當它們低垂時，小艇也籠罩在它們的陰影之下，但魚叉手依然緊握著射中頭部的長矛，當他在這個位置時，鯨魚並不能對他構成任何傷害。十二英尺長的矛，底部的木托抵著魚叉手的肚子。魚叉手努力將長矛刺得更深，直到這場長期的爭鬥結束，黑色的背部翻轉過去，露出青灰泛白的腹部。然而，就在大家亢奮歡呼的時刻——沒有人不拿起手中的槳揮舞著表達內心的興奮——這頭可憐的遭到獵捕的生物卻值得同情。鯨魚的眼睛很小，只不過比公牛的眼睛稍微大一點；我無法輕易忘記我在一頭鯨魚眼中看見的無言抗議，我只要一伸手就能觸摸到牠，而牠的眼睛隨著死亡的逼近而漸漸黯淡無光。可憐的生物，牠如何能猜到供需法則，或者，牠如何想像得到，當自然在牠的嘴裡安裝了具有彈性的濾器，[1]當人類發現用鯨鬚製成的物品極具彈性而且耐用時，牠的死亡證明書就已簽下。

當然，這是捕鯨時唯一獵取的物種，牠也是鯨魚中非常罕見的物種。常見的鬚鯨或長鬚鯨，是世界上最大的生物，牠

1　譯註：指的應該是鯨鬚。

們擺動著身上長達八十英尺毫無價值的鯨油在捕鯨船旁遊蕩，對牠們而言，任何魚叉就像小麵包一樣，起不了威脅的作用。鬚鯨一如牠們同樣毫無商業價值的遠親座頭鯨，在北極海域數量極為豐富，我曾經在晴朗的日子裡，看見牠們在遙遠海平面上噴出的氣柱，宛如繁忙工廠的煙囪噴出的煙霧一樣。同樣奇異的景象是，從船邊看著清澈的海水，可以看見深處的綠色身影逐漸變黑變大，若隱若現的鯨魚在船底下悄悄地游著。然後是詭異的呼嚕聲，一陣又像嘆氣又像哭泣的噪音隨著鯨魚傳來，聽起來像是牠們體內有隻感到滿足的豬，又像是風在煙囪裡通過的聲音！這些鬚鯨確實是應該感到滿足，因為牠們沒有敵人，除了偶然看見的劍魚。而大自然似乎對於露脊鯨獨具幽默感，它讓這個全世界最大的動物擁有最小的咽喉，但卻讓牠價值較低的兄弟[2]能一口吞下大量的東西，好讓牠能在鯡魚群中大快朵頤。

在許多書籍裡，總會看見英勇的船員站在小艇的船頭，他將魚叉高舉過頭，用力揮舞著，在他身後則是如蛇身般纏繞的魚叉繩。這些書籍，現在只能在帕特諾斯特街[3]找到。格陵蘭海域已經有一百多年沒出現過這樣的捕鯨人，因為首先而且明顯的現象是，使用魚叉槍要比用手投擲魚叉來得強勁而精確。然而，人總是執著於嬰兒時期的理想，我希望下一個世紀，書籍的卷頭插畫依然能以英勇的船員為主題，讓他繼續不可一世地揮舞著魚叉，射出遠超過人力所及的距離。迴旋的魚叉槍，就像特大號的馬槍一樣，使用巨大的填絮與二十八德拉姆的火藥粉，這種武器遠比徒手來得可靠，但表現在圖畫上卻無法那麼生動。

2　譯註：指的應是之前的鬚鯨。

3　譯註：Paternoster Row，二戰前倫敦著名的出版與書店街。

不過，用魚叉槍瞄準也是需要技術的，你想想，魚繩綁在魚叉的頸上，魚叉射出去，連帶拉著繩子出去，在這種狀況下，魚叉飛行的軌跡一定會曲折。所以，要用魚叉槍瞄準是很困難的，因此捕鯨業的行規，都會讓魚叉小艇直接朝著鯨魚駛去，然後用船頭斜頂上鯨魚柔軟略帶斜度的部位，讓船頭維持抬高的角度，再由魚叉手朝鯨魚寬闊的背部射擊，通常長四英尺的魚叉，以及後頭長十英尺的魚繩，都會沒入鯨魚體內。接下來，鯨魚是否會高高舉起尾鰭，像那幅古老的畫一樣，拍打捕鯨人的小艇呢？慶幸的是，當鯨魚受驚或受傷時，牠不會做出上述的行為，相反地，牠會把尾鰭捲到身體底部，就像喪家之犬一樣，然後如石頭般沉入水中。斜靠在鯨魚身上的船頭隨之落到水面，魚叉手站穩腳步，船員們則點起菸斗，打開雙腳，讓魚繩從船的正中間經由船首拉向海中。繩子的長度是兩英里，旁邊還有第二艘船待命，準備在繩子不夠時接上另一捆繩子，因此，繩子的末端總是鬆綁著，以便於接繩。

接下來是捕鯨時面臨的一個重大危險。魚繩在潮溼的狀態下很容易糾結在一起，因此當繩子被拖完時，很容易在船裡面打圈，然後颼的一下把人的腿捲起來。就有人曾被套索纏住雙腿拖入海中，魚叉手才剛喊出「賈克在哪？」那人早已在海中五十節的深處。或者，如果套索纏住的是小艇，那麼小艇就會像鱒魚線上的軟木一樣，艇上的人穿著捕鯨長靴若還能在水中游泳自如，一定是個游泳健將。許多鯨魚會用這種方式報復捕鯨人。幾年前，有人被繩圈纏住了大腿。「我的天啊，艾歷克被拖走了！」小艇舵手大叫，準備舉起斧頭砍斷繩索。但魚叉手抓住他的手腕。「別砍，」他叫道，「魚油錢對逝者來說可是好東西。」雖然艾歷克在這可怕的旅程中跌入海裡而喪生，但魚油錢已經安排好了。

鯨油的利潤是這些船員瘋狂投入這個行業的原因。當船員真的發現自己能捕到鯨魚時，他們會日夜不斷地工作，儘管所謂夜間工作不過是做做樣子而已，但他們仍樂此不疲。因為高級船員與普通船員的薪水都不高，他們真正仰賴的是鯨油的利潤，唯有捕到鯨魚，他們才可能衣錦還鄉。就連新加入的菜鳥每噸也都能分到一先令，因此，如果取得一百噸的鯨油，他就能額外分到五英鎊。船上實際施行的比較像是社會主義，而且比船員想像的更不民主。船長管船副，船副管魚叉手，魚叉手管小艇舵手，小艇舵手管纜繩手，以此層層節制，直到普通船員為止，而普通船員可以管新進船員。每個船員都能分到一定比例的利潤，因此不難想像，如果一個魚叉手因為技術不好或運氣不佳，而讓到手的鯨魚逃跑了，會令船上的人多生氣，而他會遭到多少人的憎恨。在這個只有五十人的漂浮小村落裡，輿論的力量是很可怕的。我認識一位頭髮灰白的魚叉手，有一回他未能命中鯨魚，當他看著鬆垮的魚繩時，居然痛哭失聲起來，而亞伯丁（Aberdeen）的船員可是出了名的強悍。

雖然格陵蘭海域一年可以捕到二十或三十頭鯨魚，但上個世紀的大量屠殺或許已經造成鯨魚數量遽減，現在實際存在的可能只有數百頭。當然，我指的是露脊鯨，至於其他種類的鯨魚，我說過，數量仍非常多。要計算這片廣大水域與遼闊冰原上有多少物種是非常困難的事，然而儘管如此，在獵捕時卻經常出現同一艘捕鯨船連續數次發現獵物都是同一頭鯨魚的事，顯示這些鯨魚的數量有多麼稀少。我記得有一頭鯨魚，牠之所以好認，是因為牠的尾鰭上長了一塊形狀大小類似蜂窩的疣。當我們降下小艇時，船長對我們說，「我追捕過牠三次。他在六一年逃脫了。六七年魚叉射中了牠，但被牠掙脫。七六年濃霧救了牠。奇怪的是，我們現在又碰上牠了！」我心想，如果要打賭的話，我一定認為這不是同一條鯨魚，然而結果證明，那個長著大疣的尾鰭至今依然拍打著北極海的洋面，顯然我想錯了。

我永遠忘不了第一次看見露脊鯨的感覺。我們發現小冰原的另一邊有鯨魚的蹤影，但是等到所有的船員全衝到甲板上時，鯨魚已經潛進水裡。十分鐘過去了，我們等待鯨魚浮出水面，此時我的眼光稍微離開水面，但在眾人充滿驚訝的喘息聲中，我趕緊抬頭，發現一頭鯨魚居然騰空出現。牠的尾鰭捲曲著，就像一條跳躍的鱒魚，亮晃晃的鉛色身軀完全脫離了水面。我驚訝得說不出話，這一點也不奇怪，因為即便有三十年航海經驗的船長，也是頭一次看到這個景象。捕到這頭鯨魚之後，我們發現牠的體外覆蓋了一層厚重的、紅色的、如螃蟹般的寄生蟲，每隻大約一先令大小，我們猜測大概是寄生蟲攪得鯨魚很不舒服，牠在惱怒之下，做出了如此狂野的舉動。如果一個人擁有短小而無指甲的鰭狀肢，並且在背部長滿了蝨子，想必在搔不到癢的情況下，這個人也會做出發狂的事吧。

捕到魚之後（捕鯨船員經常直接把鯨魚叫作魚），船會開到鯨魚的一側，然後以一種奇妙而行之有年的方式來固定魚的頭部與尾部，這樣子無論放鬆還是拉緊繩索，鯨魚巨大身體的每個部分才能拉到船上頭。巨大的嘴巴足以容得下一整艘小艇，船員用斧頭砍開十英尺長的骨頭，其他人則用尖鏟割下厚重的脂肪，這是仁慈的大自然給予它體格過於龐大的孩子的外衣。幾個小時後，割下的東西全存放在船槽裡，白色突出的骨頭置於一旁，當繩子一鬆脫，骨頭就像石頭般沉入海底。幾年前，有個船員還站在鯨魚背上，當滑車鬆開時，他的腳不小心被鯨魚肋骨勾到，多年後，也許這兩具骨骸——其中一具吊在另一具上——將會陳列在亞熱帶格陵蘭博物館裡，或者是讓斯匹茲卑爾根解剖研究所的學生大吃一驚。

除了這些耗費體力的事，對於深入極地的人來說，北極地帶仍是個充滿魅力的地方。我想到那位頭髮斑白的老船長，他在臨終前下床，穿著睡衣蹣跚地走著，最後被護士發現他走到離屋很遠的地方，嘴裡還念念有詞，「往北走」。有一隻北極狐，我有個朋友努力想馴養牠，但還是被牠逃跑了，幾個月後，牠在凱斯尼斯（Caithness）中了陷阱。[4] 這隻北極狐

4 譯註：凱斯尼斯是位於蘇格蘭北端的郡。

不斷往北走，我們能說牠是看著羅盤才知道怎麼往北走的嗎？極地是個純粹的世界，有著白色的冰與藍色的海，方圓千里之內杳無人煙，冰原上的微風完全未受到污染。此外，極地也是個浪漫的地方。你站在未知之地的邊緣，你射下的每一隻鴨子，砂囊裡留存的小石子都來自地圖尚未繪出的地方。

這些捕鯨船長宣稱要前往北極並不難。當然，在抽菸喝酒開懷暢談時，不可避免話會說得滿一點，但這些船長的想法確實有著驚人的一致性。他們的說法可以簡述如下。

探險家想從格陵蘭與斯匹茲卑爾根群島之間前往北極，此時橫亙在他面前的是巨大的漂浮冰礁，科學探險家稱之為「永凍海」，而捕鯨人則用更生動的「障礙物」一詞來表現。在巨大浮冰前尋找進路的船隻，發現自己位於北緯八十一度上，前方是一整塊密不透風的冰牆，找不到一絲縫隙讓船頭能開進去一探究竟。這些浮冰處於永凍的狀態，充滿奇特的瘤狀隆起與尖突，厚度也很驚人，不可能穿越過去，而表面也充滿砍削與鋸齒狀的痕跡。一八二七年，勇敢的帕里駕著雪橇抵達的緯度（如果我記的沒錯的話，是北緯八十二度三十分）刷新了以往的紀錄。就他所看到的狀況，這片永凍的浮冰一直延伸到北極。

這就是前往北極的障礙物。但在捕鯨人眼中，這是可克服的。

他們說，浮冰再怎麼廣大，終究漂浮在水上。在某些海域上，這些浮冰會一直往南移動，讓整片浮冰的凝聚力減弱，再加上北風的吹襲，冰牆會龜裂成條狀，因此產生許多巨大的海灣。根據捕鯨人的說法，長期持續的凜冽北風可能隨時吹出一條航路，船隻或許可以經由這條航路直達北極。捕鯨人在捕鯨季節於北緯八十二度作業，發現當地完全沒有浮冰，更重要的是，他們也看不出更往北有任何浮冰存在。然而由於捕鯨人是為公司工作，他們在那裡的目的是捕鯨，因此沒有誘因吸引他們冒著可能喪失船隻、貨物的風險前往北極。

嘗試前往北極並不費事，也不會耗費太多金錢。選擇一艘堅固的木製炮艇，船身短而穩定，引擎老舊也沒有關係，但必須擁有一百匹馬力。船員要以從皇家海軍退役的蘇格蘭與昔德蘭船員為主軸，其餘輔助人員可以是年輕人，但必須受過航海訓練。前幾次航行除了海軍軍官，還必須有一兩位有經驗的冰區領航員隨行。必須找像馬克罕這樣的人擔任船長。然後每年六月與七月出航，前去視察障礙物，並且嚴令他們除非有非常清楚的水道，否則不許接近厚重的浮冰。也許會有六年的時間一無所獲。也許到了第七年，在強勁的北風吹襲下，會出現開闊的水域。無論如何，這麼做所需的費用最少，也最不危險，年輕船員找不到比這更好的訓練機會。他們會發現夏天的格陵蘭海要比以往他們派去訓練的亞速群島或馬德拉島更為衛生與宜人。整個航行可能在一個月內就能完成。

北方的水域不乏各種事件，老捕鯨人有的是古怪的故事可說，也許是個人的經驗，也許是口耳相傳的軼聞。其中有個故事總是讓我特別感興趣，我認為它是我聽過的故事中最特別的。幾年前，「蝕缺」號的大衛．格雷船長——他是捕鯨業的老前輩，他與他的兄弟約翰及阿雷克是著名捕鯨家族的代表——在往北遠航時，曾看見一隻大鳥在冰上振翅飛翔。他降下小艇，射中了這隻鳥，並且帶上船，但沒有人知道這是什麼鳥。帶回彼得赫德之後，馬上就被認出這是尚未成年的信天翁，現在這隻信天翁陳列在彼得赫德博物館，在牠長蹼的腳趾邊放了一張小牌子，說明鳥的種類。

信天翁是南極鳥類，我們很難想像這隻信天翁是怎麼從地球的另一端飛到北方來。牠還是隻幼鳥，也許在眼花下飛來北方，但牠的體力實在不足以支持牠做到這一點。那麼是什麼原因使牠出現在北方？也許有些流浪的信天翁生活在靠北的位置。然而，如果另有一群信天翁生活在北方，那麼也許北極周邊地區的氣候跟我們所想的大不相同。或許康恩的猜測並不離譜，他認為北極周邊是一片開闊的海洋。也許兩極是一片平坦的地形，我小時候曾經想像造物主在讓地球旋轉之前，曾經用祂的手指捏著兩極，而地形平坦對氣候的影響很可能遠超過我們的想像。然而，如果真是如此，那麼一旦吹起北風，我們的探險船豈不是能輕易地從浮冰的裂縫一路開往北方。

在七個月的捕鯨航行中，我曾看到一小塊陸地。這個奇異的孤島是揚馬延島，巨大的死火山覆蓋著白雪，山峰高聳入雲。在捕鯨業繁盛的時期，荷蘭人曾在當地設了鍋爐站，現在，島上遺留著大石頭與鐵環，並且散置著生鏽的船錨，但整體來說依然保存著絕對的蠻荒景象。我們也看到了斯匹茲卑爾根島，它的黑色峭壁與白色冰河，景象令人望而生畏。我們的船曾為了躲避暴風而進入浮冰的縫隙裡，那是我第一次也是最後一次看見斯匹茲卑爾根島雄偉而令人戰慄的景色。到了捕鯨季快結束時，捕鯨船開始南行到北緯七十二度線，朝著格陵蘭的東南角航行，如果你——在離岸八十英里處——能捕捉到岸邊隱現的懸崖景象，如果你是個愛做夢的人，那麼這樣的景致足以提供你充分的夢境材料。這裡的景色，總會讓你產生各種最有趣的疑問，等待著你去解答。

當然，我們都知道冰島是歐洲文明的中心之一，冰島人在格陵蘭建立殖民地，然後繁衍茁壯，留下了許多傳說故事，並且對斯克林人（Skraeling）與愛斯基摩人發動戰爭。他們喜歡唱歌、打鬥與飲酒，行為粗魯且性嗜血腥。格陵蘭日漸繁榮，居民甚至建立教堂，派人到丹麥請主教前來。當時，格陵蘭的產業並無任何保護措施。然而，主教卻因為突然的氣候變遷而無法前往自己的教區，當時冰島與格陵蘭之間全凍成了冰，而從那時（十四世紀）到現在，一直沒有人越過廣大的冰原，也無法確認古代城市或居民是否依然存在。他們是否保存了自己的文明，他們是否依然唱歌、喝酒與打鬥，並且等著主教前來？他們是否遭到仇視的斯克林人消滅，或者更可能的是，他們是否與斯克林人混血，因而生下頭髮枯黃蓬亂、四肢粗壯的愛斯基摩人？我們必須等待像南森那樣的人進行探險，才能得知實際的狀況。目前，這只能說是一個有趣的歷史問題，就像被貝利撒留趕到非洲內陸的汪達爾人一樣，他們的命運至今未解。當我們對地球的了解更多，過去的浪漫與詩意將因此被驅除得一乾二淨，再也不會像隔著薄霧那樣充滿藝術的想像。

我還有很多關於北極的事要說，例如熊，例如海豹，例如獨角鯨，例如劍魚，以及其他許許多多有趣的事物，這些集合起來構成北極魅力無窮的來源；然而，正如一些好意的批評者說的，已經有人介紹過這些事物，而且他們說得更精采。然而，北極地區還有一個面向是一般人未注意到的，那就是醫療的部分。達沃斯普拉茨（Davos Platz）[5]已經證明寒冷對於治療肺結核相當有效，但在北極圈充滿生機的空氣中，卻鮮少帶有毒性的細菌能夠生存。在北極圈，唯一能奪走捕鯨人性命的疾病，就是具爆炸性的子彈。我敢這麼預言，不管過了多少年，當每年夏天蒸汽遊艇載著肺癆患者來到北方時，這些病人會發現，大自然的冰屋要比蒸汽浴更有益健康。

5　編註：位於瑞士東部，由於其乾燥、清新的空氣而成為肺病患者的休養勝地。

格陵蘭捕鯨船上的生活

編輯說明：柯南．道爾的這篇文章刊登在一八九七年一月號《河濱雜誌》上。到了三月，加上副標題「北極海域的個人冒險紀錄」之後，刊登於美國的《麥克魯爾雜誌》。柯南．道爾在寫作時顯然沒有完全根據他在「希望」號上寫的日記，因為裡頭的細節有一些出入，特別是他說「希望」號返鄉的時間是九月，但他的日記寫的卻是一八八〇年八月。這篇文章後來成為柯南．道爾一九二四年的自傳《回憶與冒險》第四章〈在北極海捕鯨〉的藍本。

我的人生能有這麼一段經歷，實在是一件非常幸運的事，因為現在幾乎已不可能再獲得同樣的體驗。雖然捕鯨船——無論來自英國還是美國——仍持續前往戴維斯海峽的格陵蘭漁場作業（亦即位於格陵蘭與斯匹茲卑爾根島之間的漁場），但過去十年來，這裡已很難捕到鯨魚，因此逐漸遭到放棄。「希望」號與「蝕缺」號（這兩艘都來自彼得赫德）是最後兩艘仍堅持捕鯨的船隻。捕鯨業過去曾盛極一時，甚至可以支撐起一支數量達一百艘的捕鯨船隊；「希望」號在知名的捕鯨船長約翰．格雷的帶領下，我也忝列其中，於一八八〇年參與了這次長達七個月的北極海捕鯨之行。我在船上擔任船醫的工作，但是由於我才二十歲，我的醫學知識只有醫科生大三的程度，我常想，船上應該不會出現太嚴重的病症吧。

事情是這麼起頭的。在愛丁堡一個溼冷的下午，我正坐在桌前努力準備考試，每個醫學院學生都被這些考試搞得焦頭爛額。此時有個醫學院學生走了進來，我跟他還算稍有交情。接下來他問的荒唐問題讓我的心思無法專注在書本上。

「你想不想下星期跟著捕鯨船出海？」他說，「你可以擔任船醫，一個月兩英鎊十先令，每獲得一噸鯨魚油可以分紅三先令。」

「你怎麼知道我上得了船？」我毫不思索地反問他。

「因為我自己在船上有個鋪位。我是上個月找到這份差事，但現在我沒辦法去，所以我要找個人頂替我。」

「到北極的服裝配備呢？」

「你可以用我的。」

這件事當下就搞定了，不到幾分鐘，我的人生突然轉了大彎，往全新的航道駛去。

大約一個星期後，我來到彼得赫德，在勤務員的協助下，我把少得可憐的個人行李放進我在「希望」號的鋪位底下的櫃子裡。然後，我初次上船就發生了一件愚蠢的事。我念書時，拳擊是我最喜歡的消遣活動。我發現，為了爭取時間念書，必須尋找一種能將最多運動量壓縮在最短時間完成的運動。因此，我隨身帶了兩副打扁而且褪色的拳套。剛好勤務員也有點喜歡打鬥，於是等我行李一放好，他就馬上拿起拳套，提議兩人打一場。我不知道傑克．蘭姆是不是還在人世，如果他還在，我想他一定還記得這件事。我還清楚記得他的樣子，碧眼黃鬚，個子矮小，胸膛厚實，肌肉發達，雙腿外八。我們的比賽不太公平，因為他比我矮了數寸，手臂比我短得多，而且他對拳擊一無所知，不過我毫不懷疑如果我們是在街頭打鬥，他會是一個可怕的對手。他一直衝過來，我只好用拳頭頂著他，最後，我發現他執意想找到空隙出拳，於是我只好狠狠給他一下。後來大概過了一個鐘頭，當我在大廳讀書時，聽見隔壁大副房間傳來低語的聲音，突然我聽見勤務員用確信的語調大聲地說：「幫幫我吧，柯林，他是我們手邊所能找到最好的醫生了！他把我的眼睛打青了！」這是第一次（而且幾乎可以說是最後一次）船上的人見識了我的專業能力。

這名勤務員是個好人，事後，我回想這段漫長的航行，我們足足有七個月未踏上陸地，他那和善、開朗的臉令人想到都會覺得開心。他有著美妙動人的男高音，有好幾個鐘頭，我一直聽著他的歌聲，其間伴奏著他在餐具室洗碗盤的聲響。他知道許多悲愴傷感的歌曲，當你有六個月未能看見女人的臉孔時，你才知道真正的傷感是什麼。當傑克用顫音唱著，「她明媚的笑容仍在我腦海中繚繞著」，或「甜美的貝兒．瑪紅，請在天堂門前等我」，他歌聲中那種朦朧甜蜜的缺憾打動了我們，現在的我回想起來，那感覺彷彿又回來了。而說到拳擊，他每天跟我練習，終於變成一個不可輕視的勁敵——特別是在風浪不平靜的時候，他的雙腿在搖晃的地板上不動如山。就算船已經傾斜一邊，他還是能猛衝攻擊。他也是個專業的麵包烘焙師傅，我敢說，如果當時格陵蘭是他的夢想，那麼現在格陵蘭也成了我的美夢之一。

「希望」號的人事也有耐人尋味的地方。簽約擔任大副的人是個衰老、失意的傢伙，他顯然無法履行職務。另一方面，擔任廚師助手的人卻是高頭大馬、留著紅鬍子、全身古銅色，四肢極其健壯，而且聲如宏鐘。然而，等到船一離港，那位衰老的船副隨即遁入廚房，成為專門洗餐具的人員，反過來，那位大漢卻走到船尾，成了大副。事情的真相是，其中有人有執照，但是已經從船員生活退休，至於另一個人則沒有讀寫能力，卻十足是個優秀的船員；因此——在這個約定裡，大家關注的是當事人的能力而不是資格——當船開出港口，兩人就馬上交換鋪位。

柯林．麥克林身高六英尺，有著挺拔健壯的體格。他戴著海豹皮帽，帽邊蓋住雙頰，從頰邊延伸出濃密的紅色鬍子，透顯出一股凶殘冷酷的氣質。麥克林是天生的高階船員，遠比商業局給的證書更來得令人信任。他唯一的缺點是過於熱血，一點小事就會讓他異常亢奮。我印象很清楚，某天晚上，我花了很大的力氣把他與勤務員拉開。勤務員相當魯莽地批評柯林的捕鯨方式造成鯨魚逃走。兩個人都喝了蘭姆酒，這使得其中一人變得好逞口舌，另一人變得非常暴力，而當我們三人坐在長七英尺寬四英尺的空間時，流血衝突顯然是免不了的。每一次，當我以為危險已經過去，勤務員又會愚蠢地說道，「我不是要冒犯，柯林，我只是想說，如果你捕魚時動作能快一……」我不知道這樣的話重複了多少遍，但勤務員沒有一次能把話說完；因為講到「快一」的時候，柯林就已經衝上前去勒住他的脖子，而我只能死命地抱住柯林的腰，直到我們精疲力竭為止。然後，等勤務員休息夠了，他又會重複那個可悲的句子，「快一」就成另一場衝突的發起信號。我確信如果我不在那裡，大副一定會打傷勤務員，因為大副是我所見過脾氣最暴躁的人。

在船上有五十個人，其中一半是蘇格蘭人，一半是昔德蘭人，昔德蘭人是我們經過勒維克時僱用的。昔德蘭人較為穩重、順從、安靜、規矩而且溫和，反觀蘇格蘭船員則很容易惹麻煩，但也較為壯健剛強。高級船員與魚叉手都是蘇格蘭人，但一般船員，特別是船工，昔德蘭人的表現完全能符合要求。

在船上，只有一個人既非蘇格蘭人，亦非昔德蘭人，他的出身是個謎。他是個皮膚黝黑、黑眼珠的高大男人，頭髮與鬍子都是藍黑色，外型出眾，走路時會搖晃著肩膀，流露出狂放不羈的性格。據說他來自英格蘭南方，因為犯法而遠走他鄉。他沒有朋友，沉默寡言，但他是船上最聰明的船員之一。我從他的外表推斷，他的脾氣可能相當殘暴，而他犯的罪也

COLIN MCLEAN.
From a Photo. by J. Shivas, Peterhead.

大副柯林·麥克林

許非常血腥。我們只有一次從他的眼神中看出他隱藏的怒火。船上的廚師——一名孔武有力的男子，矮小的船副只是他的助手——自己儲藏了一些蘭姆酒，他過於放縱自己喝酒，結果造成船員們連續三天沒晚餐可吃。到了第三天，我們這位沉默寡言的亡命之徒走到廚子旁邊，手裡拿著黃銅製的平底深鍋。他不發一語，只是拿著鍋子猛力朝廚子砸下去，由於用力過猛，廚子的頭穿透了鍋底，整個鍋身就這樣套在廚子的脖子上左右晃蕩。半醉半驚的廚子嚷著要打架，但他很快就發現船上的人都反對他，只好乖乖回去煮飯，但他嘴裡還是氣不過，不住地嘟囔。至於那個報復者，則是又回到原來鬱鬱寡歡的樣子，對一切視而不見。之後，我們再也沒聽過誰抱怨廚子的問題。

一艘捕鯨船上有八艘捕鯨小艇，但通常捕鯨時只會派出七艘，因為每艘小艇要坐六個人，所以派出七艘小艇時，船上就只剩下所謂的「閒人」，這些人的契約上並不包括從事船員的工作。然而，「希望」號上這些「閒人」恰好是一群積極進取與精力旺盛之人，於是我們自願搭第八艘小艇出去，而且我們成功了，至少我們做到了我們自己設定的目標，我們在獵捕海豹與鯨魚上面是全船最有效率的小艇。勤務員、大管輪與火伕，我負責划槳，紅髮的高地人擔任魚叉手，英俊的亡命之徒掌舵。我們捕到的海豹數量與其他小艇相比毫不遜色；捕鯨時，我們曾經用魚叉獵捕鯨魚，也曾負責刺穿的工作，我們的成績很優異。這份工作對我來說勝任愉快，格雷船長說，如果我願意再度跟他一起出航，他願意給我兩份薪水，一份魚叉手，一份船醫。我婉謝了船長的好意，捕鯨生活實在太吸引人了，我可以想像，如果自己投入太多，最後一定無法放棄這份工作。大多數船員並不是被人找來從事這份工作，他們是打小就開始從事捕鯨這個行業。在「希望」號上工作的船員，許多人從來沒看過農田，他們從小就上船捕鯨，往往三月出海，到九月才回港。

捕鯨的魅力之一，在於它本質上帶有賭博的元素。每個人——船長、船副與船員——都能分得獲利。如果捕鯨成功，那麼每個人都將因此致富，然後等待來年春季捕鯨季的到來。如果開著空船返港，那麼就表示這年冬天得勒緊褲帶過日子。你毋需叮囑船員，船員也會拚了命地捕鯨。只要桅頂一傳來看見鯨魚的喊聲，船員們就會馬上降下小艇，幾乎每艘小艇都在同時間降下海面。值班的船員從底下的臥鋪衝到甲板上，衣服還套在手臂上來不及穿妥，就在寒冷的極地天氣裡跳進小艇，至於上廁所的問題則留待以後有機會再解決。魚叉手與小艇舵手如果一時笨拙而讓鯨魚逃走，那麼他們接下來可要倒大楣了！他已經從船上每個存心不良的船員口袋裡拿了五英鎊的鈔票。接下來他還錢給對方時，免不了要被說個幾句。

北極地區最讓我驚訝的一點，是你很快就能抵達這個地區。我過去從不知道北極幾乎就在我們的家門口。當我們身處浮冰之中時，我想我離開昔德蘭應該才過了四天。有天早晨我被浮冰碰撞船身的巨大聲響吵醒，走到甲板一看，整片海都被冰塊覆蓋了，一直相連到天際。這些浮冰不算巨大，但相當厚實，人可以在冰塊與冰塊之間跳躍，毫無問題。浮冰白得令人目眩，相對之下，大海顯得更藍了，還有頭頂上的藍天，以及穿過鼻腔的冷冽北極空氣，這是個令人難忘的早晨。有一回，我們在如岩石般的搖晃浮冰上，看見一隻巨大的海豹，牠壯健、愛睏而且沉著，牠抬頭看著船，露出高枕無憂的表

魚叉和槍

情，彷彿知道獵捕季還要三個星期才開始。我們在浮冰上繼續前進，看見跟人很像的長形腳印，那是熊的足跡。回到船艙，玻璃杯裡的蘇格蘭雪花蓮依然新鮮。

我已經提過獵捕季，我也許可以解釋一下，挪威與英國政府之間的協議，規定兩國的人民不許在四月三日之前獵捕海豹。這麼規定的理由在於三月是海豹哺育幼兒的季節，如果母親在幼兒能獨立過活前被殺，那麼整個族群很快就會滅絕。基於哺育目的，海豹會聚集在不同的地點，牠們顯然已經預先做了安排。由於這些地點位於數百平方英里的浮冰上，要找出明確的棲息地點並不容易。但要找到這些地點的方式其實既簡單又聰明。當船在浮冰之間航行時，會看見一群群海豹游過水中。用羅盤仔細測定牠們的方向，然後在航海圖上標示出來。一小時後，或許會看到另一群海豹。也對這群海豹進行標記。當記錄了幾群海豹的方位與行進方向之後，將航海圖上標記的行進方向延長，直到這些直線相交為止。在相交的點上，或者附近，應該就是這些海豹的主要棲息地。

當你真的來到此地，那景象真是美麗。我認為這是地表上最大的生物群落——牠們棲息在從格陵蘭海岸往海上延伸數百英里的廣闊冰原上。這片棲息地大約介於北緯七十一度到七十五度之間，經度範圍則更難以確定；但海豹要找到這個地方卻毫無困難。從主桅頂端的瞭望台望去，完全看不到盡頭。在肉眼可見的最遠處，只見冰上散布著像胡椒粉般的黑點。小海豹亦躺在各個地方，像一條條雪白的鼻涕蟲，頂著小小的黑鼻子和大大的黑眼睛。空氣中充滿著牠們類似人類的叫聲；當你坐在船艙裡，此時的你其實正處於一大群海豹之中，你會以為隔壁是一間巨大的育嬰室。

「希望」號是那年最早發現海豹群的船隻，但在准許獵捕那天到來之前，我們遭遇一連串的暴風，起伏的波浪使浮冰劇烈搖晃，許多小海豹因此提早入海。結果，等到解禁之時，大自然已讓我們無事可做。然而，到了第三天拂曉，船員到浮冰上，開始收集殺戮的成果。那是一件殘忍的差事，雖然比不上為了供應國內民眾餐桌上的菜餚所做的事來得殘忍。然而深紅的池子映照著雪白的冰原，在寧靜安詳的湛藍天空下，確實予人深刻的恐怖感受。然而無可抵擋的需求創造出無可抵擋的供給，海豹的死，養活了一長串的人：水手、碼頭工人、製革工人、醃製工、食品檢驗者、蠟燭商、皮革商與油商。一端是專門宰殺動物的人，另一端則是穿著海豹皮製成的軟皮靴、過著優雅生活的人，或者是使用海豹油脂作為鑽研哲學的利器的學者。

我永遠記得第一天獵海豹的情景，因為我確實經歷了一場冒險。我說過，當天颳著強風，浮冰與浮冰猛烈衝撞著，船長認為對於一個沒有經驗的人來說，這樣的狀況太危險。於是，正當我跟著其他船員翻過舷牆時，船長命令我回來，要我待在船上。我的抗議無效，我悶悶不樂地坐在舷牆邊，兩隻腳在船側晃蕩著。我一口氣吞不下，整個身體隨著船身的搖動而上下起伏。然而，我坐的木頭上剛好結了一層薄冰，冰隆起之後產生傾斜，我一不留心，整個人滑下船，從兩塊浮冰之間跌入海裡。當我從海裡浮起時，我連忙抓住浮冰，然後再次爬上船。然而，這個意外卻導致我希望的結果，因為船長說，反正我無論如何都會摔進海裡，那麼在冰上或在船上都是一樣的。我想船長的謹慎是有道理的，因為光是那天，我就摔進海裡兩次。當我的衣服放在引擎室裡烘乾時，我必須可恥地一直待在床上。我發現我的不幸成了船長的談笑之資，使他忘了獵捕海豹不順利所造成的不愉快，如此反而讓我感到安慰，只是往後有很長一段時間，我必須忍受大家戲稱我「偉大的北方跳水員」。有一回，我差點無法死裡逃生，當時我正在剝海豹皮，但突然往後一滑，從冰緣跌進海裡。我望向四周，尋求援助，但沒有人看見我落海。冰的表面非常光滑，我找不到任何可施力的地方讓自己爬上來，而在寒凍的海水裡，我的身體很快就變得僵硬。然而，我終於抓住死海豹尾端的鰭狀肢，我像做著噩夢似地進行著拉鋸戰，要不是我把海豹也拉下海，就是我成功爬上浮冰。最後，我終於將膝蓋攀上冰緣，然後奮力翻上冰面。當我回到船上時，身上的衣服硬得跟盔甲一樣，我必須先烤融這一身發出爆裂聲的冰衣裳，才能換上新的衣物。

四月時，獵捕的海豹主要是海豹母子。五月，我們更往北走；在北緯七十七度到七十八度之間，我們遭遇到年紀較大的公海豹，要獵捕這些海豹絕非易事。牠們是小心謹慎的生物，必須在相當遠的距離射殺牠們。六月，獵海豹的工作告一段落，船繼續往北走，直到北緯七十九度到八十度之間，這裡是格陵蘭最佳的捕鯨緯度。船將在此地停留三個月，如果幸運的話，有可能捕到船主本錢三到四倍的漁獲，而船公司的每個工作人員都將荷包滿滿。如果獲利只是一般，那麼至少還可以支付捕鯨船的成本，天底下恐怕沒有比捕鯨船成本更大的營生了。

真正了解格陵蘭鯨價值的人很少。一頭巨大且骨骼良好的格陵蘭鯨在今日約值兩千到三千英鎊。之所以如此昂貴，主要來自於鯨魚骨的價值，鯨魚骨是稀有商品，而且對於某些交易來說是絕對的必需品。鯨魚骨的價值正緩步提升，因為鯨魚的數量越來越少。一八八〇年，格雷船長估計，在整片格陵蘭海域（面積約數千平方英里），或許只剩下不超過三百頭鯨魚。鯨魚的稀少可以從他認得自己追捕的每一頭鯨魚看出。有一頭鯨魚的尾鰭上長了一顆蜂窩大小的疣，格雷船長記得自己年輕時曾在父親的船上追捕過這頭鯨魚。或許，其他世代的捕鯨人也曾尾隨這個長了疣的尾鰭，因為鯨魚是非常長壽的動物。牠們能活多久，沒有人知道；但在魚叉上刻有捕鯨船名稱的年代裡，從鯨魚身上取出的舊魚叉上面的船隻名稱，早已消失於捕鯨業中，由此可以看出，鯨魚的壽命恐怕不下於一世紀。

捕鯨是件令人興奮的工作，你背對著鯨魚，若想知道鯨魚的一舉一動，必須從舵手的臉才能看出。舵手越過你的頭頂凝視前方，看著生物在水中緩慢穿梭。當他發現鯨魚的眼神起了變化，他會舉手做出停止划船的信號，而在快接觸鯨魚的時候，他會要求大家安靜。這裡有許多浮冰，只要船槳不發出聲響，那麼就算船隻靠近，也不會讓鯨魚潛入海中。所以要慢慢前進，等到距離夠近時，舵手知道可以趕在鯨魚潛水前採取行動——因為這麼龐大的身軀需要一點時間才能做出反應。你看見舵手的眼睛一亮，臉色一變，他喊道，「兄弟們，划槳，快，用力划！」巨大魚叉槍的扳機一扣，船槳在海中打出大量的泡沫。大概划了六下左右，在沉重的油脂擠壓聲中，船頭撞上某件柔軟的東西，把船上的人與船槳震得東倒西歪。但你沒有時間理會這種事，因為當你碰撞到鯨魚時，魚叉槍也發出爆裂聲，你知道魚叉已經射進鯨魚巨大而呈鉛色的曲線身體裡。鯨魚就像石頭一樣下沉，船頭再度往下敲擊水面，一面小紅旗飛奔而去，顯示魚叉已固定在鯨魚身上，此時座位底下的纜繩颼地快速往前拉扯，從你張開的雙腿之間直直朝船頭奔去。

此時正是最危險的時刻——因為在這種狀況下，很少有鯨魚會回頭來攻擊船隻。纜繩早已由專門的纜繩手纏好，確保鯨魚拉扯時不會糾纏打結。然而，如果發生打結，如果繩圈剛好圈住某個船員的四肢，那麼這個人會一下子就死於非命，速度可能快到連他的同伴都不知道他是怎麼死的。此時割斷纜繩已無濟於事，反而白白損失一頭鯨魚，因為受害者恐怕已被拉到水下幾百噚的深處。

「住手，」魚叉手叫道，一名水手正打算拿刀割斷繩子。「這條魚對逝者來說可是好東西。」聽起來很無情，卻不無道理。

射出魚叉之後，魚叉船的任務就結束了。接下來，鯨魚被魚叉刺死之後進行刺穿的工作，則更令人興奮，因為這個工作需要較長的時間完成。你會有半小時非常貼近鯨魚，近到你可以手放在牠黏滑的體側。鯨魚似乎已經沒有任何痛覺，因為當長矛刺穿牠的身體時，牠的眼睛連眨都不眨。但鯨魚的本能驅使牠的尾巴拍打小艇，而船員的本能則是將長矛插得更深並且牢牢鉤住鯨魚的體側，讓自己位在鯨魚的肩部以保持安全。然而，即使如此，我們仍必須留心各種危險，因為鯨魚可能在驚恐下抬起前鰭拍擊小艇的上方。光這麼一拍就足以讓我們沉入海底，我永遠不會忘記，我們努力從下方衝出，每個人都伸手要趕走那片巨大而充滿威脅的魚鰭——彷彿我們可以阻止鯨魚潛入水中。然而鯨魚也因此失血過多，牠並未潛入水中，反而尾鰭翻進水裡，魚肚朝天，我們知道牠已經死了。任何成功的感受都比不上這個時刻的興奮激動。

北極地區予人一種獨特的彼世感受——這種感受是如此獨特，如果你曾經到過北極地區，這種感受必定讓你終身難忘——而這種感受主要源自於這個地區的永晝現象。這裡的夜晚其實跟白晝沒什麼差異，只是多了點橙色的色調，光線也稍弱一點。有些船長會任意調整時鐘，把早餐時間定在半夜，把晚餐時間定在早上十點。這是屬於你的二十四小時，你可以任意規定作息。等一兩個月過去之後，你的眼睛就會開始厭倦永晝的世界，並且懷念起黑暗。我記得我們在返航途中，在冰島附近看到一顆星星，那是一顆精緻、閃閃發光的小東西，令人目不轉睛。我們因為習以為常，經常忽略了大自然另外一面的美麗事物。

孤獨感也凸顯了北極海予人的感受。當我們位於捕鯨的緯度時，除了船上的夥伴，方圓八百英里內一艘船也沒有。長達七個月的時間，我們毫無南方世界的音信。我們出航的時候正是局勢緊張之時。阿富汗戰役開打，與俄國的戰爭越來越迫近。我們返港時，渾然不知來自波羅的海方面的船隻，很可能像我們對待鯨魚那樣對待我們。當我們在昔德蘭群島北方看見漁船時，我們第一個問題是戰爭還是和平。在這七個月當中，發生了不少大事：邁萬德之役失敗，與羅伯茲（Roberts）著名的從喀布爾（Cabul）往坎達哈（Candahar）進軍。但這一切對我們已無法產生太大感受；直到今日，我對於這段軍事歷史依然缺乏實際的感觸。

永晝、刺眼的白色浮冰、深藍的海水，這些是讓人記憶最深刻的事物，還有乾燥、清新與令人振奮的空氣，光是這樣就讓人感到活著真好。還有，那裡有著數不清的海鳥，不斷響徹耳畔的是牠們——鷗、管鼻藿、雪鳥、北極鷗、潛鳥和海燕的鳴叫。牠們占滿了天空，而在下面，你永遠都能在海裡窺見從未見過的奇異生物。具有商業價值的鯨魚總是離你遠遠的，但其他較不受獵人青睞的同類卻是一股腦兒湧到船邊。長鬚鯨展示著長九十英尺毫無價值的鯨油，牠很清楚沒有任何捕鯨船會為牠降下小艇。體型怪異的座頭鯨、鬼魅般的白鯨、獨角鯨、醜怪的瓶鼻鯨、巨大而遲鈍的格陵蘭鯊，與可怕殘暴的殺人鯨，牠是最難對付的深海巨獸，這些生物主宰著沒有船隻的海洋。在冰上有海豹，如豎琴海豹、地海豹與巨大的冠海豹。冠海豹從鼻子到尾巴長十二英尺，當牠們生氣時，會在鼻子上吹出一個如足球般大小的血紅肉囊。偶爾會在冰上看見雪白的北極狐，但最常見的還是北極熊。在海豹棲息地附近的冰上，到處都是北極熊的足跡——可憐而無害的生物，與敏捷的深海游泳高手。北極熊為了獵捕海豹，會在冰上跋涉數百英里——而牠們有一套聰明的辦法獵捕海豹，牠們會選擇一塊廣闊而只有一個透氣孔供海豹呼吸的冰原。當海豹探出頭來，熊掌一撲就能得手，北極熊的午餐就有著落了。我們偶爾會將廚餘放進引擎室裡燒掉，產生的煙霧不到幾小時就吸引了方圓數英里的北極熊前來。

航行雖然令人愉快，但總有往南返航的時候。冬日往往突然降臨，返航太慢的捕鯨船勢必會嘗到苦頭。九月，我們收起小艇，封好鯨油槽，「希望」號啟程回港。遠處隱約可見揚馬延島的山峰，閃耀的浮冰逐漸在我們身後黯淡消失，這很可能是我最後一次看見——除了在夢裡——格陵蘭海。

「北極星」船長

編輯說明：〈「北極星」船長〉首次刊載於一八八三年一月的《聖殿關》雜誌，它代表柯南．道爾早年的重要文學成就。〈「北極星」船長〉大量援引柯南．道爾在「希望」號上的經驗，以一名在捕鯨船上擔任船醫的醫學院學生寫的日記作為表現方式，這部作品充分顯示柯南．道爾人生這段「奇異而吸引人的篇章」如何燃起他的想像力。《聖殿關》因為這部作品而付給他十基尼的優渥稿費；柯南．道爾在寫給朋友的信上表示，「我想他們喜歡這篇小說」，而他的名字也開始為英國讀者所熟知，成為一名具潛力的新短篇小說作家。

〔醫學院學生約翰．馬里斯特．雷伊的日記摘要。〕

九月十一日——北緯八十一度四十分；東經二度。仍然停泊在巨大的冰原之間。往我們北方延伸的這塊冰原——我們的冰錨就繫在上面——它的面積恐怕不下於英國的一個郡。往右與往左延伸的冰原，一直連綿不斷到地平線。今天早上，船副報告說，浮冰有往南移動的跡象。如果浮冰形成足夠的厚度，恐怕將阻斷我們返航的路線，我們將因此陷入危險，我聽說，我們的糧食已經有點缺乏。捕鯨季已接近尾聲，夜晚開始再度出現。今天早上，我在前桅最下方的帆桁處看見一顆閃爍的星星，這是五月初以來首次看見星星。船員普遍感到不滿，許多人希望及早返鄉趕上鯡魚季，因為這個時節，蘇格蘭沿岸的工資總是特別高。目前他們的不滿只是擺出個臭臉或表現出鬱悶的樣子，但今天下午我聽二副說，他們考慮派代表向船長解釋他們的苦衷。我很懷疑船長是否會接受這種做法，因為他的性子火爆，而且對於任何可能侵犯他的權利的事特別敏感。我會在晚餐後冒險跟他談談這件事。我發現，其他船員不能跟他談的事，他總是容許我發表看法。站在右舷船尾，可以看見位於斯匹茲卑爾根群島西北角的阿姆斯特丹島——一些嶙峋的火山岩，在接縫處顯現著白色，那些是冰河。想到在這個時候，世界上或許沒有人比我們更接近格陵蘭南方的丹麥聚落，內心不禁百感交集——我們和丹麥聚落的直線距離大約九百英里。當船長冒險讓船隻在這種狀況下行駛時，他必須負起最大的責任。沒有任何捕鯨船在一年中這麼晚的時節，還留在這麼高的緯度位置。

晚上九點——我已經跟克雷吉船長說了，不過結果很難讓人滿意，我必須說，他是靜靜地甚至謙恭地聽完我要說的話。當我說完時，我覺得他的決心並沒有動搖，他的臉就像平日我看到的一樣堅定，只見他在狹窄的船艙裡快速來回踱步了幾分鐘。起初，我擔心自己嚴重地冒犯了他，但他再次坐下，並且抓著我的手臂，感覺上有點像是擁抱，我想我應該沒有讓他感到不快。在他狂野的黑色眼神深處，帶著一股溫柔，這讓我頗為驚訝。

「醫生，聽好了，」他說，「很抱歉我把你拉上船——真的很抱歉——我現在願意出五十英鎊讓你安全地站在鄧迪碼頭上。這回我心裡並沒有清楚的計畫。在我們北方有鯨魚。你憑什麼搖頭呢，醫生，我明明就在桅頂瞭望台看見鯨魚噴氣？」——船長突然對我發脾氣，然而我並不覺得自己顯露出任何懷疑的樣子。「我活到這個年紀，親眼看見過二十二頭鯨魚，沒有任何一頭小於十英尺。[1] 醫生，現在我跟財富之間只隔著惱人的一小段浮冰，你是否還認為我應該離開這裡？如果明天鯨魚在北方噴氣，我們還是可以獵捕牠，並且趁著浮冰合圍之前滿載而歸。如果鯨魚在南方噴氣——嗯，我想船員們都是來賣命的，對我來說也是如此，因為我對彼世的牽掛遠比在此世為多。不過，我要坦承，我對你感到抱歉。我希望老安格斯．泰特也在船上，他上回跟我一起出航，他這個人就算出了事，也不會有人記得他，至於你——你曾經跟我說你訂婚了不是？」

「是的，」我一邊回答，一邊撥弄著項鍊盒的彈簧，項鍊盒掛在我的錶鏈上，上面嵌著芙蘿拉的半身照。

「去你的！」他吼道，從座位上跳起來，鬍子彷彿也因亢奮而顫動著。「你的終身大事與我何干？我跟她有什麼關係，你為什麼成天拿著她的照片在我面前晃呀晃？」我覺得盛怒之下的他，接下來可能要揍我一拳，但他只是嘴裡咒罵著，開門衝出艙房，快步走上甲板，留下我驚魂未定地杵在房裡。船長向來對我和善有禮，這是他頭一次對我發這麼大的火。當我寫下這些文字時，我依然可以聽見船長焦躁來回踱步的聲音。

我想描繪船長的性格，但在紙上留下這樣的紀錄似乎太冒昧放肆，而且就算我這麼想，我的腦子對船長的印象始終模

1 捕鯨人衡量鯨魚的大小不是看體長，而是看鯨魚骨的長度。

糊不清。有好幾次我以為自己已經了解船長真正的性格，但隨後再跟船長接觸的結果，卻覺得對船長又有了新的認識，因此不得不修改心中對船長的看法，這個過程讓我感到有些沮喪。不過，我現在寫下的文字不會有其他人觀看，它純屬我個人的紀錄，因此，作為一種心理研究，我想試著記錄尼可拉斯．克雷吉船長的性格特徵。

一個人的外觀通常可以顯示出內在靈魂的某些特質。船長的身材高大健壯，臉孔黝黑英俊，四肢有時會不自主地抽動幾下，令人感到好奇，我想這反映出他是個神經質的人，或者單純只是他擁有過人的精力。他的下巴與整個臉龐充滿了男子氣概與決心，但最引人注目的還是他的眼睛。船長的雙眼是深褐色，明亮而熱切，帶著魯莽大膽的神色，但有時我感覺那更像是一種驚恐的反映。一般來說，船長總是予人勇敢進取的印象，然而有時候，特別是他開始反覆思忖的時刻，恐懼的神色會開始在他臉上蔓延加深，但下一刻也許他心念一轉，整個神情又會大不相同，與之前判若兩人。這個時刻，是他深陷憤怒無法自拔之時，他自己知道這點，因為我知道他會把自己鎖在房內，不讓任何人接近他，直到這段黑暗期過去為止。他睡得不太安穩，我曾在夜裡聽見他大喊，但他的艙房和我有段距離，因此我聽不清楚他說了什麼。

這是他性格的一面，而且是最難相處的一面。我是因為在船上與他日夜相處，才知道這一點。否則的話，平日的他其實平易近人，不僅博覽群書，而且風趣詼諧，是我看過的船員中最豪邁的一位。我永遠忘不了四月初當我們在浮冰中遭受強風吹襲時，他指揮若定的樣子。我從未看過他如此開心，甚至歡欣鼓舞，這和他在某個晚上的表現如出一轍，當時風雨交加，閃電雷聲大作，只見他在船橋上來回走動，毫不感到害怕。他曾經數次告訴我，死亡的念頭令他感到愉悅，對一個年輕人來說，會這麼想實在令人感到可悲；雖然他的頭髮與鬍鬚已開始有些斑白，但他頂多三十出頭。他一定曾遭遇嚴重的打擊，使他的人生縈繞在悲傷的苦境之中。如果我失去芙蘿拉，想必也會跟他一樣吧——這點只有天知道了！我想，要不是因為她，恐怕我也不會在乎明天颳的是北風還是南風。現在，我聽到他走下艙梯，把自己鎖在房裡，這顯示他的情緒還沒平靜下來。我於是上床睡覺，我想老佩皮斯會這麼說，因為蠟燭已經燒完（由於夜晚開始出現，所以我們現在必須使用蠟燭），而勤務員又已經歇息，因此沒辦法再點下一根蠟燭。

九月十二日——平靜、晴朗的一天，我們依然停泊在相同的地點。就算有風，吹的也是東南風，而且是微風。船長心情好多了，並且在早餐時為他的粗魯向我致歉。他看起來精神有點恍惚，但眼神還是維持以往的狂放不羈，如果用高地人的說法則是「瘋瘋顛顛」——至少我們的大管輪是這麼跟我說的。大管輪在凱爾特船員中向來有著占卜師的稱號，能解讀預兆。

這些講求實際的船員對於迷信深信不疑，這點令我有些意外。除非親眼目睹，否則我對迷信是嗤之以鼻。這次出海，船上就充滿了這類迷信的問題，我因此必須使用星期六才配給的烈酒搭配鎮靜劑讓船員服用，而不久我便用光了我手邊所有的鎮靜劑。我們才剛離開昔德蘭群島不久，掌舵的船員就不斷抱怨他們聽見船的後方傳來悲傷的哭聲與叫聲，彷彿有東西跟在船後面，卻始終跟不上船。在整個航行的過程中，大家不斷以訛傳訛，到了開始獵捕海豹之後，深夜裡船員們都無心工作。顯然，他們聽到的要不是舵鏈產生的嘎吱聲，就是海鳥經過時的啼叫聲。我有好幾次硬是被船員從床上叫起來聽這些聲音，而我總是說，那些聲音聽起來並不是什麼靈異古怪的東西。然而，船員們卻愚蠢地認為這些怪聲與超自然現象有關，無論怎麼跟他們解釋都沒用。我跟船長提起這件事，令我驚訝的是，他很認真地看待此事，而且顯然對於我說的一切感到十分煩惱。我還以為至少船長不會像船員那樣有這種愚昧的妄想。

一連串對迷信的思索使我留意到一件事，我們的二副曼森先生昨晚看到鬼——或者至少是他聲稱自己看到鬼，當然這兩者沒什麼差別。在長達數月不是獵熊就是獵鯨的單調生活下，新的話題可以讓人精神為之一振。曼森信誓旦旦地說這艘船鬧鬼；他還說如果他有別的地方可去，絕不願在船上多留一天。事實上，我們的二副真的嚇壞了，今天早上我必須用三氯乙醛與溴化鉀才能讓他鎮靜下來。他對於前一晚我說他喝多了感到生氣，而我必須煞有介事地聽他講述故事，才能讓他安定下來。二副說的內容相當直接，而且活靈活現，彷彿真的一樣。

「我在船橋，」他說，「當時是凌晨四點左右，也就是夜最深的時刻。當時還能看到一點月亮，但雲剛好遮住月光，因此看不清楚遠方的事物。魚叉手約翰．麥克勞從前甲板走過來，他說船頭右舷有怪聲音。我到船頭去，我們兩人都聽見了，那聲音有時像孩子的哭聲，有時像女子的哀嚎。我在這個地區捕魚已經有十七年，從未聽過海豹——無論老的還是年輕的——有這種叫聲。當我們站在前甲板觀望時，月亮剛好從雲裡出來，我們兩人都看見某種白色的形體在冰原上移動，它出現的地方與叫聲傳來的方向一致。我們有一段時間失去了它的蹤影，但它隨後又在船頭左舷出現，我們只能看出它就像冰上的陰影。我叫另一名船員到船尾拿槍，麥克勞則與我下船接近它，我們認為那很可能是熊。我們下船來到冰上，麥克勞突然不見了，但我還是朝叫聲的來源走去。我追隨著叫聲走了一英里左右，也許還更長些，然後我感覺那叫聲繞過了冰丘，我抬頭一看，有個東西站在冰丘頂上，似乎已久候多時。我不知道那是什麼。無論如何，那不是熊。那東西高大、雪白而且站得直挺挺的，看起來不是男人，也不是女人。我敢發誓那是更可怕的東西。我使盡吃奶的力氣跑回船上，感謝老天，我終於平安回船。我的契約上規定我要做好船上的工作，如果在船上的話，那當然沒問題，但往後太陽下山之後，不管是誰叫我到冰上，打死我都不肯。」

這是曼森的故事，我已經盡可能重現他的原話。我猜想他看到的一定是——儘管他百般否認——一頭用後腳站立的年輕北極熊，熊在警戒時通常會擺出這樣的姿勢。在光線昏暗下，看起來就像人一樣，如果看的人本身處於極度害怕之下，更有可能看錯。無論那東西是什麼，這件事帶來的是不幸，因為整艘船為此而人心惶惶。大家的臉色變得更難看，不滿也全寫在臉上。船員的牢騷分成兩方面，一方面是他們急著返鄉捕撈鯡魚，另一方面是他們不願困在這艘被宣稱鬧鬼的船上，這兩件事結合起來，使船員們蠢蠢欲動。就連魚叉手——通常由船上資格最老、性格最穩定的人擔任——也禁不住受到鼓動。

撇開這種對迷信的愚蠢執迷不提，船上生活其實還算愉快。南方的浮冰已經有部分融化，海水相當溫暖，我想我們停船的地方可能剛好有灣流經過，灣流北上時會從格陵蘭與斯匹茲卑爾根島之間穿越。在船的附近有許多水母與海蛞蝓，此外還有大量的蝦子，照理說，這裡應該可以看到大量的鯨魚才對。事實上，大約在晚飯的時候，我們看見有一頭鯨魚噴氣，但是以我們的位置來說，不可能降下小艇前去獵捕。

九月十三日——在船橋上與大副米爾納先生相談甚歡。看來覺得船長神祕的不光是我而已，船員乃至於船東都搞不清楚他是什麼樣的人物。米爾納告訴我，當船隻一靠岸，薪水付清之後，克雷吉船長就消失無蹤，直到下次捕鯨季將屆之時，他會悄悄地走進公司辦公室，詢問是否有用得著他的地方。他在鄧迪沒有朋友，他早年的歷史也沒人知道。他的地位完全來自於他身為船員的技術，以及他在擔任船副時表現的勇氣與冷靜，船東因此願意委以重任，由他擔任船長一職。大家一致的看法是他絕非蘇格蘭人，他的名字也肯定不是真實姓名。米爾納先生認為，船長從事捕鯨只是因為這是他能選擇的最危險職業，他在這裡可以用各種可能的方式吸引死神。他舉了幾個例子，其中一個如果是真的，那還真是耐人尋味。有一年，克雷吉並未出現在辦公室，那年只好另外找人遞補。當年剛好是最後一場俄土戰爭。第二年春天，克雷吉再度出現在辦公室，他的脖子側面有一塊凹凸不平的傷口，他特別用領巾遮住它。船副推論那年克雷吉沒來捕鯨是因為參加了戰爭，關於這點，我雖然不敢論定對錯，但這個巧合也實在太不可思議。

風開始轉向，吹起了東風，但風力還是很微弱。我覺得跟昨天相比，浮冰離我們更近了。舉目所及，只見廣袤的一片雪白，當中偶爾出現一些裂縫或冰丘的深色陰影。南邊有一道狹窄的藍色水路，那是我們唯一的逃亡路線，而這條路線似乎每天都在變窄。船長的責任重大。我聽說馬鈴薯已經吃光了，就連餅乾也有點不足，但船長還是擺出同樣不變的表情，整天待在瞭望台用他的望遠鏡環顧整個地平線。他的舉手投足變幻莫測，似乎避免與我接觸，但他不再像那晚那樣對我有粗魯的舉動。

晚上七點半——我仔細思考後得出的意見是，我們被一個瘋子領導，否則的話，實在難以解釋克雷吉船長異想天開的行徑。幸好我還保留著這本航行日記，如果我們不得不約束他的行為——我只同意在沒有別的辦法時才這麼做——那麼這本日記將可提供有利於我們的證詞。有趣的是，正是他自己暴露了自身行為古怪的祕密，他根本是精神有問題，而不只是有怪癖而已。大約一小時前，他站在船橋上，一如往常地用他的望遠鏡瞭望著，至於我則在後甲板區不斷地上下巡邏。

大多數船員都在甲板下方喝茶，最近的輪值似乎亂了章法。我不想繼續來回走動，於是倚靠在舷牆旁，欣賞落日照耀在大片冰原上的柔和光輝。突然間，從我手肘旁傳來沙啞的聲音，使我從白日夢中醒來，我轉頭一看，原來船長已經走下船橋，站在我的身旁。他凝視著整個冰面，恐懼、驚訝與某種類似愉悅的感受輪番在他的臉上湧現，彷彿競逐著主導權。儘管寒冷，他的前額仍汗水涔涔，他顯然因害怕而興奮莫名。他的四肢像癲癇患者一樣抽動著，他的嘴唇緊繃而僵硬。

「看！」他驚呼著，抓住我的手腕，但雙眼依然望著遠處的冰面，他的頭緩慢地朝地平線的方向挪移，彷彿緊盯著某個視野中移動的物體。「看！那裡，就在那裡！在冰丘與冰丘之間！現在她從比較遠的那座冰丘後頭出現了！你看到她了嗎——你『一定』看到她了！她還在那裡！她飛起來了，老天，她離我越來越遠——她消失了！」

他低聲說出最後四個字，語氣滿是痛苦，那一幕我想我永遠也忘不了。船長抓住梯級繩，努力爬上舷牆頂部，彷彿希望再看離開的物體最後一眼。然而他力有未逮，只見他蹣跚地退到交誼廳的天窗旁，倚著窗子不停地喘氣，顯出筋疲力盡的樣子。他的臉變成青紫色，我想再這樣下去他可能會昏倒，所以馬上扶他走下艙梯，讓他躺在艙房的沙發上。我為他倒了杯白蘭地，拿到他的嘴邊，他喝了之後，蒼白的臉孔馬上泛出血色，抽動的四肢也穩定下來。他用手肘支起身體，看了一下四周，然後示意我坐在他的身旁。

「你看到了，不是嗎？」他問道，他還是一樣壓低聲調，顯得很不自然。

「不，我什麼也沒看到。」

他的頭再度往後躺回墊子上。「不，沒有望遠鏡他看不到，」他喃喃自語地說著。「他看不到。我因為有望遠鏡才看得到她，還有充滿愛的眼神——愛的眼神。我說，醫生，不要讓勤務員進來！他會以為我瘋了。幫我把門閂上，麻煩你了！」

我起身，依照他的指示去做。

他靜靜躺了一會兒，顯然陷入沉思，然後他再度用手肘支起身子，又要了一杯白蘭地。

「你應該不會認為我瘋了，是吧，醫生？」他問道，我把白蘭地放回櫃子裡。

「我認為你有心事，」我回答說，「這件事讓你心神不寧，而且對你有害無益。」

「就在那裡，小夥子！」他叫道，酒精的威力使他的雙眼閃閃發亮。「我心裡想著很多——很多事！但我還能計算經緯度，我可以操作六分儀與計算對數。你無法在法庭上作證說我瘋了，你能嗎，現在？」聽一個倒臥的人冷靜地談論自己是否神智清醒，實在是一件怪事。

「或許不行，」我說；「但我仍認為如果你明智的話，應該盡快返家，並且過上一段平靜的日子。」

「回家，是嗎？」他低聲嘀咕著，臉上露出嘲諷的笑容。「你送我一句話，那麼我就送你兩句話，小夥子。跟芙蘿拉安定下來——美麗的小芙蘿拉。噩夢是發瘋的前兆嗎？」

「有時候，」我回道。

「還有呢？發瘋一開始的症狀是什麼？」

「頭痛，耳鳴，眼前出現閃光，幻覺——」

「啊！說說那個吧？」他打斷我的話。「你說的幻覺，那是什麼？」

「看見不存在的事物，那就是幻覺。」

「但她『真的』在那裡！」他呻吟著。「她『就在』那裡！」他起身，打開門閂，緩慢而踉蹌地走回自己的艙房，我想他肯定會一覺睡到明天早上。他的思緒似乎受到可怕的衝擊，但無論如何，那都是他想像自己看到的事物。這個男人變得一天比一天神祕，我擔心他提出來的解決辦法是對的，我也憂慮他的神智已經不正常。我認為他的行為已經無法與罪惡感聯繫在一起。許多高級船員對他有相同的疑慮，現在，這種懷疑也蔓延到一般船員；但我仍找不到方法來協助他。他完全不像個犯罪者，倒像是遭受命運擺布之人，因此大家並不把他當成罪犯，而認為他是個殉道者。

今晚，風向轉為南風。往南的狹窄水道是我們唯一能回家的路，願上帝保佑。我們停泊在北極的巨大浮冰邊緣，這個地方被捕鯨人稱為「障礙物」，只要吹的是北風，圍繞在我們周圍的浮冰就有可能破碎散去，我們就得以離開此地，如果吹的是南風，那麼那些鬆散的浮冰將會朝我們聚攏，最後我們將被兩塊大浮冰夾住，無法動彈。我再說一次，上帝保佑我們！

九月十四日——星期日，也是休息日。我的憂慮成真，南方狹窄的藍色水道消失了。圍繞在我們周圍的盡是巨大靜止的冰原，上面散布著奇形怪狀的冰丘與詭異的冰峰。廣袤的冰原一片死寂，讓人感到恐怖。看不見浪濤拍岸，聽不見海鷗鳴叫與風帆張弛的聲音，整個世界完全沉靜無聲，連船員的低語與他們的靴子踩在白色發亮甲板上的吱呀聲，似乎都與這個世界格格不入。我們唯一的訪客是北極狐，這種動物在浮冰上非常罕見，通常都待在陸地上。然而，牠並未靠近船，而是從遠處看著我們之後，快速地穿過冰原離開。牠的舉動相當耐人尋味，因為一般來說北極狐沒看過人類，而基於好奇的性格，北極狐通常會趨前觀看，因此很容易捕捉。難以置信的是，即使是這樣的小事也會被船員們解讀成凶兆。「那隻可憐的野獸知道更多，唉，至少牠知道的比你我更多！」這是一名負責帶領船員捕鯨的魚叉手做的評論，而其他人都點頭稱是。嘗試與這類無知的迷信辯駁是徒勞的。船員們已經吃了秤鉈鐵了心，相信這艘船遭到詛咒，任誰說什麼他們都不會信。

船長整天把自己鎖在房裡，只有到了下午才在後甲板上短暫現身半個小時。我發現，船長一直看著昨天那東西出現的地方，似乎已做好準備等待那東西出現，但什麼事也沒發生。雖然我緊跟在他身旁，但他似乎沒注意到我。一如以往，禮拜由輪機長主持。有趣的是，在捕鯨船上，通常使用的都是英國國教會的祈禱書，但事實上船上沒有任何人是英國國教會的信眾。我們的船員清一色是羅馬天主教會或長老教會，其中尤以前者為大宗。由於儀式內容既不屬於羅馬天主教會也不屬於長老教會，因此兩邊的信徒都無法抱怨儀式是否偏袒一方，只見大家專注聆聽與禱告，顯示這個安排確實高明。

日落餘暉下，巨大的冰原宛如一座血湖。我從未看過如此美麗又詭異的景象。風轉向了。如果能二十四小時颳北風，那麼我們將轉危為安。

九月十五日——今天是芙蘿拉的生日。親愛的！她總是這麼叫我，我想她看不到我是件好事，因為此時的我正困在冰原之中，陪伴著我的只有一名瘋狂船長與僅能維持數星期的糧食。她一定每天閱讀《蘇格蘭人》報上的船運名單，想知道昔德蘭群島有沒有我們的消息傳來。我必須為船員立下模範，我必須讓自己保持愉快，並且裝出毫不在意的樣子；但上帝知道，我的內心有時感到十分沉重。

今日，溫度計顯示的溫度是華氏十九度。[2] 幾乎沒什麼風，如果有風的話，風向也來自大家不喜歡的方向。船長的精神狀況不錯；我想這個可憐的人一定在夜裡想像自己看到別的預兆或異象，因為今天一大早他跑到我的臥鋪，彎著腰低聲對我說，「那不是幻覺，醫生；那是真的！」早餐後，船長要我檢視糧食還剩多少，於是我與二副一起過去檢查。糧食

2 譯註：約攝氏零下七度。

比我們預期的來得少。往後只剩半個儲藏槽的餅乾、三桶醃肉，與所剩不多的咖啡豆與糖。在船的後艙與冷藏室裡，有許多奢侈品，例如罐裝鮭魚、湯、蔬菜燉羊肉等等，但這些東西很快就會被五十個船員吃光。儲藏室裡有兩桶麵粉，以及無限供應的菸草。總計起來，如果把配給量減為一半，那麼還可以維持十八到二十天——這已經是最大的極限了。船長在聽完我們的報告之後，馬上要所有船員到後甲板集合，他有事要向大家宣布。我想這是他最能派上用場的時候了。高大健壯的體格，黝黑熱切的臉龐，使他成為天生的領導者，他用冷靜的水手口吻討論了我們當前的狀況，並且表示他確實理解危險何在，但他並未忽略各種可能的逃生路線。

「小夥子們，」他說，「你們一定認為是我讓大家陷入這樣的窘境——如果這真的是窘境的話——而你們當中一定有人因此反對我。但你們別忘了，這麼多年來，沒有任何一艘船像我們老『北極星』號一樣來到這個地區，捕獲那麼多的鯨魚油，你們每個人都分到了利潤。當其他窮小子在教區裡追求女孩卻無人搭理時，你們全結了婚，而且留下老婆在陸地上過著舒服的日子，跟著我來這裡捕鯨。如果你們因為被困在這裡而怨我，那麼就請你們想想你們分到多少錢，我們可以在這裡彼此兩清，互不相欠。我們過去也曾面臨許多困難，而我們都一一克服了，如果我們現在面對眼前這個困境，最後失敗收場，我們也應該毫無怨言才是。再不濟，我們可以到冰原上，我們可以在海豹群中棲身，牠們的肉可以讓我們活到明年春天。然而事情不會演變到這種地步，因為不到三個星期，你們就能看到蘇格蘭的海岸。至於現在，每個人都要共體時艱，配給量減為一半，每個人都如此，沒有任何人有特權。各位要專注，切勿鬆懈，過去我們能克服那麼多危險，沒有理由過不了眼前這一關。」他的幾句話，馬上對船員起到振奮作用。他先前的不受歡迎完全一掃而空，而我提到的那位迷信的資深魚叉手則是帶頭歡呼三聲，所有的船員都由衷地吶喊助威。

九月十六日——夜裡，風向轉為北風，浮冰似乎開始出現縫隙。船員們精神奕奕，絲毫未因為配給減半而受影響。引擎室仍維持發動的狀態，只要一有逃脫的機會，就能毫無耽擱地加速前進。船長看起來心情很好，但他的表情仍帶有我先前說過的狂野與「異常」。與之前的陰鬱相比，這種突然出現的欣喜情緒反而更讓我困惑。我搞不懂。我想我在日記的前面提過，船長有許多怪癖，其中之一就是他絕不允許任何人進他的艙房，他堅持自己鋪床，許多事情都親自處理。令我驚訝的是，今天他把艙房的鑰匙交給我，要我利用正午他測量太陽高度時，到他房裡好好研究一下經線儀。那是相當小的艙房，裡頭有個臉盆架與幾本書，沒什麼貴重物品，只有牆壁上掛著幾幅畫。絕大多數是仿油畫的便宜印刷品，但其中有一幅水彩畫吸引了我的目光，那是一名年輕女性的頭像。那顯然是一幅肖像畫，而非船員們特別愛看的那種花俏的美女圖。這幅巧妙地混合了性格與虛弱的畫作，顯然不可能出自藝術家的匠心獨具。疲憊而恍惚的眼神，低垂的睫毛，貼近眼睛的粗眉，但經過細心整理而顯得柔順，與線條分明突出的下巴以及堅定的下唇形成強烈的對比。在畫作下方的角落，寫著「M．B，十九歲時畫像」。才十九歲的年紀就能在臉上顯現出如此強烈的意志力，對我來說，這實在難以置信。她一定是個不凡的女性。她的相貌深深吸引了我，雖然我只短暫看了一眼，但如果我是個善於作畫的人，我一定能在日記本上仔細地畫下她的容貌。我想著這名女子在船長的生命中占有什麼樣的地位。他把女子的肖像掛在床尾，好讓自己可以不斷地注視著她。要不是船長絕不提自己的事，否則我真想問個明白。艙房裡的其他物品並無特別之處——制服外套、摺凳、小型眼鏡、菸草盒與各種菸斗，包括一只東方的水煙筒——頂多是讓米爾納先生說的船長參加戰爭的故事略微可信一點，只不過兩者的連結還是有些牽強。

晚上十一點二十分——船長結束了漫長而有趣的話題之後，便回房睡覺了。船長其實可以成為最好相處的夥伴，他博覽群書，而且不用專斷獨行也能讓周圍的人信從。我不喜歡在思考時遭受旁人的干擾壓制。船長談到靈魂的本質，並且嫻熟而概略地描述亞里斯多德與柏拉圖的靈魂觀點。他似乎相信靈魂轉世與畢達哥拉斯的學說。在討論這些話題時，我們觸及到現代唯靈論，我開玩笑地暗示斯雷德（Slade）[3]的詐欺案。但令我驚訝的是，船長卻嚴正地提醒我不要混淆無辜與有罪，並且認為我的邏輯等於是宣稱因為猶大這個惡徒信仰基督教，所以基督教是個錯誤一樣。不久，船長與我互道晚安，然後回到自己的房間。

風勢變強，而且持續從北方吹來。現在，每日入夜後的陰暗已與英國不相上下。希望明日我們能從冰凍的枷鎖中解脫。

九月十七日——又傳來鬧鬼的消息。感謝老天，我是個粗枝大葉的人，這些小事不至於讓我煩心！這些可憐的傢伙滿腦子迷信，而他們描述的狀況，全都是發自內心，絕無一絲欺瞞，而正因如此，凡是第一次聽他們講述的人，莫不被他們的繪聲繪影嚇個半死。關於鬧鬼的事有許多說法，但每個人言之鑿鑿的部分是整晚一直有東西繞行著船邊，彼得赫德的桑迪．麥克唐納與昔德蘭的「老」彼得．威廉森都看到了，船橋上的米爾納先生也看到了——在有三名目擊者的狀況下，聽起來要比之前二副所說的來得可信。我在早餐後對米爾納說，他應該破除這些無稽之談，而且身為高級船員，他應該做個好榜樣。他那顆飽經風霜的頭不祥地搖了幾下，然後以他慣有的謹慎說道，「也許是，也許不是，醫生，」他說，「我

3　編註：斯雷德（Henry Slade, 1835-1905），美國靈媒，善於「板書魔術」（slate-writing）。一八七六年在倫敦表演板書魔術時被揭穿為騙局因而被判入獄，為了躲避坐牢而逃往美國。

沒有說我看到鬼。我沒有辦法確定我是不是看見某種可怕的東西，不過倒是有不少人宣稱他們看見更驚悚的事物。我不是膽小之輩，但如果你不是大白天時問我，而是昨晚跟我一起看見那個白色而陰森的東西，相信你一定會毛骨悚然。那東西在黑暗中叫著，就像羔羊在呼喊母親一樣。我想，你絕不會把它當成是三姑六婆在嚼舌根。」我想跟他講理是不可能了，於是只好請他幫個忙，如果再看到幽靈，一定要叫我——他同意時語氣中似乎充滿了感嘆，彷彿這樣的機會不可能再出現。

如我所希望的，我們身後的白色荒漠逐漸裂成許多細流，這些細流來自各個方向，彼此交錯。我們今日的緯度是八十度五十二分，顯示有一股往南的強大力量拉動著浮冰。如果風向持續對我們有利，不用多久南邊的浮冰就會碎裂散去。目前，我們什麼也幫不上忙，只能抽菸等待最好的情況發生。我很快就成為一名宿命論者。當面對風與冰這些不確定因素時，人真的無能為力。或許正是阿拉伯沙漠的風沙，使得穆罕默德最初的追隨者拜伏在命運之前。

這些幽靈的警訊對船長造成惡劣的影響。我擔心這件事會攪擾他的敏感心靈，因此刻意不讓他知道這件蠢事，然而遺憾的是，他在無意間聽見船員們在談這件事，於是堅持要他們一五一十向他稟報。如我所預料的，他在知道這件事之後，潛藏的精神失常變得極度誇大。我幾乎無法相信眼前的這個人前一晚還跟我大談哲學，而且表現出最敏銳的批判力與最冷靜的判斷力。他在後甲板來回踱步，像頭囚籠中的猛虎，偶爾停下，張牙舞爪一番，而後又不耐地注視著浮冰。他不斷喃喃自語，有一次他大聲喊道，「再等一下，吾愛——再等一下！」可憐的傢伙，原本意氣風發的海上男兒，博學有禮的紳士，如今卻成了這副德性；他的心智原本最懼怕的是平凡無奇的人生，然而過度的想像與幻覺，卻使他神智不清，令人唏噓不已。天底下還有人像我一樣，夾在精神失常的船長與整天嚷著鬧鬼的船副之間，窮於應付嗎？有時我覺得，我大概是船上唯一清醒的人——或許還有一個神智清楚的人，那就是大管輪。他是個喜歡沉思的人，他在紅海航行時，旁邊的人說什麼妖魔鬼怪他都充耳不聞，只要這些鬼魅之物不來煩他，也不弄亂他的工具，那麼他也懶得搭理這些話題。

浮冰的裂縫快速擴大，很可能明天早晨我們就能再度起錨航行。當我告訴家鄉的人，我所遭遇的各種怪事時，他們都以為我在編故事。

午夜十二點——我受到極大的驚嚇，不過在喝了一杯嗆烈的白蘭地之後，我終於穩定下來。然而，我還沒完全回過神來，這一點從我的筆跡可以看出。事實上，我經歷了一次非常古怪的經驗，我因此開始懷疑自己是否能合理地把船上的人稱為瘋子，只因為他們宣稱自己看見我認為不合理的事物。啐！我是笨蛋嗎？怎麼能煩心這種瑣碎小事；當我親身遭遇與先前聽過的驚恐說法一致的現象之後，我既不能質疑曼森先生的故事，也不能對船副嗤之以鼻，畢竟這一切似乎有憑有據。

話說回來，我經歷的現象並不是非常恐怖——只是聲音而已。我無法期望有人會讀到我寫的這段文字，如果有的話，想必會同情我的感受，或理解當時這種聲音對我的影響。吃完晚飯，我在回房就寢前，先到甲板上一個人靜靜抽菸。今晚的夜色特別黑——幾乎一點亮光也沒有，當我站在船尾小艇下方時，完全看不見船橋上的船員。我想我已經提過在冰凍的洋面上，寂靜的感覺有多麼明顯強烈。在世界其他地方，就算貧瘠荒涼可以與極地冰原一較高下，但置身其中的我們依然能感受到空氣中傳來的些許振動——某種微弱的低鳴聲，也許來自遙遠的人聲，或樹葉摩擦的聲音，或鳥兒的拍翅聲，或甚至是地面青草的沙沙聲。這些細微的聲音我們也許不會主動去辨識，但一旦少了這些聲音，我們馬上就會感覺到哪裡不對勁。但只有在北極海，深不可測的寂靜從四面八方包圍住我們，充滿著可怕的陰森氣氛。你發現自己的耳膜為了捕捉細微的聲音而緊繃著，渴望聽見船上任何偶發的可能聲響。我往前倚靠著舷牆，此時從浮冰，幾乎是從我的正下方傳來一陣叫聲，尖銳刺耳，劃破了寧靜的黑夜。起始的高音，非歌劇的首席女歌手所能企及，然而那高音還能輾轉攀升，直到一聲長嘯，充滿了哀怨與悲慟，那也許是迷途靈魂的最後哀鳴。可怕的嚎叫聲依然在我耳中繚繞著。哀傷，難以名狀的悲苦，全都表達在叫聲之中，還有強烈的渴望，偶爾還穿插著狂野的得意。那聲音緊鄰在我四周出現，然而當我瞪大眼睛看著黑暗，卻看不出任何東西。我等待了一會兒，但那聲音就此消失，再也沒出現，於是我回到甲板下方的艙房，與過去相比，我的想法似乎開始動搖。當我走下艙梯，剛好看見米爾納先生上來換班。「醫生，」他說，「也許那是三姑六婆在嚼舌根？你沒聽到那叫聲多悽厲嗎？也許那是迷信？你現在還這麼想嗎？」我應該向這名誠實的船員道歉，並且承認我跟他一樣感到困惑。或許明天狀況看起來會不一樣。目前，我幾乎不敢寫下自己心中的想法。往後我檢視今日的記載，也許那時的我已將此事拋諸腦後，所以現在我或許應該將自己脆弱的一面隱藏起來。

九月十八日——度過心神不寧的夜晚，我的腦子裡依然充斥著那股奇怪的聲音。船長看起來也沒睡好，只見他一臉憔悴，雙眼充滿血絲。我沒有告訴他昨晚的遭遇，也沒有這個必要。現在的他已經相當不安而亢奮，只見他一下子起身，一下子坐下，完全靜不下來。

今天早晨，浮冰終於如我預期的裂出一條水道，我們起錨，發動引擎，以每小時十二英里的速度往西南西方向前進。然後，我們被一塊浮冰擋住去路，這塊浮冰就跟我們離開的那塊浮冰一樣巨大。我們動彈不得，只好再度下錨等待浮冰裂解，如果風勢持續，相信二十四小時內我們又能繼續前進。看到幾隻冠海豹在水中游泳，射殺了一隻，牠的體長超過十一英尺，相當巨大。冠海豹是凶猛好鬥的動物，連北極熊也不是牠的對手。幸好冠海豹的行動遲緩笨拙，在冰上攻擊牠們幾乎不會有任何危險。

船長顯然不認為我們已渡過難關，我不懂他為什麼如此悲觀，每個船員都認為我們已經奇蹟似地逃脫，而且必將航抵開闊的海域。

「醫生，你是不是覺得我們已經脫險了？」船長說道，我們在晚飯後坐在一起閒聊。

「我希望如此，」我回答說。

「我們不能太肯定——但無疑地，你是對的。我們不久就會投入真愛的懷抱，不是嗎？但我們不能太肯定——我們不能太肯定。」

他沉默地坐著，若有所思，兩隻腳不由自主地前後擺盪著。「看看這裡，」他又說；「這是個危險的地方，即使在最宜人的時候，也充滿凶險。我知道一些人在這樣的地方突然死去。有時候，只要不慎失足就會送命——一旦跌入冰縫，只會看到綠色海水中有氣泡升起，顯示你跌入海中的位置。奇怪的是，」他露出神經質的微笑，「這麼多年來，我每年都會來這裡，但我從沒想過要預立遺囑。不是說我有什麼特別的東西要留給別人，而是當人們從事具有危險性的工作時，總是希望預先安排好後事，你不這麼覺得嗎？」

「當然，」我回道，搞不懂他到底想說什麼。

「一個人如果把後事都安排好了，就會感到安心不少，」船長接著說。「接下來我要說的是，一旦我有個三長兩短，我希望你可以幫我處理後事。我的艙房裡東西不多，儘管如此，我希望把這些物品賣了，賣得的錢就當作鯨魚油的利潤，依照同樣的比例分給全船所有的同仁。至於經線儀，我希望你留著，就當作這次航行的紀念。當然，這一切只是以防萬一，但我想我還是利用這個機會把事情交代給你。我想如果真有那麼一天，我可以仰賴你吧？」

「當然，絕對沒問題，」我回道，「而且既然你這麼說，我也——」

「你！你！」他打斷我的話。「你不會有事的。你到底有什麼毛病？我不是發脾氣，但我不喜歡聽年輕人——他們的人生才剛開始——動不動就說死。上去甲板呼吸一點新鮮空氣，不要在船艙裡胡思亂想，順便也鼓勵我這麼做。」

這段對話，我越想越不對勁。為什麼這個人偏偏在我們即將脱險的時刻交代後事？在他狀似瘋狂的背後，一定存在著某種念頭。難道他想自殺？我記得他曾嚴詞抨擊自殺是十惡不赦的事。然而，我必須留意他的一舉一動，雖然我無法隨意闖入他的艙房，但只要他在甲板上，我不會讓他離開我的視線。

米爾納先生對我的憂慮嗤之以鼻，他説那只是「船長一時興起」。他自己倒是對當前的處境十分樂觀。米爾納認為，後天我們就能脱離浮冰，再過兩天會經過揚馬延島，一個多星期後就能看見昔德蘭群島。我希望他不要太樂觀了。與船長的陰鬱謹慎相比，米爾納的意見似乎穩健許多。米爾納是個資深而經驗豐富的船員，説話之前總是多所斟酌。

＊＊＊

長久以來一直聽説會有災難出現，終於，災難發生了。我實在不知道該怎麼記錄這起事件。船長消失了。他也許會活生生地再次出現在我們面前，但我想恐怕不會有那麼一天。現在是九月十九日早上七點。昨天一整晚，我和一群船員橫越我們面前的廣大冰原，希望發現船長的蹤影，但最終一無所獲。我應該試著陳述船長消失的來龍去脈。如果有人偶然間讀到我寫下的文字，我相信他們一定會記得，我不是基於猜測或傳聞而寫，我身為一名神智清楚與受過良好教育之人，所描述的完全是我親眼目睹之事。當中的推論完全出自我個人的思考，但我的思考完全根據事實。

船長在跟我談過話之後，心情依然愉快。然而，他似乎有點緊張與不耐煩，他一直走來走去，四肢的擺動有點像舞蹈症患者一樣毫無規律，但這似乎是他的身體特徵，他有時就是會如此。才過十五分鐘，他已經走上甲板七次，但在甲板上快速走了幾步之後，又馬上走下甲板。每一次我都緊跟著他，因為他的表情讓我深信絕不能讓他走出我的視線之外。他似乎知道自己的行為產生的影響，因為看得出來他裝出一副極度開心的樣子，對於極其普通的笑話也開懷大笑，彷彿為了讓我寬心似的。

晚餐後，船長再度走向船尾，而我尾隨其後。夜晚黑暗而平靜，只有風吹過圓杆的聲音，令人感到些許愁悶。西北方湧現厚厚的雲層，前端零亂的觸手延伸到月亮前方，最後，只能從雲層的縫隙處透出一點月光。船長快速地來回踱步，然後他看見我還死纏著他不放，於是走過來暗示我，他認為我最好到甲板下——毫無疑問，他這麼做更加強了我待在甲板上的決心。

之後，我想他似乎是忘了我的存在，只見他靜靜地倚在船尾欄杆上，望著廣大的雪白荒原，其中有部分隱沒在陰影中，有部分則在月光下閃爍著朦朧的亮光。有好幾次，我看見他在看錶，還有一次他低聲說了簡短的句子，我只能聽見「準備好了」這四個字。坦白說，當我看見船長高大的影子逐漸拉長隱沒在黑暗中時，突然一陣毛骨悚然的感覺席捲全身，我想到船長該不會是跟什麼人有約吧，那是跟誰呢？一旦心裡起了這樣的念頭，我便一股腦兒將一個個事實依次串連起來，但我終究未準備好面對最後將發生的事。

突然間，他的態度突然專注起來，我覺得他應該看見了什麼。我悄悄走到他的身後。他以渴望而疑惑的眼神看著前方的環狀霧氣，風強勁地吹著，那塊霧氣與船成一直線。那是一團朦朧的雲氣，看不出形狀，在月光的照射下，時而清楚，時而模糊。稀薄雲霧的頂端發出明亮的光輝，宛如銀蓮花的外層，連月亮也為之失色。

「來吧，我的愛人，來吧，」船長叫著，他的聲音充滿無限的溫柔與關愛，宛如得償所願似的安慰著對方，無論是施予還是收受都同感滿足。

接下來是轉瞬間發生的事。我無力阻止。船長一躍上了舷牆，然候再一躍落到了冰上，幾乎是跟隨在白色的霧狀身影之後。他伸出手，似乎是想抓住那團霧氣，只見他張開雙臂，嘴裡喊著愛戀的話語，就這樣跑進黑暗之中。我仍然站著，只是全身僵硬，一動也不動，眼睜睜看著他的身影越來越模糊，直到他的聲音在遠處消失為止。我原本認為不可能再看到他了，但此時月光從雲縫照射下來，照亮了廣大的冰原。我看見船長的深色身影已經離船非常遙遠，而且以驚人的速度在結凍的平原上前進。這是我們最後一次瞧見他的身影——說最後一次並不算錯。我們派出小隊尋找他，我也跟著前往，但隊員們似乎都無心尋找，最後無功而返。幾個小時內，還要再派出第二隊。我真不敢相信，當我寫下這些事時，我居然還沒做夢或做過可怕的噩夢。

晚上七點三十分——筋疲力盡地返回船上，第二次還是沒有任何發現。浮冰非常廣大，雖然我們至少在上面行進了二十英里，還是看不到盡頭。冰原上結成的霜變得十分堅硬，仿佛花崗岩一樣，我們無法在上面留下足跡，作為引導我們回程的指標。船員認為我們應該放棄尋找任務，趕緊上船，發動引擎向南航行，因為浮冰在夜裡已經敞開，遠遠望去，地平線上已可看見海洋。船員們認為克雷吉船長顯然已經死了，我們不需要冒著生命危險進行毫無意義的搜尋，而應該把握機會趕緊脫離此地。米爾納先生與我苦口婆心地勸他們搜尋到明晚，並且承諾屆時若找不到就馬上開船，絕不延誤。我們提議大家小睡片刻，然後進行最後一次搜尋。

九月二十日，傍晚——今天早上，我跟一個小隊搜尋浮冰南半部，米爾納先生則往北搜尋。我們走了十到十二英里，沒有看見任何生物的蹤跡，只看見一隻鳥從我們頭上飛過，我從牠飛行的方式判斷，牠可能是一隻老鷹。冰原的極南端逐漸消褪成一道細長的尖端，插入海中。當我們來到這個海岬與冰原連接的地方時，船員們停住腳步，但我懇請他們繼續走到最前端的地方，好讓我們能竭盡所有可能，不要留下任何遺憾。

我們才走不到一百碼，彼得赫德的麥克唐納就大聲呼叫，他發現前方有東西，於是開始奔跑。我們也看到了，大家一擁而上。起初，我們只覺得在雪白的地面上有個深色的物體，等到接近時一看，是個男人的樣子，最後我們終於認出他就是我們尋找的人。他臉朝下躺在冰凍的岸上。他的身上覆蓋著一層小冰晶與羽狀的雪花，在他深色的船員大衣上閃閃發亮。當我們接近船長時，一陣旋風捲起了這些冰晶與雪花，將它們帶往空中，有一部分又再度落下，然後再度被捲上去，最後加速往海上飛去。在我看來，那只是一陣風雪，但許多船員卻堅稱那構成了一個女人的形體，那女人俯在船長身上，親吻他，然後快速穿越浮冰而去。我已經學乖了，這回無論多麼荒誕，我都不輕易表示那是無稽之談。顯然克雷吉船長死前並不痛苦，因為在他已經青紫的臉上掛著燦爛的微笑，他的雙手依然張開著，彷彿抓住了那個召喚他走到陰暗世界進入死亡的神祕訪客。

當天下午，我們舉行海葬，我們用船的旗幟包裹船長的遺體，並且在腳上綁了三十二磅重的鉛塊。我閱讀葬禮的禱文，一些平日粗枝大葉的船員此時哭得跟小孩一樣，他們許多人其實深受船長的照顧，只是他在世時的一些詭異行徑，壓抑了船員們對他的感情。他的遺體從格柵滑入水中，只濺起了些許暗色的水花，我看見船長在綠水中不斷下沉、下沉、下沉，直到他就像一塊白色的小拼布，懸浮在永恆的黑暗邊緣。最後，就連白色的小點也被陰暗吞噬，他消失了。他將與他胸中的祕密與謎團一起長眠此地，直到偉大的日子來臨，大海將放棄他的遺體，克雷吉從冰裡浮現，臉上依然帶著笑容，僵直的手臂依然伸展著向眾人打招呼。我祈禱他在彼世能比在此世過得幸福。

我的日記到此為止。我們的返鄉之路平順而清楚地呈現在我們面前，廣大的冰原很快就將成為記憶的一部分。要從近來這起事件中平復，需要一段時間。當我開始記錄我們的航行過程時，我沒有想到自己居然是在如此無奈的狀況下停止書寫。當我獨自一人在艙房裡撰寫時，我有時會開始想像自己聽見了死去的船長在上面的甲板快速而緊張地走著。今晚，我進到他的艙房，這是我的職責，我必須製作他的財產清冊，並且將它們記在官方日誌裡。房間裡跟我之前看到的完全一樣，但我之前提過的那幅掛在船長床尾的畫，已經從畫框消失，看起來是用刀子割下來的，只有這張畫不見了。在記下這段奇異證據鏈的最後一個環節之後，我闔上了這本「北極星」號航行日記。

〔約翰．馬里斯特．老雷伊醫生的註記——我讀完了我兒子的日記，裡面提到與「北極星」船長的死有關的種種怪事。我相信，我的兒子已經把事情的來龍去脈詳細描述出來，而且我十分肯定他所言不虛，因為他是個沉穩堅毅、不妄自想像的人，而他對於真實的追求向來不遺餘力。然而，這則故事乍看之下晦澀難懂，而內容又涉及怪力亂神之事，因此我長久以來一直反對出版。然而，最近幾天，我突然得到了獨立的證言，使我對整件事有了新的想法。我之前曾到愛丁堡參加英國醫學學會會議，在那裡偶然地遇見P醫生，他是我在大學時代的好友，現在在德文郡的薩爾塔什執業。我向他轉述兒子的親身經驗，他對我說，他與這個人相熟，並且向我描述這個人的特徵，我大吃一驚，因為他所說的跟我兒子日記上描述的人分毫不差，唯一的不同是他口中的那個人比較年輕。根據P醫生的描述，這個人之前與住在康瓦爾郡海邊的一名美麗女子訂婚。在他出海的時候，他的未婚妻因為某起恐怖的事件身亡。」

黑彼得懸案

編輯說明：雖然福爾摩斯探案不乏對船隻與船員的描述，但沒有任何一篇小說像〈黑彼得懸案〉一樣清楚反映出柯南．道爾在「希望」號上的經驗。在這篇小說中，捕鯨船船長的胸部遭魚叉貫穿，「就像釘在紙板上的甲蟲一樣」。柯南．道爾幾名傳記作家提到，〈黑彼得懸案〉於一九〇四年三月刊登於《河濱雜誌》，之後引起約翰．格雷的抗議，這位「希望」號船長似乎從惡形惡狀的彼得．凱瑞身上看見自己的影子。但這是不可能的事，不僅因為凱瑞在敵對的鄧迪港受到歡呼，也因為格雷船長早在這篇小說刊登前十二年於家鄉彼得赫德去世。

我從來沒有見過我的朋友身心有如在一八九五年那般健壯。他不斷上漲的名聲為他帶來龐大的工作量，而我只要稍微暗示到訪我們貝克街寒酸的事務所那些有頭有臉的人物是誰，也會被視為輕率、不夠慎重。然而，福爾摩斯就跟古往今來那些偉大的藝術家一樣，他似乎只為藝術而活，除了霍德尼斯公爵的案子外，我很少聽說他為了自己不眠不休的調查而索求高額的報酬。福爾摩斯視錢財如無物——或者你也可以說，他只專注於追尋自己想做的事——如果案子無法勾起他的同情心，那麼即使客戶是位高權重家財萬貫之人，他也會推辭；反之，如果案子的詭譎與戲劇性觸動了他的想像或令他百思不解，那麼即使客戶阮囊羞澀，他也會不辭勞苦地花上數星期進行調查。

一八九五年是值得紀念的一年，在這年，一連串耐人尋味且充滿玄機的案子吸引福爾摩斯的注意，從著名的托斯卡樞機主教猝死案——由教宗親自出面拜託他進行調查——到他逮捕威爾遜這名惡名昭彰的金絲雀訓練師，為倫敦東區去除了禍害。緊接在這兩件大案子之後的是伍德曼宅的悲劇，以及圍繞在彼得·凱瑞船長之死那些極其離奇難解的狀況。

如果不提這起極不尋常的案件，那麼夏洛克·福爾摩斯探案史便不算完整。

七月的第一個星期，我的朋友經常不在我們的住所內，而且時間相當長，我知道他肯定有事。這段期間，有幾個看起來不修邊幅的傢伙來找他，並且問起巴塞爾船長的事，我知道福爾摩斯一定喬裝易容、改名換姓，隱藏自己的身分在某處祕密調查。他在倫敦至少有五個藏身處，用來轉換自己的身分。他未向我透露任何訊息，而我也沒有探聽隱私的習慣。他給我的第一個有關他的調查方向的訊息非比尋常。他在早餐前出門，當我坐下來準備吃早餐時，他走進房間，手臂夾著一根長矛，矛尖是帶著倒鉤的魚叉頭，他夾在腋下，彷彿當它是一把雨傘。

「我的天哪，福爾摩斯！」我叫道。「你該不會想告訴我，你帶著這東西在倫敦各處亂逛吧？」

「我搭車去肉販那兒，然後回來。」

「肉販？」

「而且我帶著絕佳的胃口返家。毫無疑問，親愛的華生，早餐之前運動確實有助於胃口大開。但我已經準備好要打賭，你絕對猜不到我做了什麼運動。」

「我並不打算猜測。」

他咯咯地笑著，一邊為自己倒了杯咖啡。

「如果朝阿勒代斯後頭的店鋪看進去，你會看見一頭死豬掛在天花板的鉤子上，豬的身體還在那兒晃蕩著，一名穿著袖套的男子猛烈地用我手上拿的這個武器刺那頭豬。我就是那個使勁刺豬的人，而我對自己感到滿意，因為我不需要用太多力氣，就能一次刺穿那頭豬。或許你也想試試？」

「我沒興趣。你到底在那裡幹什麼？」

「因為我覺得這跟伍德曼宅懸案有著間接的關聯性。啊，霍普金斯，我昨晚接到你的電話，我正想著你的事呢，過來加入我們吧！」

我們的訪客警戒性極高，三十歲，穿著素淨的花呢西裝，但身體還是相當筆挺，顯然他已習慣穿著官方的制服。我馬上認出他是斯坦利．霍普金斯，一名年輕的督察，福爾摩斯對他的未來寄予厚望，而他也如同弟子一樣，對福爾摩斯的科學辦案手法充滿仰慕與敬意。霍普金斯愁容滿面，他坐下來，一副垂頭喪氣的樣子。

「不，謝謝你，先生。我在來之前已經吃過早飯。我晚上待在倫敦，我昨天來此回報。」

「你要回報什麼？」

「失敗，先生——一敗塗地。」

「你毫無進展嗎？」

「毫無進展。」

「真是的！看來我必須看看這個案子了。」

「我很希望你能了解一下案情，福爾摩斯先生。這是我第一個大好機會，但我的聰明才智已到了極限。看在老天分上，請助我一臂之力。」

「嗯，好吧，碰巧我才剛讀過所有的證據資料，包括死亡驗屍報告，我讀得還算仔細。順便問一下，你對於犯罪現場發現的那個菸草袋有何看法？一點線索也沒有嗎？」

霍普金斯露出驚訝的表情。

「那是死者的菸草袋，先生。袋子裡繡著死者姓名的首字母。菸草袋是用海豹皮做的——他是個資深的獵海豹人。」

「但他沒有菸斗。」

「沒有，先生，我們找不到菸斗；事實上，他很少抽菸。他的菸草也許是他幫朋友保管的。」

「我想是的。我提這件事只是因為如果是我偵辦本案，我會把菸斗當成調查的起點。然而，我的朋友華生醫生對本案一無所知，我再聽一次案情也不會有什麼損失。就請你簡單告訴我們事件的始末吧。」

斯坦利．霍普金斯從口袋裡掏出一張紙條來。

「我這裡有幾個日期，你們聽了之後就能了解死者，也就是彼得．凱瑞船長的職業。他生於一八四五年——五十歲。他是最大膽與最成功的獵海豹人與捕鯨人。一八八三年，他擔任來自鄧迪的蒸汽船『獨角鯨』號的船長，這是一艘專門用來獵捕海豹的船隻。他曾連續數次出海，每次都豐收，隔年，也就是一八八四年，凱瑞退休。之後，他旅行數年，最後在薩塞克斯郡佛瑞斯特街附近買了一間小住宅，稱為伍德曼宅。他在那裡住了六年，一個星期前，他陳屍在家中。

「這個人有一些奇特之處。平日，他是個嚴謹的清教徒——沉默寡言、性情陰鬱。他的家庭成員包括他的妻子、二十歲的女兒與兩名女僕。女僕經常更換，因為凱瑞家顯然不是一個令人愉快的工作場所，有時候甚至可以說令人難以忍受。凱瑞是個酒鬼，情況時好時壞，當酒癮犯了的時候，他便成為一個不折不扣的惡魔。眾所皆知，他曾經在大半夜把妻子與女兒趕出家門，並且在公園裡鞭打她們，她們的慘叫聲把城門外的村民都給驚醒了。

「他曾因為暴力攻擊牧師而遭到傳喚，而先前牧師曾為了他的野蠻行為上門勸戒他。簡單地說，福爾摩斯先生，你要找到比彼得．凱瑞更凶暴的人恐怕相當困難，而我聽說他在船上也是用同樣的脾氣對待下屬。同行給他取了綽號，叫黑彼得。不只是因為他的膚色黝黑、且留著黑色大鬍子，也因為他令人生畏的火爆脾氣。我想不用我多作解釋，各位也能理解鄰居有多討厭他，對他避之唯恐不及，而他的慘死，我也沒聽過他的鄰居說過一句難過的話。

「福爾摩斯先生，你肯定已經讀過死因調查報告裡對於死者艙房的描述；但你這位朋友或許並不知道裡面寫了什麼。凱瑞在屋外又為自己另外蓋了一間木造房——他總是稱這間小屋為『艙房』——這間木造房離他的屋子約數百碼，他每晚都睡在這間木造房裡。房子很小，只有一個房間，長十六英尺，寬十英尺。他隨身攜帶小屋的鑰匙，自己鋪床，自己打掃，不讓任何人進這間屋子。屋子的每一面都裝了窗戶，窗門緊閉，窗簾也總是拉上。其中一扇窗對著大馬路，夜裡當屋內點起蠟燭時，人們總是指指點點，猜想黑彼得在屋內做什麼。福爾摩斯先生，根據死因調查報告，就是這扇對著馬路的窗戶給了我們幾個正面的證據。

「你記得有一個石匠名叫斯雷特，他在凌晨一點左右從佛瑞斯特街走來——這是謀殺案前兩天的事——當他經過小屋附近時，停了下來，看見樹林之間有塊方形的亮光透了出來。斯雷特信誓旦旦地說，有個男人的側臉陰影清楚地映照在窗簾上，斯雷特與凱瑞很熟，他知道那個影子顯然不是凱瑞。那是個蓄鬍的男子，但鬍子較短而且樣子跟凱瑞不太一樣。話是這麼說，但斯雷特在此之前已經在酒館待了兩個鐘頭，而且他是站在路邊望向窗戶，兩者其實隔了一段距離。此外，斯雷特看到的時間是星期一，而犯罪時間卻是星期三。

「星期二，彼得．凱瑞心情其差無比，他喝得酩酊大醉，野蠻粗暴，活像危險的野獸。他在自家附近閒晃，妻女一聽到他來了，馬上躲得遠遠的。晚間，他回到自己的小屋。隔天凌晨兩點左右，他的女兒——她睡覺時通常開著窗——聽見小屋的方向傳來悽厲的叫聲，但凱瑞喝醉時經常會吶喊咆哮，因此她不以為意。到了七點起床時間，一名女僕注意到小屋的門是開著的，然而大家實在太懼怕凱瑞了，因此直到中午才有人敢進屋去一探究竟。他們從門口窺探，看到的景象使他們嚇得魂飛魄散、面無血色，一溜煙地逃回村裡。一小時內，我到了現場，並且由我負責這個案子。

「嗯，福爾摩斯先生，你知道的，我這個人膽子向來很大，但我要坦白跟你說，當我探頭到那間小屋時，居然渾身抖了一下。蚊蠅四處飛舞亂竄，如小風琴般發出嗡嗡的聲音，地上與牆壁沾滿血跡，活像座屠宰場。凱瑞把這間小屋稱為船艙，而它確實像個船艙，因為走到裡面你會覺得自己是在一艘船上。在屋子的一端擺著臥鋪，水手櫃、地圖與海圖，『獨角鯨』號的照片，書架上擺著一排航海日誌，這些全是船長艙房裡的物品。屋子的中央是死者，他的臉如失落的靈魂飽受折磨般扭曲，灰白的大鬍子也因痛苦而豎立上指。一根鋼製魚叉從他的寬闊胸膛直穿而過，刺進他身後的木牆上。他就像釘在紙板上的甲蟲一樣。當然，他已經死了，而且應該是在他發出最後一聲哀嚎的那一刻死的。

「我知道你的方法，先生，而我會照你的方法做。我要求維持現場原貌，然後我非常仔細地檢查屋外的地面以及屋內的地板。沒有任何足跡。」

「意思是說你沒看見任何足跡？」

「我向你保證，先生，沒有任何足跡。」

「親愛的霍普金斯，我調查過許多犯罪，但我從未看過會飛的動物犯下的案子。只要犯人是用兩隻腳走路，那麼科學辦案者一定能找出壓痕、刮痕或微不足道的變化。這間濺滿血污的房間，說是找不到任何能協助我們辦案的證據，實在令人難以相信。事實上，我從死因調查結果發現，你有好幾個地方忽略了沒有好好檢視。」

這名年輕的警督察聽見我的夥伴的尖刻評論，整個人變得畏縮起來。

「福爾摩斯先生，我實在太蠢了，居然沒有通知你來。然而，現在追悔也無濟於事。是的，房間裡的確有幾件物品值得特別關注。」

「首先是魚叉，也就是殺人凶器。它是從牆壁架子上拿下來的。架子上還有兩根魚叉，並且還有空位擺放第三根魚叉，那就是行凶的魚叉原來擺放的位置。魚叉柄上刻著『蒸汽船「獨角鯨」號，鄧迪』。這應可證明凶手是在一時氣憤下殺人，而魚叉是他順手抄起的武器。犯罪發生的時間是在凌晨兩點，但彼得．凱瑞卻衣著整齊，顯示他與凶手有約，這點可以從桌上擺著一瓶蘭姆酒與兩個用過的杯子得到證實。」

「好的，」福爾摩斯說：「我想兩個推論都可以成立。除了蘭姆酒外，房裡還有其他的酒嗎？」

「有的，水手櫃上的透明酒櫃，裡面有白蘭地與威士忌。不過，這些酒對我們來說並不重要，因為它們都裝得滿滿的，也就是說，這些酒並未開瓶。」

「儘管如此，這些酒還是有意義的，」福爾摩斯說。「不管怎麼樣，讓我們聽聽看你的說法，你認為哪些物品與案情有關。」

「桌上放著這個菸草袋。」

「桌子的什麼地方？」

「桌子的中間。菸草袋是用粗海豹皮做的——直毛皮，上面有用來綁袋口的皮帶。袋口內緣繡著『P·C』。袋內裝著半盎司多的菸草。」

「很好！還有什麼？」

霍普金斯從口袋裡掏出一本黃褐色封皮的筆記本。本子的外皮粗糙破舊，內頁也已經褪色。第一頁寫著首字母「J·H·N」，與年份「一八八三」。福爾摩斯把筆記本攤在桌上，用自己的方式仔細檢視一番，霍普金斯與我也在一旁觀看有無異樣。第二頁印著字母「C·P·R」，然後是連續數頁的數字。某頁的頁首寫著「阿根廷」，另一頁寫著「哥斯大黎加」，還有一頁則是「聖保羅」，這些標題頁後面都附隨著數頁的符號與數字。

「這些看起來像是證券交易所的證券清單。我想『J·H·N』是某個股票經紀人的首字母，而『C·P·R』可能是他的客戶。」

「試試加拿大太平洋鐵路公司（Canadian Pacific Railway），」福爾摩斯說。

霍普金斯忍不住罵了一句髒話，掄起拳頭重重朝自己大腿一擊。

「我真蠢！」他叫道。「當然C·P·R就是你說的加拿大太平洋鐵路公司。這麼一來，我們只需要破解『J·H·N』

這個首字母。我已經看過證交所過去的證券清單，以一八八三年的紀錄來說，證交所內外的經紀人，沒有人的姓名首字母相符。然而我覺得這是我目前掌握的最重要線索。福爾摩斯先生，你應該會同意，J·H·N這個首字母很可能就是當時在現場的人——換句話說，這個人很可能就是殺人凶手。我會要求將大量證券相關文件列入調查，這會是第一次我們藉由證券資料來釐清犯罪動機。」

福爾摩斯的臉顯示他對於這個新發展充滿困惑。

「我不得不接受你的觀點，」他說。「我必須說，死因調查報告中並未提到這本筆記本，它的出現改變了我原先的想法。我先前設想的犯罪過程，當中並未包含這本筆記本。這上面提到的證券，你打算每家公司都去調查嗎？」

「這方面的調查工作，局裡已經在進行，我擔心的是南美洲股東的完整登記資料可能放在南美洲，這樣的話，恐怕要等上幾個星期才能追蹤股份。」

福爾摩斯用放大鏡仔細檢查筆記本的封皮。

「確實，這裡有一些污漬，」他說。

「是的，先生，那是血跡。我曾告訴你，這本書是我從地板上撿起來的。」

「血跡是在上面還是在下面？」

「在側面，在封面旁邊。」

「這證明筆記本是在犯罪發生後才掉到地上。」

「一點沒錯，福爾摩斯先生。我同意這點，而且我猜測是凶手在倉皇逃逸時掉的。因為筆記本掉落的地點接近門邊。」

「我想死者的財產中應該沒有證券吧？」

「沒有，先生。」

「有任何理由懷疑這是一宗搶劫案嗎？」

「不，先生。看來屋內的東西沒被動過。」

「哎呀，這可真是一件有趣的案子！然後，還有一把刀子不是嗎？」

「一把鞘刀，刀還收在鞘裡。這把刀放在死者腳邊。凱瑞太太認出來，這是她丈夫的東西。」

福爾摩斯沉思了好一陣子。

「嗯，」他終於說話了，「我想我必須到現場去看一下。」

霍普金斯不禁歡呼起來。

「感謝你，先生。這真是讓我如釋重負。」

福爾摩斯對著警督察搖搖指頭。

「如果在一個星期之前，這件事會比較容易處理，」他說。「然而即使如此，我現在到現場勘查也未必沒有收穫。華生，如果你能撥出時間，我會很高興有你作陪。霍普金斯，如果你能叫來四輪馬車，我們就能在十五分鐘內前往佛瑞斯特街。」

我們在路邊小站下車，搭車經過數英里，沿途是砍伐過的森林。這片森林原本是更廣大的森林的一部分，過去，這裡曾是抵禦撒克遜人入侵的要地——易守難攻的「森林地帶」，有六十年的時間一直充當著守護不列顛的堡壘。現在，這片森林泰半已砍伐一空，因為這裡是鋼鐵業最初興起的重鎮，所有的樹木全送進火爐裡冶煉礦物。現在，北方更加茂密的森林原野吸引產業北上，只留下此地的斷株殘幹，地表上巨大的砍削傷痕也成了冶煉業曾在此駐足的明證。在綠意盎然的山丘上有一處空地，上面矗立著一棟長形的低矮石屋，一條道路穿過原野，最後在石屋附近拐彎。離道路更近一點的地方有一間外屋，三面圍繞著灌木叢，正對我們的方向剛好有一扇窗，大門也面朝我們。這裡就是命案現場。

霍普金斯走在前面帶著我們進屋，他向一名面容憔悴、頭髮斑白的婦人說明我們的來意。這名婦人就是死者的遺孀，她那張枯瘦而皺紋深刻的臉龐，紅腫的眼睛深處隱藏著恐懼的目光，那是多年來忍受煎熬苛待的結果。站在婦人身旁的是她的女兒，一個蒼白的金髮女孩，她滿臉不在乎地看著我們，並且說她對父親的死感到高興，她會為殺死父親的凶手祝福。這真是個可怕的家庭，而這一切全是黑彼得．凱瑞自己造成的。此時太陽再度露臉，陽光普照，我們鬆了一口氣，於是我們沿著死者平常走過的小徑，穿過原野。

這間外屋是一棟極其簡易的木造房，連屋頂也是簡易的木板，屋門旁有一扇窗，另一面也開了一扇窗。霍普金斯從口袋裡拿出鑰匙，彎腰準備開鎖，當他停下來檢視門鎖時，臉上露出驚訝的神情。

「有人破壞門鎖，」他說。

毫無疑問，木頭有切削的痕跡，表面的漆也刮落了，破壞的人顯然相當匆促。福爾摩斯也檢查了窗戶。

「這個人還想破窗而入。無論他是誰，他最終還是未能進入屋內。這個人肯定是個窮愁潦倒的小偷。」

「這實在太奇怪了，」警督察說；「我敢說昨天傍晚還沒有這些破壞的痕跡。」

「或許是村裡某個好奇的人幹的，」我說。

「不太可能，村民平日就不敢來此，更甭說闖進小屋了。福爾摩斯先生，你認為呢？」

「我認為幸運之神待我們不薄。」

「你的意思是，這個人會再出現？」

「很有可能。他原本預期小屋的門沒鎖。因此身上只帶了非常小的小刀。光憑小刀的刀刃是無法打開門鎖的。接下來他會怎麼做？」

「隔天晚上再來，並且帶著能夠開門的工具。」

「所以我必須說，如果我們不在這裡恭候他的到來，那就是我們的不是了。現在，讓我看看屋內的樣子。」

悲劇的痕跡已經清除，但家具依然維持犯罪當晚的樣子。持續兩個小時，福爾摩斯極其專注地依序檢視每樣物品，但他的表情說明他並未獲得有用的資訊。但他在耐心調查的過程中，只停頓了一次。

「霍普金斯，你有沒有拿走架上的東西？」

「沒有；我什麼也沒動。」

「有東西被拿走了。架子的這個角落灰塵比別處少。這裡可能原本橫放著一本書，也可能放了一個箱子。好吧，我只能做出這樣的推測。華生，現在讓我們去美麗的林子散散步，留幾個小時給那些花鳥樹木。霍普金斯，我們待會兒見，也許我們能與昨晚未能成功闖進屋內的紳士見上一面。」

當我們做好埋伏時，已是晚上十一點多。霍普金斯想讓小屋的門開著，但福爾摩斯認為這麼做會讓對方起疑。這道門鎖是相當簡易的門鎖，只要夠強韌的刀子就能打開它。福爾摩斯也建議我們不要躲在屋內，而是躲在遠側窗戶外圍的灌木叢裡。這樣我們可以看見闖入者——如果他點燈的話——並且觀察他深夜偷偷摸摸來此的目標是什麼。

監視是漫長而鬱悶的，但它也讓人感到緊張興奮，就像獵人躲在池邊，等待口渴的野獸前來一樣。什麼樣的野獸會從黑暗中逼近我們？牠是否會是一頭凶猛的老虎，在乖乖就擒前可能得先扭打一番，抑或牠是一隻躲躲藏藏的胡狼，只有軟弱而毫無防備的人才覺得牠危險？我們俯在灌木叢裡默不作聲，等待對方出現。起初，有幾名晚歸的村民或村裡的聲音引起我們的注意；然而，當這些無關緊要的聲音消失之後，四周又陷入絕對的寧靜，只有遙遠教堂的鐘聲，告訴我們夜越來越深，細雨開始打在遮蔽我們的樹葉上，發出窸窣的低語聲。

兩點半，鐘聲響起，此時是黎明前最黑暗的時刻，我們聽到門的方向傳來微弱但清晰的聲響，我們不敢大意。有人走在屋前的道路上。接下來又是漫長的沉默，我開始擔心這回可能又弄錯了，但從小屋另一邊傳來輕悄的腳步聲，隨後便聽到有人撬動金屬的聲音。有人想開鎖！這回這個人技術更好了，或者使用了更好的工具，因為鎖很快被撬開來，我們聽到門鉸鏈拉動的聲音。接著火柴一劃，下一刻，燭光照亮了屋內。透過薄薄的窗簾，我們目不轉睛地注意屋內的狀況。

這名深夜訪客是個年輕人，看起來相當瘦弱，黑色八字鬍使他的臉格外慘白。這個人頂多二十出頭。我從未看過有人怕成這副德性，看得出來他的牙齒不住地打顫，四肢也抖個不停。他的穿著像是個紳士，諾福克外套與燈籠褲，頭上戴著低頂圓帽。我們看著他四處張望，眼神流露著恐懼。然後，他把燭火放在桌上，走向其中一個角落，從我們的視野消失。他回到桌旁時，手裡拿著一本大書，那是從架子上那一排航海日誌拿下來的。男子倚靠著桌子，快速翻著書頁，直到他找到想要的條目為止。然後，他突然握緊拳頭，似乎非常生氣，只見他闔上書，把書放回角落，然後熄滅了燈火。他還沒來得及轉身離開小屋，就被霍普金斯揪住領子，他發現自己被逮個正著，在驚恐下只是不斷地大聲喘氣。燭火重新點著，被我們的警探一把抓住的可憐俘虜，一邊顫抖，一邊露出畏縮的樣子。他軟趴趴地靠在水手櫃上，無助地看著我們每一個人。

「現在，這位仁兄，」霍普金斯說道，「你是誰，你在這裡幹什麼？」

這名男子振作精神，努力想用冷靜的態度面對我們。

「我想，你們是警探吧？」他說。「你們以為我跟彼得．凱瑞船長的死有關。我向你們保證，我跟這件事一點關係也沒有。」

「我們很快就會知道答案了，」霍普金斯說。「首先，你叫什麼名字？」

「我叫約翰．霍普利．聶里根（John Hopley Neligan）。」

我看到福爾摩斯與霍普金斯彼此對望了一下。

「你在這裡做什麼？」

「我能夠不公開透露嗎？」

「不，當然不行。」

「我為什麼得告訴你？」

「你不說的話，在法庭上對你不利。」

年輕人畏縮了。

「好吧，我會告訴你們，」他說。「我為什麼要隱瞞呢？然而我不想讓舊醜聞重新受到注意。你們聽過道森與聶里根嗎？」

我從霍普金斯的表情可以看出，他沒聽過這個東西；但福爾摩斯顯然非常有興趣。

「你說的是西南英格蘭的銀行家，」福爾摩斯說道。「他們虧空了一百萬，毀了康瓦爾郡半數的家庭，然後聶里根消失無蹤。」

「沒有錯，聶里根就是我父親。」

終於，我們有進展了，但潛逃的銀行家與被自己的魚叉釘死在牆上的彼得．凱瑞船長，兩人之間實在看不出有什麼瓜葛。我們所有人因此聚精會神地聆聽這名年輕人說下去。

「真正牽涉其中的是我父親。道森早就退休了。當時我才十歲，但我的年紀已足以讓我感到羞恥與恐懼。世人都說我父親帶走所有的證券潛逃。但事實並非如此。父親相信，如果給他足夠的時間，他會實現這些證券的利益，並且還清所有的債務。父親在逮捕令發布前，就搭乘小遊艇前往挪威。我還記得前一晚他與母親道別的情景。他把他帶走的證券擬了一份清單給我們，他發誓，他返家時將會恢復他的名譽，屆時信任他的人都將苦盡甘來。然而，此後我們再也沒有他的音訊。不僅遊艇，就連他本人也完全從世上消失。母親與我都認為，父親與遊艇，連同他帶走的證券，全已石沉大海。我們有個忠實的老友，他是個商人。前一陣子這位朋友發現父親帶走的證券居然再度在倫敦市場上出現。你可以想像我們有多麼驚訝。我花了幾個月追查股票的來源，最後，歷經無數次的懷疑與艱辛，我發現最早的賣家是彼得．凱瑞船長，也就是這間小屋的主人。

「因此，理所當然地，我開始追查彼得．凱瑞的下落。我發現，他曾經是捕鯨船船長，他從北極海返航的時間，正好也是我父親渡海前往挪威的時間。那年秋天，風暴的日子特多，有很長一段時間連續吹著強勁的南風。父親的遊艇很可能因此被吹往北方，並且在那裡遇見了彼得．凱瑞船長的船。若是如此，我父親之後到底去了哪兒？無論如何，如果我能證明是彼得·凱瑞而非父親在市場上賣出這些股票，那麼就表示父親並未為了一己之私而拿走這些證券。

「我來薩塞克斯，是想與船長見上一面，但就在我上門之前，居然發生這場可怕的命案。我在死因審理時讀到一段有關他的艙房的描述，裡面提到他過去在船上的航海日誌全放在這間小屋裡。我因此想到，如果我可以查閱一八八三年八月『獨角鯨』號的航海日誌，或許可以解開父親的命運之謎。我昨晚想來這裡查看日誌，但無法開門。今晚再嘗試一次，終於成功了，但卻發現日誌裡關於一八八三年八月的部分已被撕掉。就在這個時候，我成了你們的階下囚。」

「就這樣？」霍普金斯問道。

「是的，就這樣。」他說話時眼神晃了一下。

「你沒有別的事要告訴我們？」

他露出猶豫的樣子。

「不，沒有了。」

「昨晚之前，你沒來過這裡？」

「沒有。」

「那麼，你如何解釋這個？」霍普金斯不假辭色地逼問，一邊拿出該死的筆記本，上面第一頁就寫著被我們抓住的人姓名的首字母，而筆記本的封面也沾著血跡。

這個可憐的年輕人崩潰了。他把臉埋在手裡，全身顫抖。「你在哪裡拿到的？」他呻吟著說。「我不知道。我想我是在旅館遺失的。」

「夠了，」霍普金斯嚴厲地說。「不管你要說什麼，都留到法庭上說吧。現在請你跟我到警局一趟。福爾摩斯先生，非常感謝你和你的朋友的協助。接下來就交給我們警方吧，我想我可以自己順利偵破這個案件。我已經為兩位在布蘭伯泰旅館訂好房間，我們可以一起走到村子。」

「華生，你覺得如何？」隔天早晨，我們返家之後，福爾摩斯問道。

「看得出來，你不是很滿意。」

「喔，當然，親愛的華生，我非常滿意。但同時我並不欣賞霍普金斯的方法。我對霍普金斯感到失望。我原本期望他能做得更好。我們在設想可能的線索時，也要思考其他的可能。這是刑案調查的第一原則。」

「那麼，可能的線索是什麼？」

「我調查的線索，很可能讓我們一無所獲。我說不出理由。但至少我必須把這條線索調查到底。」

在貝克街，已有數封信等著福爾摩斯。他拿起其中一封信，打開信封，然後禁不住發出勝利的笑聲。

「太好了，華生。我說的線索有眉目了。你有電報紙嗎？你只需要幫我寫幾個訊息：『薩姆納，船運經紀人，瑞克利夫公路。找三個人，叫他們明天早上過來。——巴塞爾。』這是我在那一區的化名。另一封是『斯坦利·霍普金斯警督察，勳爵街四十六號，布里克斯頓。明日九點三十分，請來舍下共進早餐。重要。若不克前來，請回電報給我。——夏洛克·福爾摩斯。』華生，聽好了，這個懸案糾纏我十天了。我這次要完全擺脫這件案子。明天，我相信會是我們最後一次討論此案。」

時間一到，霍普金斯警督察準時出現，我們一起坐下享用赫德森太太為我們準備的豐盛早餐。年輕的警探正為自己的成功沾沾自喜。

「你真的覺得自己的想法是對的？」福爾摩斯問道。

「我想不到更能解釋的理由了。」

「但在我看來，我覺得還不是定論。」

「你的話讓我很吃驚，福爾摩斯先生。對於這樣的結論，誰還能要求什麼呢？」

「你的說法能解釋每個爭議點嗎？」

「毫無疑問。我發現那個叫聶里根的年輕人在凶案發生當天住進布蘭伯泰旅館。他宣稱來這裡打高爾夫球。他的房間位於一樓，他可以隨意進出。當天晚上，他前往伍德曼宅，看見彼得·凱瑞在小屋裡，於是與他爭吵，最後用魚叉殺死他。然而，他對於自己犯下的罪行感到驚慌，於是奪門而出，途中不慎弄丟了筆記本，而這本筆記本是他用來質問凱瑞證券的事的。你會發現筆記本裡有些證券名稱打了勾，但絕大多數並未打勾。打勾的證券可以追溯到倫敦市場；但其他未打勾的很可能仍在凱瑞手裡，根據聶里根的說法，他急於取回這些證券好清償父親的債務。他逃走之後，有一段時間不敢再靠近木屋，但最後他還是鼓起勇氣前來，想得到他需要的資訊。這些犯罪事實豈不是簡單而明確？」

福爾摩斯微笑著搖搖頭。

「在我看來，霍普金斯，你的推論只有一個瑕疵，但光這個瑕疵就足以推翻你整個推論。你有否試過用魚叉刺穿一個人的身體？沒有？嘖！嘖！親愛的督察，你必須專注在這些細節才行。我的朋友華生可以告訴你，我一整個早上都在練習刺魚叉。這可不是件容易的事，手臂必須強健而且習慣投擲才行。而且命案的魚叉顯然使用了極大的力量，魚叉的尖端不僅刺穿了被害者，而且刺進了牆內。你能想像這名虛弱的年輕人能有這麼大力氣做出這麼可怕的攻擊嗎？你認為這名年輕人就是在深夜裡與黑彼得一起喝著蘭姆酒交談的人嗎？命案發生的兩天前，深夜窗簾映照著的人影，是否就是這個年輕人？不，不，霍普金斯；那另有其人，而且這個人更加可怕，我們應該找出這個人。」

福爾摩斯不斷地說著，警探的臉色越來越難看。他的希望與野心全在福爾摩斯面前摔個粉碎。但他仍想據理力爭。

「你無法否認聶里根那晚在場，福爾摩斯先生。這本筆記本證明了這點。我想，即使你有辦法從中挑出瑕疵，我還是有足夠的證據說服陪審團。此外，福爾摩斯先生，我已經抓住了我認定的凶手。至於你說的那個恐怖傢伙，他在哪兒呢？」

「我想，凶手也許現在正上樓到我們這兒來，」福爾摩斯冷靜地說。「華生，為了以防萬一，你最好把左輪手槍放在你可以隨時拿到的地方。」福爾摩斯拿起一張寫了字的紙放在邊桌上。「現在，我們準備好了，」他說。

外頭傳來粗啞的談話聲，赫德森太太開門進來說，外頭有三個人要找巴塞爾船長。

「一次一個人，讓他們依序進來。」福爾摩斯說。

第一個進來的人，他的臉頰紅潤，讓人聯想到里布斯頓皮平的小蘋果，並留著蓬鬆的白色鬢角。福爾摩斯從口袋裡掏出一封信。

「你叫什麼名字？」他問道。

「詹姆斯．蘭開斯特。」

「我很抱歉，蘭開斯特，但鋪位已經滿了。為了補償你撥冗前來，這裡是半英鎊金幣，請你收下。接下來請你在這個房間裡待幾分鐘。」

第二個人是個細長乾癟的生物，頭髮稀疏，臉色灰黃。他的名字叫休・派廷斯。他也遭到婉拒，收了半英鎊金幣，也被要求在房間裡等待。

第三名應徵者有著引人注目的相貌。凶猛的鬥牛犬臉孔，配上一頭亂髮與鬍鬚，在濃密下垂的睫毛後面，兩顆深色的眼珠閃爍著無畏的光芒。他行禮，並且採水手的站姿，把帽子摺圓握在自己手裡。

「你的名字是？」福爾摩斯問道。

「派屈克・凱恩斯。」

「魚叉手？」

「是的，先生。二十六次的航海經驗。」

「鄧迪人，我猜？」

「是的，先生。」

「隨時可以上船？」

「是的，先生。」

「薪水呢？」

「一個月八英鎊。」

「你能馬上開始工作嗎？」

「我只需要回家拿工具箱就可以開始。」

「你有證件嗎？」

「有的，先生。」他從口袋裡掏出一份破舊而油膩的文件。福爾摩斯瀏覽了一下又還給他。

「你正是我要的人，」他說。「邊桌上放著合約，你簽字之後，這件事就這樣定了。」

這名水手走到房間的另一邊，拿起筆。

「我應該簽在這裡嗎？」他彎腰趴在桌上問道。

福爾摩斯傾身向前，從水手的後頭出手。

「這樣就行了，」他說。

我聽到鋼鐵的喀嚓聲，以及如憤怒公牛般的吼叫。下一刻，福爾摩斯與這名水手倒在地上扭打翻滾。他是個孔武有力的壯漢，即使福爾摩斯巧妙地將他上了手銬，但若不是霍普金斯與我趕緊上前協助，他還是能輕易壓倒我的朋友。直到我把左輪手槍的冰冷槍口對著他的太陽穴，他才知道抵抗是沒有用的。我們用粗繩綁住他的腳踝，結束了這場驚險的打鬥。

「我必須向你致歉，霍普金斯，」福爾摩斯說道。「恐怕炒蛋已經涼了。然而，剩下的早餐想必你會吃得更津津有味，因為這件案子終於水落石出了，不是嗎？」

霍普金斯驚得說不出話來。

「我不知道該說什麼，福爾摩斯先生，」終於，他脹紅了臉，脫口說了這些話。「我覺得自己從一開始就是個傻子。我現在了解，這點我永遠也不會忘記，我是學生，而你是老師。即使現在我親眼看見你做了什麼，但我還是不知道你怎麼做到的，或者這麼做的意義是什麼。」

「嗯，這個嘛，」福爾摩斯愉快地說。「我們全是從經驗中學習，而這回你學到的是，絕不能忘記有別的可能。你太專注於聶里根，因此完全忽略了派屈克．凱恩斯，也就是真正謀殺彼得．凱瑞的人。」

水手沙啞的聲音打斷了我們的對話。

「呃，先生，」他說，「我遭受如此粗暴的對待，並無怨言，但我希望你能正確地陳述事情。你說，我謀殺了彼得．凱瑞；而我則說，我『殺』了彼得．凱瑞，這兩件事不一樣。也許我說的話你不相信，甚至認為我只是在編故事。」

「不，」福爾摩斯說。「讓我們聽聽你的說法吧。」

「我會說的，我向天發誓，我說的話句句屬實。我了解黑彼得，當他抽出刀子時，我便準備朝他丟擲魚叉，因為我知道在這種情況下，不是他死就是我亡，因此他死了。你可以說這是謀殺。反正我很快就要被吊死了，就跟黑彼得拿刀刺進我的心臟沒有兩樣。」

「你為什麼會來這裡？」福爾摩斯問道。

「我會從頭說起。但是先讓我坐直身體，這樣我可以舒坦一點說話。那是一八八三年——事情發生在當年的八月。彼得．凱瑞是『獨角鯨』號船長，而我是候補的魚叉手。我們出了浮冰，開始返航，當時吹起了逆風與連續一星期強勁的南風，然後我們看到了一艘被風吹到北邊來的小船。有個人在船上——但這個人並非討海為生。我們的船員認為他的那艘大船已沉沒，他是靠著船上的救生艇前往挪威海岸。我猜那艘船上應該沒有人生還。於是，我們讓這個人上船，他與船長在艙房裡談了很長的時間。他隨身的行李只有一個鐵盒子。直到現在，我都不知道那個人的姓名，因為他在第二晚就從船上消失，彷彿原本就不存在一樣。有人說，他是自己跳下海的，也有人說，他是在風強雨急之下意外跌入海中。只有一個人知道發生了什麼事，那就是我。我親眼看見船長綁住他的腳跟，趁夜深的時候把他丟下船，這是我們看見昔德蘭群島燈塔前兩天的事。

「嗯，我把這件事藏在心裡，在一旁觀察事情的演變。當我們回到蘇格蘭時，這件事就這樣煙消雲散，沒有人提出疑問。一名陌生人意外喪生，有誰會在意呢？不久，彼得．凱瑞放棄捕鯨，而我花了很久時間才找到他。我猜測，他是為了鐵盒裡的東西而殺人，而我想向他追索一點封口費。

「透過一名曾經與他在倫敦見面的水手，我得知他的行蹤，因此我來這裡找他要錢。第一晚，他很講道理，而且願意給我一筆錢，讓我從海上生活退休。我們決定兩天後的晚上談妥這件事。當我來到小屋時，我發現他已經有七分酒意，而且脾氣暴躁。我們坐下來一起喝酒，談起以前的事，但他越喝臉色越不對勁。我看到牆上放著魚叉，我心想，必要時我可以用上這個東西。終於，他開始對我發火，又吐口水又罵髒話，他的眼中透著殺意，手裡拿著刀子。但他刀子還沒出鞘，就被我的魚叉射中。我的天！他叫得實在太悽慘了；他猙獰的表情實在太不真實，我搞不清楚我是清醒的還是在夢裡！我站在那裡，他的血噴得我滿身都是，於是我等待了一段時間；但外頭靜悄悄的，於是我再度鼓起勇氣。當我查看屋內，發現架子上放著那個鐵盒。無論如何，我跟彼得．凱瑞一樣有權擁有這件東西，於是我帶著盒子離開小屋。我太疏忽了，居然把菸草袋忘在桌上。

「現在，我要告訴你們這個故事最奇怪的部分。我才走出小屋，就聽見有人來了，於是我躲進灌木叢裡。一名男子偷偷摸摸地過來，走進小屋，他大聲叫喊，彷彿看到鬼一樣，並且沒命地跑出屋外，直到不見蹤影為止。他是誰，他想做什麼，我完全不知道。至於我，我走了十英里，在坦布里奇維爾斯搭乘火車前往倫敦，我做的事完全沒人發覺。

「當我檢視盒子裡的東西時，發現裡面沒有錢，只有文件，但我不敢賣這些東西。我無法從黑彼得身上拿到錢，身無分文的我只能困在倫敦，無法動彈。我能仰賴的只有我的專長。我看到僱用魚叉手的廣告，薪水很高，於是我到船運公司，由他們介紹我來這裡。這就是我知道的一切，我要再說一遍，如果我殺了黑彼得，那麼法律應該感謝我，因為我為他們省了一條麻繩。」

「非常清楚的陳述，」福爾摩斯說道，他起身點了他的菸斗。「霍普金斯，我想你最好馬上將你的犯人帶到安全的地方。這個房間不適合充當牢房，派屈克．凱恩斯先生占的空間太大了。」

「福爾摩斯先生，」霍普金斯說，「我不知道如何表達我的謝意。即使是現在我仍不知道你是怎麼做到的。」

「我只是運氣好，一開始我便找到了正確的線索。如果我起初就拿到這本筆記本，我的思緒很可能被引導到別的地方，就跟你一樣。然而我聽到的一切訊息都指向同一個方向。驚人的力量、使用魚叉的技巧、蘭姆酒與水、海豹皮製成的菸草袋與粗劣的菸草——這一切都指向水手，而且是捕鯨船的水手。我相信菸草袋上的首字母『P．C．』只是碰巧跟彼得．凱瑞一樣，因為彼得．凱瑞很少抽菸，在他的小屋裡也找不到菸斗。你還記得我問你屋裡有沒有威士忌與白蘭地。你說有的。不以捕魚為生的人，家裡已經有威士忌與白蘭地，為什麼還要喝蘭姆酒？是的，我相信在場的人一定是個水手。」

「那麼，你是怎麼找到他的？」

「親愛的霍普金斯，這個問題反而是最簡單的。如果他是水手，那麼就只能是『獨角鯨』號上的水手。就我所知，彼得．凱瑞從未在別的船上工作。我花了三天發電報到鄧迪，最後終於確認了一八八三年『獨角鯨』所有船員的名單。當我發現魚叉手裡有個人名叫派屈克．凱恩斯（Patrick Cairns）時，我知道真相已經大白。我認為這個人可能在倫敦，而且這個人很可能急著想離開國內。因此，我花了幾天時間在東區，編造一個北極探險的計畫，提出誘人的條件吸引魚叉手來為巴塞爾船長工作——於是就出現了你眼前這個結果！」

「太精采了！」霍普金斯叫道。「真是太精采了！」

「你必須立即釋放聶里根，」福爾摩斯說道。「我必須說，你應該向他道歉。鐵盒也應該還給他，當然，彼得·凱瑞賣掉的證券已經找不回來了。馬車來了，霍普金斯，你可以把你的犯人帶走。如果你需要我出庭作證，我與華生的地址將會在挪威的某處——我日後會再通知你。」

亞瑟・柯南・道爾搭乘北極捕鯨船「希望」號

船醫航海日誌摹本

（一八八〇年二月二十八日到八月十一日）

6 13 20 27
7 14 21 28
8 15 22 29
9 16 23 30

EBRUARY.

7 14 21 28
1 8 15 22
2 9 16 23
3 10 17 24
4 11 18 25
5 12 19 26
6 13 20 27

MARCH.

7 14 21 28
1 8 15 22 29
2 9 16 23 30
3 10 17 24 31
4 11 18 25
5 12 19 26
6 13 20 27

Wed..... 7 14 21 28
Thur.... 1 8 15 22 29
Fri...... 2 9 16 23 30
Sat...... 3 10 17 24

MAY.

Sun...... 2 9 16 23 30
Mon..... 3 10 17 24 31
Tues.... 4 11 18 25
Wed..... 5 12 19 26
Thur.... 6 13 20 27
Fri...... 7 14 21 28
Sat... 1 8 15 22 29

JUNE.

Sun...... 6 13 20 27
Mon..... 7 14 21 28
Tues.... 1 8 15 22 29
Wed..... 2 9 16 23 30
Thur.... 3 10 17 24
Fri.... 4 11 18 25
Sat...... 5 12 19 26

Wed..... 7 14 21 28
Thur.... 1 8 15 22 29
Fri...... 2 9 16 23 30
Sat...... 3 10 17 24 31

AUGUST.

Sun..... 1 8 15 22 29
Mon...... 2 9 16 23 30
Tues..... 3 10 17 24 31
Wed..... 4 11 18 25
Thur.... 5 12 19 26
Fri...... 6 13 20 27
Sat...... 7 14 21 28

SEPTEMBER.

Sun...... 5 12 19 26
Mon...... 6 13 20 27
Tues...... 7 14 21 28
Wed..... 1 8 15 22 29
Thur.... 2 9 16 23 30
Fri...... 3 10 17 24
Sat...... 4 11 18 25

Wed..... 6 13 20 27
Thur.... 7 14 21 28
Fri... 1 8 15 22 29
Sat... 2 9 16 23 30

NOVEMBER.

Sun...... 7 14 21 28
Mon..... 1 8 15 22 29
Tues.... 2 9 16 23 30
Wed..... 3 10 17 24
Thur..... 4 11 18 25
Fri...... 5 12 19 26
Sat...... 6 13 20 27

DECEMBER.

Sun..... 5 12 19 26
Mon..... 6 13 20 27
Tues. ... 7 14 21 28
Wed..... 1 8 15 22 29
Thur.... 2 9 16 23 30
Fri..... 3 10 17 24 31
Sat...... 4 11 18 25

Wed..... 5 12
Thur.... 6 13
Fri...... 7 14
Sat... 1 8 15

FEBRUAR

Sun..... 6
Mon..... 7
Tues.... 1 8
Wed..... 2 9
Thur.... 3 10
Fri...... 4 11
Sat...... 5 12

MARCH

Sun...... 5
Mon..... 6
Tues..... 7
Wed..... 1 8
Thur.... 2 9
Fri...... 3 10
Sat...... 4 11

TABLE

the number of days from any given day of one month, to e day in any other month. In leap-year add 1 if February 29 calculation.

me of	Jan.	Feb.	Mar.	Apr.	May	June	July	Aug.	Sept.	Oct.	Nov.	Dec.
	FROM ANY DAY OF											
....	365	334	306	275	245	214	184	153	122	92	61	31
....	31	365	337	306	276	245	215	184	153	123	92	62
....	59	28	365	334	304	273	243	212	181	151	120	90
....	90	59	31	365	335	304	274	243	212	182	151	121
....	120	89	61	30	365	334	304	273	242	212	181	151
....	151	120	92	61	31	365	335	304	273	243	212	182
....	181	150	122	91	61	30	365	334	303	273	242	212
....	212	181	153	122	92	61	31	365	334	304	273	243
....	243	212	184	153	123	92	62	31	365	335	304	274
....	273	242	214	183	153	122	92	61	30	365	334	304
....	304	273	245	214	184	153	123	92	61	31	365	335
....	334	303	275	244	214	183	153	122	91	61	30	365

)R 56 YEARS, FROM 1844 TO 1899.

PLANATION.

ne year you want. Above Dominical letter. Look part of the Diary for the in the line opposite the ed. Above that letter you s o the week, and on the of the month. Leap years ters; the first serves till ebruary. Leap year is the divides evenly by 4; but will not be a Leap year.

C	BA	G	F	E	DC
47	48	49	50	51	52
75	76	77	78	79	80

FE	D	C	B	AG	F
56	57	58	59	60	61
84	85	86	87	88	89

A	G	F	ED	C	B	A
65	66	67	68	69	70	71
93	94	95	96	97	98	99

29	Su	Sa	Fr	Th	W	Tu	M
30	M	Su	Sa	Fr	Th	W	Tu
31	Tu	M	Su	Sa	Fr	Th	W
	W	Tu	M	Su	Sa	Fr	Th
	Th	W	Tu	M	Su	Sa	Fr

PUBLIC HOLIDAYS.

LONDON—*Exchequer, and India House.*—Good Friday and Christmas.

Law Offices.—Good Friday and three following days, Whit-Monday and Whit-Tuesday, Queen's Birth-day and Accession, Christmas, and three following days.

Excise, Stamp and Tax Offices.—Good Friday, Queen's Birth-day, June 28, Nov. 9, and Christmas.

Docks and Customs.—Good Friday, Queen's Birth-day, and Christmas.

IRELAND—*Customs.*—Good Friday, Queen's Birth-day, and Christmas.

Excise, & Stamp Offices.—Good Friday, Queen's Birth-day, June 28, Nov. 9, and Christmas.

SCOTLAND—*Customs*—Good Friday, Queen's Birth-day, Sacramental Fasts, & Christmas

Excise and Stamp Offices.—Jan. 1, Good Friday, Queen's Birth-day, (Fair Saturday, Glasgow), Sacramental Fasts, and Christmas.

BANK HOLIDAYS.

ENGLAND AND IRELAND.

Good Friday, Easter Monday, the Monday in Whitsun week, the first Monday in Aug., Christmas, & the 26th of Dec. if a week day.

SCOTLAND.

New Year's Day, Christmas Day, (if either of these fall on a Sunday the following Monday shall be a Bank Holiday,) Good Friday, the first Monday of May, the first Monday of August, and any day which may be appointed by Royal Proclamation. Upon Sacramental Fast-days and other local Holidays, the Bank Offices

POSTAGES.

INLAND LETTERS AND PACKAGES.

The rate of postage to be prepaid on inland letters and parcels of all sorts, closed or open, is as follows:—

Not exceeding 1 oz. in weight, ...1 *d.*
Above 1 oz. and not above 2 oz.,.........1½*d.*
Do. 2 " do. do. 4 " ....2 *d.*
Do. 4 " do. do. 6 " ....2½*d.*
Do. 6 " do. do. 8 " ....3 *d.*
Do. 8 " do. do. 10 " ....3½*d.*
Do. 10 " do. do. 12 " ....4 *d.*

A letter above the weight of 12 oz. is liable to the charge of 1*d.* for every ounce, commencing with the first ounce. For instance, a letter between 12 and 13 oz. weight must be prepaid 1*s.* 1*d.* As a general rule, the postage if not paid in advance, is double the foregoing; and if the payment in advance be insufficient, double the deficiency is charged. An inland letter, for example, weighing more than an ounce, and not exceeding two ounces, and prepaid one penny only, is on delivery charged *double* the deficiency of one halfpenny, viz. one penny, and so on. —A letter directed to a person, and the person not found at the address, and the letter re-directed, single additional postage only is charged. The Post Office cannot undertake the safe transmission of valuable inclosures in unregistered letters. Letters when once posted cannot be given back upon any pretence whatever. Letters to warm climates should be gummed or wafered, not sealed with wax, as the wax is liable to get melted, to the injury of other letters.

A postmaster is not bound to re-direct letters for a person temporarily leaving his home and not having a private bag or box, unless the house be left uninhabited, or the letters would be delayed in their transmission by being sent to the house to be re-directed there. In all cases of re-direction, a written authority, duly signed by the person to whom the letters are addressed, must be sent to the postmaster.

REGISTERED LETTERS.

An inland letter or book-packet can be registered on payment of 4*d.* in addition to the postage of such letter or packet. The full amount in stamps for postage and registration, must be on the letter or book-packet, and it will require to be posted half an hour before the closing of the box for the mail by which it is to be despatched, otherwise a late fee of 4*d.* will be charged till the closing of the letter-box. A letter to be registered should be presented at the window and a receipt obtained for it, and must not be dropped into the letter-box. Any letter marked "Registered" which shall be posted without at the same time being registered shall, if observed, be afterwards registered by the post-office, and be forwarded to its destination, charged with double the ordinary registration rate of postage. All letters containing coin are treated as registered, even though they be posted without registration, and are charged on delivery with a double registration fee, in addition to the ordinary postage. Any person sending money or jewellery in a letter, if lost or mis-delivered, has no claim on the Post-office. The most secure mode of sealing is first to wafer or gum the letter and then to

BOOK PACKET

Or plain, written, or printe out a cover, or in a cover ends or sides, may be sent—
Not exceeding 2 oz. in weigh
" 4 oz. "
" 6 oz. "
" 8 oz. "
" 10 oz. "
" 12 oz. "
And ½d. for every additiona

The postage to be prepai stamps affixed. If the wh not prepaid, the unpaid pa double on delivery. The pa tain any number of separate photographs (when not on cases containing glass), map or vellum, either printed or w ing printed or lithographed le mixed, but not letters, seale anything sealed or closed ag tion. Marking or writing allo of the nature of a letter. An stating who sends the book, is sent, is not regarded as a name and address of the send permitted but recommended, cover come off, or for any oth packet cannot be forwarded, turned. In books and prints, binding, mounting, or coverin or of a portion thereof, will b also markers and rollers, (whe or otherwise), and whatever is the safe transmission of litera matter or usually appertains the greater security of the packet may be tied at the ends The postmaster is authorise string, but must refasten the wards. No packet can be rec ceeds 5 pounds in weight, length, and 9 inches in width in depth, except petitions to

INLAND PATTERN

All parcels are forwarded desires, whether closed or open is limited to 12 oz., and the siz in length by 9 inches in depth in width. The postage is the for letters, and must be prepa stamps.

INLAND MONEY OR

For sums under 10*s.*, - -
" 10*s.* and under £1, -
" £1, " " 2, -
" 2, " " 3, -
" 3, " " 4, -
" 4, " " 5, -
" 5 " " 6, -
" 6, " " 7, -
" 7, " " 8, -
" 8, " " 9, -
" 9, " " 10, -
" 10, - - - -

No order to contain a fractio penny. No money order ca unless the applicant furnish in full, and at least one in Christian name of the per who sends the order, and of t

day of	Jan.	Feb.	Mar.	Apr.	May	June	July	Aug.	Sept.	Oct.	Nov.	Dec.
January..........	365	334	306	275	245	214	184	153	122	92	61	31
February	31	365	337	306	276	245	215	184	153	123	92	62
March	59	28	365	334	304	273	243	212	181	151	120	90
April............	90	59	31	365	335	304	274	243	212	182	151	121
May	120	89	61	30	365	334	304	273	242	212	181	151
June..............	151	120	92	61	31	365	335	304	273	243	212	182
July	181	150	122	91	61	30	365	334	303	273	242	212
August	212	181	153	122	92	61	31	365	334	304	273	243
September	243	212	184	153	123	92	62	31	365	335	304	274
October	273	242	214	183	153	122	92	61	30	365	334	304
November.........	304	273	245	214	184	153	123	92	61	31	365	335
December........	334	303	275	244	214	183	153	122	91	61	30	365

DIARY FOR 56 YEARS, FROM 1844 TO 1899.

EXPLANATION.

Look for the ear you want. Above t find its Dominical letter. Look n the lower part of the Diary for the ame letter in the line opposite the nonth wanted. Above that letter you nd the days of the week, and on the eft the days of the month. Leap years ave two letters; the first serves till he end of February. Leap year is the ear which divides evenly by 4; but he year 1900 will not be a Leap year.

F	E	D	C	BA	G	F	E	DC
844	45	46	47	48	49	50	51	52
872	73	74	75	76	77	78	79	80
B	**A**	**G**	**FE**	**D**	**C**	**B**	**AG**	**F**
853	54	55	56	57	58	59	60	61
881	82	83	84	85	86	87	88	89

E	D	CB	A	G	F	ED	C	B	A
862	63	64	65	66	67	68	69	70	71
890	91	92	93	94	95	96	97	98	99

PUBLIC HOLIDAYS.

LONDON—*Exchequer, and India House.*—Good Friday and Christmas.

Law Offices.—Good Friday and three following days, Whit-Monday and Whit-Tuesday, Queen's Birth-day and Accession, Christmas, and three following days.

Excise, Stamp and Tax Offices.—Good Friday, Queen's Birth-day, June 28, Nov. 9, and Christmas.

Docks and Customs.—Good Friday, Queen's Birth-day, and Christmas.

IRELAND—*Customs.*—Good Friday, Queen's Birth-day, and Christmas.

Excise, & Stamp Offices.—Good Friday, Queen's Birth-day, June 28, Nov. 9, and Christmas.

SCOTLAND—*Customs*—Good Friday, Queen's Birth-day, Sacramental Fasts, & Christmas

Excise and Stamp Offices.—Jan. 1, Good Friday, Queen's Birth-day, (Fair Saturday, Glasgow), Sacramental Fasts, and Christmas.

BANK HOLIDAYS.

ENGLAND AND IRELAND.

Good Friday, Easter Monday, the Monday in Whitsun week, the first Monday in Aug., Christmas, & the 26th of Dec. if a week day.

SCOTLAND.

New Year's Day, Christmas Day, (if either of

4 "	do.	do.	6 "	........2½d.
6 "	do.	do.	8 "	........3 d.
8 "	do.	do.	10 "	........3½d.
10 "	do.	do.	12 "	........4 d.

ter above the weight of 12 oz. is to the charge of 1*d.* for every ounce, ɪencing with the first ounce. For ɪce, a letter between 12 and 13 oz. t must be prepaid 1*s.* 1*d.* As a al rule, the postage if not paid in ɪce, is double the foregoing; and if ayment in advance be insufficient, e the deficiency is charged. An in- letter, for example, weighing more an ounce, and not exceeding two s, and prepaid one penny only, is on ry charged *double* the deficiency of alfpenny, viz. one penny, and so on. etter directed to a person, and the ɪ not found at the address, and the re-directed, single additional post- ɪly is charged. The Post Office can- ɪdertake the safe transmission of val- inclosures in unregistered letters. rs when once posted cannot be given upon any pretence whatever. Let- o warm climates should be gummed fered, not sealed with wax, as the s liable to get melted, to the injury er letters.

ostmaster is not bound to re-direct s for a person temporarily leaving his and not having a private bag or box, s the house be left uninhabited, or the s would be delayed in their transmis- y being sent to the house to be re- ed there. In all cases of re-direction, ten authority, duly signed by the to whom the letters are addressed, be sent to the postmaster.

REGISTERED LETTERS.

inland letter or book-packet can be ered on payment of 4*d.* in addition postage of such letter or packet. The mount in stamps for postage and re- tion, must be on the letter or book- t, and it will require to be posted half ɪr before the closing of the box for the y which it is to be despatched, other- late fee of 4*d.* will be charged till the g of the letter-box. A letter to be ered should be presented at the win- ɪd a receipt obtained for it, and must dropped into the letter-box. Any let- arked "Registered" which shall be without at the same time being regis- shall, if observed, be afterwards regis- by the post-office, and be forwarded to tination, charged with double the or- registration rate of postage. All let- ontaining coin are treated as register- en though they be posted without ...

,,	8 oz.	,,	.........2 d.
,,	10 oz.	,,	.........2½d.
,,	12 oz.	,,	.........3 d.

And ½d. for every additional two ounces.

The postage to be prepaid by postage stamps affixed. If the whole postage be not prepaid, the unpaid part is charged double on delivery. The packet may contain any number of separate books, prints, photographs (when not on glass nor in cases containing glass), maps, parchment or vellum, either printed or written, including printed or lithographed letters, plain or mixed, but not letters, sealed or open, nor anything sealed or closed against inspection. Marking or writing allowed when not of the nature of a letter. An entry, merely stating who sends the book, or to whom it is sent, is not regarded as a letter. The name and address of the sender is not only permitted but recommended, so that if the cover come off, or for any other reason the packet cannot be forwarded, it may be returned. In books and prints, all legitimate binding, mounting, or covering of the same, or of a portion thereof, will be allowed; as also markers and rollers, (whether of paper or otherwise), and whatever is necessary for the safe transmission of literary or artistic matter or usually appertains thereto. For the greater security of the contents, the packet may be tied at the ends with a string The postmaster is authorised to cut the string, but must refasten the packet afterwards. No packet can be received if it exceeds 5 pounds in weight, 18 inches in length, and 9 inches in width and 6 inches in depth, except petitions to Parliament.

INLAND PATTERN POST.

All parcels are forwarded as the sender desires, whether closed or open; the weight is limited to 12 oz., and the size to 18 inches in length by 9 inches in depth and 6 inches in width. The postage is the same as that for letters, and must be prepaid in postage stamps.

INLAND MONEY ORDERS.

For sums under 10*s.*,	1*d.*
" 10*s.* and under £1,	2*d.*
" £1, " " 2,	3*d.*
" 2, " " 3,	4*d.*
" 3, " " 4,	5*d.*
" 4, " " 5,	6*d.*
" 5 " " 6,	7*d.*
" 6, " " 7,	8*d.*
" 7, " " 8,	9*d.*
" 8, " " 9,	10*d.*
" 9, " " 10,	11*d.*
" 10,	1*s.*

...6 13 20 27
hur.... 7 14 21 28
ri. ...1 8 15 22 29
t.....2 9 16 23 30

FEBRUARY.

ın...... 7 14 21 28
on..... 1 8 15 22
ues. ... 2 9 16 23
ed..... 3 10 17 24
hur.... 4 11 18 25
ri...... 5 12 19 26
t...... 6 13 20 27

MARCH.

ın...... 7 14 21 28
on..... 1 8 15 22 29
ues. ... 2 9 16 23 30
ed.... 3 10 17 24 31
hur.... 4 11 18 25
i 5 12 19 26
t...... 6 13 20 27

Wed..... 7 14 21 28
Thur.... 1 8 15 22 29
Fri...... 2 9 16 23 30
Sat...... 3 10 17 24

MAY.

Sun...... 2 9 16 23 30
Mon...... 3 10 17 24 31
Tues..... 4 11 18 25
Wed..... 5 12 19 26
Thur..... 6 13 20 27
Fri....... 7 14 21 28
Sat... 1 8 15 22 29

JUNE.

Sun...... 6 13 20 27
Mon...... 7 14 21 28
Tues. ... 1 8 15 22 29
Wed..... 2 9 16 23 30
Thur.... 3 10 17 24
Fri...... 4 11 18 25
Sat...... 5 12 19 26

Wed..... 7 14 21 28
Thur.... 1 8 15 22 29
Fri....... 2 9 16 23 30
Sat...... 3 10 17 24 31

AUGUST.

Sun. 1 8 15 22 29
Mon...... 2 9 16 23 30
Tues..... 3 10 17 24 31
Wed..... 4 11 18 25
Thur.... 5 12 19 26
Fri....... 6 13 20 27
Sat...... 7 14 21 28

SEPTEMBER.

Sun...... 5 12 19 26
Mon...... 6 13 20 27
Tues...... 7 14 21 28
Wed..... 1 8 15 22 29
Thur.... 2 9 16 23 30
Fri...... 3 10 17 24
Sat...... 4 11 18 25

Wed..... 6 13 20 27
Thur.... 7 14 21 28
Fri... 1 8 15 22 29
Sat... 2 9 16 23 30

NOVEMBER.

Sun...... 7 14 21 28
Mon..... 1 8 15 22 29
Tues. ... 2 9 16 23 30
Wed..... 3 10 17 24
Thur..... 4 11 18 25
Fri....... 5 12 19 26
Sat....... 6 13 20 27

DECEMBER.

Sun. 5 12 19 26
Mon...... 6 13 20 27
Tues. ... 7 14 21 28
Wed..... 1 8 15 22 29
Thur.... 2 9 16 23 30
Fri. 3 10 17 24 31
Sat...... 4 11 18 25

Wed.....
Thur....
Fri.......
Sat.... 1

FE

Sun. ....
Mon......
Tues. ...
Wed.....
Thur....
Fri.......
Sat......

M

Sun......
Mon......
Tues. ...
Wed.....
Thur....
Fri. .....
Sat......

TABLE

wing the number of days from any given day of one month, to e same day in any other month. In leap-year add 1 if February 29 in the calculation.

To the same day of	FROM ANY DAY OF											
	Jan.	Feb.	Mar.	Apr.	May	June	July	Aug.	Sept.	Oct.	Nov.	Dec.
uary...........	365	334	306	275	245	214	184	153	122	92	61	31
ruary..........	31	365	337	306	276	245	215	184	153	123	92	62
rch............	59	28	365	334	304	273	243	212	181	151	120	90
ril............	90	59	31	365	335	304	274	243	212	182	151	121
y..............	120	89	61	30	365	334	304	273	242	212	181	151
e..............	151	120	92	61	31	365	335	304	273	243	212	182
y..............	181	150	122	91	61	30	365	334	303	273	242	212
gust...........	212	181	153	122	92	61	31	365	334	304	273	243
tember.........	243	212	184	153	123	92	62	31	365	335	304	274
ober...........	273	242	214	183	153	122	92	61	30	365	334	304
ember..........	304	273	245	214	184	153	123	92	61	31	365	335
ember..........	334	303	275	244	214	183	153	122	91	61	30	365

ARY FOR 56 YEARS, FROM

1844 TO 1899.

EXPLANATION.

ok for the ear you want. Above nd its Dominical letter. Look e lower part of the Diary for the letter in the line opposite the th wanted. Above that letter you the days o the week, and on the he days of the month. Leap years two letters; the first serves till nd of February. Leap year is the which divides evenly by 4; but ear 1900 will not be a Leap year.

E	D	C	BA	G	F	E	DC
45	46	47	48	49	50	51	52
73	74	75	76	77	78	79	80
A	**G**	**FE**	**D**	**C**	**B**	**AG**	**F**
54	55	56	57	58	59	60	61
82	83	84	85	86	87	88	89

D	CB	A	G	F	ED	C	B	A
63	64	65	66	67	68	69	70	71
91	92	93	94	95	96	97	98	99

15	22	29	Su	Sa	Fr	Th	W	Tu	M
16	23	30	M	Su	Sa	Fr	Th	W	Tu
17	24	31	Tu	M	Su	Sa	Fr	Th	W
18	25		W	Tu	M	Su	Sa	Fr	Th
19	26		Th	W	Tu	M	Su	Sa	Fr

PUBLIC HOLIDAYS.

LONDON—*Exchequer, and India House.*—Good Friday and Christmas.

Law Offices.—Good Friday and three following days, Whit-Monday and Whit-Tuesday, Queen's Birth-day and Accession, Christmas, and three following days.

Excise, Stamp and Tax Offices.—Good Friday, Queen's Birth-day, June 28, Nov. 9, and Christmas.

Docks and Customs.—Good Friday, Queen's Birth-day, and Christmas.

IRELAND—*Customs.*—Good Friday, Queen's Birth-day, and Christmas.

Excise, & Stamp Offices.—Good Friday, Queen's Birth-day, June 28, Nov. 9, and Christmas.

SCOTLAND—*Customs*—Good Friday, Queen's Birth-day, Sacramental Fasts, & Christmas

Excise and Stamp Offices.—Jan. 1, Good Friday, Queen's Birth-day, (Fair Saturday, Glasgow), Sacramental Fasts, and Christmas.

BANK HOLIDAYS.

ENGLAND AND IRELAND.

Good Friday, Easter Monday, the Monday in Whitsun week, the first Monday in Aug., Christmas, & the 26th of Dec. if a week day.

SCOTLAND.

New Year's Day, Christmas Day, (if either of these fall on a Sunday the following Monday shall be a Bank Holiday,) Good Friday, the first Monday of May, the first Monday of August, and any day which may be appointed by Royal Proclamation. Upon Sacramental Fast-days and other local Holidays, the Bank Offices ...

POSTAGES.

INLAND LETTERS AND PACKAGES.

The rate of postage to be prepaid on inland letters and parcels of all sorts, closed or open, is as follows:—

Not exceeding 1 oz. in weight, ...1 *d.*
Above 1 oz. and not above 2 oz.,..........$1\frac{1}{2}$*d.*
Do. 2 " do. do. 4 " ....2 *d.*
Do. 4 " do. do. 6 " ....$2\frac{1}{2}$*d.*
Do. 6 " do. do. 8 " ....3 *d.*
Do. 8 " do. do. 10 " ....$3\frac{1}{2}$*d.*
Do. 10 " do. do. 12 " ....4 *d.*

A letter above the weight of 12 oz. is liable to the charge of 1*d.* for every ounce, commencing with the first ounce. For instance, a letter between 12 and 13 oz. weight must be prepaid 1*s.* 1*d.* As a general rule, the postage if not paid in advance, is double the foregoing; and if the payment in advance be insufficient, double the deficiency is charged. An inland letter, for example, weighing more than an ounce, and not exceeding two ounces, and prepaid one penny only, is on delivery charged *double* the deficiency of one halfpenny, viz. one penny, and so on. —A letter directed to a person, and the person not found at the address, and the letter re-directed, single additional postage only is charged. The Post Office cannot undertake the safe transmission of valuable inclosures in unregistered letters. Letters when once posted cannot be given back upon any pretence whatever. Letters to warm climates should be gummed or wafered, not sealed with wax, as the wax is liable to get melted, to the injury of other letters.

A postmaster is not bound to re-direct letters for a person temporarily leaving his home and not having a private bag or box, unless the house be left uninhabited, or the letters would be delayed in their transmission by being sent to the house to be re-directed there. In all cases of re-direction, a written authority, duly signed by the person to whom the letters are addressed, must be sent to the postmaster.

REGISTERED LETTERS.

An inland letter or book-packet can be registered on payment of 4*d.* in addition to the postage of such letter or packet. The full amount in stamps for postage and registration, must be on the letter or book-packet, and it will require to be posted half an hour before the closing of the box for the mail by which it is to be despatched, otherwise a late fee of 4*d.* will be charged till the closing of the letter-box. A letter to be registered should be presented at the window and a receipt obtained for it, and must not be dropped into the letter-box. Any letter marked "Registered" which shall be posted without at the same time being registered shall, if observed, be afterwards registered by the post-office, and be forwarded to its destination, charged with double the ordinary registration rate of postage. All letters containing coin are treated as registered, even though they be posted without registration, and are charged on delivery with a double registration fee, in addition to the ordinary postage. Any person sending money or jewellery in a letter, if lost or mis-delivered, has no claim on the Post-office. The most secure mode of sealing is first to wafer or gum the letter and then to ...

BOOK P

Or plain, written, or
out a cover, or in
ends or sides, may be
Not exceeding 2 oz. i
" 4 oz.
" 6 oz.
" 8 oz.
" 10 oz.
" 12 oz.
And ½d. for every a

The postage to be
stamps affixed. If t
not prepaid, the un
double on delivery.
tain any number of s
photographs (when
cases containing glas
or vellum, either prin
ing printed or lithogr
mixed, but not letter
anything sealed or c
tion. Marking or writ
of the nature of a lett
stating who sends the
is sent, is not regard
name and address of t
permitted but recom
cover come off, or for
packet cannot be forv
turned. In books and
binding, mounting, or
or of a portion thereo
also markers and rolle
or otherwise), and wha
the safe transmission
matter or usually app
the greater security
packet may be tied at
The postmaster is au
string, but must refas
wards. No packet ca
ceeds 5 pounds in w
length, and 9 inches i
in depth, except petit

INLAND PAT

All parcels are forw
desires, whether close
is limited to 12 oz., an
in length by 9 inches i
in width. The postag
for letters, and must
stamps.

INLAND MON

For sums under 10*s.*,
" 10*s.* and under £1,
" £1, " " 2,
" 2, " " 3,
" 3, " " 4,
" 4, " " 5,
" 5 " " 6,
" 6, " " 7,
" 7, " " 8,
" 8, " " 9,
" 9, " " 10,
" 10, - - -

No order to contain
penny. No money
unless the applicant f
in full, and at least
Christian name of
who sends the order, a

Log of the S. S. 'Hope' 1880.
Greenland whale and seal fishing
Vol I - II.

D002

.....		5	12	19	26
.....		6	13	20	27
[Th]ur....		7	14	21	28
[F]ri. ...	1	8	15	22	29
[S]at.....	2	9	16	23	30

FEBRUARY.

Sun......		7	14	21	28
Mon.....	1	8	15	22	
Tues....	2	9	16	23	
Wed.....	3	10	17	24	
Thur....	4	11	18	25	
Fri......	5	12	19	26	
Sat......	6	13	20	27	

MARCH.

Sun......		7	14	21	28
Mon.....	1	8	15	22	29
Tues....	2	9	16	23	30
Wed.....	3	10	17	24	31
Thur....	4	11	18	25	
Fri	5	12	19	26	
Sat......	6	13	20	27	

Tues....		6	13	20	27
Wed.....		7	14	21	28
Thur....	1	8	15	22	29
Fri......	2	9	16	23	30
Sat......	3	10	17	24	

MAY.

Sun......	2	9	16	23	30
Mon.....	3	10	17	24	31
Tues.....	4	11	18	25	
Wed.....	5	12	19	26	
Thur....	6	13	20	27	
Fri.......	7	14	21	28	
Sat... 1	8	15	22	29	

JUNE.

Sun......		6	13	20	27
Mon......		7	14	21	28
Tues....	1	8	15	22	29
Wed.....	2	9	16	23	30
Thur....	3	10	17	24	
Fri.......	4	11	18	25	
Sat......	5	12	19	26	

Tues....		6	13	20	27
Wed.....		7	14	21	28
Thur....	1	8	15	22	29
Fri......	2	9	16	23	30
Sat......	3	10	17	24	31

AUGUST.

Sun.....	1	8	15	22	29
Mon.....	2	9	16	23	30
Tues.....	3	10	17	24	31
Wed.....	4	11	18	25	
Thur....	5	12	19	26	
Fri.......	6	13	20	27	
Sat......	7	14	21	28	

SEPTEMBER.

Sun......		5	12	19	26
Mon......		6	13	20	27
Tues.....		7	14	21	28
Wed.....	1	8	15	22	29
Thur....	2	9	16	23	30
Fri......	3	10	17	24	
Sat......	4	11	18	25	

Tues.....		5	12	19	26
Wed.....		6	13	20	27
Thur....		7	14	21	28
Fri...	1	8	15	22	29
Sat...	2	9	16	23	30

NOVEMBER.

Sun......		7	14	21	28
Mon......	1	8	15	22	29
Tues....	2	9	16	23	30
Wed......	3	10	17	24	
Thur.....	4	11	18	25	
Fri.......	5	12	19	26	
Sat.......	6	13	20	27	

DECEMBER.

Sun.		5	12	19	26
Mon......		6	13	20	27
Tues. ...		7	14	21	28
Wed.....	1	8	15	22	29
Thur....	2	9	16	23	30
Fri......	3	10	17	24	31
Sat.......	4	11	18	25	

Tues.....		4	11	18	25
Wed......		5	12	19	26
Thur.....		6	13	20	27
Fri........		7	14	21	28
Sat....	1	8	15	22	29

FEBRUARY.

Sun.		6	13	20	27
Mon......		7	14	21	28
Tues. ...	1	8	15	22	29
Wed......	2	9	16	23	
Thur.....	3	10	17	24	
Fri........	4	11	18	25	
Sat.......	5	12	19	26	

MARCH.

Sun......		5	12	19	26
Mon......		6	13	20	27
Tues. ...		7	14	21	28
Wed.....	1	8	15	22	29
Thur....	2	9	16	23	30
Fri.	3	10	17	24	31
Sat......	4	11	18	25	

TABLE

Showing the number of days from any given day of one month, to the same day in any other month. In leap-year add 1 if February 29 is in the calculation.

To the same day of	FROM ANY DAY OF											
	Jan.	Feb.	Mar.	Apr.	May	June	July	Aug.	Sept.	Oct.	Nov.	Dec.
January..........	365	334	306	275	245	214	184	153	122	92	61	31
February..........	31	365	337	306	276	245	215	184	153	123	92	62
March..........	59	28	365	334	304	273	243	212	181	151	120	90
April..........	90	59	31	365	335	304	274	243	212	182	151	121
May..........	120	89	61	30	365	334	304	273	242	212	181	151
June..........	151	120	92	61	31	365	335	304	273	243	212	182
July..........	181	150	122	91	61	30	365	334	303	273	242	212
August..........	212	181	153	122	92	61	31	365	334	304	273	243
September..........	243	212	184	153	123	92	62	31	365	335	304	274
October..........	273	242	214	183	153	122	92	61	30	365	334	304
November..........	304	273	245	214	184	153	123	92	61	31	365	335
December..........	334	303	275	244	214	183	153	122	91	61	30	365

DIARY FOR 56 YEARS, FROM 1844 TO 1899.

EXPLANATION.

Look for the [y]ear you want. Above it find its D[om]inical letter. Look on the lower pa[r]t of the Diary for the same letter in the line opposite the month wanted. Above that letter you find the days o[f] the week, and on the left the days of [t]he month. Leap years have two letters; the first serves till the end of February. Leap year is the year which divides evenly by 4; but the year 1900 will not be a Leap year.

GF	E	D	C	BA	G	F	E	DC
1844	45	46	47	48	49	50	51	52
1872	73	74	75	76	77	78	79	80
B	**A**	**G**	**FE**	**D**	**C**	**B**	**AG**	**F**
1853	54	55	56	57	58	59	60	61
1881	82	83	84	85	86	87	88	89

E	D	CB	A	G	F	ED	C	B	A
1862	63	64	65	66	67	68	69	70	71
1890	91	92	93	94	95	96	97	98	99

1	8	15	22	29	Su	Sa	Fr	Th	W	Tu	M
2	9	16	23	30	M	Su	Sa	Fr	Th	W	Tu
3	10	17	24	31	Tu	M	Su	Sa	Fr	Th	W
[illegible]	11	18	25		W	Tu	M	Su	Sa	Fr	Th
[illegible]	19	26			Th	W	Tu	M	Su	Sa	Fr
[illegible]	20	27			Fr	Th	W	Tu	M	Su	Sa
[illegible]	21	28			Sa	Fr	Th	[illegible]	Tu	M	Su

PUBLIC HOLIDAYS.

LONDON—*Exchequer, and India House.*—Good Friday and Christmas.

Law Offices.—Good Friday and three following days, Whit-Monday and Whit-Tuesday, Queen's Birth-day and Accession, Christmas, and three following days.

Excise, Stamp and Tax Offices.—Good Friday, Queen's Birth-day, June 28, Nov. 9, and Christmas.

Docks and Customs.—Good Friday, Queen's Birth-day, and Christmas.

IRELAND—*Customs.*—Good Friday, Queen's Birth-day, and Christmas.

Excise, & Stamp Offices.—Good Friday, Queen's Birth-day, June 28, Nov. 9, and Christmas.

SCOTLAND—*Customs*—Good Friday, Queen's Birth-day, Sacramental Fasts, & Christmas

Excise and Stamp Offices.—Jan. 1, Good Friday, Queen's Birth-day, (Fair Saturday, Glasgow), Sacramental Fasts, and Christmas.

BANK HOLIDAYS.

ENGLAND AND IRELAND.

Good Friday, Easter Monday, the Monday in Whitsun week, the first Monday in Aug., Christmas, & the 26th of Dec. if a week day.

SCOTLAND.

New Year's Day, Christmas Day, (if either of these fall on a Sunday the following Monday shall be a Bank Holiday,) Good Friday, the first Monday of May, the first Monday of August, and any day which may be appointed by Royal Proclamation. Upon Sacramental Fast-days and other local Holidays, the Bank Offices will be open only between the hours of 9 and 11 a.m.

POSTAGES.

INLAND LETTERS AND PACKAGES.

The rate of postage to be prepaid on inland letters and parcels of all sorts, closed or open, is as follows:—

Not exceeding 1 oz. in weight, ...1 *d.*
Above 1 oz. and not above 2 oz., ...1½*d.*
Do. 2 " do. do. 4 " ....2 *d.*
Do. 4 " do. do. 6 " ....2½*d.*
Do. 6 " do. do. 8 " ....3 *d.*
Do. 8 " do. do. 10 " ....3½*d.*
Do. 10 " do. do. 12 " ....4 *d.*

A letter above the weight of 12 oz. is liable to the charge of 1*d.* for every ounce, commencing with the first ounce. For instance, a letter between 12 and 13 oz. weight must be prepaid 1*s.* 1*d.* As a general rule, the postage if not paid in advance, is double the foregoing; and if the payment in advance be insufficient, double the deficiency is charged. An inland letter, for example, weighing more than an ounce, and not exceeding two ounces, and prepaid one penny only, is on delivery charged *double* the deficiency of one halfpenny, viz. one penny, and so on. —A letter directed to a person, and the person not found at the address, and the letter re-directed, single additional postage only is charged. The Post Office cannot undertake the safe transmission of valuable inclosures in unregistered letters. Letters when once posted cannot be given back upon any pretence whatever. Letters to warm climates should be gummed or wafered, not sealed with wax, as the wax is liable to get melted, to the injury of other letters.

A postmaster is not bound to re-direct letters for a person temporarily leaving his home and not having a private bag or box, unless the house be left uninhabited, or the letters would be delayed in their transmission by being sent to the house to be re-directed there. In all cases of re-direction, a written authority, duly signed by the person to whom the letters are addressed, must be sent to the postmaster.

REGISTERED LETTERS.

An inland letter or book-packet can be registered on payment of 4*d.* in addition to the postage of such letter or packet. The full amount in stamps for postage and registration, must be on the letter or book-packet, and it will require to be posted half an hour before the closing of the box for the mail by which it is to be despatched, otherwise a late fee of 4*d.* will be charged till the closing of the letter-box. A letter to be registered should be presented at the window and a receipt obtained for it, and must not be dropped into the letter-box. Any letter marked "Registered" which shall be posted without at the same time being registered shall, if observed, be afterwards registered by the post-office, and be forwarded to its destination, charged with double the ordinary registration rate of postage. All letters containing coin are treated as registered, even though they be posted without registration, and are charged on delivery with a double registration fee, in addition to the ordinary postage. Any person sending money or jewellery in a letter, if lost or mis-delivered, has no claim on the Post-office. The most secure mode of sealing is first to wafer or gum the letter and then to seal it with wax. No article of a dangerous kind can be sent by post. Scissors, knives, [illegible] may be sent if packed in

BOOK PACKETS,

Or plain, written, or printed paper, without a cover, or in a cover open at the ends or sides, may be sent—

Not exceeding 2 oz. in weight, ... ½*d.*
" 4 oz. " ....1 *d.*
" 6 oz. " ....1½*d.*
" 8 oz. " ....2 *d.*
" 10 oz. " ....2½*d.*
" 12 oz. " ....3 *d.*

And ½d. for every additional two ounces.

The postage to be prepaid by postage stamps affixed. If the whole postage be not prepaid, the unpaid part is charged double on delivery. The packet may contain any number of separate books, prints, photographs (when not on glass nor in cases containing glass), maps, parchment or vellum, either printed or written, including printed or lithographed letters, plain or mixed, but not letters, sealed or open, nor anything sealed or closed against inspection. Marking or writing allowed when not of the nature of a letter. An entry, merely stating who sends the book, or to whom it is sent, is not regarded as a letter. The name and address of the sender is not only permitted but recommended, so that if the cover come off, or for any other reason the packet cannot be forwarded, it may be returned. In books and prints, all legitimate binding, mounting, or covering of the same, or of a portion thereof, will be allowed; as also markers and rollers, (whether of paper or otherwise), and whatever is necessary for the safe transmission of literary or artistic matter or usually appertains thereto. For the greater security of the contents, the packet may be tied at the ends with a string The postmaster is authorised to cut the string, but must refasten the packet afterwards. No packet can be received if it exceeds 5 pounds in weight, 18 inches in length, and 9 inches in width and 6 inches in depth, except petitions to Parliament.

INLAND PATTERN POST.

All parcels are forwarded as the sender desires, whether closed or open; the weight is limited to 12 oz., and the size to 18 inches in length by 9 inches in depth and 6 inches in width. The postage is the same as that for letters, and must be prepaid in postage stamps.

INLAND MONEY ORDERS.

For sums under 10*s.*,	- - - -	1*d.*
" 10*s.* and under £1,	- - - -	2*d.*
" £1, " " 2,	- - -	3*d.*
" 2, " " 3,	- - -	4*d.*
" 3, " " 4,	- - -	5*d.*
" 4, " " 5,	- - -	6*d.*
" 5 " " 6,	- - -	7*d.*
" 6, " " 7,	- - -	8*d.*
" 7, " " 8,	- - -	9*d.*
" 8, " " 9,	- - -	10*d.*
" 9, " " 10,	- - -	11*d.*
" 10,	- - - - - -	1*s.*

No order to contain a fractional part of a penny. No money order can be issued unless the applicant furnish the surname in full, and at least one initial of the Christian name of the person or firm who sends the order, and of the person or firm to whom the money is to be sent, unless the remitter or receiver is a peer or a bishop, then his ordinary title is suffi-

Log of the "Hope" Vol ~~II~~ I.

D004

Saturday February 28.

Sailed at 2 o'clock amid a great crowd and greater cheering. The 'Windward' Captain Murray went out in front of us, their Captain bellowing 'Port' and 'Starboard' like a Bull of Bashan. We set about it in a quieter and more business like way. We are as clean as a Gentleman's yacht, all shining brass and snow white decks. Saw a young lady that I was introduced to but whose name I did not catch waving a handkerchief from the end of the pier. Took off my hat from the Hope's quarterdeck though I don't know her from Eve. Rather rough outside and the glass falling rapidly. Beat about the bay for several hours and had dinner with champagne in honour of Baxter and grandees on board. Pilot boat came and fetched them all off at last, together with an unfortunate Stow-a-way who tried to conceal himself in the Tween decks. Sailed for Shetland in a rough wind, glass going down like oysters. As long as I stick on deck I'll do.

Sunday March 1st

Got into Lerwick at 7.30 PM. Deuced lucky for us as

D006

a gale is rising and if we hadn't made the land we might have lost boats and bulwarks. We were uneasy about it, but we sighted the Bressay light about 5.30. Captain very pleased. We got in before the Windward, though they had 5 hours start.

Monday March 1st

Blowing a hurricane. Windward got in at 2AM only just in time. The whole harbour is one sheet of foam. Feel very comfortable aboard. Have a snug little cabin. Telegraph gone wrong between this and Peterhead. Pokey hole.

Tuesday March 2nd

Glass down at 28.375. Captain has never seen it so low. Blowing like Billy outside. Made out the hosiery list. Tait on religion and atheism. He is our Shetland agent, not half such a fool he looks.

Wednesday March 3rd.

Fine day - Glass still very low. Went on shore with the Captain after breakfast. Enlisted our Shetland hands. Fearful rush and row in Tait's small office. 'Jan Meyen' & 'Victor' came in. Murray a

Windward seems a decent fellow. Captain and
were going from Tait's shop when a drunken
ellander got hold of him. "Capn. I'm (hic!)
in' with you. Oh Such a Voyage, Captain,
ch a voyage as never was landed! hic (!)
ee hundred and fifty tons, sir, I've brought
luck with me". Gray turned back in the
ack room, and seemed annoyed. I said
'll turn him out if you like, Captain' He
id 'Ah, I know fine you'd like a smack
him, Doctor; I would mysel but it
ouldna do." We had locked the door
the back room when there was an apparition
a hand and arm through the smoked Glass
ndow which formed the upper half of the door.
ang! Crash! Wood and Glass came rattling
to the room, and we saw our indomitable
ellander, with his hands cut and bleeding,
oking through the hole. "Wood and iron
won't keep me from you, Captain Gray. Go I
ill." The Captain coolly smoked his pipe the
hole time and never moved from the Stove.
he man was carried off, kicking & thumping

D008

t the Gaol, I suppose, though the infirmary
would have been a far better place. If ever
I saw D T that was it. Had Murray of Windw
and Tait to dinner, talk of masonry, whaling &c
Dispute with Murray about efficacy of drugs. P
of good wine going. Finished the evening with
Captain very pleasantly. By the way another
Stowaway turned up today, a wretched looking
animal, The Captain was frightening him after
by telling him he'd have to go back, but he
finally signed the Articles

Thursday March 4th

Gave out Tobacco in the morning. Slept forenoo
Went ashore in the evening. Went first wi
second mate and Stewart to the Queen's a
had something short as he calls it. Then we
to Mrs Brown's and lost sight of them. Ha
a very hospitable reception there. Told me
make their home my home. Went down to
the Commercial where an F & E was going o
Heard some good songs and sang Jack's Yar
Chat with Captain about Prince Jerome. &c.

[Sun]day March 5th

Captain and I were invited to Taits for dinner: [b]oth thought it a horrid bore. Went to the Queen's [a]nd played billiards. Then toddled down to Taits. [Me]t Murray of the Windward and Galloway, the [l]atter a small lawyer, insufferably conceited — [h]ate the fellow. Had a heavy weary dinner with [v]ery inferior champagne. Old Tait expressed great [s]urprize at my saying I was RW's nephew - the old [c]row, I found out afterwards that the Captain had [j]ust been telling him about it. He has a dog [w]ho has been taught to love the name of Napoleon, [if] you talk of shooting Napoleon he will make a [st]art at you, and probably leave with some things [of] yours in his mouth, muscles and clothes and [th]ings. Murray talked about putting three men [u]nder the ice, seeing ten men shot in a mob row [a]nd several curious things. We got the boat [a]t nine o'clock and were both delighted to get [o]n board again, and stretch our legs quietly. [W]ind rising. Saw what the Captain says is a Roman Camp, but I think it is a Round Pictish [T]ower.

D010

Saturday March 6th

Raining and blowing hard. Did nothing all day. Colin McLean and men went ashore in the evening and hailed for boat which we had to give though it was rather rough. Began Boswell's life of Johnson.

Sunday March 7th

Nothing doing except that the mail steamer St Magnus came in with a letter from home and one from Letty, also a week's Scotsmen. Satisfactory news. We shifted our berth the other day in the harbour and now lie apart from the other ships with the Windward. Colin the mate was at the Queens last night among a lot of Dundeemen who spoke of those two W–d Peterheadmen who went and moped by themselves. Colin got up and after proclaiming himself a "Hope" man ran a muck through the assembly knocking down a Dundee Doctor. He remarked to me this morning when I was giving him a pick me up "It's lucky I was sober, Doctor, or I might have got into a regular row." I wonder what Colin's idea of a regular row is. Lerwick is a dirty little tow

th very hospitable simple inhabitants. Main Street
is designed by a man with a squint, builded
the lines of a corkscrew. Noticed today that
me of the ships in harbour flew Freemason
ags, Murray has the Royal arch up, Compasses
a blue ground. Fishermen sell cod
e at 6/ a hundred weight, and
ve caught as much as 25 Cwt in
night. By the way the Engineer of the Windward
t his two forefingers crushed in machinery
sterday and I had to go over before breakfast
d dress them. Twenty sail of whalers in the
y.

onday March 8th.

Nothing like a quill pen for writing a Journal
th, but this is such a confounddedly bad one.
ent ashore today and after knocking about some
me went up to see a Football match between
rkney and Shetland – Play rather poor. Met
aptains of Jan Meyen (Deuchars), Nova Zembla,
nd Eric, also a London man, Brown, Doctor of
e Eric. Six of us went down to the Queens
ter the match and started on bad whiskey

D012

and went in to Coffee. Then Brown ordered a bottle of Champagne, and Murray and I followed suit. Cigars and pipes. I think we all had quite enough liquor. Brown was wrecked in the Ravenscraig last year. Says he is a very superior sort of chap. Captain and I got home about half past nine.

Tuesday March 9th

Went ashore with Captain before dinner. Jack Wil[illegible] was drunk and playing old Harry in the streets. Captain got hold of him and sent him on board the Hope in the pilot boat, but when he got half way he sprang over and swam ashore again. Cain and a boat's crew captured him afterwards. Had a very dull morning going from shop to shop. We will sail tomorrow if it is any way fair. Tait came on board afterwards and we had a pleasant talk. He is a sensible fellow tho' rather a bore. Looked over Scoresby. Captain told me some curious things about whaling. The great distance at which they can hear a steamer and how it frightens them. oil is about £50 a ton and bone £800 or so

ll bone goes to the continent. Sea Unicorns are
ery common, so are sharks, and dolphins
ut the curiosity of the place are the Animalcule
hich the Whale eats.

Vednesday. March 10th

North Wind prevented our getting off. The old
clipse steamed in grandly about four o'clock
eing cheered by each ship as she passed. Went
n board and saw Captain David, Alec and Crabbe.
Went ashore in the evening and played Captain;
lso had the honour of beating Crabbe at billiards.
e has a great local reputation. Left my meershaum and Gloves in the smoking room.

Thursday March 11th

big day for Leith. The ships began to steer out from
Lerwick sound after breakfast. It was a pretty thing
n the beautifully clear and calm day to hear the
men singing across the bay to the clank clank of the
nchors. Every ship as it passed out got 3 cheers
from all the others. Captain and I went ashore,
nd the boat's crew and I went in search of that
beggar Jock Webster. We found him at last and
wo of us carried him, cursing horribly down the

D014

main street of Lerwick to the boat, where I had to hold him to keep him from jumping overboard. We left about one o'clock and steamed through islands till about seven when we came to an anchorage with the Jan Meyen, Eric, and Active in a little Voe. We raced the Jan Meyen up from Lerwick and beat her all the way, anchored within a stonethrow of the Eric. Talking to McL and Captain about getting to the pole in the even. There is no doubt about it that everyone has been on a wrong tack. The broad ocean is the way to find a way up to the pole, not by going up a drain which gradually grows narrower and down which the ice naturally runs, as it does in Davis' Straits.

Friday March 12th

We'll have to stay here all day, I fear, for it is blowing half a gale tho' the glass is high. Nothing to do all day. The land is a succession of long low hills with peat cuttings and funny little thatched cottages here and there. Captain went over to the Eric in the evening. They seemed to be catching fish but we had no proper bate, so Mate and I

went ashore with a boat's crew to get some clams.
It was nearly dark so we couldn't gather again
but we went the round of the little cottages begging.
Such dismal hovels, the esquimeaux have better
houses. Each has a little square hole in the ceiling
to let out the smoke of a large peat fire in the
middle of the room. They were all civil enough
met one rather pretty but shy girl even in this
barbarous spot. Got some razor fish as bait
and departed triumphant. Up to our thighs in
mud coming and going. Revenue Cutter
boarded us this evening and Lieutenant was
only pacified by the present of a stick of baccy.
Am afraid Colin will eat all our bait. Captain
rather annoyed about being kept in this hole.
Glass high

Saturday March 13th.

Wind high and raining hard. Active and Jan Meyen
are off already. We follow them soon. They are
pulling up the anchor now and singing "Goodbye,
Fare-thee-well, Goodbye Fare-thee well". A pretty
song it is too. Sea was not very rough outside -
went through the islands, keeping Uyll at the right

D016

at the extreme north of Shetland we passed some curious rocks in the sea called Ramna Stacks.

Ramna Stacks.

Raining hard all day. raced with the Eric and had rather the best of it. a bit seasick. Saw Burrafiord Holms the extreme north point of Great Britain, and then lost sight land about four P.M. Ran with an oblique w and three quarter steam all night. Dreamed being beaten by a Gorilla, and of pulling in the Oxfo boat. 167 miles

Sunday March 14th

Eric rather a head of us and only occasionally in sight. Heavy Atlantic swell doing the Gran

Northward Ho! all day under steam and sail. Northward Ho! ran about 150 miles. About getting to the pole the gulf stream runs up past

Heavy Atlantic Swell.

Spitzbergen so of course that is the way to go. It is one of the most extraordinary delusions in history how ship after ship has run up into a cul-de-sac for Davis' Straits is nothing better. Read Boswell. Don't agree with McCauley at all about Boswell bein

a man of no intellect. If ever a man was afflicted with what he calls 'morbus Boswellianus' It is Lord McCauley himself in the case of Willy the Silent.

Monday March 15th

First under Steam and Sail, and then under Sail alone. Must have got about half way today. Kept in the cabin until evening. Read Boswell. Like that old boy Johnson for all his pomposity. A Thorough old fellow, I fancy. He was in Plymouth, it seems, for a couple of days, and there was considerable ill-feeling between the townsmen and the men about the docks. Johnson who had nothing in the world to do with it was often heard to exclaim "I hate a docker" I like that sort of thing. Sky looked like ice this evening. Surface temperature fallen from 44 to 38 in one day.

Tuesday March 16th

All under canvas, wind continues fair. I've brought luck with me. Two bottle nose whales were playing round the ship in the morning but I did not see them. It seems we are crossing a very favourite feeding ground of theirs. Expect to come on the ice tomorrow. We made 159 miles yesterday.

are hundreds of miles north of iceland, about
sixty south east of Jan Meyen. Old hands on
board say they never knew such a good passage,
however we mustn't crow until we are out of the
wood. Water temperature has fallen 2° since 12 o'c
which looks like ice. White line on the sky. Everyo
seems to think we will see ice before tomorrow. We ca
tell that we are under the lea of ice by the calm. Captai
told me about some curious dreams of his, notabl
about the Germans and the black heifers

Wednesday March 17th

Dies cretâ notanda. About five o'clock I heard th
second mate tell the Captain, that we were amon
the ice. He got up but I was too lazy. Passed a
Norwegian about 8 o'clock. When we rose at nin
the keen fresh air told me it was freezing. I went
on deck and there was the ice. It was not in a
continuous sheet but the whole ocean was covere
with little hillocks of it, rising and falling w
the waves, pure white above and of a wonderful
green below. None were more than 4 or 6 feet o
of the water but they were of every shape. No Sea
Put up the crow's nest in the morning.

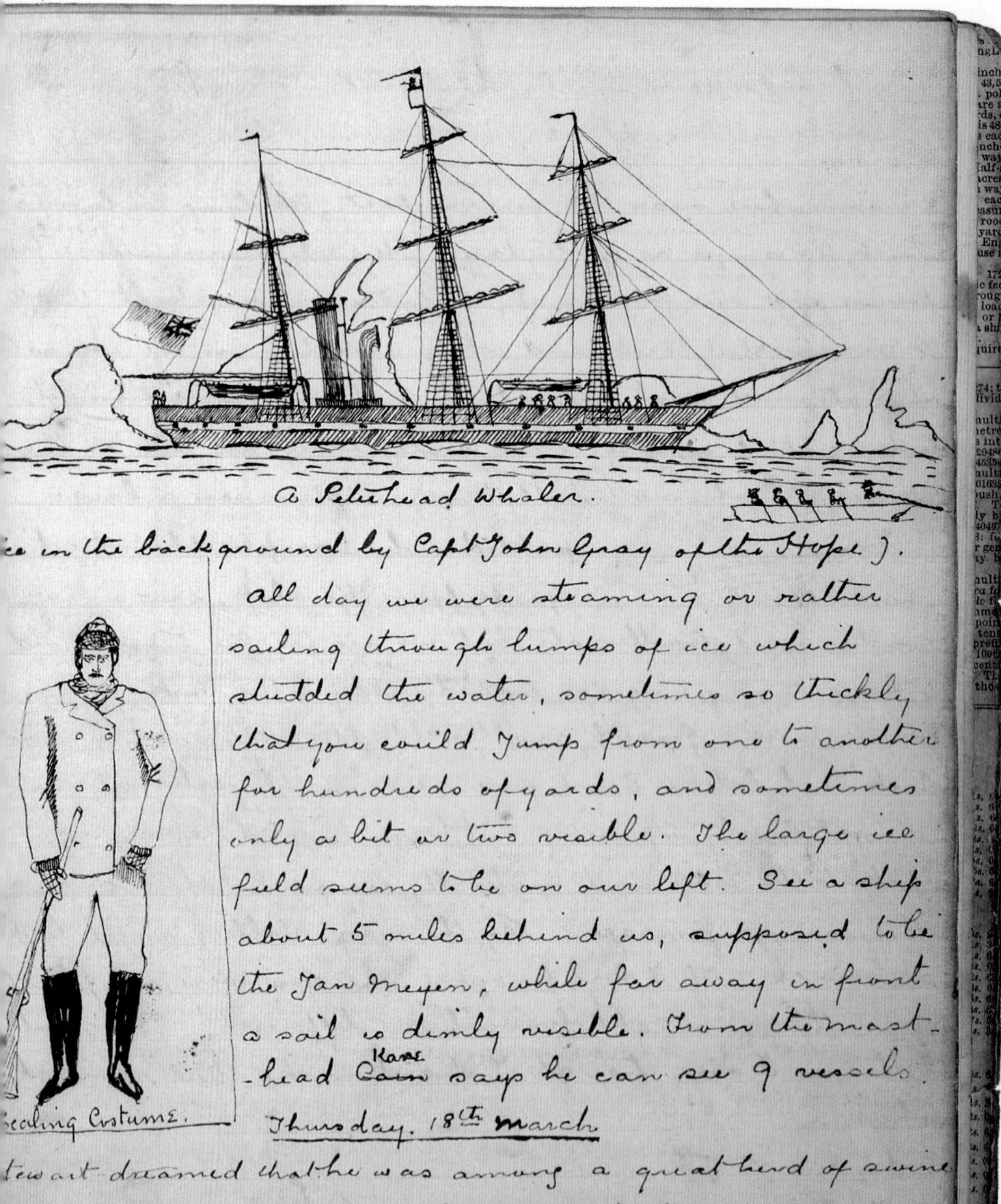

A Peterhead Whaler.

ce in the background by Capt John Gray of the Hope].

All day we were steaming or rather sailing through lumps of ice which studded the water, sometimes so thickly that you could jump from one to another for hundreds of yards, and sometimes only a bit or two visible. The large ice field seems to be on our left. See a ship about 5 miles behind us, supposed to be the Jan Meyen, while far away in front a sail is dimly visible. From the mast-head ~~Cain~~ Kane says he can see 9 vessels.

Sealing Costume.

Thursday. 18th March

tewart dreamed that he was among a great herd of swine ast night, so we are sure to see seals today. If a man reams of anything agricultural it always means that seals

D020

are somewhere near. A curious fact. Ice lying in lumps much the same as yesterday. Stewarts dream seems true for we saw our first seal, a bladder nose, about 11 AM. It was speckled black and white and lay on the ice as the ship steamed past, only about a dozen yards from it, looking at it quietly. Poor brute if they are all as tame it seems a shame to kill them. Captain saw a large

our first seal

speckled owl a couple of hundred yards from the ship, saw a few roaches and Guillemots but we are too far from land to have many. We are considerably to the North of Jan Meyen now. Passed another bladder nose and a saddle-back seal later. Some were seen in the water afterwards. A most lovely morning but hazy towards evening. Spoke to the Eric and mutually congratulated each other on our passage. By the way Walker said to me at Lerwick "If I had known who you were, sir, last year, things might have been different." I'm a lot better as I am, though I didn't make that remark to him.

Friday March 19th

A thick haze with the lumps of ice looming out of it. Could see about a hundred yards in each direction.

assed two large bladdernoses, male & female on a bit
ice. We tried the whistling and certainly the male
d stop and listen to it, the female wasn't so susceptible
t shunted at once. The male was about 10 feet long
should think, the female 7 or 8. I wish the haze
ould clear up. Drizzling a little. Haze continued
ll day so we lay to at night. Lane and Stewart were
sparring in the evening. Talk on literature with the
ptain, he thinks Dickens very small beer beside
hackeray. Buckland seems to be a lively sort of cove.

Saturday March 20th

nly a week from Shetland and here we are far into

are somewhere near. A curious fac
much the same as yesterday. Sle
for we saw our first seal, a bladd
It was speckled black and white a
ship steamed past, only about a
looking at it quietly. Poor brute
it seems a shame to kill them.

our first seal

speckled owl
yards from
roaches and Guillemots but we
to have many. We are considerably to the North
Meyen now. Passed another bladder nose and
-back seal later. Some were seen in the water a
A most lovely morning but hazy towards even
Spoke to the Eric and mutually congratulated
other on our passage. By the way Walker sa
at Lerwick "If I had known who you were, si
year, things might have been different." I'm
better as I am, though I didn't make that re
to him.

Friday March 19th

A thick haze with the lumps of ice looming out
Could see about a hundred yards in each direc

among loose ice. March 16th 1880

Norwegian sail to North 1880 [illegible]

passed two large bladdernoses, male & female on a bit of ice. We tried the whistling and certainly the male did stop and listen to it, the female wasn't so susceptible but shunted at once. The male was about 10 feet long I should think, the female 7 or 8. I wish the haze would clear up. Drizzling a little. Haze continued all day so we lay to at night. Lane and Stewart were sparring in the evening. Talk on literature with the Captain, he thinks Dickens very small beer beside Thackeray. Buckland seems to be a lively sort of cove.

Saturday March 20th

Only a week from Shetland and here we are far into

the icefields. It has certainly been a splendid voyage. Beautiful day, wonderfully clear. Icefields, snow white on very dark blue water as far as the eye can reach. We are ploughing through in grand style. Five sail in sight, one the Eric. Stewart insists on my accepting a pretty Esquimeaux tobacco pouch; I suppose he means it as a quid pro quo for the Pipe I gave him. No seals seen as yet. Got near heavy ice in the evening and lay to. Several bladder noses playing about the ship. about a couple of hundred seals visible from the Crow's nest, so we seem to be coming near the pack. Eleven sail in sight. Adam Carner saw the steps of a bear in the ice

Sunday March 21st.

Lay to all day owing to the thick haze. Bladdernoses by the dozen are all round us. A few Saddle backs. The captain thinks the pack is about 20 miles or so in front of us. Johnny had a meeting in the evening, the singing sounded well from the deck. Split a bottle of port after dinner. Captain tells me he tried fixing a cone full of prussic acid onto the end of the harpoon. He fired it into a finner from his small steamer. The brute went away at such a rate that it very

early set the bows on fire by the friction. The line
roke and it got away, but seems to have died
as no dog fish were seen on the coast for some
ays. Many finners are 120 feet long. By the way
arner taught me some esquimeaux. Amalang
yes). Pioo (very good) Pioo smali (bad) kisi-
nicky (ice-dog-is bear).

Monday March 22nd

ery foggy again, but we have drifted among a few
addlebacks with their little fat yellow off spring.
ot the quarter boats out, and the rifles. A long
me to wait yet, though, till April 3d, Saturday week.
og lasted all day so that we lay to. Boxed in evening.
Finished Boswell Vol I. Dreamed of G. P.

Tuesday March 23d

Clear morning, a good few seals in sight. Eclipse
ame in atlast, and Captain boarded it before dinner.
teamed a few miles in the right direction. Blowing
gale all day. 11 degrees below freezing point. Very
old wind. Rigging covered with ice. Climbed up to the
Crow's nest before tea, but the
Captain called me down
Just as I got up to it, as

Male, female & Young Saddleback

he thought I might get frost bitten. Got a fine pouch from Cane. Carner tells me at New Orleans before the war a dock labourer could make £1 a day. Now the make a dollar only. Captain saw blockade runne leaving Liverpool during the war, long spider like steamers of great speed, and painted the colour of the ocean. Cargo mostly quinine, needed hardly any crew. Glass rising again.

Wednesday. March 24th

Another big day for Leith. We have seen the pack, and an enormous pack it is too. I have not seen it from the nest yet but it extends from one side of the horizon to the other, and so deep that we can see no end to it. The nearer we steam towards it, the bigger it grows. Colin says he never saw such a one in his life. It is certainly the largest collection of big animals in the world at present, at least I know no other beast that goes in herds of millions, covering a space about 15 miles long and 8 deep. We ought to have a good voyage now, my old luck. All the ships are lying round now and taking up their positions. Wind-ward steamed past us today flying her Jack, and dipped it as a salute. 10 days yet to wait. Oysters.

urs day March 25th

urrah for a quill pen! 19° below freezing point this evening.
ve been taking up our position, and mounting boats and
aning guns all day. Edge of pack can be seen from the
idge now. Good many isolated ones about the ship. I can
ar the young ones squeaking as I write. It is a noise
tween the mew of a cat and the bleat of a lamb.
y look a sort of cross between a lamb & a gigantic
ug. Our only fear now is that some of these great
undering Norwegians or Dundeesmen go and put
ir foot into it. If we get less than 50 tons I'll be
appointed, if we get less than 100 I'll be surprized.
ptain is going to teach me to take the latitude and
ngitude. Saw a clever couplet today

"Till Silence, like a poultice comes,
To heal the blows of Sound:"

olmes' I think. Sported my sea boots today.

riday March 26th

rost still continues, 17° today, 20° during the night.
is is Just what we want to fill up gaps in the
efield and make it safe walking. Steamed very
ittle. The mate says the seals are lying in an
lmost solid mass. He says there are more than
. 1855, and in that year 50 vessels were among

there, and all got filled. We are 23 vessels now all told so the prospect is cheery. Bar Earth--quakes we'll make a voyage of it. It is very trying work waiting, though this Close time is an excellent provision. The poor brutes used to be killed before they had pupped. Eclipse g[ot] a bear today, and we saw the steps of one o[n] the snow beside our ship. They are cowardly brutes unless in a corner. Captain killed one once with a boat hook. Engineer told me how one chased a crew for miles across the snow once, and how they had to throw down article after article to engage his attention, so that they got to the ship nearly naked and in a blue funk. There is no specimen of a right whale in any British museum, except a foetus. Saw the young seals suckling today. Hurt my hand boxing with the Steward. Stuffed old Keith's tooth, and cured young Keith's Colly wobbles. It seems to be the family's day out.

Saturday. March 27th

This day week is our day. Got my knife and my

[h]appiness today, and asked Carnes to see about my
[c]lub. Beautiful day, still lying on the skirts of the pack,
all seem satisfied except the Captain and he
grumbles a bit, but I think he is only Joking.
[W]e Saw another bear's footsteps. The Eclipse
[h]as killed two and we have never seen one.
[T]hey tell me bears go in flocks of 20 or 30
[v]ery often. Rifles given out tonight. Steamed a
[l]ittle. Hoggie Milne better tonight. No news. Wrote
[m]y "Modern Parable".

[S]unday March 28th

[H]oggie bad again so I gave him some Chlorodyne.
[C]aptain went on board the Eclipse and in a little
[t]he boat came off for me for dinner. Had a very
[p]leasant feed with good wine afterwards. The
[c]onversation turned upon the War, politics, the
[N]orth Pole, Darwinism, Frankenstein, Free trade,
[W]haling and Local matters. Captain David seems
[t]o take a sinister view of our case. Says we'll
[b]e lucky if we get 20 tons; he may say it, but
[I] don't think he thinks it. Saw his bear's Skins.
By the way he told us some strange stories which
[I] will try to write as he told them.

"When I was a young fellow," he said "I happened to be in London with a gold watch and a good deal of money. I was at the Lyceum one night and wanted to get back to my lodgings in Holborn but wandered about a long time unable to find my way. At last I saw a respectable looking man and asked him the way to Holborn, adding that I was a stranger. He said he was going that way himself, and that he was Captain Burton of the 17th Lancers. We walked on together and Captain Burton by turning the conversation on the danger of carrying money about in London, learned about my watch and gold, and warned me against it. We shortly afterwards turned into an open door and the Captain said "What shall we have here, I'll have some Cognac." I said "Coffee is strong enough for me". The waiter who brought in the things was the most repulsive looking ruffian I ever clapt eyes on, and I saw him stick his tongue in his cheek and leer at the Captain. It was then that I first suspected that I had got into a trap.

I threw half a sovereign on the counter and rose to go out, but the waiter put his back against the door and said "We don't allow our visitors to leave us like this." The Captain said "Come on, sir, and we'll make a night of it; hullo give us some Sherry out of bin No 3". The waiter called "Janet" and a girl appeared rather pretty and very pale. He said "Bin No 3". The girl said "Surely, Surely you don't need that bin tonight. He said "Do what you are told." As she brought in the wine she whispered to me "Pretend to sleep". I drank a little of the wine, but spilled most of it. Then I sank down & closed my eyes. Soon the two villains came over and whispered together, and one passed the Candle over my eyes and said "He is off". They whispered a little again, and one said "Dead men tell no tales" The other said "Then we had better get the bed ready" And they both left the room. I flung open the window and was off down the street like a shot, and ran about half a mile before I saw a

lobby, and then I found it impossible, with my imperfect knowledge of London to find the house again. I heard no more of it. Get out another bottle of Port, Doctor": The conclusion of the story was considered to be a very able effort. He told us another story about how he acted as a Spy in the Boer service, and murdered 3 Kaffirs in their sleep, and shot a German through the body.
He saw a Walrus eating a Narwhal once. He is a fine fellow, and Dr Walker seems a very decent chap too. He thinks more whales are found at night than in the day, so when he gets North into the Twilight land, he has his breakfast at 10 P.M. Dinner at 2 in the morning. And Supper at 7 A.M. Then he sleeps all day. He says whales leave a very characteristic odour behind them and you often smell them before you see them.

March 29th Monday

Our time is coming now. Thick day with

driving snow. Nothing particular going on. Had
pleasant evening in the mate's berth. Songs all
und. Sang "Jack's Yarn" "The Mermaid" and
t'arm Arm". Good fun. By the way Colin the
nate payed me a high compliment today. He
id "I'm going to have every man working hard
hen we start sealing. I've no fears of you,
rgeon, I'll back you to do a day's work with
y man aboard. You suit me, and I liked the
ks of you the first time I saw ye. I hate your
an-handed gentlemen". This was a high com-
liment from taciturn Colin.

rch 30th Tuesday

thing much doing. Windward came along-
de and Murray came on board. He seemed
have small prospects, 10 tons was more than
expected, he said. Told us about Sir John Ross
ing his gun through the window of a house
ause his mate was inside & he wanted him.
ray was one of the Franklin searchers. Ross
d "Every step onwards, boys, is honour and
y to us. Death before dishonour", when they
starting sledging. Sparred with Colin & Stewart.

D034

Wednesday. March 31st
Very little doing all day. A heavy swell has set in and we are uneasy about the result. If it continues until Saturday it will make our work both difficult and dangerous. The ice is not a solid sheet, but made up of thousands of pieces of all sizes floating close to each other now in a swell these pieces alternately separ-ate and come together with irresistible force. If a poor fellow slips in between two pieces as is easily done, he runs a good chance of being cut in two, as actually happened to several Dundeesmen. Men played leap frog on a big piece. I started a story "A Journey to the Pole", which I intend to be good. We are going to write to Gladstone and Disraeli when the Dundeesmen go home.

Thursday April 1st
Swell continues and things look badly. We steamed a bit during the day. This is the first time for 3 years that I have not been examined today. Sent the Chief Engineer to the Captain with a cock and bull story

-ount curtain rings. Johnny's dignity was very
-uch hurt. By the way I was at the mast
-ad yesterday, and also on the ice some
-ime. Saluted the Harold Haarfager tonight
-.30. Swell Still on.

D036

March 31st
toing all day. A heavy swell has set
are uneasy about the result. If it
until Saturday it will make our work
ult and dangerous. The ice is not
ut, but made up of thousands of
all sizes floating close to each other.
swell these pieces alternately separ-
come together with irresistible force.
fellow slips in between two pieces
ly done, he runs a good chance of
in two, as actually happened to
Dundeesmen. Men played leap frog
piece. I started a story "A Journey
"; which I intend to be good. We are
write to Gladstone and Disraeli
Dundeesmen go home.

April 1st
times and things looks badly. We
a bit during the day. This is the
for 3 years that I have not
mined today. Sent the Chief Engineer
him with a cock and bull story

about east a
much hurt.
head yesterd
time. Salut
7.30. Swell

D037

...ngs. Johnny's dignity was very
...the way I was at the mast
...and also on the ice some
... Harold Haarfager tonight
...on.

...g up their positions among the seals - Birds eye view. March 26th 1880

D038

Friday April Second

Swell still on and the pack growing more scattered. I'm afraid our prospects will not be realized. However every man must do his best, and then we can do no more. Stayed up until 12 o'clock to see the close time out.

Saturday April 3d

Up at 2.30 AM. Swell still on, so as to make good work impossible. Lowered away our boats in the sludge about 4.30. I stayed aboard at the captain's command much against my will and helped as well as I could by pulling the skins up the side. The old seals who can swim are shot with rifles, while the poor youngsters who can't get away have their skulls smashed in by clubs. It is bloody work dashing out the poor little beggars brains while they look up with their big dark eyes into your face. We picked the boats up soon and started packing, thats to say all hands getting over the ships side and jumping along from floating piece to piece, killing all they can see, while the ship steams after and

Seal Club

cks up the skins. It takes a lot of knack to
ow what ice will bear you, and what not.
was ambitious to start but in getting over the
ps side I fell in between two pieces of ice and
s hauled out by a boathook. I changed my
thes and started again, & succeeded in killing
couple of seals and dragging their remains
ter I had skinned them to the ship's side. We
t 7.6760 seals today. Poor work, I believe
t we hope for the best. After all whales are
e things that pay.

nday April 4th

king all day. I fell into the Arctic Ocean three times
day, but luckily someone was always near to pull
e out. The danger in falling in is that with a heavy
well on as there is now, you may be cut in two
etty well by two pieces of ice coming together and
pping you. I got several drags but was laid
, in the evening as all my clothes were in the
gine rooms drying. By the way as an instance
abstraction of mind after skinning a seal today
walked away with the two hind flippers in my
nd, leaving my mittens on the ice. Some of

our hands work very well, while others, mostly Shetlanders with many honourable exceptions, shirk their work detestably. It shows what a man is made of, this work, as we are often killing far from the ship away from the Captain's eye with a couple of miles drag, and a man can skulk if he will. Colin the mate is a great power in the land, energetic & hard working. I heard him tell a man today he would club him if he didn't work harder. I saw the beggars often walk past a fine fat seal to kill a poor little 'Toby' or newly pupped one in order to have less weight to drag. The Captain sits at the masthead all day, looking out with his glass, for where they lie thickest. Took about 460 today.

<u>Monday April 6th</u>

Went out with Colin this morning for some regular hard work but began proceedings by falling into the sea again. I had just killed a seal on a large piece when I fell over the side. Nobody was near and the water was deadly cold. I had hold of the edge of the

e to prevent my sinking, but it was too
smooth and slippery to climb up by, but
last I got hold of the seals hind flippers
nd managed to pull myself up by them.
he poor old 'flappy' certainly heaped coals of
ire upon my head. Got off again with the
tewart and did some good work. Took
bout 400 again.

uesday April 6th

ut on the pack in the morning with Colin
nd actually did not fall in. The Captain
alls me 'the Great Northern Diver'. We
ok a good number of young and old
nd then steamed outside to see if we could
ind anything for ourselves. Shot two large
laddernoses, both were easy shots at
bout 70 yards, but as I fired after all
he harpooners had missed I felt cocky.
hey were huge brutes, I am keeping the bone
f one which was 11 feet long. They are also
alled Sea Elephants. They have a vascular
ag on their snouts which they distend to
ny extent when they are angry. Saw the

D042

Jan Meyen and others, with all their boats on killing old seals. Took 270 young & 58 old

Wednesday April 7th

Poor work today, seals are scarce and we only took 133. Maggie Milne is very bad I fear he will die. He has intussusception with faecal vomiting & constant pain. It is not hernia. Gave soap & castor oil injection today.

Thursday April 8th

Put our letters on board the 'Active' today. Had short notice and only wrote one letter though I would willingly have written more. Did a wretched days work, only about 30 seals. However most of the other ships have done worse than us, & that with crews of 80 men to our 56. Gale in the evening.

Friday April 9th

Gale continuing so that we have done no work at all. Heavy swell on. Got under the lee of the point. Wretched day. Did nothing but sleep & write up my log. The

[we a]re commencing to cut the blubber off the hides.
[I']m afraid tomorrow will be as bad.

Waiting for the mother

Dragging Seals Skins

Clubbing a Young one.

a big load

my Accident

A Dangerous Bit

Hunting a seal

April 10th Saturday
Poor Andrew Milne is almost beyond hope. At suc[h] an age and with such an illness recovery was almost hopeless. Blowing fitfully and with a heavy swell on. Nothing doing all day. Began Carlyle's "Hero worship". A great and glorious book.

April 11th. Sunday
A dark day in the ship's cruise. Poor Andrew was very cheery and very much better in the morning, but he took some plum duff at dinner, and was taken worse. I went dow[n] at once, and he died within ten minutes in my arms literally. Poor old man. They were very kind to him forwards during his illness, and certainly I did my best for him. Made a list of his effects in the evening. Rather a picturesque scene with the corpse and the lanterns and the wild faces aroun[d]. We bury him tomorrow. Picked up seals all day on large pieces in the slush about 60 I think.

April 12th Monday
uried poor old Andrew this morning. Union Jack
as hoisted half mast high. He was tied up in
nvas sack with a bag of old iron tied to his
t, and the Church of England burial service
as read over him. Then the stretcher on which
was lying was tilted over and the old man
ent down feet foremost with hardly a
plash. There was a bubble or two and a
ugle and that was the end of old Andrew.
knows the great secret now. I should
ink he would be flattened out of all
mblance to humanity before he reached the
ottom, or rather he would never reach the
ttom but hang suspended half way down
ke Mahomets coffin, when the weight of the
on was neutralized. The Captain & I agree that
these occasions three cheers should be given
the coffin disappears, not in levity, but
a genial hearty fare-thee-well wherever
u are. Did a fair day's work about
0 I should think. Made a bad miss in
evening. "Polynia" has 2050 seals, worse than
us.

Tuesday April 13th

Boiled Beef day again (Tuesday - Tough-day - Toug[h] day - Boiled Beef day). The worst dinner in the week except Friday. Lay to on account of the gale all da[y]. Had the gloves down in the Stokehole in the evenin[g] and some fine boxing. No Seals.

IN. MEMORIAM. ANDR. MILNE
APRIL. 11th 1880

Wednesday April 14th

Knocking along among the ice under sail and canvas picking up seals. Made a good days work, about I should think bringing us up to 2460 about. Stood on the Folksel head all day and reported progress. Rather cold work had a shot or two tho'. Someone told me that in the South Seas when a man died the first comer got his property, and that when a man fell over board you might see half a dozen standing by the hatchways to run down for the plunder whenever he was drowned.

Thursday April 15th

Beautifully fine day but we did a poor days work, about 46 I think. Assisted in shooting 2 bladders. They took five balls each. A pretty little bird with a red tuft on its head, rather larger than a Sparrow came and fluttered about the boats. No one had ever seen one like it before. Rather a long beak, feet not webbed, white underneath, with "pee-wheet - pea wheet". A sort of Snowflake. Georgey Grants got his trousers torn by a young Sea Elephant in the evening.

Friday. April 16th
Steamed hard to the North West all day to see if we could see anything of the seals. Failed in seeing many, and only picked up half a dozen. Jack Buchan shot a hawk in the evening which the Captain with his eagle eye discerned upon a hummock, and detected even at that great distance to be a hawk. About 18 inches high with beautifully speckled plumage.

my idea of a hawk.
(~~[illegible]~~).
Had the Smallpox in its youth.

The Captain's idea of a hawk (N.B. Looking out for prey).

~~The prey the Captain's~~
The prey the Captain's hawk is looking out for.

Saturday April 17th
Nothing doing all day - only half a dozen seal again. We are steering South now with the "Iceberg" a Norwegian. If we could only make

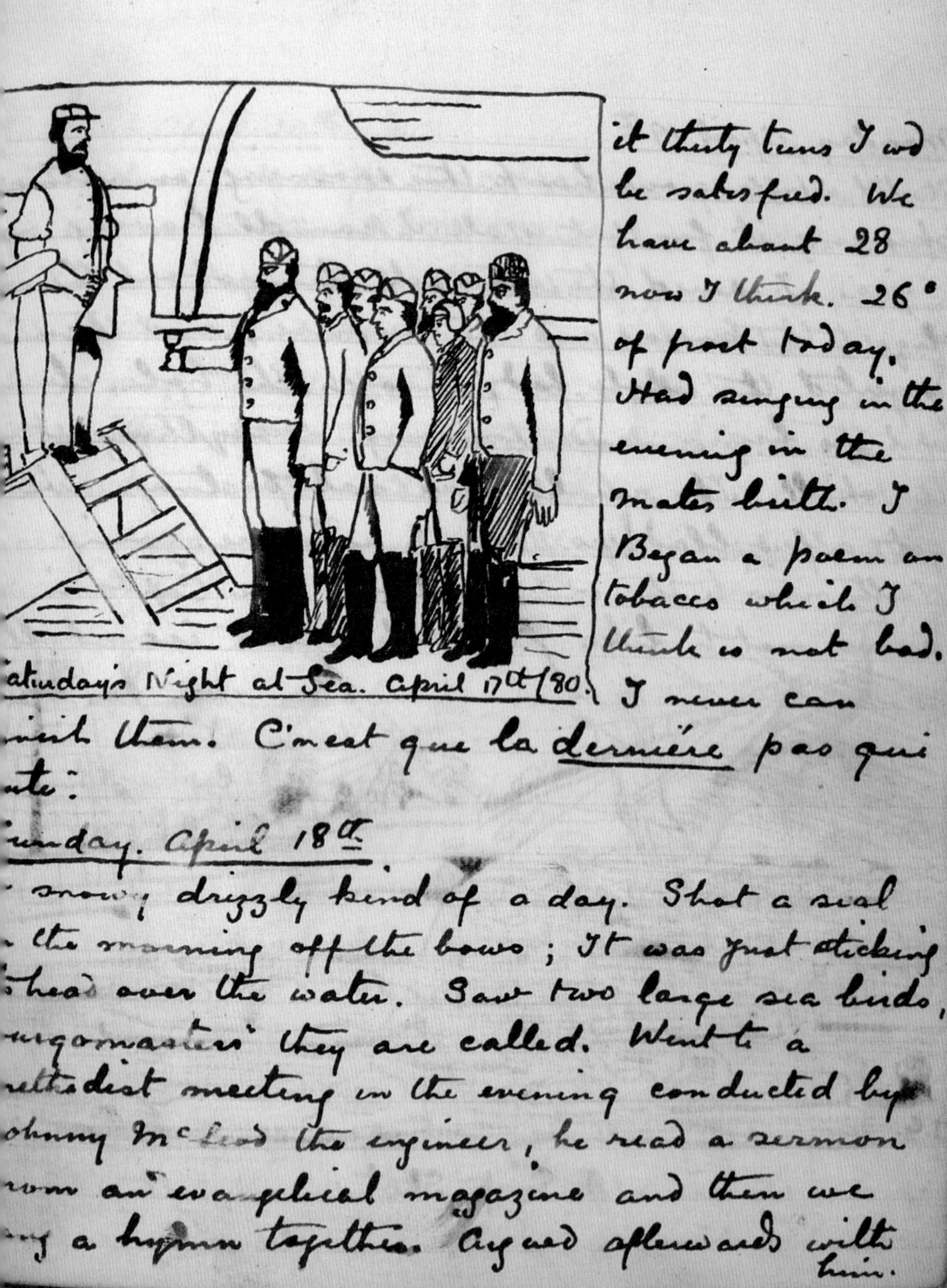

it thirty tons I wd
be satisfied. We
have about 28
now I think. 26°
of frost today.
Had singing in the
evening in the
mates birth. I
Began a poem on
tobacco which I
think is not bad.

aturday's Night at Sea. April 17th /80.

I never can
inish them. C'n'est que la dernière pas qui
ute:

unday. April 18th

snowy drizzly kind of a day. Shot a seal
the morning off the bows; It was just sticking
head over the water. Saw two large sea birds,
urgomasters they are called. Went to a
ethodist meeting in the evening conducted by
ohnny McLeod the engineer, he read a sermon
rom an evangelical magazine and then we
g a hymn together. Argued afterwards with
him.

Monday April 19th

Started Stuffing our hawk this morning, or rather skinning it for that is all I can do having no wires. I opened the stomach, then got out the legs to the knees and the humeri, and then inverted the whole body through the hole, cleaned out the brain, and removing everything except the skull. The result was satisfactory. We got a few bladders today, and are going North now to the old sealing. The Captain seems not to like the look of the ice at all.

J. G.

AC

A. Snap. Shot.

usday
unday. April 20th
thing doing all day. We didn't take a single seal.
iled and Steamed to the North East. 72-30 today.
ared a couple of Seals' flippers for tobacco
uches, rubbed alum over our hawk's Skin
ednesday. April 21st
bsolutely nothing to do except grumble, so we
id that. A most disagreeable day with a
asty cross sea and swell. No seals and
othing but misery. Felt seedy all day. Was
nocked out of bed at 1 AM to see a man
rwards with palpitations of the heart. That
idn't improve my temper
ursday April 22nd
heavy swell still on. Took about 13
which I shot two. Bad but better than
sterday. Thick fog. Got a newly pupped
al, it seems rather late in the season
r that. I have shot hitherto about 15
als. I intend to count them after this.
day. April 23rd
d rather better today taking 36 seals. I
de a bag of 11, that is 26 altogether.

The shooting was uncommonly bad on the whole. Looks like a gale this evening. Captain saw another hawk. It is an extraordinary thing that we have not fallen in with a bear yet. Captain saw a meteoric stone fall into the water once within a hundred yards of the sh The Magnetic Pole is in King Williams Land Lat 69°. There is another for South Pole, a thing that I never knew before.

Our Evening Exercise.

Saturday. April 24th

We have been steaming North West all day. Saw a fine flock of Eider ducks, the males are black and white, the females bronze with a green head. Picked up 17 more young seals. I think we are not very far from the old ones. Had a pleasant evening in the mates birth. No Shooting today. Sparred in the morning. Have a tip to teach Jimmy.

as talking to Hutton, one of our best harpooners, about oological curiosities. He says that during a gale between uebec and Liverpool he saw two fish lying on the urface of the water. They were about 60 feet long nd spotted all over, exactly like leopards. An nknown Species. The Captain fell in with another pecies in Lat 68°. the hide of which was so thick at no harpoon would pierce it. Here is my list Northern Whales.

Right Whale. proper Greenland whale. yield 10-20 tons of oil. Bone sells at £1000 a ton. Value of one is £1500-£2000 found in far North between the ice fields

Finner Whale Found in every sea in hundreds. Are longer and stronger than the Right Whale, but very worthless. Some 120 feet long. Razor Backed. Spout two Jets, proper whale has only one.

Bottle Nose Whales Found South of the ice, & round Iceland. Only 30 feet long. Give a ton of oil (£80). Skin Valuable.

White Whale (Beluga) found everywhere, including Westminster Aquarium. Chiefly at mouths of American Rivers. Oil valuable. 16 ft long.

Black Whale a rare variety. Captain has only seen one. Valuable. Americans get them sometimes off North Cape.

Hutton's whale (Balaena variagatum)

Capt Gray's whale (Balaena Ironsidum)

Sunday. April 25th.

Got among a currant of young bladders in the morning and took 22. I did good shooting before dinner, hitting seven in eight shots from the bow. Shot one after dinner and missed two which w poor. We have 2502 now. Saw one old seal. Boxed with Stewart and sang hymns with Johnny Drew a fine picture of Young Sealing.

Saw a good parody.

"Oh the wild Rhymes he made,
Small poets wondered
To see in the 'Light Brigade'
'Hundred' and 'Thundered'

Monday April 26th

Sailing N and NW all day trying for old seals. They lie on the points of heavy ice stretching out into the sea, but you never know exactly where you can come across them, you must just

All h

oast along the heavy Greenland ice until you
nd them. We are in 74° North today. Took one
oung seal yesterday, and saw several. We
ave nobler game in view. Boxed in evening.
hallenged Stewart to run a hundred yards,
understand this sealing business thoroughly
now

nd everywhere, including Westminster
at mouths of American Rivers. Oil
s
e variety. Captain has only
me. Valuable. Americans
m sometimes off North Cape.
laena variagatum)
laena Ironsidum)

of young bladders in the
2. I did good shooting before
in eight shots from the bows.
and missed two which was
e now. Saw one old seal.
nd sang hymns with Johnny.
of Young Sealing.

Rhymes he made,
ts wondered
'Light Brigade'
and 'Thundered'

ll day trying for old seals.
of heavy ice stretching out
w never know exactly where
s them, you must just

All han

coast along the heavy
find them. We are in
young seal yesterday
have nobler game in
Challenged Stewart to
I understand this se

r the bows — Young Sealing. 1880.

and ice until you
North today. Took one
l saw several. We
. Boxed in evening.
a hundred yards,
business thoroughly
now

Plan of Greenland Seal fishing

Tuesday April 27th

Steaming N and NW all day. We have been among young bay ice and are trying to make the heavy where we may expect seals. Looks as if we were not far off towards evening. Did nothing all day. The skin of my hawk is just ruined. Drew Milne's funeral again at night for his brother who is aboard.

Wednesday April 28th

Made the heavy Greenland ice early in the morning and when I came on deck after breakfast it was

hitching along the whole horizon. Heavier ice
than any I have seen yet. The effects of the
Arctic refraction are very curious. Here are two
views at the distance of a mile and close up

Heavy ice close up.

Heavy ice at a mile

Saw marks of large herd on seals on the ice.
A few in water steaming Northward. Was close
to the Victor of Dundee in the evening. Beggar
has no right to be there. Have the best prospects
for tomorrow.

Thursday. April 29th

Our prospects have not been realized, for although
we saw a few schools of seals in the water, we
have not reached their head quarters though we
have been steaming North all day. Capt Davidson
of the Victor boarded us this morning – a poor
specimen of a man, hairy also. Was our mate
once, and had the reputation of being a sulky
beggar. The effects of refraction were extraordinary
tonight, many pieces of ice appearing high up

in the air with the sky above and below them
Victor steamed after us all day. We are not
far from the seals I'll bet. Saw many Snow
-birds about which is a good sign. In
Latitude 75°. 11.

Friday April 30th

Morning broke very inauspiciously with a
Southerly wind and a hazy sky. We are beginnin
to feel a bit downhearted as our sealing should
be begun by this time. Steamed North East after
the haze rose, water was like a lake with a
great deal of bay ice and numerous Looms
and Petrels. Just before tea we saw a point
of heavy ice ahead, and hope to find the seal
at the other side of it. I am rather doubtfu
as we have seen none in the water as yet
The night is very nearly as light as the day
now, I can read Chambers's Journal at mid
-night easily. Served out Grog this evenin
as tomorrow is the first of May. The ice
looks well for the whaling. 10.PM As I thought
there are no signs of seals upon the ice, so we
have come to the conclusion that we are probably

[th]e North of them. "Mine too, Mammy." They [ge]nerally shave new-comers on the first of May [an]d a boatsteerer told me this evening that I was [to] be a victim, but I told him they would have [to] call two watches to do it. ~~[illegible]~~

Saturday May 1st.

[In] the morning there was a heavy swell on and [ou]r prospects were of the darkest. Before dinner [ho]wever there was a change for we saw a [you]ng bladder on the ice, and shortly afterwards [a] considerable school of seals in the water going [be]fore the wind. The Captain and all of us [we]re rather gloomy at dinner time, but the [m]oment he mounted the Crow's Nest after dinner [do]wn came the welcome shout "Call all hands". [I] was in the Second Mate's boat and we lowered [a]way about 4.30. PM. It was a fine sight [to] see the seven long whale boats springing

through the blue water as we made for the ice. The seals seemed a good deal whiter than when I saw them last. Mate fired and missed, and not a shot could I ge[t] as he took the boatsteerer with his club an[d] left me to find my way, and test the ice with the butt end of my rifle as best I could. Which was rather scurvy conduc[t]. It was dangerous work on the ice as I co[uld] see no one, and twice only just saved myself from falling in when I should in all probability have been drowned. It i[s] more dangerous work than the young sealing, for the sea undermines these lumps of heavy ice, so that when you think you are perfectly safe on a large piece the whole thing may crumble thro'. Never got a shot the whole time. Mate slew one. Most miserable work, the wor[st] boat of the lot. If he could shoot as well as I, or I could walk on ice as well as hi[m] we would have had a different tale to tell. However it is jolly to get to work again.

als were soon frightened off the piece. Went
to the Westward. Here is our day's fishing
uchan's Boat. 14
nnie's Boat 13
rner's Boat 10
lin's Boat 10 Total 69.
atheson's Boat 10.
ulton's Boat 9.
M'Kenzie's Boat 2.
ane's Boat 1

Sunday May 2nd

howers, heavy ice, snow and wind all conspiring
ruin us. We steamed North in the teeth of a
le all day persevering manfully. In the
vening the Captain came down from the mast-
ead almost in despair, and pointed out a
link' in the sky showing heavy ice ahead.
the seals are not there', he said 'I must
rn South again'. We steamed along and
en to my delight after tea 'All Hands'
ere suddenly called. A considerable body
seals were in sight but as others were
en coming on to the ice, it was thought

advisable to leave them tonight & attack
them tomorrow. The great thing is to try
and get a turn at them before the 'Victor'
sees what we are doing. This Dundee
ship is the only one in sight. The Captai
of her is a sumph. Turned in early fo
an early rise.

Monday May 3d

Boats lowered away about 6 AM. The
moment they were down the Victor, who
is about five miles off, turned & steame
furiously towards us. I went with
Peter McKenzie, the last of the harpooners.
We call our boat The 'mob'. It is manned
by all the rag tag and bobtail of the ship,
but I think has as good a crew as any.
There is Pete harpooner, Jack Coull Steerer
The Doctor, Steward, Second engineer, an
Hieth the oldest man in the ship. We wer
the last to leave the ship as the boats we
dropped one here, one there. The ice was
very heavy and good. At first we had
a bad berth and only shot 2 seals, but

e poked and pushed our way by sheer
ard work through the ice and got into a
ine bay lined with seals. Peter and I
prang out with our guns and wriggled
ur away along the ice, while the crew
rept after us to skin what we shot. I
aw Peter shoot two, and then I floored
ne. Then I got behind a hummock and
hot mine, five all in a line on the edge
- one piece. I was just thinking we
ould make a good bag and had shot
nother, while I could hear the ring of
eter's rifle a hundred yards off, when
came the Victors boats, pell mell all
a heap right at the back of us. The
en sprang out, rushing across the ice
ring without aiming, jumping up on
e top of hummocks, shouting, and
aking the most fearful mess of it.
ey scared the seals and spoilt our
ork and their own too. I don't suppose
ey got fifty seals all together. Our boat
ad 27 and the united total of ours

morning's work was 234, Hutton headin the poll with 68, and Cain having only Our Captain lowered the ensign 3 times to the Vict as an ironical "Thanks for your politeness". moment the boats were aboard we set off at great rate as the Captain saw a fresh and a larger batch of seals. We had a mouthful o dinner it being 2.P.m. When we came on de after it we found the Victor had already land her boats, so choosing another spot off we went. There was an enormous body of seal but very shy, so that we had to make lon shots. We got 28 this time and the total came to 287 or so. Altogether today we got 540 ▬▬, a splendid days work, about tons of oil. Felt tired as I had been pulling and crawling on my face all day. Capta sees another patch of seals for tomorrow.

Tuesday May 4th

at it at 6 AM again. Boats lowered away and dropped here and there as usual. Peter and I got behind a hummock and shot 7 each, when the Captain saw he

ad not got the thick of them, so he hoisted
e Jack as a signal to the boats to return,
e took the first five that came up, including
r noble selves in tow, and away he steamed
full speed right past the Victor's boats
d dropped us in among a fine patch. It
s an energetic and sensible action. I suppose he towed us about 15 miles or so.
e made good use of our chances then and
hot away hard. The "mob" distinguished
self killing 41, Buchan was best with
, then Colin with 51, Carner 42, We 41 and
e rest very poor. We took 275 and did
ot lower away again. a Norwegian ship
e Diana came in on our flank but
id not get very many. One of ~~our~~ them boats
ame alongside ours and we asked them
f they had seen the Eclipse to the North, they
aid they had, but I doubt if they understood
o. Victor had its men out all night last
ight - a very short sighted policy.

Wednesday May 5th

teamed to the NE. open water round us.

miles, 2025 yards
tical miles
mmon Engl
14 square inch
yard, and 43,5
yds. in a pol
ur roods are a
quare yards, o
Anacre is 484
20½ inches eac
ards 14 inche
ards each way
mile. Half-a
y, is 160 acres
yards each way
220 yards eac
Scotch measur
40 falls a rood
was 77½ yard
res are 61 Eng
a general use i
There are 172
t; 27 cubic fee
c feet of rough
hewn is a load
of earth, or
A ton of a shi
each way.
re, and 20 quir
ide by 277·274; to
s to litres, divide
r yards, multi
rds into metre
logrammes int
iply by 2·20486
nes by 0·45359
c inches, multi
rary by 0·01639
imperial bush
ry, 0·36347. T
es, multiply by
res by 0·40467
, by 0·62138: fo
6102. For gen
ometre may b
e.
ted into multi
refixing deca fo
imes, by kilo f
, 1000 gramme
e decimal poin
right for tens
o divide, prefi
ti for the 100th
th part, as cent
a gramme. Th
are Greek, tho
S,
ontaining a
s and Mar-
Pages, with
nac, &c. cl., 1s.
pockets, ...1s.
1, 2 pockts, 2s.
..........4s.
..........5s.
lling wallet, 5s.
wallet, ...7s.
wallet,) ...1s.
Days on 2
for Cash,
..........0s.
..........1s.
kets, ...1s.
d, 2 pockets, 2s.
t clasp, ...2s.
..........4s.
lling wallet, 4s.
g wallet, ...7s.
wallet,) ...1s.
2,) 7 Days
ges for Cash,
..........0s.
ockets, ...1s.
d, 2 pockets, 1s.
t clasp, ...2s.
..........2s.
se, ...3s.
lling wallet, 3s.
ng wallet, ..6s.
r wallet,) ..1s.
y 2 1-8th,)
ges, ...0s.
ockets, ...1s.
lt clasp, ...1s.
lling wallet, ..2s.
r wallet,) ...0s.
y for a Y

Five Bulls at a hundred Yards
May 3d 1880.

Hardly expected any seals - All hands were called however Just before dinner - The Diana got the better of us rather, having all her boats in the heart of the pack before we lowered away The seals were lying very thick but not over any great extent of ice. Our fellows muddled it completely, each being anxious to get the best position and beat the others. The seals were finally scared off after we had taken 71. Captain seems displeased, and quite right too.

End of Volume I. Log of Hope.

	May 1.	3	4.	5.	14	15				
Colin	10	85	51	8	7	[illegible]				
Cane.	1	36	20	2	13					
Carner	10	61	42	11	2					
Hutton	9	112	11	6	12	14				
Buchan	14	87	75	18	20					
Rennie	13	68.	26	7	2					
Mathieson	10	47	10	11	2					
McKenzie	2	55	41	8.	5					
	69	540	275	71	63	32				

Scrummidge. 56.

69
540
275
71
119
32
1106
2502
3608

Game Bag of the "Hope". Voyage. 1880.

			My B
April. 3.	760. Young Seals.	50 Old Seals.	1 Old S
4	450 Young Seals.	10 old Seals.	
5	400. y. s.		
6	270 y. s.	6 Bladders. 57 Old Seals.	2 Bl
7	133 y. s.		
8	30 y. s.		
9	50 y. s.		
10	72. y. s.		2 Sea
11			
12			
13			
14	80 y. s.		2 Seal
15	46 y. s.	2 Bladders. 2 Seals.	1 Blad
16	6. y. s.	a Hawk.	
17	10. y. s.		2 Seal
18	10 y. s.		1 Seal.
19	6. y. s.		
20			
21			
22	13 y. s.		2 Seal
23	36 y. s.		11 Sea

April 24. 17. Y. S.
25 22. Y. S. 8 Seals.
26
27
28
29
30.

May. 1 69 Old Seals
2
3 540 Old Seals 27 Seals
4 275 Old Seals 10 Seals.
5 71 Old Seals.
6
7
8
9
10
12
12
13
14. 119 Old Seals
15. 32 Old Seals.

May 16.
17. 6 Old Seals.
18
19
20
21
22
23
24
25
26
27
28
29
30. 2 Ground Seals 31. 1 Flaw Rat.
June 1 1 Bladdernose.
2 4 Roaches. 7 Loons.
3
4
5 1 Bladdernose
6 1 Narwhal. 2 Raw Ducks.
7 [illegible]
8 1 Roach. 1 Loon.

9. 1 Roach. 6 Snowbirds
10 1 Kittiewake. 1 Maulie. 3 Loons
11. a whiting
12 a Bear
13
14
15
16
17
18 a Bear & 2 Cubs.
19
20 a Bear
21
22
23
24
25
26 a Greenland whale
27
28
29
30. a Burgomaster - Snowbird - 5 Loons. 1 Haw Rat.

Log of the Hope Vol II.

D076

May 6th Thursday.
The Captain has come to the conclusion that we had better go South a bit for seals, and let the Diana and Victor go on to the North. We are in 77.20 today, and expected to see the West coast of Spitzbergen. All hands are making off. There is a heavy swell and no signs of seals as yet.

Pull
Old Sealing

May 6th Thursday.
The Captain has co
better go South a l
and Victor go on
today, and expect
bergen. All han
a heavy swell a

…e conclusion that we had
… seals, and let the Diana
… North. We are in 77.20
… see the West coast of Spitz-
… making off. there is
… signs of seals as yet.

Pull, boys, pull!
… Sealing. Drawn in a heavy swell.

Steamed SW all day but saw no seals. We have about 50 tons now.

Process of making off in Sealing
(i.e. Separating the blubber from the skin).

Friday May 7th

The Diana seeing us lying to yesterday night thought we saw something splendid so she came down at a fearful rate to share the booty under steam and canvas. After burning 30/ worth of coals it began to dawn upon the Norwegian mind that the whole thing was a 'do' and a sell, so with a howl of disgust it flitted off again, to Iceland we believe. Under sail all day to N.E. Saw some schools in the water.

Saturday May 8th

Steaming N.W. Victor in sight going in the same direction. He follows us as a Jackal

ollows a lion. Ice all marked with seals.
. beautiful day. Gave out tobacco and sugar
n the evening. Was amused by a sailor's auction
Manson Turville a Shetlander was auctioneer &
vas particularly eloquent about a very delapid-
ated and seedy old coat of his which he wanted
palm off. "Going at five plugs of tobacco,
t five plugs! Nobody bid any more? A coat
warranted to keep out anything under 190
egrees of frost - No advance on five plugs?
entlemen! Gentlemen! Five plugs and a half.
ank you, sir! Going at five and a half!
e figure of a beaver will be found on one
ide of the lining and a rattlesnake on the
ther. Not sold but given away! Going. Going
ow or never. Gentlemen, now's your chance
or a bargain. Gone." I bought a pair of
ealskin trousers from Henry Polson.

Not Sold but Given away.

Sunday May 9th

Why are seals the most holy of animals? Because it is mentioned in the Apocalypse that at the last day an angel shall open six of them in heaven. None of them to be seen today. The thing is growing monotonous as Mark Twain said when the cow fell down the chimney for the third time while he was composing poetry below. A cloudy day. Have been reading Scoresby's book on whaling. Some of the anecdotes are too big to be swallowed at a gulp, they need chewing. He saw a whale caught in the bight of a rope that held another whale fast. Saw a man go a quarter of a mile on a live whale's back. However on the whole it is an eminently readable book, and very accurate as far as I can judge! Nothing all day. Was down in the Harpooner's berth in the evening, conversation ran on Zoology, murders, executions and Ironclads. Steaming to the NorthWest.

Monday May 10

We are down in 73.20 now or only Just to the N of the place where we were young sealing. We are going North again I am glad to say. No Seals.

-erved out tol coffee and tea in the morning. Glass
-ad a tremendous fall after tea, and it came on
-hick rain and wind. I hope we are going to
-ave a bit of a hurricane. anything to wake us
-p. A Codfish has been brought up through the
-umps in a case of a big leak.

Tuesday May 11

- heavy gale during the night, and nearly all
-ay. We hardly feel more than the force of the
-ind however, as the ice forms fine natural "
-arbours. Running North all day. It is too bad
-is - after we began our old sealing so well too.
-owever this is a trade of ups and downs, and
- must wait for the swing of the pendulum. Old
-tie got a nasty cut over the eye brought from
- rope, and seemed to think he was blinded,
-ut I set him right again. Misery & desolation.

Wednesday May 12.

- most beautiful day. Blue sky which is rare up
-ere as the sky is usually rather peasoupish. A
-ood many seals in the water but none on the
-e. As clear at midnight as during the day.
"Finner" whale was seen spouting near the

ship after dinner, but I was asleep myself at the time. I would have liked to have seen it. Balæna Physalis is its scientific name, and it is the swiftest, strongest, biggest and most worthless of the whale tribe, so hunting them is rather a losing game. However there is a regular Finner fishery. They are worth to abo £120 each, and our whale about £1500, so we are on the right side of the bargain. Played Catch the ten in the mate's berth for love. The last time I had a card in my hand was at Greenhill Place. Saw a Flaw ra today swimming round the ship. It is the smallest variety of seals. Captain's idea for the cure of baldness. Pick hairs out of another man's head by the roots. Then bore little holes in your head and plant them. He dreamed it

Thursday May 13th

I hear from the engine room that Mr McLeod, our chief engineer, has done me the honour to read my private log every morning, and make satirical comments upon it at table, and among his own foremen. Now I would as soon that he read my private letters as my Journal, in fact a good deal sooner, and it is just one of those things which I

on't stand from any man. If any man meddles
ith my private business I know how to deal with
im. I am only astonished that a man professing
eligious principles, should act with such a want,
I won't say of gentlemanly honour, but of common
onesty. If he does it after this warning he shall
nswer for it to me. A sensible man might be
usted, but a man who will talk about my
rejudices against boiled beef &c in the engine
oom must be suppressed. I hope this may
ueet his eye in the morning.

Saw a 'Finner' whale today. I had no idea of
e size and sleekness of the brutes before. His blast
ooked like a puff of white smoke. He was a good
uarter of a mile from the ship but when he dived
could see every fin. A most enormous creature.
rospects look brighter this morning as seals have
een seen on the ice, and a good many in the
ater. Cane came running down about 11. PM to say
at he saw a good strip on the ice.

Friday May 14th

oats lowered away about 9 A.M. Seals would not lie
tall though. They have come up all the way from the

Labrador coast, and are nothing but skin and hair after their month's travelling. Our boat was one of the highest with 5. We took 63 in the boats & then came aboard. The harpooners were sent over the bows to attack the remainder of the pack and killed 56 mo making a total of 119. It is pleasant to get started again. Cane was frightened by an enormous Walrus with a head like a barrel coming up beside him while he was flinching a seal on the ice. He fired 4 shots into it, but it only seemed amused, and swam away.

Poking the 'mot' boat through heavy ice. May 14th 1880

Saturday May 15th

Sent away two boats in the morning, Colin's and Hutton's, to a small patch of seals. Took 32 of them. Steamed and Sailed North afterwards but saw no more blubber. The time is rapidly approaching now when we must coil our whale lines and go North

nless we fall among seals in the next two days
e must give it up. We think the eclipse and the
indward are North already, we have seen nothing
f them since more than a month ago, when they ran
own to Iceland for the bottlenosing. Reading Scoresby's
urnal of his discoveries between Lat 69° & 74° on
e coast of East Greenland. The lost Danish
ettlements on that coast are a very curious
roblem. He found no trace of them.

Sunday May 16th

o seals. Lat 76·33 at noon. Banging away
the North as hard as we can go. Port Wine.
d Cooper Tumbled down the hatch and broke
is arm nearly.

Monday May 17th

Beautiful day. Steamed to the North all day.
at 77° Long 5 East. About 100 miles West of
pitzbergen. Got 6 from a small patch of seals
fter dinner. They are getting very thin. The ones
e have captured lately we consider to be, not
reenland seals, but seals from the Labrador coast
hich after their month's travelling could hardly
e expected to be in prime condition. Rigged up

the harpoon guns this evening. Fearfully cumbrous things working on a swivel with a pull of 28 lb. Has to be let off by pulling at a string. Carries a harpoon about 80 yards with some accuracy. Bore about 1½ inches.

Tuesday May 18th

Cleaned out the boats and made all straight for whaling. During dinner a sail was seen to the N.W., which turned out on closer

Capt. J.G. inspection to be the Windward, which we thought was South with the Eclipse at the Bottle-Nose fishing. We hauled our yards aback & waited for him. Murray came aboard with a very dismal tale to tell. After the Young Sealing he had been too ambitious to content himself with the modest work that we had stuck to, picking up half a ton a day or so, but he had run right away North at once to Spitzbergen after whales, not taking a single old Seal. The result of this ambition is that we have about 52 tons now, and he about 28. He has been

[th]ree three weeks and never seen a fish. He [g]ives a most discouraging account of the [w]hole thing, and will, I think, go away after [th]e Bladders. A heavy gale blew from the SW during the evening, a most awkward direction [fo]r us.

[W]ednesday & Thursday. May 19 & 20

[B]lowing a hard gale both days. We are [t]acking and turning between the ice and [S]pitzbergen. We can make out the Windward [i]n the lulls, sometimes ahead, sometimes astern. [Se]a running very high, and sky as dark [a]s possible. Took a sea aboard on Wednesday, [g]iving the Watch a fine ducking. My old foe, [t]oothache, has it seems followed me all the [w]ay from Scotland, and been hiding about the [s]hip the whole voyage. Yesterday it came out [f]rom its concealment and said "Oh, mine [e]nemy, and have I found thee?", whereupon [it] seized hold of me by one of my incisors [a]nd twinged it so, that my whole face is [d]istorted today. (Addison). On Thursday we saw [th]e wild bleak coast of Spitzbergen breaking

through the rifts of the Storm. A great line of huge black perpendicular crags running up to several thousand feet, as black as coal but all seamed with lines of snow. A horrible looking place. We were thinking of running in and anchoring in King's Bay, but the chart was mislaid. Toothache.

Friday May 21st

Spitzbergen still in sight about 50 miles to the North East. A complete lull in the wind but the sky very dark, and a heavy swell on from which we think we will have a change of wind. Windward went South, and in the evening we saw the Eclipse coming up in the distance. As we had not seen her for a month we were anxious to know what she had done. The Captain boarded her and after three hours came back with the news that she had been down to Iceland and had managed to capture 32 Bottle-nose whales, a very large take. They yield on an average a ton apiece, and as Captain David had also as many young and old seals as we he has managed to beat us so far. 90 Tons I believe

e has got. This wind has done us terrible injury
y packing all the ice up close, and destroying
ll the bights or bays in it in which whales are
sually found. However we must just keep up
ur peckers, and hope for the best.

<u>Saturday May 22nd</u>

heavy swell all day. I come of age today.
Rather a funny sort of place to do it in, only
00 miles or so from the North Pole.

of the Storm. A great line of
[p]endicular crags running up t[o]
[..] feet, as black as coal but
[..] lines of snow. A horrible
we were thinking of running
[..]ing in King's Bay, but the
[..]id. Toothache.

[..]

[..]ll in sight about 50 miles
a complete lull in the wind
dark, and a heavy swell on,
think we will have a change
[..]ward went South, and in the
the Eclipse coming up in the
[h]ad not seen her for a month
to know what she had done.
her and after three hours came
[..]s that she had been down to
managed to capture 32 Bottle-
[v]ery large take. They yield on an
[..]ice, and as Captain David had
[yo]ung and old seals as we he
[..]at us so far. 90 Tons I believe

he has got. This we[..]
by packing all the[..]
all the bights or ba[..]
usually found. [..]
our pickers, and t[..]

Saturday May 22

A heavy swell all [..]
Rather a funny so[..]
600 miles or so f[..]

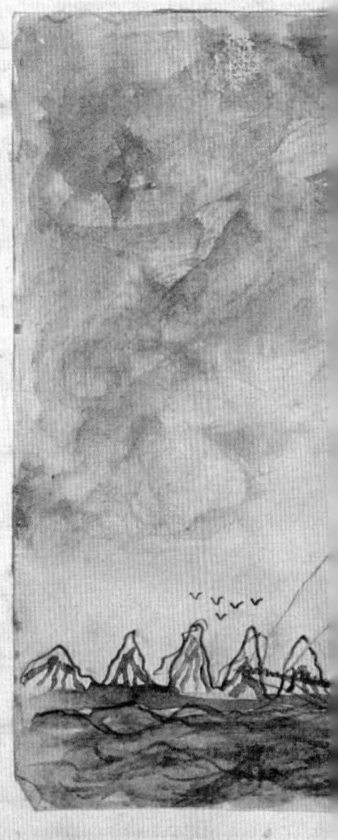

s done us terrible injury
up close, and destroying
it in which whales are
ver we must just keep up
for the best.

I come of age today.
place to do it in, only
the North Pole.

The "Hope" in a gale off Spitzbergen.
May 20th 1880.
"The Seven Icemountains" to the Left.

Had rather a doleful evening on my birthday, as I wa
very seedy from some reason or another ~~in the evenin~~
The Captain was very kind and made me bolt two
enormous mustard emetics which made me feel
as if I had swallowed Mount Vesuvius, but did
me a lot of good. Eclipse sailing near us all da
Ice is sadly damaged.

Sunday May 23d

Plum Duff day again – a fine day, the swell all
gone. Sailing in to the West again down the tight
ice. The Captain and I have been making mo
villainous parodies of Jean Ingelow's "Sparrow
Build"

~~"When Sparrows build & the L~~

"When 'Burgies' Build their Greenland nest,
My Spirit groans and pines
For I know there are Seals in the Nor' Nor' West
But its time to 'coil our lines.'
Far down in the South the 'Bladders' lie
But the Devil a one near me,
And the 'Unis' are sticking their horns on high
As they plunge & play in the sea

Chorus

But oh the Whale, and the right, right, whale!
And the Whale we all love so
Is there never a 'bight' in the Greenland 'tight'
Where a ~~whale has room~~ 12 foot whale can to blow.

Thou didst set thy foot on the ship and fare,
To that ~~sad~~ cold and lonely shore,
Thou wert sad for the seals were all skin & hair,
And they came from Labrador.
And 'Meg' he came and scared away
Some Twenty mile at the least,
And how could we tell where the 'Flappies' lay,
With a great bay flaw to the east.

Chorus.

We shall never again sail back in May,
As we oft before have done
Or take four thousand 'Young' in a day
And go home with two hundred ton,
We shall never be full with seals alone
For all our work and toil,
But we'll never say die while whales yield bone,
And 'Bladders' give up their oil

Chorus.

Monday May 24th

Another fine day. We are going to have a little luck at last I hope. 6.P.m. No, we are not though. We are certainly awfully unlucky this year. A strong wind has set in from the East and is packing up a nice little bight which was forming, and playing the deuce with our prospects. Colin says we have a Jonah aboard. Eclipse near us. Got our harpoon guns stuck up.

Tuesday May 25

Worser and Worserer. Wind still blowing from the East and murdering the ice. All hands disgusted. Eclipse set sail for the South but seemed to think better of it and came back again. Horrible!

Wednesday May 26th

A fine day but the ice is ruined. Wormed our way through it as best we could. I was smoking my afternoon pipe on the quarterdeck when there was a cry of 'A Bear - close to the Ship' Captain was at the masthead and sang out at once to 'Lower away the Quarter Boat'. I ran down for my shooting iron and succeeded in getting

seat in the boat. I could see the bear - a great
rute - looking quite tawny against the white
now, and running very fast in a direction
arallel to the ship. Then he crouched down in a
ole of water about a couple of hundred yards
f, and hid with just his nose above surface.
ratheson was harpooner of the boat and we
ulled off, but had to make a bit of a circuit
get through the ice. We lost sight of him;
nd when we saw him again he was standing
ith his fore paws on the top of a hummock, and
is head in the air, staring at us and sniffing.
e were within shot then but we thought he
ould let us get nearer, so we bent to our
ars. ~~again~~ But some associations connected
ith boats seemed to dawn on his obtuse
ntellect, for he suddenly got off the hummock
nd we lost sight of him. Then we saw the
ignal hoisted for the boat to come aboard,
nd spied Bruin travelling over the ice at
great rate, and a long way off, so we
ad to give it up as a bad job. Wind still
asterly.

Average for the Old Sealing

Buchan	14 + 87 + 75 + 18 + 20 =	214
Colin	10 + 85 + 51 + 8 + 7 =	161
Hutton	9 + 112 + 11 + 6 + 12 =	150
Carner	10 + 61 + 42 + 11 + 2 =	126
McKenzie	2 + 55 + 41 + 8 + 5 =	111 (mob)
Rennie	13 + 68 + 26 + 7 + 2 =	116
Mathieson	10 + 47 + 10 + 11 + 2 =	80
Kane.	1 + 36 + 20 + 2 + 13 =	72
	Scramble	55
	Young Sealing	141
	Total.	1216 Old Seal

The Bear we did not shoot
May 26th 1880

Thursday May 27th

Ice began to close round us fast in the morning, and we had to steam our way out to the open sea as best we could, to save ourselves from being beset or nipped. Had a difficult job to get out. Eclipse kept in our wake. Captain went on board her to dinner and stayed till about eight. I drew, slept, played draughts and boxed while he was away. We are going off to 80° North Latitude to see what is up there, right up to the Northern Barrier in fact. The terror of the seas up here is an animal which is called the Swordfish, but is not a swordfish at all. It is one of the whale tribe with a long snout like a mackerel, and great pointed teeth the whole length of its Jaws. It attains the length of 25 feet, and is distinguished by a high curved dorsal fin. It feeds on the largest sharks, on seals and on whales. Yule of the "Esquimeaux" took six whales the other year in the straits, which actually came and cowered under the ship for protection, because one of these monsters was in the vicinity. The Captain tells me that he was in the Crow's Nest one day

when he saw a great hubbub a head of the ship
on examination with the glass he made out
that it was an enormous sea elephant which
was sitting on a piece of ice very little
larger than itself. In the water round it were
half a dozen of these blood thirsty fish, which
were striking the poor creature with their
long fins, trying to knock him off his perch
when they would have made short work o
it him. As the ship came up the Captain say
he never shall forget the look which the po
seal cast towards it with its big eyes, and
suddenly taking an enormous bound off
the bit of ice, it squattered along the Surface
of the water, and took such a leap toward
the ship's side, that its head was above the
taffrail, and it very nearly gained the deck
A boat was lowered when the great 12 foot
creature climbed into it, and was knocked
on the head. Balls had to be fired into the
fish to keep them from attacking the boat
they were so riled at the disappearance of
their prey.

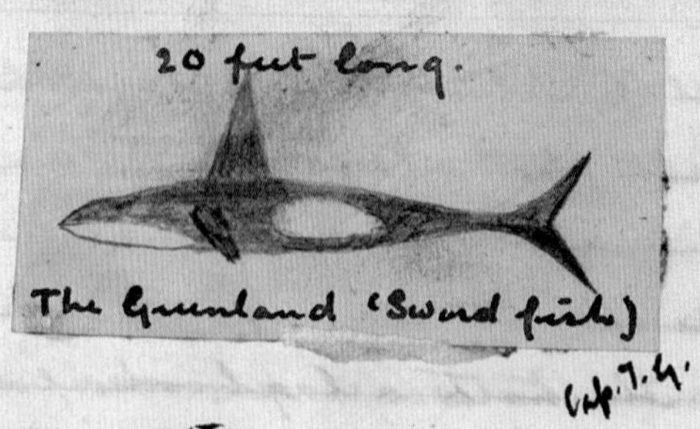

Cap. T. G.

<u>riday May 28th</u>

Steaming North and North East all day, in
mpany with the "Eclipse". It is clear we are not
oing to have any whales in May, and we can
nly hope for the best in June. Thick fog in the
ening and we had to blow our steam whistle
nd fire guns for several hours before we could
ind the "Eclipse" which was also screaming loudly
ook a bang at some loons on the ice at a
ng range with my rifle, since signals were
e order of the day, but although I hit the piece
nd knocked the snow all over them I slew none.

<u>Saturday May 29th</u>

The less said about Saturday
the better. Let Saturday sink
into oblivion. Nothing doing.
Fog in the evening. Lat
9.10 North at noon. Played cards in evening.

The 'Loon' or Lesser Auk.

Sunday May 30th

Captain David came aboard in the morning and expressed great dissatisfaction at the state of ice, in fact he said he had never seen it worse. Dr Walker came afterwards with a logbook for me which the Captain very kindly sent. In the morn we espied two objects swimming near the ice, whi the Captain made out to be two Ground Seals, a rare variety, nearly as large as Bladdernoses. We lowered away a boat and after an exciting c and an exhibition of bad shooting on the part of t harpooner we nailed them both. They were a fem and young one, the former about 8 ft. 6. By the way talking of Bladdernoses Colin killed one on which measured 14 feet long. It charged the boa and nearly bit the harpoon gun in two. We hope we may have a turn in the luck now after this small capture. By the way one of the most interesting things in Arctic Zoology was the captur last year of a large Albatross by Capt David, in 80° North Latitude. Where did the breed come from? It looks as if the temperature of the Pol was semitropical

onday May 31st

Dreamed about whales in the Caledonian Canal
d how frightened we were lest some of the barges
horses would scare them. There were 17 of them,
bottlenoses under a bridge. A very curious
eam. The wind this morning is WNW which
excellent, and the water is of a greenish hue
hich is excellenter.

a Capture.

t

id came aboard in the morning
eat dissatisfaction at the state of the
id he had never seen it worse. Dr
rwards with a logbook for me
very kindly sent. In the morning
jects swimming near the ice, which
e out to be two Ground Seals, a
arly as large as Bladdernoses.
a boat and after an exciting chase,
n of bad shooting on the part of the
illed them both. They were a female
the former about 8 ft. 6. By the
laddernoses Colin killed one once
l 14 feet long. It charged the boat
the harpoon gun in two. We hope
turn in the luck now after this
By the way one of the most
in Arctic Zoology was the Capture
large Albatross by Capt David,
ude. Where did the breed come
as of the temperature of the Pole
l

Monday May 31st

Dreamed about
and how frightened
or horses would sc
all bottlenoses unde
dream. The wind th
is excellent, and the
which is excellenter.

a Captu

s in the Caledonian Canal
ere lost some of the barges
tern. There were 17 of them,
bridge. A very curious
orning is WNW which
is of a greenish hue

ordfish in pursuit of a school of Seals

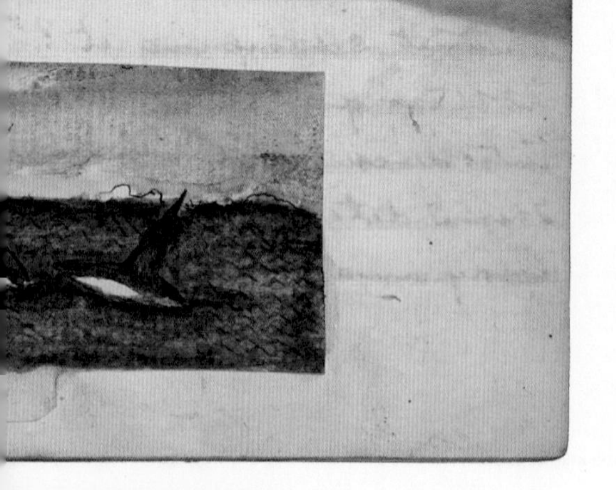

By the way I haven't half exhausted my curious dream. While we were away killing the whales under the canal bridge I heard it strike two o'clock, and it suddenly came into my head that my final professional was to have begun at one. Horrified I abandoned the whales and rushed to the University. The Janitor refused me admission to the examination room, and after a desperate hand to hand struggle he ejected m Even then I did not wake but dreamed that someone handed me out a paper to see wha the questions were like. There were four question but I forget the two middle ones. The first wa "Where is the water ten miles deep near Berlin" The last was headed NAVIGATION, and the question was this word for word "If a man and his wife and a horse ~~was~~ were in a boat, how could the wife get the man and the horse out of the boat without swamping it?" I grumbled very much at these questions, and said it was not fair to introduce Navigation into a medical Examinatio Then I determined to send the paper to Captain Gray and get him to answer it, and then at las

woke up. Certainly the most connected dream, s well as the most vivid I ever had.

This evening our foretop yard came down with run owing to the breaking of a shackle, and nashed the halliards. We put up a spare spar nd made all right again within four hours, a ne bit of seamanship. Captain has gone up to Nest and I am writing this before the cheery cabin e. I hear the hammering on deck as they do up broken yard, and just outside the door the ward is remarking in a really first class tenor t 'at midnight on the Sea-heas - Her Bright Smile unts me still'. It seems to haunt him at mid-ight, and then he employs the odd 23 hours in mmenting upon the fact." Captain David was on ard in the evening, and lent me a pamphlet on ales. I was experimenting on the 'mollies' in e evening. I took 4 pieces of bread and soaked m, one in Strychnine, one in Carbolic Acid, one Sulphate of Zinc, and one in Turpentine. Then I ew them over to the birds to see which would work ickest, but to my horror and old patriarch pped forward and swallowed the whole four pieces,

and strange to say he didn't seem a bit the wor

Tuesday June 1st

I trust that we may have better luck this month than last. We can see the Northern Barrier along the whole horizon. Eclipse is getting up steam and I suppose we are going to have a look a the bight in Lat 78° out of which we were driven, and then we will run away to Scoresby Sound on the Liverpool Coast if nothing turns up. Water is full of animalculae and olive green in Colour,

Balaena Mysticetus!
Balaena Mysticetus!
If we were animalculae
You wouldn't take long to eat us.

Captain says he has seen whales spouting so thick that it looked like the Smoke of a large tow a very good description. By the way the water rose 8 degrees yesterday from which we think we are in the Gulf Stream. Passed a piece of a fir tree floating in the water. It has come many thousands of miles drifting down the Obi or Yenesei rivers in Siberia and so into the Arctic seas by the NW current.

Saw
[..]t two bladdernoses in the evening but only got
[o]ne on account of bad shooting. Hoped to get away
[a]nd shoot roaches in the evening but there weren't
[a]ny. Buchan shot four in the morning.
~~Tuesday 1~~ Wednesday June 2.
[P]lying West and South under canvas. Captain
[s]uffering from Ablubberomnia – Very cold, as cold
[a]s it was in April. My hair is coming out and I
[a]m getting prematurely aged. Read a good story
[th]at a doctor was buried in the middle of a large
[c]hurchyard, and a professional brother suggested as
[a]n epitaph 'Si monumentum quaeris, circumspice'
[Ve]ry witty, I think. It is very disheartening to be kept
[o]ff the whaling banks like this by the ice. As the Steward
[s]ays 'it makes a lad inclined to Jump up, and never
[c]ome down again'. Sydney Smith said of Jeffrey
[']His body is too small to cover his mind. Jeffrey's
[in]tellect is always indecently exposed'. Very clever too.
[S]aw the marks of a large bear in the evening, also
[a] Bladdernose in the water. Things look rather more
[h]opeful this evening, as we have made considerable
[w]ay to the Westward, and are close to the whalebanks.

Thursday June 3rd

Very cold again, a great hoar frost is on. Strong wind from the North. We are in the most promising place we have seen yet and if the wind holds we ought to catch some of the minnows we are after. Came on a fog in the evening. I have my cod line overboard baited with pork but have not had a bite. About 60 sail of Russians come to Spitzbergen this month to hunt cod, so there must be some knocking about. Had the bag net out tonight and towed it to see if there was any food. Brought up a most beautiful Clio or Sea Snail, a couple of inches long, looking like some weird little fairy. I have stuck him in a pickle bottle and christened him 'John Thomas'. I hope he will live, we have put some butter and pork into his house. Saw a good many narwhals knocking about, one very large one, almost snow white and quite 15 feet, ricochetted past the Stern, making the peculiar grunt they give when they rise. Also saw some beautiful medusae.

[Fr]iday June 4th

John Thomas is in an awful passion. We left [th]e pickle bottle far from the fire, and as there [we]re 11 degrees of frost it froze up and John [h]as caught cold. He is sitting in a corner [w]ith his tail in his mouth, just as a sulky [b]aby sticks its thumb into its potato box. I [h]ave drawn John's attention to the butter & Pork [a]nd he took a hurried breakfast, but seems [to] have business of importance down at the [b]ottom of the bottle. He's thinking perhaps of

'Where his Rude Shell by the Gulf Stream lay,
There were his little Sea Snails all at play,
There their Amoeboid mother, He their sire
Butchered to make a Whale's holiday.

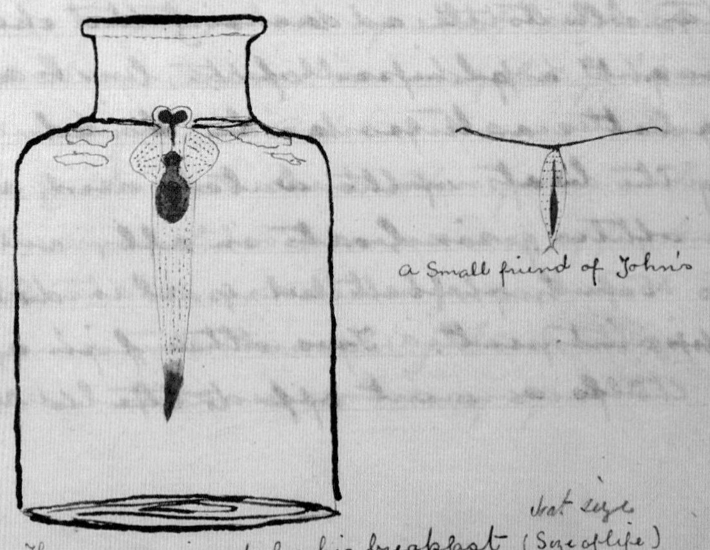

a Small friend of John's

John Thomas coming up for his breakfast (Size of life) that size

Just after one o'clock I was standing on deck talking to Andrew Hutton about the general bleakness of affairs. He is one of our best harpooners. I happened to ask "By the way, Andrew, when a man does see a whale I suppose he never sings out 'There she blows' as put in books." He said "Oh they cry 'There's a fish' or any thing that comes into their head, but there's Colin going up to the masthead, so I must go on the bridge". Up he went on the Bridge and the moment he got there he bellowed out 'There's a fish'! There was a rush for the boats by the watch but the Captain put a stop to it "Do things quietly", he said "and man the boats when I give the word". We could see two blasts ahead among the ice, and I caught a glimpse of the back of one of the great creatures as he dived. We lowered away the boats of the watch and afterwards four others, six boats in all, and our hopes ran high but were alas doomed to disappointment. Two other fish appeared, and the four went off to the W N W. The

-ats kept after them for four hours, but it was
-o go, something (heavy ice) seemed to have scared
-em. However it is something to be on their
-ail. We see a flaw water ahead and hope we
-e going to have a fine time of it in there.
-e Eclipse was also after two fish but lost them
-ing to the unskilfulness of their second mate
-ho lost his post in consequence.

Saturday June 6th

-hn is well and hearty. Saw a great many
-arwhals today, but none of what we want.
-pt a lookout on the bridge from breakfast
Dinner. We saw a large Sea Elephant on
-e ice about noon, and Andrew Hutton &
-went away and shot it. About 9 feet
-ng and very fat. We opened its stomach
-nd found it contained a very large assort-
-ment of Cuttlefish. Captain went aboard
-e Eclipse in the evening. The guano here
blood red, and has a curious effect. Plenty
birds about. Wind coming round to the
-outh. It is a most exciting business; the
-nsion on the nerves is very great

Sunday June 6th

John was up before me and took a heavy breakfast. He is now operating on the top of his bottle surveying his new kingdom apparently and meditating a map. I put him in a bucket every evening where he wanders fancy free for an hour or two. Wind is round to SW I am glad to say, it was SSW yesterday. We may see fish any moment now, the water is a peculiar dark grey green. I thought I smelled a fish yesterday from the deck. You can often smell the queasy smell long before you see them. Aaron our Shetland boy the son of old Peter the prophet was in the crew of the boat that visited the Eclipse yesterday when he came back I heard him go straight to his father and begin with "Father, Peter Shene's been dreaming!" (Peter Shene is the rival prophet of the Eclipse)

'Ay, boy, What?

'Peter Shene's had a dream, Father.'

nd what did he tream, Joy?'

He treamed he saw them killing cows on
board the Hope.'

Oh a good tream, Joy, a goot tream. That
means that the Hope will have the first
ish. A very goot tream.

So we still have some hopes.

Saw a large Cuttle fish under the surface, and a
ood many medusae and Clios. About 3 PM
Word came that the Eclipse Boats were away.
hey were several hours after their fish but
nally they were recalled by the hoisting of the
ucket. About 6 PM Adam Carner saw a
ast a long way off from the masthead. Four
oats were sent off in pursuit, but failed
ven to catch a glimpse of the whole. Jack
uchan, who by the way started in his shirt
nd trousers Just as he tumbled out of bed,
aided a Narwhal or Sea Unicorn about 13
et long, with a horn of 2 feet. The Harpoon
ut its throat most beautifully. It was
owed by the four boats and hoisted aboard.
eautifully speckled with Black and Grey.

after flinching it we opened the Stomach which we found to be full of a very large shrimps, which I take to be the 'Mountebank' shrimp, and with bits of Cuttlefish. It had two distinct sets of para-sites upon it, one like a long thin worm in the drum of its ear. The other seed like at the root of the horn.

Two very rare ducks were seen behind the ship this evening. The Captain went off himself in a boat and nailed them both with a right and left barrel. No one on board has seen the species before They have a yellowish beak with an Orange Callosity stretching up in a curve from the base of the beak towards the eyes. They are rather larger than our ducks, dark brown on the head, white on the neck, dark brown on the back, lighter silvery brown on the breast. All the plumage very soft & delica

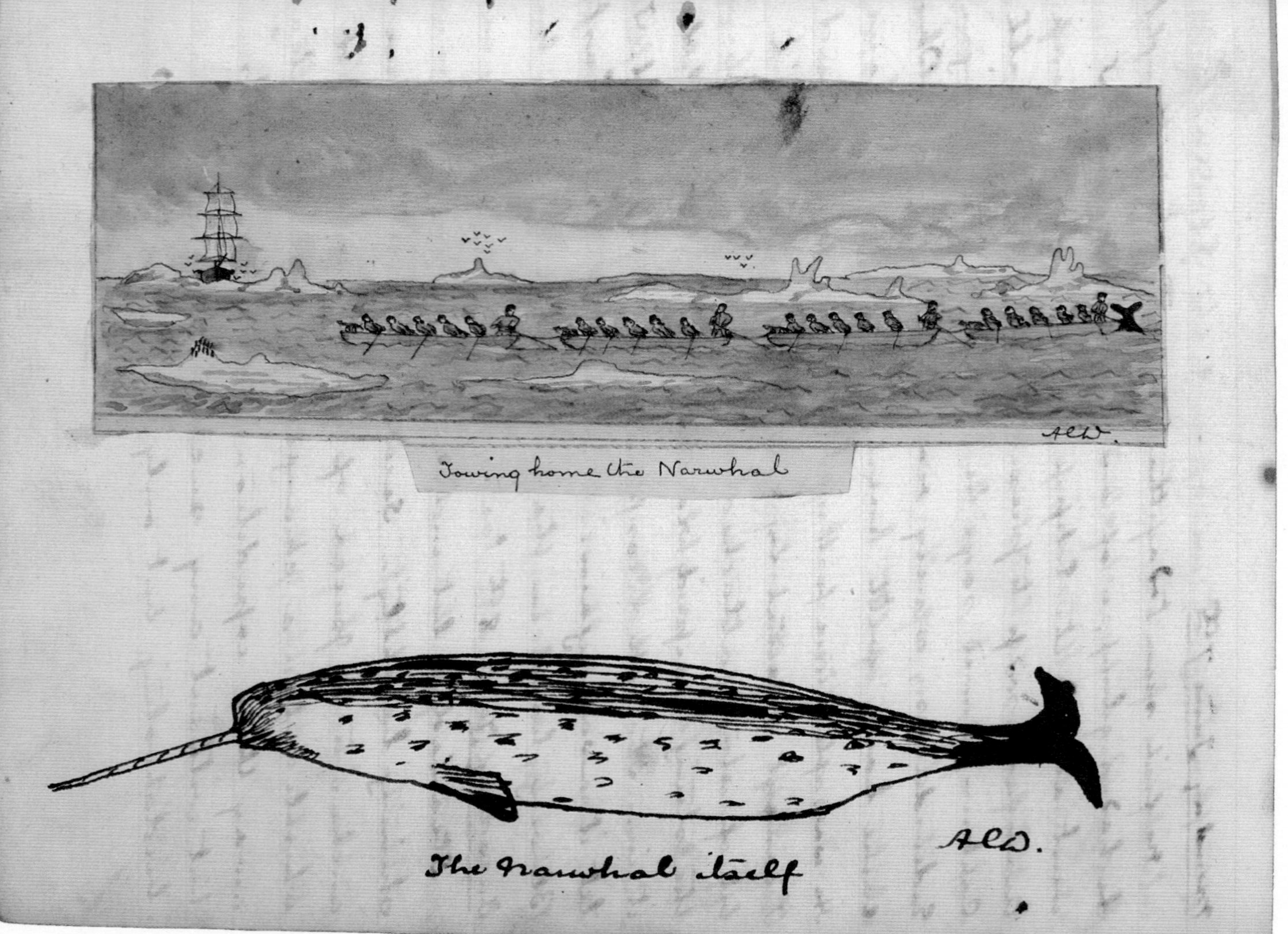
ALD.
Towing home the Narwhal
The Narwhal itself
ALD.

Monday June 7th

No fish seen today though the Captain thought he had a glimpse of one in the evening. I went aboard the Eclipse after tea to get some arsenical soap to preserve our ducks with. Captain David says he thinks they are King Eider ducks, a very rare bird. Captain David came back with me and stayed an hour. He was after three fish yesterday but got none. I caught a petrel by flinging a lead with a bit of string attached over its head, when the string warped round it and I hauled it in. It looked confoundedly astonished. I let it away again. Wind North & North East Blowing hard in the morning

Tuesday June 8th.

Steamed a bit in the morning. Sun shining brightly. Secured the ship by an anchor to a piece of floating ice, and whistled for a change of wind. Sent away three expeditions after Narwhals but without any success. Went away birdshooting but only got two shots

lling a Roach and maiming a loon.
pped a Flaw Rat but it got away. Grant
w the steps of an Arctic fox on the ice.
d a pleasant day on the whole. Captain
ys if I will load my own cartridges I may
aze away until all is blue. Made sail
ain in the evening. Played 'Nap' in the
gine Room. Almost dead calm.

Wednesday June 9th

e were forced to come out towards the open sea
gain today on account of changes in the ice.
lipse and we moored ourselves on to one
ece of ice in the evening. Captain David &
Walker came aboard us about ten P.M.
nd stayed until two. They shot a very
arge bear upon the ice today. It was sitting
unching away at the head of a narwhal
hich it had dragged on to the ice, while a
eat shark was wiring into the tail which
ung over into the water. How the bear got a
arwhal onto the ice is a mystery. Went away
Two o'clock in the morning to shoot birds.
ey were very scarce however and I was

only enabled to get a roach and 6 Snowbird Saw a large Bladdernose but were unable get a shot at it. Came back at 4 P.M.

Thursday June 10th

Still trying hard to get in to where we know the whales are lying. Made some progress under steam and then anchored with the "Eclipse" to an iceberg. Shot a Kittiewake and a Loon off the deck, and then got two more loons while picking up the first. Amused myself in the afternoon by catching petrels by flinging a lead over the heads of them and warping the string round their wings something like the South American 'Bolas' By the way when I shot a roach the other day a great Maulie seized it the moment it fell and regardless of the shouts of the boats crew, and my frantic howls proceed to bear it away, but I shied a boats stretcher at it and scared it off.

Maulie Stealing our Roach

John Thomas
died on the 8th of June, regretted
by a large circle of acquaintances.

He was a right thinking and high minded Clio,
istinguished among his brother sea snails for
is mental activity as well as for physical
erfection. He never looked down upon his
maller associates because they were protozoa
hile he could fairly lay claim to belong to the

End of Volume II. Log of Hope.

igh family of the Echinodermata or Annulosa.
never taunted them with their want of a
ter vascular system, nor did he parade his
wn double chain of Ganglia. He was a modest
nd unassuming blob of protoplasm, and
uld get through more fat pork in a day
han many an animal of far higher pretensions.
is parents were both swallowed by a whale
his infancy, so that what education he had
as due entirely to his own industry and
bservation. He has gone the way of all flesh
o peace be to his molecules.

Zoological List of Whaling Voyage

INVERTEBRATA

I Protozoa.

Any number in whale's food

II Infusoria

Rice food.

III Annulosa

Common Louse (On a Shetlander) Clio Helecina

Shrimp (Common) Horn louse of Narwhal

Clio Borealis (John Thomas) Ear louse of Narwhal

Shrimp 'Mountebank' Whale Louse (Ocima)

IV Echinodermata

Medusa gileus 78·40 N.

Medusa —? 78.40 N.

Flask Shaped Medusa 78·5 N.

V. Mollusca

Sepia —— 78·40 N.

ERTEBRATA

I. AVES

tic Petrel or 'Maufie' (Procellaria Glacialis) —
lish Guillemot or 'Loon' (Colymbus Troile) —
ach (Arca Alle) —
veca (Colymbus Grylle) —
rgomaster (Larus Glaucus) —
tiwake (Larus Rissa) —
owbird (Larus Eburneus) —
ow Bunting (Emberiza Nivalis) —
dpoll. (Fringilla Linaria) 75 N.
ffin or 'Tammy Norie'. (alca artica) 78 N.
atswain (Larus Crepidatus) 78.12 N
land hawk (Falco Icelandicus) 73.40 N
eat white owl. (Styx) 71 N.
at Tern or Sea Swallow (Sterna hirundo) 78.18 N
ntGeese. (Anas Bernicla) 78 N
der duck (Anas mollissima) —
a Gull (Larus Communis)
ag. (Lerwick).
ick (Calos?). Very rare. King Eider. 78.50 N.
tic Starling 78.6 N.
ndpiper 75.30 N.
tic Gull. 69°N

PISCES

Flaw fish (Rather like a whiting) 78.40 N.

Silver Fish 78.12 N.

Herring. 69°N.

Squalus Greenlandicus or Greenland Shark

MAMMALIA.

Horsesaddle Seal. (Phoca Vitulina)

Bladdernosed Seal

Flaw Rat.

Ground Seal 79 N.

Walrus. (Trichecus Rosmarus) 77.30 N.

Whitefaced Seal.

Fresh Water Seal. (78 N)

rca Gladiator. The Greenland Swordfish. Lat 69 N.
ottle nosed Whale (Delphinus Deductor) 68 N.
azor back Whale (Balæna Physalis)
Narwhal (Monodon Monoceros)
ight Whale (Balæna mysticetus).
alæna Musculus (Hunchback whale) 68° N.
rsus Maritimus or Polar bear

nis Lagopus or Arctic Fox

Additional birds seen on passage.

olan Goose.
Fien Chuck
Stormy Petrel.
Black Back Gull.
Sparrow hawk
rallet

D126

D127

Log of the Steam Ship "Hope".
Greenland whaling & sealing.
Summer 1880.
Vol. III

Friday June 11th.

We made a few miles in the right direction. The Eclipse shot two bears this morning. About one o'clock a fish came up near the Eclipse but was not captured. We made fast to an iceberg in the evening. Caught a curious fish today, the first I have seen in Greenland. It looked rather like a whiting, but was not one. Jack Williamson one of our hands got a terrible blow from the wheel ~~today~~. It exposed the bone of his skull for about 5 inches. Stitched it up and sent him to bed. Steward the boatsteerer and I were walking on the ice in the evening and both distinctly saw the blast of a fish about half a mile off among the pack ice. It could not however be reached by boats

Saturday June 12th.

The ice is shutting rather than opening. Hope deferred maketh the heart sick. Men shot a bear off the side about eight o'clock. I was asleep and so missed the fun. Stomach was

full of seal oil but he was very thin [illegible] shots. Went aboard the Eclipse at dinner time with the Captain. Had a pleasant feed and chat. Captain David seems far from despairing. Strong wind from W and SW – ought to do us good. Ice began to close round us so rapidly that we had to steam out 30 miles or so to prevent being nipped or beset. Had a difficult job to get out as it was. The sea this morning was actually swarming with Narwhals.

Sunday June 13th

Got a fine opening towards the Westward and worked in again about as far as we came out, going W & SW. Saw nothing but one seal in the water the whole time. Need about 20 miles North to take us into whaling ground. 'Thou art so near and yet so far'. It does seem hard after our penetrating impenetrable packs, and leaving forty miles of shifting heavy ice between us and the sea, exposing ourselves to every danger of storm and flood, and putting ourselves in the way of losing our ship and ourselves, or of being beset and wintering out, that we shd

e no better off than the half hearted beggars who shun
he whole concern, and go South after small game.
t is a shame and a sin, and can't last long. The
clipse and ourselves are the last of ten generations
f daring Arctic seamen, the breed has deteriorated
nd we are the sole survivors of the men who
sed to harry Greenland from the 80 to the 72,
nd here we are stuck in the mud & helpless.
It would make a saint swear.

Monday June 14th.

Thick fog in the morning. Blew foghorns but got
no answer from the Eclipse. Jack Williamson, the
man with the head is doing very well. Things look
s bad as they can be and worse. I hope we will go
nd hunt bladdernoses instead of persevering at
this. The whales are only 20 miles off but an
impassable barrier of ice intervenes, and the wind
is such as to pack the ice firmer together, rather
than to open it out. We want wind from the W.
W or NWW and we are getting it all from the
South. ὦ ποποι ποποι! 53 tons! Such is life!

Tuesday June 15th

The only difference in the weather is that the fog is thicker and the wind more utterly odious and depraved. However we are at the bottom of our woes for nothing could make our situation worse, so 'there's an end on't' as old Sam Johnson used to say. Captain went aboard the Eclipse at dinner time. I do hope we'll go and slay bladdernoses or Bottle-noses or any other animal who has some peculiarity about its nose, and carries blubber on its carcase. Browsed over Boswell all day.

Wednesday June 16th

The Eclipse lowered away after a whale about 8 AM and pursued it until noon, but did not get it. The fact is we are not upon the grounds, and any we see are stragglers on the march, and not stopping to feed. Wind Westerly, so far so good. Calm in the evening, sea looks like quicksilver, the whole place covered with Narwhals, great brutes 15 & 16 feet long. You hear their peculiar 'Sumph!' in every direction.

I saw one pass like a great flickering white Ghost
underneath the keel. Reading "Tristram Shandy"; a
coarse book but a very clever one.

Thursday June 17th

An eventful day – for the Eclipse at any rate. In the
morning about 10 AM Colin saw a whale from the Crow's
Nest about five miles off while the Eclipse had her
boats after another. We made sail and reached up
towards Colin's fish but did not see it again until
about 1 PM when it suddenly appeared within 50
yards of the ship, accompanied by another one. The
two were gambling and frisking in the water like a
couple of lambs. We lowered away four boats, Colin's,
Turner's, Rennie's and Peter's which all pulled up for
a piece of ice where the fish were likely to reappear.
They came up there near Rennie's boat, but he unfortunately is not a man of much decision of
character, and he hesitated to fire into the nearest
fish for fear of scaring the other, which was turned
head on to him. The fish separated one disappearing
and the other leading the boats a most exciting

a most exciting chase to Windward. From the deck I could see its blast rising apparently just in front of the boats, and its great tail waving in the air, but our men could never get quite within shot of it. The Eclipse seeing the way the whale was heading came round that way and dropped two boats in front of it; The whale came up in front of one, the second mates, and in a moment we had the mortification of seeing the boats Jack flying, as a sign they were fast to our fish. It is hard to see a thousand pounds slip through your fin-gers so. They killed the fish during dinner and had it aboard before 8 P.M. Rennie got a fine wigging from the Captain when he came aboard.

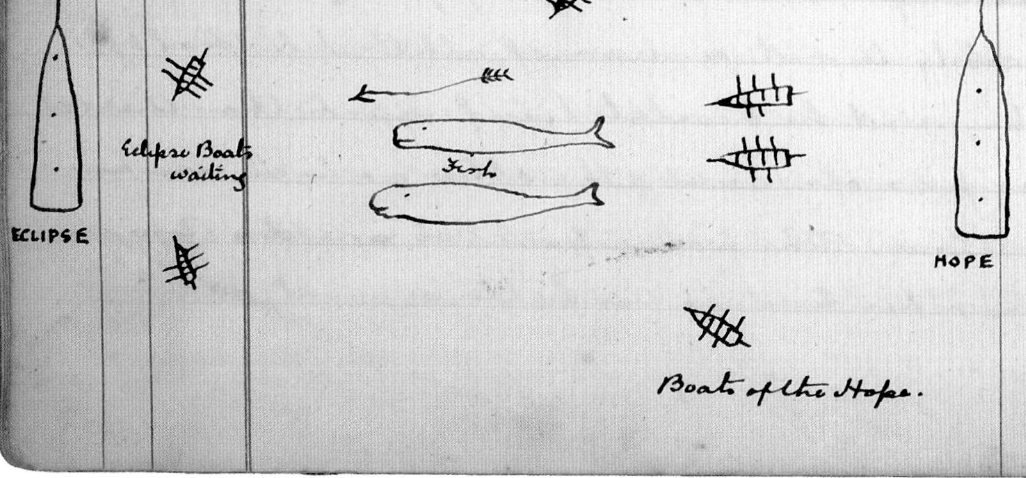

After dinner we saw a large bear on a point of
e apparently in a great state of excitement, probably
ue to the smell of the whale's blood. I got off in the
at with Matheson to kill it. We got out on the ice,
great flaw many miles across, with our rifles,
d could see the bear poking about among some
ummocks about 40 Yards away from us. Suddenly
caught sight of us and came for us at a great
peed, running across the pieces of ice towards us,
nd lifting up his fore feet as he ran in a very
line way. Matheson and I were kneeling down
the ice, and I intended not to fire until the
ute was right on the top of us. Matheson how-
ver let blaze when it was about 15 yards off and
ist grazed its head. It turned and began trotting
way from us, and as it only presented its stern
was compelled to put my bullet into that. It
as wounded but went went off across the ice
t a great rate, and we never saw it more.

Saw a 'Boatswain' Gull today. ~~Boa~~ Row in
e mate's berth in the evening

Friday June 18th

Eclipse stuck another fish during the night and had it aboard before breakfast. Lucky dogs!. Buchan shot a fine bear and two cubs during the night. By the way my bear of yesterday when it had escaped some distance got up on its hind legs on the top of a hummock like a dancing bear, to have a good look at us. I had no idea they did that in a state of nature. Cruised about all day in search of blubber but found none. Our boats and the Eclipse were after one fish at night but they never got a start. Ice is closing round us and we are cut off from the sea, so that unless there comes a change of wind we may easily be beset. We are all very melancholy.

Our Bear.

Saturday June 19th

Calm as a fishpond, water like quicksilver. A good many Narwhals about. The ice is remaining stationary or thereabouts. No fish seen today at all. A Shark was seen to come up alongside and nail a

[illegible]manba out of the water. We wouldn't mind being
unsuccessful if others shared the same fate, but it
is maddening that the Eclipse should make £3000
while we have not made a penny. Our Captain
is as good a fisherman as ever came to Greenland,
there are no two opinions on board on that point,
quite as good as his brother David, but somehow
the luck seems to be with the others. They have seen
from first to last about 14 fish to our 5.

Sunday June 20th

A large fish was seen during breakfast, but
after a short pursuit it got among pack ice
where it was impossible to follow it. It was very
nearly within reach once. This is terrible to see
fish and not to get them. No man who has not
experienced it can imagine the intense excitement
of whale fishing. The rarity of the animal, the
difficulty attending any approach to its haunts,
its extreme value, its strength, sagacity and size
all give it a charm. A large bear was shot
during the night

D138

Ice closed round us during the day but relaxed towards evening. Captain David came aboard during the day, and our Captain went and had supper with him. One of his harpooners was attacked in his boat by a bear the other day when he had no rifle with him, but he banged the hard wad of the harpoongun through it, which was ingenious. That was nothing however to what one of our harpooners did a few years ago, which would be incredible if I did not know it to be true. Buchan was sent to shoot a bear and two cubs on the ice, but they took to the water before he reached them. He passed the noose of a rope over the head of each, as they swam and snarled at him, and tied the ends of the three ropes to his thwarts. All the oars were then run in except the steer oar, and Buchan standing in the bows and banging them on the head with a boathook whenever they offered to turn, guided the boat right back to the ship the ~~boats~~ bears towing it the whole way. The Steward who saw it, says the roaring could be heard a mile

f. Some hopes for tomorrow

Monday June 21st

Hopes not realized as usual. We are shut up in
small hole of water with nothing but great ice
elds as far as we can see. If it goes on shutting up
will be beset and our chances of any success
uined. Colin bad with a Sore throat. No fish about.
ught a beautiful Sea Lemon yesterday floating on
surface but it died shortly after being brought on
ard. Saw a very curious sight at midnight, which
u might come North a lifetime and never see.
ere were three distinct suns shining at the same
ne with equal brilliancy, and all begirt by
utiful rainbows, and with an inverted rain-
w above the whole thing. A most wonderful
ectacle.

A Family party
(Seen from the deck of the Eclipse).

Tuesday June 22nd

An utterly uneventful day. We are still cooped up in this hole of water. Caught a rare & indeed un-described medusa in the evening (Medusa Doilea Octostripata). Misery and Desolation

Wednesday June 23d

Made our way out of our prison, by a most delicate and beautiful bit of manoeuvring under steam. We came out about 60 miles among very heavy ice, the smallest piece of which could have crushed our ships like eggshells. Often we squeezed through between floes where the ships sides were grinding against the ice on each side. Steamed S and E. Eclipse went after a fish but never got a start. Glass falling rapidly

Thursday June 24

Captain and I were knocked up at 6 AM by the mate's thrusting his tawny head into the Cabin, singing out 'A Fish, sir', and disappearing up the Cabin stairs like a Lamplighter. When we got on deck the mate's and Peter's boats

ere already on the seat of action where the fish
ad been seen. They caught another glimpse of
about a mile to leeward and pulled down
wards it, but lost sight of it again. Meanwhile
nother very fine whale came up astern very
ear the ship and Hutton's and Rennie's boats
ere lowered away after it. The four boats

We are still cooped up
rase & indeed un-
ry (Medusa Woilea
olation

son, by a most
anoeuvring under
miles among very
which could have
. Often we squeezed
ships sides were
ch side. Steamed
s fish but never
pidly

up at 6 AM by
head into the Cabin,
d disappearing
nplighter. When
d Peter's boats

Boats of the Eclipse an

were already on the seat of
had been seen. They caught
it about a mile to leeward
towards it, but lost sight o
another very fine whale ca
near the ship and Hutton's
were lowered away after it.

ps in pursuit of two whales. June 17th 1880.

where the fish
the glimpse of
pulled down
again. Meanwhile
p astern way
Rennie's boat
four boats

pursued it for a couple of hours, when it began to blow extremely hard and a heavy sea arose so that some of the boats' head sheets were right under water. We had to get them on board, and let the whale alone. Blowing a very hard gale from the North East all day, 9 Wind Force

Friday June 25th

Wind is still very strong though not so much so as before. Nothing seen during the day but a large Finner whale which is a bad sign. It is of no use to us, and it drives the right whale away from its feeding grounds. Played Nap in the evening. Wind only a fresh breeze now, have begun to steam to the North after the Eclipse

Saturday June 26th

Things looked dark enough all day, but suddenly took a turn for the better. Nothing had been seen all day and I had gone down to the cabin about 10 o'clock when I heard a sort of bustle on deck. Then I heard the Captain's voice from the masthead

ower away the two waist boats!" I rushed into the
ates' berth and gave the alarm, Colin was dressed
t the second mate rushed on deck in his shirt
th his trousers in his hand. When I got my
ad above the hatchway the very first thing I saw
as the whale shooting its head out of the water
d gambolling about at the other side of a
ge "sconce" piece of ice. It was a beautiful
ght, with hardly a ripple on the deep green
ter. In Jumped the crews into their boats, and
officers of the watch looked that their guns
e primed and ready, then they pushed off
d the two long whale boats went crawling
ay on their wooden legs one to one side of
bit of ice, the other to the other. Carner had
rdly got up to the ice when the whale came
again about forty yards in front of the
at, throwing almost its whole body out of
water, and making the foam fly. There
s a chorus of "Now, Adam – now's your
ance!" from the line of eager watchers on

the vessel's side. But Adam Carner, a grizzled and weatherbeaten harpooner knows better. The whale's small eye is turned towards him and the boat lies as motionless as the ice behind it. But now it has shifted, its tail is towards them – Pull, boys, pull! Out shoots the boat from the ice – will the Fish dive before he can get up to it? That is the question in every mind. He is nearing it, and it still lies motionless – nearer yet and nearer. Now he is standing up to his gun and has dropped his oar – "Three strokes, boys"! he says as he turns his quid in his cheek, and then there is a bang and a foaming of waters and a shouting, and then up goes the little red flag in Carner's boat and the whale line runs out merrily.

But the whale is far from taken because it is struck. The moment the Jack appeared in the boat there was a shout of 'A fall' on board, and down went other six boats

help the 'fast' boat and nail the whale on its
appearance. I got into the mate's boat and
way we pulled. Of course the whale may
me up any where within a radius of the
ne it has taken out, which may amount
three or four miles, so our seven boats
ad to spread out over a considerable area.
ve minutes passed - ten - fifteen - twenty and
ter being away 25 minutes the brute came
between the second mate's and Rennie's
ats, who fired into her and dispatched her.
e proved to be a small fish, about 40 feet
ng, with 4 ft 1 in of bone, worth between
o and £300. We gave three cheers and towed her to
ship. She was covered with very large crab lice
hich accounted for her erratic conduct in the
ater. Had her flinched and stowed away by 3
clock AM. I went to the Crow's nest during the process
look out for another which I didn't see. Went
bed at 6 AM and got up at 12.

4ft. 1.

Adam Carner.

Sunday June 27th

Not a thing to be seen all day, but about 4 AM Colin saw a very large fish in the distance. Eclipse lowered away 2 boats as well as we, and after getting one start they lost scent of her. She seems to have been a tremendous brute.

Monday June 28th

Nothing

Tuesday June 29th.

Master aboard the Eclipse last night until 2 AM. Lay to in a calm all day - nothing doing. Waiting for a chance of getting North but ice looks bad. Got away to shoot at midnight and came back at 4 PM. Got a Burgy, a Snowbird and five Loons. These Burgies I think are the biggest of Gulls after the Albatross. They usually are about 5 feet from tip to tip

Wednesday June 30th.

Slept nearly all day after last night's exertion. Went aboard the Eclipse ~~boat~~ and had a great talking. Worked with a microscope aboard. Buchan shot a flaw Rat. Hutton skinned my birds

[Thu]rsday and Friday July 1 & 2.

Lying to in a thick fog as we have been ever since last [Su]nday. Nothing to chronicle except that Colin got a large [n]arwhal early on Thursday morning. It took out a whole [l]ine (120 fathoms) and made a great fuss about being [k]illed. A Unicorn is worth about £10. The skin is [of] considerable value. I have a very decent Arctic mu-[s]eum by this time including a lot of interesting things. [I] have at present

1. An Esquimeaux pair of Sealskin Trowsers
2. An Iceland Falcon
3. My Sealing knife and Steel.
4 Bone of Bladdernose - Shot myself.
5. 2 Bones of Old Seals
6. 2 Foreflippers of Young Bladdernose
7. 2 Foreflippers of a Ground Seal
8. A Bear's head
9. Bristles of a Bladder
10 A Burgomaster
11. Drums of Whale's ears
12 2 King Eider ducks

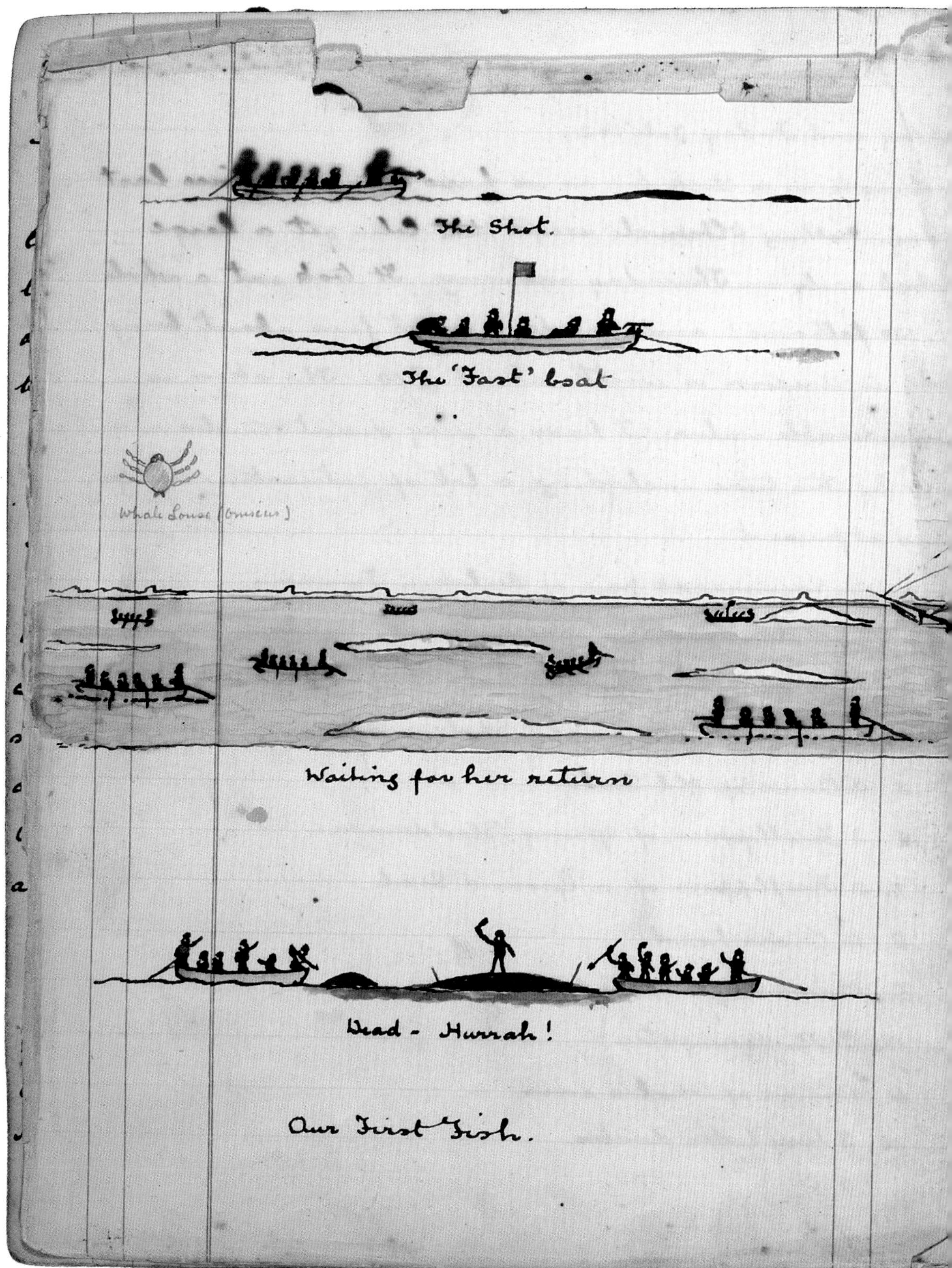
The Shot.
The 'Fast' boat
Whale Louse (Oniscus)
Waiting for her return
Dead - Hurrah!
Our First Fish.

13. Bits of Lava found in King Eider duck.

14 (?) A Unicorn's horn.

Added 2 Esquemeaux pouches
A Kettiewake
A Bear's Claw

Saturday July 3d

It has cleared up and we are off to the happy hunting grounds. Sailed Nor' and Nor' West all day. Saw nothing but an extraordinarily small seal on the ice, about the size of a rabbit. It seemed as much amused at the appearance of the ship as we were at it. We are all despairing. The Stewart stuffed my Ground Seal's flippers very nicely with sawdust.

Sunday July 4th

Sailed North and then South again. Everything looks bleak and discouraging. No trace of whales or even of whale's food. A Bladdernose was seen on the ice. A small bird something like a starling or thrush was flying round the ship. Saw a puffin. Have no heart to write much in the Log. Reading Morley's Rise of the Dutch Republic"; a very fine history.

Monday July 5th

~~Monday J.~~ Steamed into a flaw water, made fast in the evening. Saw several Finner whales. Eclipse mistook

one for a fish and lowered away his boats, which however were promptly recalled. Nothing else of interest seen during the day. Got some delicious fresh water off the salt water ice

Tuesday July 6th

Dead calm. Sun beating down in a tropical manner though the temperature was only 36°. Tremendous glare from the ice flaws. Went aboard Eclipse in morning. Got away to shoot and nailed altogether 7 Loons, a roach, a Kittiwake, a Snowbird, and a flaw Rat. We had great fun securing the latter as our small shot did not suffice to kill it, and after a chase of atleast half an hour, we harpooned it with boathooks when swimming under the water. We brought it aboard alive but the Captain humanely put it out of its misery. Got away again at night but found no game. A couple of Sea Swallows played round the ship. Saw several Finners.
A very Jolly day!

Wednesday July 7th

Steamed 20 or 30 miles South, and then on seeing indications of fish made sail. Captain David

came aboard in the evening with his Engineer and caught a rare shrimp. Feel very much the better for yesterday's outing. Cooked Red Herring for supper in a very scientific manner.

Thursday July 8th

Another memorable day. Sailed along the edge of a great flaw among very blue water with the Eclipse ahead of us. About 1 o'clock a whale, the first seen since Sunday week came up close to Captain Davids ship; he lowered away three boats after it and chased it until 4.15 P.m when he succeeded in getting fast, and had her alongside by 8 P.m and flenched by midnight. We dodged about hoping his fish would come in our direction when we would have been Justified in securing it, but about 4 o'clock the welcome shout came from the masthead "there's another fish on the Lee Bow, Sir!". Mathieson and Bob Cane lowered away after it, and were soon lost sight of among the ice, while we crowded along the side of the deck and waited. Then a groan went up as a large Finner whale rose near the ship, for Finners and 'right' whales are

deadly enemies, and we were afraid our quarry would be scared. I went down to the Cabin to sooth my disappointment with a smoke, when I heard the Captain yell "A fall! A fall!" from the masthead, which is the signal that the fish is struck. Up we tumbled many of the men only half dressed, and away went five long green whaleboats to the support of the 'fast' boat and its' companion. I got into Peter McKenzie's boat. We had hardly got clear of the ships side when the boatsteerer announced that the fish was up, and was lashing out, fin and tail. Then we knew our work was cut out for us, for when a fish stays a very short time under water after being struck, it is reserving all its strength for a struggle with the boats. If the whale goes down and stops away half an hour it is generally so exhausted on returning to the surface that it falls an easy prey. The boats pulled up and Hutton and Carner fired into her and got fast. We were the next boat up and pulled on to

fishes head, where we lanced her deep in the neck. She gave a sort of a shudder and started off at a great rate along the surface. Buchan pulled his boat on to her head as she advanced, by which senseless manoevre the prow of the boat was lifted up in the air, and finally the whole boat landed on the animal's back amid a shouting of men & snapping of oars and Buchan roaring "Pull! Sweep! Back! Hold Water! Pull! What the devil are you feared at!" I said to Peter "Stand by to pick them up!" but they managed to shove the boat off without accident. The beast now made for a flaw and got beneath it, but soon reappeared when both Buchan and Rennie fired into her. She went under again but once more reappeared right among our three boats and then the fun began. We pulled on to her and in went our lances for five feet or so. The three boats tried to keep well at the side of her while she was always slewing round to bring her ~~tail~~ formidable tail to bear upon us. She nearly had our boat over once by coming up underneath

it, but we managed to get it righted. Then we stood off from her while she went into her dying flurry, whipping the water into a foam, and then she slowly turned up on her back and died. We stood up in our boats and gave three hearty cheers. We towed her up to the ship and by 10 P.m had her aboard. She was a fine fish, each lamina of whale bone being 9 foot 6 inches, yielding about 12 tons of oil. It is worth quite £1000 and has secured our voyage from being a failure. A large and very ugly shark came up and superintended the process of flinching the fish in spite of numerous knives passed through its body. I asked the Captain to let the Stewart and me go off in a boat and harpoon it, but he refused.

Whale

Buchan's Boat on the top of the fish

Friday July 9th.

Nothing doing. Everybody in a state of reaction after yesterday's capture. The Captain says Bob Cane managed the affair very well. Several Finner whales seen during the day. Beautiful sunshine.

to get it righted. Then we
hile she went into her dying
water into a foam, and then
on her back and died. We
ts and gave three hearty
up to the ship and by 1 P.M
he was a fine fish, each
ne being 9 foot 6 inches,
ons of oil. It is worth quite
ed our voyage from being
and very ugly shark
r intended the process of
spite of numerous knives
body. I asked the Captain
d me go off in a boat
t he refused.

foot. 6 in.
b. Cane.

B

Friday July 9th.
Nothing doing. E
yesterday's captu
-aged the affair
seen during the

hale dragging 2 fast boats through water
July 8th 1880

Boat on the top of the fish

dy in a state of reaction after
he Captain says Bob Lane man-
well. Several Finner whales
Beautiful sunshine.

It is a curious fact that the last whale the Eclipse captured only had one eye, and our friend of yesterday was also restricted to the same meagre allowance. The socket was perfectly empty. It may be that there is a breed of one eyed Greenland whales

Saturday July 10.

We have made a mistake, I think, in heading North again. The South seems to me a greasier locality. Had the boat away after a Bladder which we did not get. Played Euchre four hours in the evening in the Engine room. Query. Who did Adam & Eve's children marry?

Sunday July 11.

Got up late, and would have liked to have got up later, which is a sad moral state to be in. Eclipse got a Bladder in the morning. Steamed to the Eastward with the Eclipse in the evening, by which proceeding we scared a whale. Saw many Finners. About seven P.m a steamer was reported

about 20 miles to the Eastward. This is the first ship we have seen since the beginning of May. We steamed out and soon recognized it as the new discovery yacht of Leigh Smith's the 'Eira'. He is going to try for the Pole if the ice is favourable, which it isn't, and in any case to explore Franz-Joseph Land and shoot deer. He is a private gentleman, a bachelor with £4000 a year, and has taken Spitzbergen to himself as a wife. When our ships came up we saluted the little Eira with ensigns and three cheers, which they returned. Her men are in naval reserve uniform, officers in gold lace. The Captain went aboard her, while their Doctor, Niel, the photographer, the Engineer and 2 mates all boarded us. The Captain came back about 1 PM and he and I with the Eira's photographer & Doctor made a night of it on champagne and sherry. We had tinned salmon at 5 AM and turned in at 6.30.

Monday July 12.

Anchored to a flaw with the Eclipse and Eira. Unshipped our rudder which was damaged by

ice. By the way we got our home news up to June 18th from the Eira. Got no letter from Edinburgh but a very pleasant and cheerful one from Lottie. Surprised to hear that the Liberals have got in, disgusted also. Invited aboard Eclipse to meet Leigh Smith and Gang at dinner. Had Mock Turtle Soup, fresh Roast Beef with potatoes, French beans and Sauce, Arrowroot pudding and pan-cakes with preserves, winding up on wine & cigars. A very respectable whaler's feed. Went aboard "Eira" afterwards, She is beautifully fitted up aft. Had more cigars and Champagne. Got aboard at 12, after being photographed in a group. They came up by Jan Meyen and saw millions of bladdernoses in the 72·30, I hope we may come down for them.

Tuesday July 13.

Steamed 20 miles South and stopped short, I don't know why. I fancy we might fill our ship now if we went straight down for those Bladders but we must go at once. We are vacillating here too

much, I think, however it is for the Captain to decide. The success of our voyage depends on these few days, its our last chance of making a hit. Eclipse chased a bear and killed it in the water close to our ship. Left the Erna in the morning wishing them all success. A pleasant ship and a pleasant crew. She is black with a line of gold, about 200 tons burden and 50 horse power engines. I think I should like to be going out in her, although the prospect of seeing home again is pleasant. They left their letters with us. Fog in the evening

Wednesday July 14

Steamed and Sailed South and Sou' West. Eclipse had their boats away in the evening, but it was only a finner which they mistook for a right whale. Foggy nearly all day. No news of any sort. Read our papers ~~all day~~

Thursday July 15.

Another uneventful day. Lounged about & smoked. Absolutely nothing to do. Very thick and foggy and all that is reprehensible. Saw a small scene of Goethe's

'Faust' which I am reading which I think is as vivid and weird as anything I ever read, far more gruesome than Shakespeare's witches.

Night --- An Open Plain

Faust. Mephistopheles rushing past on black Horses

Faust- What are these hovering round the Ravenstone?

Meph- I know not what they're shaping & Preparing

Faust- They wave up - wave down - They bend - They stoop.

Meph. A band of witches

Faust. They sprinkle and Charm

Meph. On! On!

That is very awful I think.

Friday July 16.

Still foggy. Eclipse had four boats away during the night, but without success. We do not know yet if he really saw a fish. Boarded him in the evening and learned that it most certainly was a fish, and that they very nearly secured her. They got near enough to touch her with a boathook as she swam under water. Captain David still seems to be ver

sanguine. Some of our stores are running short, we got some potatoes however from the Eira ~~[illegible]~~. Stayed till 2 AM on the Eclipse. Got some more papers. Many seals seen during the day in the water.

Saturday July 17.

Absolutely nothing to do or to be done. It has been thick fog now for nearly a week. Steamed about 20 miles S and E. Captain David came aboard at night. We intend now to try the Liverpool coast right down in West Greenland near the land Lat 73° N. Many heavy fish have been taken there late in the season by Capt David, notably in '69 when he took 12, striking the first on the 16th of July, and the last on the 4th of August. I remember I used to think that when a whaler saw a whale they always got it, as a matter of fact the average is about one fish in 10 attempts.

Sunday July 18.

A little clearer today, not very much. Strong SSW breeze changing to a gale in the evening. Blew very hard all day, and all night. Dodged about under

the lea of ice flaws to escape its fury. I wonder if Leigh Smith's vessel is caught in it. By the way I was photographed among a distinguished group on the quarterdeck of her, but as I was smoking a cigar during the operation I am afraid I'll be rather misty

Monday July 19.

Blowing a gale all day. Nothing to do and we did it.

Tuesday July 20.

Cleared up a little and we did a good day's work steaming among great icefields about 40 miles S & W. If it keeps clear we may do something yet. There is an enormous accumulation of ice this year round the land, more than has ever been seen. We are 240 miles from it now, and the fields are almost continuous. I'm afraid we won't get in

Wednesday July 21.

Thick again, this fog is paralyzing - We are groping in the dark. Anchored to a flaw in the evening and the Captain and I went aboard the Eclipse. Had

Flinching (i.e. Cutting up) a whale. July 8th 1880

Nox Ambrosiana from 8 to 2 AM. The Late Mr Procter.
Captain David tells me of a fish he captured which had a lump the size and shape of a beehive on the fluke of its tail. He entered into a critical analysis of Goethe's Faust comparing it with some of Shakespeare's plays, and showing where the former borrowed from the latter, so we are not altogether barbarous up here.

Thursday July 22.

Still foggy and we continue anchored to the flaw. In the half deck in the morning discussing the loss of the Atalanta. Saw 2 'Boatswains', very rare birds at a considerable distance over the flaws and was going to hunt them but they absconded. Got a shot at a flaw rat's head about 60 yards off in the water, and blew it clean off with a rifle ball. Unfortunately the body sank.

Friday July 23.

Steamed S and SW as it became clearer. Continued to ply under sail all night in the same direction among very heavy ice fields. Wind coming round to

the Westward.

Saturday July 24.

Steamed SW again all day. Went through some ice that would have made Sir George Nares and the whole Arctic Committee turn up the whites of their eyes. Looking back it seemed solid as far as the horizon, and you could hardly conceive that two ships had wormed their way through it. We have one or two faintheasted ones aboard who have the terrors; it is not the going in it is the going out again, they say and we only have a fortnights provisions left. If we got beset we should certainly have to go on uncommon short commons. We are leaving 200 miles of heavy ice between us and the sea.

Sunday July 25

A very clear day with occasional fogs. Steamed 10 miles West. Made sail in the evening. Saw a great number of 'boatswains'. We have been exulting rather during the last few days as we have been getting on to Westward very well, but our way seems to be barred now by an immense chain of flaws, which

we hope to circumvent.

Monday July 26.

Sailed West and South West. Made our Longitude 6 ¼° W, and our Latitude 73-56 N. Captain went aboard Eclipse in evening. Water swarming with food but no animal life to be seen save 9 mallies and a school of Phoca Vitulina. Wrote a POM, about a Meerschaum Pipe

It lies within its leather case,
As it has lain in years gonebye,
Trusty friends and Comrades true,
Are that old Meerschaum pipe and I.

For it was young when I was young
And many a Jovial reckless night,
We students drank, and smoked and sung,
While yet my meerschaum pipe was ~~young~~ white

And it was hardly brown before,
From home and friends I first did part,

But bound for Russia's hostile shore,
I bore my meershaum next my heart.

And there upon the bloodstained ground,
Where many came and few went back,
With death and pestilence around
'Twas there I smoked my meershaum black.

And when the day our Colonel died,
We charged and took the Malakoff,
A Russian bullet grazed my side,
And shot my meershaum's amber off.

But I am grizzled now and bent,
Death's sickles near – His crop is ripe,
I fear him not but wait content,
I wait and smoke my meershaum pipe

ACD

Tuesday July 27th

Plying under sail about SSW. Latitude at noon gave us 73.29 N. A large Finner whale, the first we have seen for some time came up below the quarter boats. It seems to be a disputed point whether they are a good or a bad sign, the majority affect the latter opinion, but Captain David Gray throws his very weighty verdict on the minority. From my own experience I should say that the presense of Finners is not by any means a bad sign.

Blew a fresh breeze in the evening, ice moving at a great rate. Spent some time in the halfdeck. 'Eric' built a house as a depot in Davis Straits. On returning one season they found a polar bear lying asleep in one of the beds on the top of the blankets. Reading Maury's 'Physical Geography of the Sea. He explains the weed of the Sargasso sea (in the triangle between Cape de Verdes, Azores and Canaries) by saying it is the centre of the whirl of the Gulf stream, as when you whirl the water in a basin, you find floating corks at centre. He also remarks that railway trains always run off the line to the right hand side whether going North or South.

Wednesday July 28.

Another disagreeable day. Blowing hard from the South East, which is about the worst possible direction. This is the longest interval we have ever had. The ship has not drawn blood since July 8th, except a flaw-rat I shot. Blew from Eastward in the evening. As thick as pea soup and ice closing upon us rapidly. We have hopes that there is the open sea to the South of us from the fact that seals are coming through from the South. I thought too there was a swell from the same direction which would settle the question.

Tuesday July 27th

Plying under sail about SSW. Latitude at noon gave us 73.29 N. A large Finner whale, the first we have seen for some time came up below the quarter boats. It seems to be a disputed point whether they are a good or a bad sign, the majority affect the latter opinion, but Captain David Gray throws his very weighty verdict on the minority. From my own experience I should say that the presence of Finners is not by any means a bad sign.

'Flinching a Fish'. Sketched by Capt David [Gray]
S.S. Eclips[e]

Blew a fresh breeze in the evening, ice moving at a great rate Spent some time in the halfdeck. 'Eric' built a house as a depot in Davis Straits. On returning one season they found a polar bear lying asleep in one of the beds on the top of the blankets. Reading Maury's 'Physical Geography of the Sea. He explains the weed of the Sargasso sea (in the triangle between Cape de Verdes, Azores and Canaries) by saying it is the centre of the whirl of the Gulf stream, as when you whirl the water in a basin, you find floating corks at centre. He also remarks that railway trains always run off the line to [illegible] de whether going North or South

28

[illegible] day. Blowing hard from the South East, [illegible] worst possible direction. This is the [illegible] have ever had. The ship has not drawn [illegible] except a flaw rat I shot. Blew from [illegible] ning. As thick as peasoup and ice [illegible] rapidly. We have hopes that there is the [illegible] th of us from the fact that seals are [illegible] m the South. I thought too there was a [illegible] e direction which would settle the question.

A 'Right' and 'Left' among the Loons.

A very anxious and disagreeable night for us all, blowing hard, thick fog and ice everywhere. Captain and I could not turn in till 4 AM.

Thursday July 29

Horrible contemptible pusillanimous thickness over all. made fast to a flaw, and waited for better days. Went on a Journey over the ice, accompanied by our newfoundland Sampson. Were out of sight of the ships and had great fun. Came across a most extraordinary natural Snow house, about 12 feet high, shaped like a beehive with a door and a fine room inside in which I sat. Travelled a considerable distance, and would have gone to the pole but my matches ran short and I couldn't get a smoke. Got a long shot at a Boatswain but missed

-hum. Steamed SE when it cleared, but as it grew thick again we had to anchor once more. Eclipse shot at a Bladder but missed it. Got a curious fungus on the ice.

Natural Ice house. Lat 73.15. Long 6 W.

-in and Tobacco at night

Friday July 30

Suffered for the Gin and Tobacco. A most lovely day 72.52. N. -n Mayen bearing SW about 100 miles and not visible. Steaming SE at 6 knots. Took no dinner but went to the masthead in preference enjoying a pipe and the welcome sunshine. Fell in with one or two small bladdernose seals of which we shot two, one fell to my rifle, the other was the object of the worst exhibition of shooting I ever had the misfortune to witness, I fired my only cartridge at a long range and missed, whereupon two harpooners took the Job in

hand, and fired 3 shots each, or 7 shots in all before the unfortunate seal dropped its head.

Saturday July 31st

Out in the open sea pitching and tossing like Billy and with her head WSW bound for the Bottle Nose Bank. It is very problematical whether we will get any of the creatures, as I suppose they shift their ground like all other animals in these regions, and because Captain David got them there in April is no reason why we should see them again in August. No ice in sight. I shall never again see the great Greenland floes, never again see the land where I have smoked so many pensive pipes, where I have pursued the wily cetacean, and shot the malignant Bladdernose. Who says thou art cold and inhospitable, my poor ice fields? I have known you in calm and in storm and I say you are genial and kindly. There is a quaint grim humour in your bobbing bergs with their fantastic shapes. Your Floes are virgin and pure even when engaged in the unsolicited 'Nip'. Yes, thou art virgin, and drawest but too often the modest veil of Fog over thy charms.

I can apostrophize the icefields, but hang the word will I say in favour of Spitzbergen, the Jotunheim of the Scandinavian mythology which I saw in a gale and left in a gale, a barren rugged upheaval of a place. Sailed West and Sou'West all day. It fell calm in the evening and we lay in a long rolling swell our sails flapping and a thick mist around.

Sunday August 1st

Eclipse out of sight – has probably been steaming in the fog all night. Steamed W and SW through calm water and thick mist. We hope we may find Bottle-nose whales about 80 miles SE of Jan Meyen, and from there to Langaness in Iceland. Keeping up our spirits. Saw some drift wood today. Hove a bottle overboard in the evening with our Longtitude and Latitude and a request to publish where it was picked up. Bottlenose fishing has never as yet been atall developed, several ships have tried it in a half hearted way and failed. The Jan Meyen got 9 in 6 weeks which did not pay them, Capt David this year got 32 in a month which did pay him. Fell in with very greasy water tonight, with a strong smell of

herrings and swarming with clios, I caught about 100 of the shelled variety. One would think the Bottlenoses would be near such tempting Grub. Heard a Finner whale blowing away in the mist like an empty beerbarrel. Lat 70.59. Long 0° 15 E. Passed 2 dead maulies and another bit of drift wood from Siberia. Several more 'finners' seen.

Monday August 2nd

Sea calm and hardly any wind. The top of Mount Beerenberg is in sight bearing WNW about 80 miles. Saw several puffins, seaswallows and eider ducks, birds only seen in the vicinity of land. About two o'clock four Bottlenose whales, two old and two young came in sight and two boats were lowered away in pursuit. They made straight for Cane's boat but when within shot they dived and though we pursued them two hours we never got another chance. About 5 o'clock two more came up and Colin was sent after them but they disappeared. The Eclipse is in sight and had his boats away also without success. They are funny looking brutes in the water, with high dorsal fins like finner whales. They are worth about £60 each. Quite warm now, have all our flannels off.

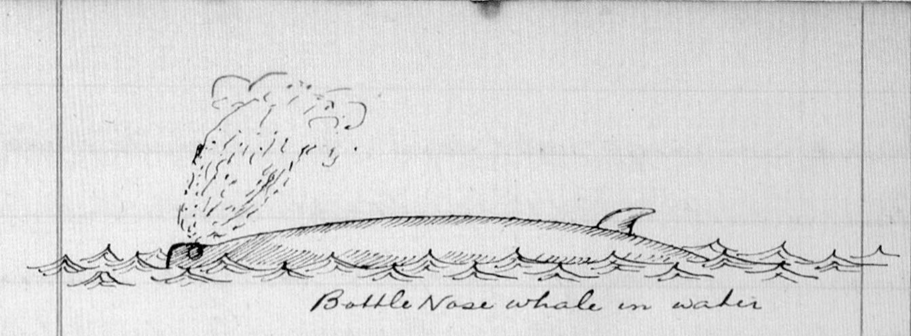
Bottle Nose whale in water

Tuesday August 3rd

Things don't look as well this morning as there is more wind and not so many birds or food in the water. Sailing Westward. Nothing seen during the day

Wednesday August 4th

Came into better ground this morning, there being very many birds and much grease on the water. Watched the Bósun gulls, who are very bad fishers, chasing the poor old Kittiewakes until they disgorged their last meal, which the bullies devour in its semidigested condition. Sea was swarming with cetaceans about noon which we lowered away 2 boats for thinking they were bottlenoses but they proved to be young finner whales, worthless brutes and so powerful that they would run out all our lines, so the boats were recalled. Captain shot a 'Boatswain'. Saw many Eider ducks. Several swordfish also seen. One of them was chasing a 'Finner' whale round the Eclipse. The poor

brute was springing right out of the water and making an awful bobbery. Carner put a rifle bullet into one young one about 40 feet long, which went away in a great hurry to tell its ma what they had been doing to it. This sea from Jan Meyen to Iceland might be called the Feather sea. The surface is literally covered with feathers in many parts. This Bottlenosing is an awful spree.

'Hope' in a calm among Cetaceans. Aug 4th 1880.

Was called up about 11 PM by the Captain to see a marvellous sight. Never hope to see anything like it again. The sea was simply alive with great hunchback whales, rather a rare variety, you could have thrown a biscuit on to 200 of them, and as far as you could see there was nothing but spoutings and great tails in the air. Some were blowing under the bowsprit, sending the water on to the

forecastle, and exciting our Newfoundland tremendously. They are 60-80 feet long, and have extraordinary heads with a hanging pouch like a toad's from their under jaw. They yield about 3 tons of very inferior oil, and are hard to capture so that they are not worth pursuing. We lowered away a boat and fired an old loose harpoon into one which went away with a great splash. They differ from finner whales in being white under fins and tail. Some of them gave a peculiar whistle when they blew, which you could hear a couple of miles off

School of Hunchback Whales south of Jan Meyen.

Thursday August 5th

Nothing seen today. A stiff breeze arose towards evening and pitched and tossed us about confoundedly. We think the Eclipse has gone home. Steering SW

Friday August 6th

Gave it up as a bad Job and turned our head ESE for Shetland. Dense fog and rain with very little wind. Utterly beastly weather. We are all dejected at having to turn home with so scanty a cargo, but what can we do? We've ransacked the country and taken all we could get, but this is an exceptionably unfavourable year owing to the severity of last winter which has extended the Greenland Ice far to the Eastward, and locked the fishes feeding ground inside an impenetrable barrier. Here is our whole game bag for the season according to my reckoning

2 Greenland Whales

2400 Young Seals

1200 Old Seals

5 Polar bears

2 Narwhals

12 Bladder noses.

3 Flaw rats

1 Iceland Falcon

2 Ground Seals.

2 King Eider ducks &

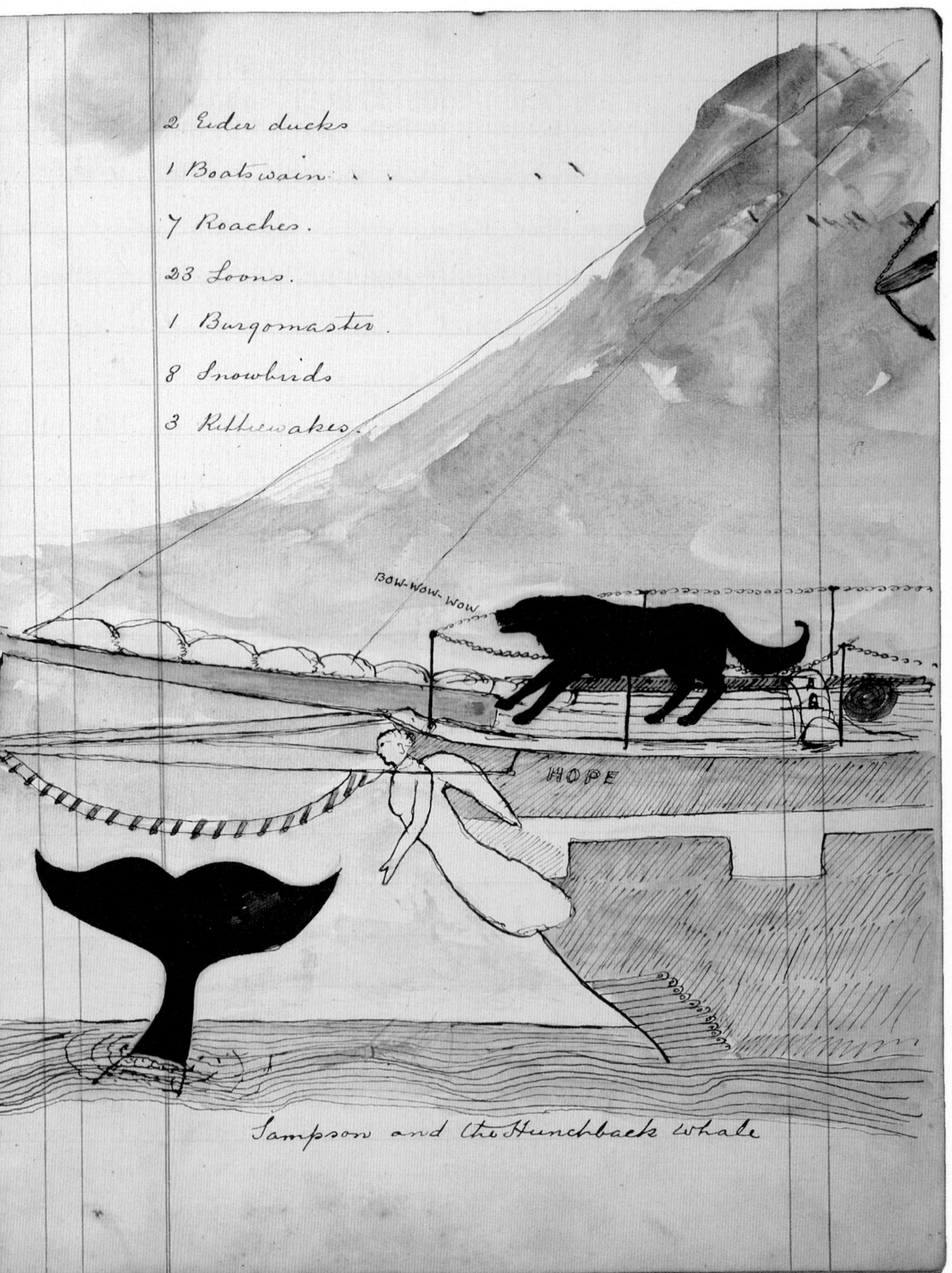

Sampson and the Hunchback Whale

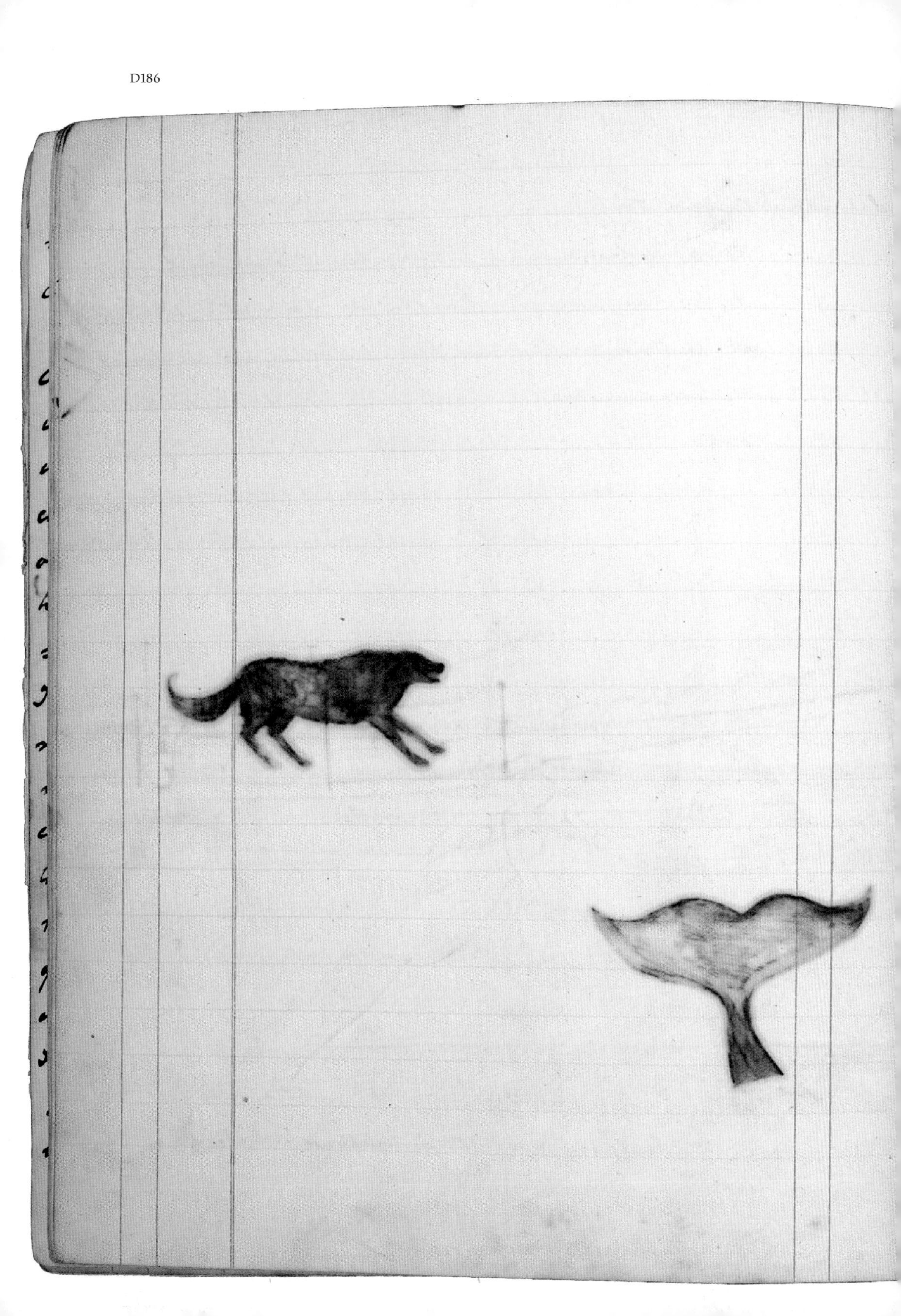

D186

Saturday August 7th

Groping homeward under steam and sail in such a thick fog that we can hardly see the water from the side of the ship. Took in the two Funnel boats. We have not got our reckoning now for several days, and as we have been dodging about zig zag after these bottlenoses, our dead reckoning is very uncertain. It isn't nice to be steaming along in the North sea in a fog with Iceland and the Faroe Islands knocking about in front of us. Several puffins and other land birds seen.

Sunday August 8th.

Cleared up a little although it was raining nearly all day. Had a mackerel line over all evening but got nothing. Sighted land about 8 PM which proved to be the North end of Faroe island. A nice Job if we had come on it in the dark. Saw a Schooner running North about midnight, probably bound for Iceland from Denmark. Men busy drying our whale lines

Monday August 9th

A beautiful clear day with a blue sky and a bright sun. Wind from the NE a good strong breeze

before which we are flying homeward with all sail set, and the bright green waves hissing and foaming from her bows. No mackerel again. Ship all covered with whale lines drying. Expect to make the land late tonight. Saw a Solan Goose and a little bird called a Steen chuck, also some stormy petrels. The kittiewakes down here are a smaller breed, I think, than those further north. All hands on the look out for land

Tuesday August 10th

Up at 8 AM to see the land bearing WSW on the Starboard bow. Half a gale blowing and the old Hope steaming away into a head sea like Billy. Hence the feebleness of my hand writing. The green grass on shore looks very cool and refreshing to me after nearly 6 months never seeing it, but the houses look revolting. I hate the vulgar hum of men and would like to be back at the Floes again

'There is society where none intrudes

Upon the sea, and music in its roar!'

Passed the skerry light, and came down to Lerwick but did

not get into the harbour as we are in a hurry to catch the
tide at Peterhead, so there goes all my letters, papers and
everything else. A girl was seen at the lighthouse waving a
handkerchief and all hands were called to look at her. The
first woman we have seen for half a year. Our Shetland
crew were landed in four of our boats and gave 3 cheers
for the old ship as they pushed off, which were returned
by the men left. Lighthouse keeper came off with last
week's weekly Scotsman by which we learn of the defeat
in Afghanistan - Terrible news. Also that the Victor
has 150 tons the dirty skunk. Took our boats aboard
and went off for Peterhead full pelt. Fitful head and
Sumburgh light twinkling away astern like a star.
Herring fishing seems to be a success. Saw a large
grampus.

Wednesday August 11th

Dead calm and the sun awfully awful. Saw Rattray
Head at 4 P.m. The sea black with fishing boats.
Hurrah for home! Pilot boat came off at 6 P.m and
we lay off for high water at 4 in the morning. hundreds
and hundreds of herring boats around us. Crew getting

on their shore logs. Well here we are at the end of the log of the Hope, which has been kept through calm and through storm, through failure and success; every day I have religiously Jotted down my impressions and anything that struck me as curious, and have tried to draw what I have seen. So there's an

End of the Log of the SS Hope.

D192

Our Illustrations

Vol II

Old Sealing

Making off Seal's blubber

Not sold but Given away

Poking the mob Boat

Harpoon Gun

Hope off Spitzbergen in a gale

The Bear we did not shoot.

Greenland Sword fish

The Lesser Auk (Loom)

Swordfish chasing Seals

A Capture

John Thomas & his friend

Towing the Narwhal home

A narwhal

Maulie stealing our roach

Vol III.

Capture by Eclipse's boats

Our bear

Bear and Shark devouring Narwhal.

Boats after 2 fish.

Our First Fish

Whale and 2 fast Boats

Buchan's Boat

Ship flinching a whale (Capt J Gray)

do do do (Capt David Gray)

A Right and Left among Looms.

Natural Ice house

Bottle Nose Whale.

Hope among Cetaceans

Hunchback whales.

Sampson and the Fish

Game Bag of the Hope. (Continued)

July	1	1 Narwhal.
	2	
	3	
	4	
	5	
	6	1 Haw Rat 7 Loons 1 Roach 1 Kittiewake. 2 Snowbirds
	7	
	8	a Greenland Whale.
	9	
	10	
	11	
	12	
	13	
	14	
	15	
	16	
	17	
	18	
	19	
	20	
	21	

22

23

24

25

26

27

28

29

30

31. 2 Bladdernose seals.

August

1

2

3

4. A Boatswain

5. 2 Eider ducks

My Own Gamebag.

Young Seals and Young Bladders xxxxxxxxxx· xxxxxxxxxx· xxxxx

xxxxx· xxxxxxxx

Old Seals. xxxxxxxxxx· xxxxxxxxxx· xxxxxxxxx

Bladdernoses xxx

Loons xxxxxxxxxx·

Roaches xxx

Maulies x

Snowbirds xx

Kittiwakes xxxx

Haw Rats xx

＊此頁為日誌封底，請從書尾開始翻閱